THE POLITICS OF SURVIVAL

THE POLITICS
OF SURVIVAL

Peirce, Affectivity, and Social Criticism

LARA TROUT

FORDHAM UNIVERSITY PRESS
NEW YORK   2010

Library of Congress Cataloging-in-Publication Data

Trout, Lara.
The politics of survival : Peirce, affectivity, and social criticism / Lara
Trout.—1st ed.
p.   cm.— (American philosophy series)
Includes bibliographical references and index.
ISBN 978-0-8232-3295-6 (cloth : alk. paper)—
ISBN 978-0-8232-3297-0 (ebook : alk. paper)
1. Discrimination—Social aspects.   2. Prejudices.
3. Cognition—Philosophy.   4. Peirce, Charles S. (Charles Sanders),
1839–1914.   I. Title.
HM1091.T76   2010
303.3′85—dc22
2010005584

Printed in the United States of America
12 11 10   5 4 3 2 1
First edition

To
Lisa Kammerer
and
Samantha Kolinski

Contents

Abbreviations

CP   *Collected Papers of Charles Sanders Peirce* (1958–65)

EP   *The Essential Peirce* (1992, 1998)

RLT   *Reasoning and the Logic of Things* (1992)

W   *Writings of Charles S. Peirce: A Chronological Edition*, Vols. 1–3 (1982–86)

Acknowledgments

I have many people to thank. Doug Anderson is very much at the top of the list. The support he has given me for my unconventional reading of Peirce's work has been vital to this project's growth. Thank you, Doug! Thanks, too, to Helen Tartar at Fordham University Press, who believed in this project and helped me bring it into its finished form.

I thank Vincent Colapietro, whose love for Charles S. Peirce and classical American philosophy helped to form and fuel my own. Shannon Sullivan has been a model for me of the fruitfulness of bringing classical American philosophy into dialogue with feminism and race theory. She has also very generously provided comments on my work whenever I needed her to. Nancy Tuana also has been an important mentor for me in my formation as a feminism and race theory scholar. Other key supporters of my work on Peirce and social criticism are Mitchell Aboulafia, Dan Conway, Claire Katz, and Cathy Kemp. Without all these individuals, with whom I worked at Penn State University when I was a graduate student there (2005–6), my work in this book would not have stable roots. I also thank Terry McGrail, Staci Kelly, Toni Mooney, and Mona Muzzio, who provided me with friendship and technical support during my years at Penn State. Other friends to this project include Leigh Johnson, who let me sit in on her Philosophy and Race class at Penn State University in the spring of 2005. The connections I was able to draw between race theory and Peirce's ideas benefited a great deal from what I learned in her class. I also had many fruitful conversations about Peirce's ideas with classmates Daniel Campos, David O'Hara, and Michael Ventimiglia.

In the transformation process through which this book has grown into its present form, I have had the support of many. Roberto Frega and Roger Ward each gave my penultimate manuscript a thorough and critical read. I thank them both for their many criticisms and suggestions. Dwayne Tunstall provided invaluable critiques and also helped me frame my work in better dialogue with race theory issues. Bill Lawson took the time to talk with me about my work, challenging me to frame my project more rigorously on the race theory front. Daniel Campos provided insightful feedback and suggestions, as well as encouragement. Judith Green has been a wonderful source of support and advice about the book-writing process. Lisa Heldke has served in this capacity as well and has offered content suggestions when I needed them. And Marcia Moen—thank you so much for all your support and advice in the specific world of Peirce, affectivity, and social criticism.

My thanks to the University of Portland for supporting my work on this book through funding from the Butine Grant. I thank Norah Martin for being an incredibly supportive department chair who goes out of her way to support my research. Alex Santana has been an extraordinarily generous interlocutor, happy to give me feedback as I was working through my ideas at various points. Jeff Gauthier read my introduction with a fine-toothed comb and gave me many detailed and helpful comments. Rayne Funk was always there to help me with technical support. Kaycie Rueter, Jayme Schroeder, Tyler Bryan-Askay, Megan Smith, and Chelsea Egbert have also provided technical support. Thank you all! Thanks too to Richard Askay, Jim Baillie, Caery Evangelist, Thom Faller, Jessica Logue, and Peg Hogan, all of whom have been wonderful colleagues to work with throughout this process. Thanks, as well, to Fay Beeler, Devon Goss, Melanie Gangle, Kenneth Laundra and Amanda Mosher for fielding short-notice questions from me as I was completing work on the final manuscript. Thanks too to my Philosophy and Feminism and Self and Identity students over the years at the University of Portland.

They have helped me develop my work on this project through their own engagement with Peirce's ideas in conjunction with issues in social criticism.

I thank the many audience members who gave me feedback about my work at conferences for the Association for Feminist Epistemologies, Methodologies, Metaphysics and Science Studies; the Society for the Advancement of American Philosophy; the Society for Women in Philosophy (Pacific Division); the Summer Institute in American Philosophy; PhiloSOPHIA; the International Meeting on Pragmatism; and Pedagogy and Theater of the Oppressed. I also received helpful audience feedback at a presentation I gave at Lewis and Clark College, in Portland, Oregon.

Thank you very much to Eric Newman, Nicholas Frankovich, and Sonia Fulop at Fordham University Press, who helped prepare the manuscript for publication.

I have been blessed with many stalwart friends who have supported me through thick and thin throughout this project, many of whom have already been mentioned. I need to add several names to this list. Kelly Burns and Samantha Kolinski are dear friends whom I have known from way back. Evgenia Cherkasova is a newer friend who was a blessing in my life during the years we were in State College, Pennsylvania, together. Thank you to Bobbi Hokenson for the idea for the cover photo, and for the photography itself. And thanks to Milo, John, and Stephanie Salomone for posing for the cover photo. I really appreciate your help! Thanks, too, to Dr. Leigh Kochan Lewis, Dr. Suzanne Lady, and Lovejoy Chiropractic, as well as Virginia Fidel and Robin Rice.

Dad and Mom, thank you for the love of learning you have fostered in me for as long as I can remember. Eric and Mandy, thank you for believing in me. Parker and Sydney, thank you for being your adorable selves! And, of course, Lisa, who has given me so very much; Dan; and their incredible children, Eva (Mayo!), Natalie, and Ben, whose love helps me keep my center. *Y Absa, gracias a ti también. Eres un regalo.*

Thank you to the University of Illinois Press for giving me permission to adapt material for my conclusion from my article "Attunement to the Invisible: Applying Paulo Freire's Problem-Posing Education to 'Invisibility,'" *The Pluralist* 3, no. 3 (2008): 63–78. Material from Chapters 1, 2, and 5 has also appeared in "C. S. Peirce, Antonio Damasio, and Embodied Cognition: A Contemporary Post-Darwinian Account of Feeling and Emotion in the 'Cognition Series,'" *Contemporary Pragmatism* 5, no. 1 (2008): 79–108, and "'Colorblindness' and Sincere Paper-Doubt: A Socio-political Application of C. S. Peirce's Critical Common-sensism," *Contemporary Pragmatism* 5, no. 2 (2008): 11–37.

THE POLITICS OF SURVIVAL

INTRODUCTION

I use the philosophy of classical American pragmatist Charles Sanders Peirce to teach my students about unintentional racism. Many of these students, almost all of whom are Euro-American white,[1] report a transformation—from not believing in the possibility of unintentional racism to fully acknowledging this phenomenon.[2] The type of racism I focus on in class—and in this book—is white racism against people of color, which includes denying or restricting, based on race,[3] a person or group's access to societal recognition, respect, resources, and protection. Racism in this sense can take on both everyday forms (such as rudeness) and systemic forms (such as denial of equal access to education). By *unintentional* racism, I mean racist behavior—or behavior that supports racism—that is not consciously willed.

Traditional Peirce scholars may wonder how Peirce can be so pedagogically effective for this social critical consciousness-raising.[4] Scholars in social criticism may also have this question coupled with curiosity about the specifics of Peirce's philosophy. I would answer that Peirce's work provides nuanced descriptive and prescriptive resources for grasping societal ills that often elude the understanding of those belonging to socio-politically dominant groups, such as Euro-American whites, the economic middle class, men, heterosexuals, and others. I use "socio-political" and its derivatives to signify a relation to institutional power dynamics that influence how humans treat each other within communities, including factors such as societal recognition and respect, as well as the distribution of resources, legal rights, and citizenship.

The Politics of Survival: Peirce, Affectivity, and Social Criticism details these Peircean resources in the context of a provocative engagement with the affective dimensions of Peirce's philosophy.[5] This engagement lends itself to a demonstration of the rich compatibilities between Peirce's thought and social criticism. By "social criticism" I mean any type of critique, such as feminism and race theory[6] (my foci in this book), that acknowledges the reality of oppression,[7] as well as the theoretical and practical mechanisms by which oppression can be perpetuated. I understand social justice to be the ultimate goal of social criticism. Social justice includes, without being limited to, a society's giving fair and dignified treatment, as well as rendering its resources, opportunities, and protections concretely available, to all groups.

I do not pretend that Peirce himself—a Euro-American white man who lived from 1839 to 1914 and was born into the socio-economic elite of Cambridge and Boston—intended his thought to be feminist or conducive to race critique (Brent 1998, 26).[8] He certainly was not a social reformer on these fronts. Although he was a Northerner who was of age to fight in the Civil War, Peirce was not interested in fighting and was relieved to be exempted because of his work with the U.S. Coastal Survey. He was not against slavery either (Brent 1998, 61–62; Menand 2001, 161). And he was also against women's suffrage (Brent 1998, 319).

I also do not intend to somehow vindicate Peirce on a personal level by showing how his philosophy can be used to promote social justice. Nonetheless, it is significant to note that in his later years Peirce experienced poverty, which in many respects removed him from the high-society circles in which he had formerly moved. His later writings, such as his essay "Evolutionary Love" (1893), suggest a corresponding sensitivity to the perspective of the poor. In a letter to his good friend William James, dated March 13, 1897, Peirce notes that "a new world of which I knew nothing, and of which I cannot find that anybody who has written has really known much, has been disclosed to me, the world of misery" (quoted in Brent 1998, 259–60; cf. 261–62).[9] While Peirce's sensitivity to misery did not extend to the plight of people of color and women in the United States, it did give him footing from which to give philosophical voice to those considered "weak" by society.[10]

Moreover, Peirce was a fallibilist who was committed to the evolution of his ideas. He valued self-critique and self-correction as indispensable qualities of human reason and actively sought out critical feedback from his contemporaries. He also realized that he was immersed enough in his culture to be blind to some of his own prejudices, saying that "[t]ruly to paint the ground where we ourselves are standing is an impossible problem in historical perspective . . ." (CP 4.32).[11] My guess is that Peirce expected and hoped that after he died his work would go on living and growing. My project engages his ideas in this spirit.

Taking an infinitely inclusive community of inquiry as its ideal, Peircean science *requires* social justice. As ideally practiced, it also demonstrates fallibilism, self-control, and agapic love, whereby it embraces new ideas as sources for ongoing growth and self-critique, even and especially when these ideas challenge existing beliefs. It follows, therefore, that the Peircean community of inquiry eschews exclusionary prejudice. Moreover, Peirce's epistemological doctrine of Critical Common-sensism (CCS) calls humans to expand self-control over their common-sense beliefs and provides conceptual tools to address gaps that exist between his communal ideal and the concrete realities of heterosexism, racism, sexism, and other social ills, which undermine actual inquiry and growth in flesh-and-blood communities.

My style of argument in this book reflects Peirce's injunction that philosophical reasoning "should not form a chain which is no stronger than its weakest link, but a cable whose fibers may be ever so slender, provided they are sufficiently numerous and intimately connected" (W 2:213). I articulate a Peircean, social critical narrative within and by means of an argument by demonstration. Regarding the latter, I argue that the affective dimensions of Peirce's philosophy point to compatibilities between his thought and social criticism. I present many fibers, or what Doug Anderson would call "strands,"[12] of Peircean thought in dialogue with thinkers who help draw out its social critical potential. These strands are, indeed, "numerous and intimately connected."

My demonstration calls on the contemporary neuroscientific work of Antonio Damasio, as well as the philosophical, social critical work of thinkers including Linda Alcoff, Susan Babbitt, Lorraine Code,[13] Marilyn Frye, bell hooks, María Lugones,[14] Peggy McIntosh, Charles Mills, Shannon Sullivan, Nancy Tuana, Patricia Williams, and others. I use Damasio's work to give voice to the latent embodiment and post-Darwinian themes in Peirce's work. This in turn highlights the inescapable bias that characterizes human cognition. By "bias" I mean "perspective" in its various inflections, such as embodied, personal, socio-political, etc. For Peirce the bias in human cognition points to the need for a *communal* inquiry into reality and knowledge, in conjunction with scientific testing. A solitary Cartesian knower simply will not do. I use work in social criticism to draw out the social critical implications of Peirce's communal epistemology and metaphysics.

These implications form the strands of my Peircean narrative, which traces affective, social critical themes, chronologically, through three of Peirce's major published essay series and his writings on association: the Cognition Series, published in the *Journal of Speculative Philosophy* in the late 1860s; the Illustrations of the Logic of Science series, published in *Popular Science Monthly* in the late 1870s; and the *Monist* "Cosmology Series" and association writings, from the 1890s.

It culminates in a study of Peirce's mature doctrine of Critical Common-sensism, which he articulated in the 1900s.

The narrative begins with the uniquely embodied human organism. It acknowledges, as Peirce does, that humans begin life as children whose habits are shaped by the social, and by implication *sociopolitical*, habits of their caretakers and society in general. This means that children, dependent and vulnerable as they are, can internalize oppression-perpetuating beliefs (or habits) before they are old enough to examine them critically. By "internalization" I mean the incorporation, by means of reinforcement or trauma, of a belief into one's personal comportment and worldview, such that the belief is difficult to eradicate rationally.[15] In hegemonic societies, this internalization can be continually reinforced through messages that portray a privileged experience as a societal norm. By "privilege" and its derivatives, I mean the increased advantages, opportunities, and resources available to those who are members of socio-politically dominant groups in society, such as the economically middle class, Euro-American whites,[16] heterosexuals, men, and so on. By "hegemonic," I mean reflective of a *closed* circle of power representing and enforcing only self-interested perspectives. In hegemonic societies, mainstream societal habits are imposed by those in power and leave out non-hegemonic perspectives. Historically in the West, societies have been hegemonic to the extent that they have limited social inquiry to Euro-American white, propertied males, who were also Christian and heterosexual. Historically non-hegemonic perspectives have included people of color, the poor, and women, as well as non-Christians and GLBTQs.[17] In conjunction with this societal hegemony, children who belong to groups privileged by race, sex, economic security, and/or other factors can grow into adults who perpetuate oppressive social structures—such as racism, sexism, and discrimination against the poor and/or other groups—*without intending to*. This is because children's vulnerability and dependency on others makes their internalization of discriminatory beliefs likely. Such internalized beliefs can become so deeply rooted that they function *undetected* in adulthood. Peirce has resources to address these social critical concerns. In addition to its inclusive and agapic ideals, the Peircean community of inquiry abides by the doctrine of Critical Commonsensism, whereby it calls into question its background or commonsense beliefs, which is where nonconscious discriminatory beliefs can dwell.

My project takes up Charlene Seigfried's invitation, in her book *Pragmatism and Feminism*, to embrace the compatibilities between these two domains of philosophical discourse, namely pragmatism and feminism (1996, 4). It is "pragmatist-feminist" in this regard.[18] Like Seigfried, however, I do not wish to be limited by this description, placed into a box (9). Pragmatist-feminism describes a sensibility that deeply informs my work, even as my project extends into neuroscience and social criticism broadly construed. Regarding its feminist sensibilities, in addition to the description of social criticism just given, my work more specifically acknowledges the oppression of women and the significance of gender categories (femininity and masculinity) for both men and women in the West.[19] In addition my work takes on the mantle of feminist or liberatory epistemology, by critiquing modernist epistemological assumptions as a means of promoting social justice.[20] I prefer the term "liberatory epistemology" to "feminist epistemology" because the former is broader, just as I prefer the term "social criticism" to simply "feminism" because I prefer to envision the axes of social reform—such as economic class, race, sex, sexuality, and so on—as interweaving.

Regarding its pragmatist sensibilities, let me note that classical American pragmatism, which I call "pragmatism" for short, is significantly different from everyday understandings of "pragmatism" as a narrow, "what's in it for me," utilitarian outlook. Pragmatism as the philosophy practiced by Jane Addams, John Dewey, Charlotte Perkins Gilman, William James, Alain Locke, George Herbert Mead, and Peirce himself is rooted in the union of thought and practice. Experience is the learning and testing ground for our ideas. Peirce's pragmatic maxim instructs that the meaning of a belief is found in

the patterns of effects, or habits, to which the belief leads.[21] For example, my belief in the importance of eradicating racism in the United
States results in habits including (but not limited to) incorporating
the work of people of color into my course syllabi and working to
unlearn my unintentional racism. For the pragmatists our beliefs are
habits. And our habits inform all our behavior, in contrast to the narrower colloquial understanding of habits as including only repetitive
or annoying activity, such as brushing one's teeth before bed or talking too loudly on one's cell phone. Habits are enacted not only by
human individuals but also by human communities and, for Peirce,
by nature itself (insofar as nature is external to humans). Through
the large-scale habits of society and nature, individual habits are inescapably shaped. In human habits body and mind come together, and
so do emotion and reason, individual and society, and self and others,
as well as the personal and the political.[22]

This brings us to several points where pragmatism and feminism,
as well as other forms of social criticism, often converge, via challenging the traditional dichotomies erected by modern philosophy and
the Cartesian confidence that an individual thinker can achieve certain knowledge, as long as she fully transcends all sources of bias,
such as her body and emotions.[23] Pragmatism embraces inclusively
communal, scientifically grounded, fallibilist pursuits of knowledge
that compensate for and celebrate the fact that individuals are inescapably situated. It is here that pragmatism can offer epistemological
and metaphysical insights to feminism and social criticism. At the
same time feminism and social criticism offer to pragmatism insights
about the socio-political blind spots—regarding economic class, race,
religion, sex, sexuality, and other factors—that can undermine the inclusiveness of pragmatism's ideal for communal, scientific inquiry
into knowledge and reality (cf. Seigfried 1996, 9–10).

In addition to responding to Seigfried's pragmatist-feminist invitation, I also issue an invitation of my own, for a continued expansion
of the road of inquiry into both Peircean affectivity and Peircean social criticism. In many respects, my book only scratches the surface.
Regarding Peirce's works, I stay to the beaten path of his published

works. While this approach is aimed at helping introduce many of Peirce's major essays to a larger audience, it also leaves to one side the infinitely fertile ground of Peirce's unpublished manuscripts. Even as I am excited to present innovative interpretations of Peirce's work to readers of various stripes, I am aware that there is much more to be done beyond the work I offer here.

On the social criticism front, first of all, I limit my primary focus to the unintentional perpetuation of racism and, to a lesser extent, sexism. Below I will explain my specific treatment of unintentional discrimination. Here I want to stress that limiting my framework to unintentional racism and sexism is not meant to imply that other types of oppression are less prevalent or less important. Rather, I engage this narrower focus because it enables me to go into more depth than I would be able to otherwise. This depth allows me to show some of the complexities that are involved in any particular kind of oppression, such as racism, and how these complexities relate to unintentional discrimination. Were I to try to address as many types of oppression (and corresponding unintentional "isms") as possible, I would need to sacrifice depth in order to keep my project within bounds in terms of length and clarity of presentation. I invite the reader, throughout the chapters that follow, to extrapolate from my presentations of racism and sexism, in order to find similarities and differences regarding the complexities involved in other types of oppression. For my part, I continually gesture beyond racism and sexism, to remind the reader to engage in this extrapolation.[24] My work is the tip of the iceberg and is meant to be an invitation to go far beyond the limited breadth I am able to cover in this book.

Second, my treatment of thinkers from feminism and race theory is selective and insight focused. It is selective in that I do not pretend to give a full panorama of work being done in feminism and race theory that can relate to Peirce's thought. I invite others fill in gaps I have left behind. My incorporation of specific thinkers is insight focused in that I target specific, circumscribed points of connection between a given thinker and Peirce's work. For example, in Chapter 2, I describe Charles Mills's conception of "subpersonhood," which he explains in his book *The Racial Contract*, to help foreground the social critical insight latent in a reference Peirce makes to the power of testimony to convince someone she is "mad" (W 2:202; Mills 1997, 53–62). I do not, however, explicitly engage the larger project of *The Racial Contract*, despite my agreement with its argumentation. Proceeding in this insight-based way is intended to create a narrative that balances introducing (for those who need it) many voices from feminism and race theory with giving a manageable presentation of Peirce's ideas.

My audience includes both Peircean and social critical scholars, whom I want to introduce to each other properly. I have met few social criticism scholars who are aware of the potential of Peirce's work for social critical ends. I have also met few Peirce scholars who are familiar with work in social criticism. I would like for all these scholars to get to know each other better. My audience also includes those readers interested in the intersection of Antonio Damasio's work and philosophy, as well as nonspecialists who are willing to brave the technical discussions to follow. I provide many concrete examples in order to make my presentation approachable. I beg the patience of each of these audiences as, throughout the book, I explain concepts basic to various specialists, in order to keep all my audiences on the same page.

The narrower, scholarly genealogy of my project begins, quite simply, with my interest in two dimensions of Peircean scholarship that are underdeveloped: the latent post-Darwinian affective themes in Peirce's work and the compatibility between Peirce's work and social criticism. By "affectivity" I mean the ongoing body-minded communication between the human organism and her or his individual, social, and external environments, for the promotion of survival and growth. This communication is shaped by biological, individual, semiotic,[25] social, and other factors. My treatment of Peircean affectivity includes feelings, emotion, instinct, interest, sentiment,[26] sympathy, and agapic love, as well as belief, doubt, and habit.

There is a tendency within Peircean scholarship to underemphasize, or overlook altogether, the post-Darwinian and embodiment

themes that inform Peirce's writings. Even studies of Peircean emotion and sentiment neglect them.[27] Moreover, so do studies of Peirce's
account of the agapastic evolution of the universe (that is, evolution
by means of agapic love).[28] Yet Peirce viewed the human person as an
animal organism whose survival depends on the successful navigation
of an environment outside of her or his control. He makes regular
reference to post-Darwinian and/or embodiment themes throughout
his work.[29] Moreover, Peirce is aware of the *uniqueness* of the human
organism's body, a uniqueness that goes hand in hand with the inescapable bias and resource found in an individual human's cognition.

It is understandable that Peircean scholarship has consistently
overlooked embodiment and survival themes in Peirce's work. After
all, he does not engage in extended discussions of these issues, often
making only abbreviated or implicit references. It can seem that he
backgrounds these themes because they are not important. I would
argue, however, that Peirce considers them to be *too obvious to require
his attention.* Those who know anything of Peirce's life know that he
was—to put it mildly—a brilliant, focused, and impatient man who
had little tolerance for spelling things out to slow or stubborn inter-
locutors. He was loath to make connections for his readers that they
could make for themselves (EP 2:301). This tendency is unfortunate
in the present case, given that his audience was (and often still is)
steeped in modernist habits of thought and composed of formally educated, economically advantaged persons. It would have been (and
still can be) all too easy for them to forget that embodiment and survival issues affect *all* humans. Even persons with assured access to
food, shelter, and physical protection are vulnerable, embodied organisms who must interact successfully with their environment in
order to survive. My reading of Peirce is therefore a proactive one,
which foregrounds the individualized human embodiment and survival concerns of the human organism. This approach provides a
richer account of Peircean affectivity, which flows naturally into social justice issues, because human affective engagement involves encountering not only natural large-scale habits, such as gravity, but

also socio-political large-scale habits, such as those informing hetero-sexism, racism, sexism, and other social ills.

My reading of Peirce is also proactive regarding the social critical implications I continually highlight in his work. On this front, the contributions of classical American pragmatism to contemporary dis-cussions of addressing and ameliorating concrete oppressive condi-tions are readily acknowledged by many scholars in this field. Peirce, however, tends to be sidelined in these discussions, noted as the founder of pragmatism yet given little more than superficial acknowl-edgement.[30] The reasons for this are not difficult to hypothesize. First of all, Peirce was no social reformer, as noted earlier regarding his racist and sexist views. Moreover, Peirce can be perceived as an elitist scientist whose level of technicality forecloses dialogue regarding so-cial concerns (Seigfried 1996, 22, 281 n. 20). In all fairness, Peirce's personal track record is indisputably dubious, and his writing style and level of technicality can, at times, be elitist and off-putting. None-theless, Peirce's ideas *do* support social inclusiveness and critique.

Peirce's philosophy provides significant resources to add to con-temporary discussions of social criticism. The broad strokes of his ex-plicitly antimodern epistemology and metaphysics are compatible with efforts to grasp (while avoiding postmodern extremes) the socio-political dimensions of "reality," which structure our beliefs, concepts, and habits. For Peirce, humans are not equipped with an immediate epistemic grasp of their world. Instead, they are depen-dent on communal scientific inquiry, whereby they pool the re-sources of their perspectives. Knowledge and articulations of reality are products of this ongoing communal venture, whereby hypotheses are continually tested against the external world. Ideal scientific in-quiry, as noted above, involves an infinitely large community of in-quiry that extends over an indefinite period of time. This breadth of scope is required so that humans may have the best grasp possible of the habits of nature, which are infinitely complex, grow, and elude capture in absolute natural laws. Scientific inquiry is not a finite en-deavor. Any particular articulation of reality is *fallible* and thus sub-ject to further revision. Therefore it is a reflection of immaturity for an individual person or a finite community to decide that they have a lock on truth. Such hubris would be in violation of Peirce's oft-repeated admonition: "Do not block the way of inquiry" (EP 2:48).

In "Fixation of Belief" (1877), Peirce's discussion of the authority method is, in fact, a portrayal of a hegemonic society in which inquiry *is* blocked. Peirce was aware that communal articulations of inquiry can be usurped to oppressive ends by those in power. When this occurs, exclusionary societal habits are enforced and preemptive measures are taken to forestall growth. These measures involve educating children and the public *against* questioning the status quo. His later writings reassert his attunement to this danger, calling for an inclusive communal inquiry that does not shun society's "weak" but embraces them as integral to an agapic community whose growth depends on the sympathetic continuity of all its members.

Beyond these broad affinities to social justice, Peircean thought makes at least three contributions. First of all, the sophistication of Peirce's phenomenology provides conceptual tools to articulate how socio-political factors are integral to a person's experience. I will be calling on his category of secondness,[31] by which he means environmental resistance to one's movement in the world. Secondness, in a socio-political inflection that I introduce, allows us to describe how, for example, people of color in the United States often encounter racism-based obstacles that Euro-Americans do not experience. There can also be secondness as a result of economic classism, sexism, heterosexism, and so on. Since U.S. mainstream culture tends to represent the Euro-American white, male, middle-class, heterosexual, Christian, etc., experience as a neutral view of "human experience" in general,[32] people in any of the corresponding hegemonic groups can internalize a concept of "human experience" that does not involve racial obstacles, or obstacles because of sexism, economic classism, heterosexism, or religious beliefs. This perpetuates racism (and other "isms") by failing to acknowledge the contemporary reality of racial (and other forms of) discrimination in the United States.

Second, Peirce's account of human cognition lends unique support to the social critical position that no one can achieve a "god's-eye" view on the world. Any point of view is a situated one. For Peirce, cognition is embodied and therefore inescapably affective. This affectivity is semiotic in nature, as each of us naturally makes personal signs out of the objects in our world, according to our experience of them. Thus the flow of a person's cognition is informed by a deeply personalized attunement to the world outside of her, a unique attunement that makes each individual an epistemological resource to her community, even as her perspective reflects inescapable bias. It is by means of communal inquiry that humans pool the resources of their varied epistemological perspectives, discovering points of rational or intellectual communion in the midst of their idiosyncratic bodily orientations toward the world. This approach reflects the metaphor of the blind people standing stationary at different points around an elephant, who pool their perspectives (tail, legs, ears, trunk, and so on) to achieve the best description possible of the elephant, given their limitations in perspective. Communal inquiry, then, does not eliminate bias but reflects the best efforts of the inescapably biased individuals who undertake it. Any communal agreement about how reality is best articulated (in light of scientific testing) reflects the situatedness of the inquirers and is amenable to future critique and growth.

Third, Peirce articulates the *nonconscious* influence that our habits can have on our reasoning process. Since our habits are shaped from childhood by socio-political factors, this means that oppressive societal habits can find their way *unnoticed* into a person's habitual orientation toward the world. In this respect, Peirce's ideas on habit-taking and reality enable a nuanced articulation of how individuals *come to embody* socio-political bias by means of internalized habits.[33] This brings us back to Peirce's doctrine of Critical Common-sensism, which calls for the engagement and enhancement of human self-control, by requiring an epistemological, communal self-critique. In this self-critique, community members work to bring nonconscious exclusionary beliefs to light, such as those that perpetuate economic classism, heterosexism, racism, sexism, and other social ills. I argue that members of oppressed groups, such as the poor, GLBTQs, people of color, and women, play pivotal roles in this respect, since the beliefs in question may not be detectible to those who are privileged by them (the economically secure, heterosexuals, Euro-American whites, and men). The various types of socio-political secondness encountered by those in oppressed groups are experiential evidence that discriminatory beliefs are still in play.

A further point to address in the context of Peirce's contributions to social criticism is that his conceptions of the terms "intellect," "rationality," "objectivity," and "reasonableness" do not lend support to the racist and sexist bias so prevalent in the traditional Western philosophical canon, a canon that often portrays people of color and women as incapable of fully exercising or achieving what these terms have represented. Peirce is explicit that *all* humans possess the rational/intellectual capacity to grasp the regularities of the world around them and to form aims for their own conduct (W 3:285; EP 2:348). This capacity is linked to natural selection and survival. It unifies humans, rather than dividing them into those who can be rational and those who cannot. Objectivity, for Peirce, reflects the extent to which knowledge is endorsed by the community as a whole. This precludes a limited community of inquiry from proclaiming that their research results are "objectively" true, come what may. Peirce—who admonishes us *not* to block the road of inquiry—would frown on epistemological procedures that result in objective-as-infallible knowledge. Peircean objectivity implies that communal endorsement has been *achieved*, not seen as unnecessary (W 2:270–71; CP 7.259, 266).[34]

Finally, Peircean reason involves growth in diversification (EP 2:254–55, 343–44; CP 1.174; EP 1:310). At the level of human thought and behavior, reasonableness manifests as our beliefs/habits grow in complexity, which can fruitfully be applied to social critical issues. To use racism as an example: When I was younger I thought racism no longer existed in the United States, except in an individual here or there. I believed the civil rights movement in the 1960s had brought an end to institutional racism in this country. This belief was unreasonable in its extreme lack of diversity, reflecting my very limited white, middle-class, suburban experience. As my consciousness was raised by my work as a teacher with African American students, my belief about the existence of racism grew in reasonableness to embrace experience outside of my own—thus becoming more diverse, by accounting for both my white experience and the experience of many African Americans. It was still unreasonable in that my view of racism was only a black-white paradigm, which assumed only African Americans experienced racism. More reasonableness has been achieved as I have rendered more sophisticated my understanding of racism to apply to many more types, such as white racism against Asian Americans, Latino Americans, and Native Americans. There is still much more reasonableness for me to achieve, as I learn about the diversity within the classification Asian American, for example, as well as issues that arise for those of mixed race.[35]

That Peirce himself was not sensitized to reform regarding race (or women's) issues underscores the significant contribution social criticism can make to Peirce's work. Social criticism offers insight in identifying socio-political blind spots, in order that his infinitely inclusive agapic and scientific ideals are not undermined by nonconscious racism, sexism, or other exclusionary beliefs. It is, thus, a two-way street. Peirce's ideas are fortified by, even as they make contributions to, contemporary scholarship in social criticism. The following epistemological-metaphysical questions are common to both: Whose perspectives are reflected in how reality is articulated? Whose perspectives are *left out*? How can articulations of reality perpetuate oppression? Social criticism helps Peirce's philosophy extend its reach by extending its inclusive ideals beyond the borders of an imagination limited by hegemonic viewpoints that are circumscribed by whiteness, maleness, economical security, heterosexuality, and so on (cf. Code 2001). In other words, social criticism helps Peirce be more Peircean.

As a means of ongoing synthesis and illustration of the interrelationships between the affective and social critical elements of Peirce's thought, I will examine issues of racism and (to a lesser extent) sexism in the United States.[36] As I said above, I do not pretend to give a thoroughgoing analysis or the final word as to how Peirce's ideas can be applied in this context. Rather, I use U.S. history and mainstream culture as an extended concrete example of social problems that Peirce's ideas can help detect and address. Cornel West comments on the distinct failure of classical American thinkers, like Peirce, to address issues of race in the United States, even as these issues were undeniably part of the fabric of U.S. society when they were writing: "If a Martian were to come down to America and look at the American pragmatist tradition, they would never know that there was slavery, Jim Crow, lynching, discrimination, segregation in the history of America. This is a major indictment" (2004, 225; cf. 1989, 5). My efforts in this book retroactively address this lacuna with regard to Peirce.

The connections I draw in this respect are oriented toward a specific problematic. Within the United States, an actual agapic and inclusive community of inquiry is especially difficult to achieve because of the nonconscious influence of internalized, exclusionary habits that are shared among *well-intentioned* whites (and/or others in hegemonic groups). By "well-intentioned" whites (and/or others in hegemonic groups), I mean people who repudiate racism (and/or other forms of discrimination). I do not mean to imply that all whites repudiate racism; this would be naive. Many white people, however, think that racism is abhorrent yet can inadvertently perpetuate racism because of the influence of nonconscious racist habits. The same scenario applies to men and sexism, heterosexuals and heterosexism, and so on. Coupled with the historical exploitation and underrepresentation of people of color, women, GLBTQs, and so on, these nonconscious habits promote the *continued* marginalization of these groups.

In fact, this same group of well-intentioned white people is my primary audience, insofar as I think Peirce's ideas can truly help white people, including myself, raise our consciousness about the prevalence of racism in the United States.[37] Peirce's ideas can also foster consciousness-raising for men about sexism and for others in hegemonic groups regarding other forms of discrimination. This is not to imply that conscious racism, sexism, heterosexism, and other social ills no longer exist. The critiques presented in the following chapters are easily extended to such bigotry.[38] Rather, for rhetorical purposes, I wish to focus on nonconscious habits of exclusion, in order to challenge a folk assumption common among Euro-American whites (and others) living in the United States—namely, that prejudices such as racism, sexism, heterosexism, etc., are only a matter of conscious intent. According to this assumption, if I am not consciously racist, sexist, heterosexist, etc., then I cannot act or think in a racist, sexist, heterosexist, etc., fashion.[39] Linda Alcoff puts it this way, addressing racism: "[I]t is commonly believed that for one to be a racist one must be able to access in consciousness some racist belief, and that if introspection fails to produce such a belief then one is simply not racist" (2006, 188). This naive yet prevalent attitude undermines a sensitivity, among whites (and others in hegemonic groups), to the *current* racist (as well as sexist, heterosexist, and other discriminatory) structures that continue to inform U.S. society (cf. Bernasconi 2001, esp. 287, 295). Also undermining that sensitivity is the fact that, according to mainstream U.S. discourse, both racism and sexism have been largely eradicated in the United States, as a result of the civil rights and women's movements. In this respect, racism and sexism are different from heterosexism and prejudice against non-Christians, the latter prejudices still finding significant numbers of supporters in mainstream U.S. society.

In the chapters to follow, I address elements of Peirce's thought that help explain how this naïveté about racism and sexism comes about, and also how it might be addressed epistemologically through a synthesis of his ideals of infinite inclusiveness and agapic love operating in conjunction with his doctrine of Critical Common-sensism. In Peirce's system, there is hope amid the most indurate of habits, because there is always room for spontaneity and self-control. In concrete communities of inquiry in the United States, this spontaneity may take the form of an individual or group of community members who can identify racist and/or sexist beliefs that other community members cannot see. The majority members in such communities are called to exercise self-control by resisting the temptation to reject this testimony about racism and/or sexism, in order to embrace it as a legitimate hypothesis and potential source of communal growth past limiting, nonconscious beliefs.

In Chapter 1, I introduce Peircean affectivity, within an explicitly post-Darwinian context, as the ongoing body-minded communication between the human organism and her or his individual, social, and external environments, for the promotion of survival and growth. This communication is shaped by biological, individual, semiotic, social, and other factors. I use Antonio Damasio's work to give voice to the latent affective and post-Darwinian themes in Peirce's work. I also introduce Peirce's phenomenology, including a socio-political inflection of his concept of secondness, or environmental resistance, which I apply to heterosexism, racism, sexism, and other forms of discrimination. Finally, I use this initial chapter to give the reader the Peircean background necessary for my chronological study of three of Peirce's essay series, in Chapters 2, 3, and 4, respectively.

My work in these middle chapters shows that dialogue with social criticism *both* foregrounds the social criticism potential of Peirce's ideas *and* pushes Peirce's ideas to better address the very issues they help to describe and diagnose. Chapter 2 examines Peirce's Cognition Series published in the *Journal of Speculative Philosophy* in the late 1860s. My starting point is the uniquely embodied human organism whose cognition is inescapably biased by both personal and social factors, which points to the need for a *communal* inquiry into knowledge and reality. I use work in social criticism to highlight the socio-political implications of Peirce's communal epistemology and metaphysics, especially as these pertain to child development. Children, dependent and vulnerable as they are, can internalize discriminatory beliefs (or habits) from a young age, which can remain intact nonconsciously in adulthood.

In Chapter 3, I examine the Illustrations of the Logic of Science series published in *Popular Science Monthly* in the late 1870s, to address how communities can best avoid perpetuating the internalization danger just outlined. The scientific method is lauded by Peirce in this series as a superior method for "fixing" (establishing) belief-habits. This is because of its grounding in an infinitely inclusive communal inquiry into truth and knowledge, where beliefs are not brutally imposed or arbitrarily adopted (as in the authority and a priori methods); rather, beliefs are tested against external reality. While Peirce's infinitely inclusive communal ideal bodes well for social justice, social criticism concerns still push Peirce beyond his work in this Logic of Science series, because he does not address the nonconscious discriminatory background beliefs that that can enter scientific method through the back door, leading to the rejection of feedback from non-hegemonic groups about discrimination occurring within the scientific community. Thus applying the scientific ideal in actual communities falls prey to nonconscious discrimination.

Chapter 4 takes up Peirce's *Monist* "Cosmology Series" and association writings, from the 1890s, showcasing an additional communal ideal, one that can help mitigate a community's rejection of input coming from perspectives that differ from the norm. Agape is this ideal; it is a love characterized by an embrace of the different, even and especially when this difference is threatening. This ideal can be especially helpful for those in hegemonic groups to adopt in relation to feedback about discrimination that they may not want to hear. Nonetheless, here, too, work in social criticism points to an analogous application problem. Agape, like scientific ideals, can be undermined in practice by the nonconscious functioning of exclusionary beliefs that can override the conscious intent of those in hegemonic groups.

My project culminates, in Chapter 5, in a study of Peirce's mature doctrine of Critical Common-sensism, which he articulated in the 1900s. I show how Critical Common-sensism (CCS)—once pushed to its full potential through dialogue with social criticism—addresses the application problem plaguing the scientific method and agapic love, because CCS requires the scrutiny of individual and communal common-sense (or background) beliefs. CCS forms a synthesis with the infinitely inclusive ideal of the scientific method and the agapic ideal, to create a richly textured ideal of reasonableness that takes seriously the deep influence of socialized instinctive beliefs, which can include heterosexist, racist, sexist, and other discriminatory beliefs. This synthesis does not completely *solve* the application problem by offering suggestions and/or strategies for structural change regarding heterosexism, racism, sexism, and other social ills. Peircean reasonableness does, however, promote consciousness-raising and concomitant openness among those in hegemonic groups who wish to unlearn unintentional discriminatory beliefs (or habits).

Before ending this introduction, I need to make a clarification and to address two objections to which my project gives rise. The clarification is that my choice of the term "people of color" to describe "nonwhite" people is intended to work against the grain of white-dominant United States discourse. I wish to invoke a chromatic metaphor in which white is considered *lacking* in color, not because white people are race-less,[40] but because white-dominant ways of thinking are lacking in richness. As my work in the following chapters will show, Euro-American whiteness is a raced perspective that proclaims itself to be neutral and universal but is actually an exclusionary view limited to those who enjoy white privilege. Epistemologically and metaphysically, white-dominant discourse is deeply unreasonable in a Peircean sense to the extent that it fails to include and/or embrace the many, many perspectives on knowledge and reality that would allow for deep transformation of thinking and behavior within hegemonic societies. Such transformation involves not merely adding color to an artwork designed by and for whites but displacing this white self-absorption in order to allow for the creation of a tapestry whose genesis and growth are polychromatic. My work thus points beyond itself, as it focuses on consciousness-raising for whites and others in hegemonic groups. It provides conceptual tools to describe and diagnose problems, to promote opening the road of inquiry into epistemological, metaphysical, and social transformation. How this transformation might take shape is beyond the scope of my project.

The first of two objections I need to address is that I am not respecting the sharp line Peirce tended to draw between the formal practice of science, on the one hand, and the everyday world on the other hand.[41] There are several responses to make to this concern. First of all, the formal practice of science cannot be fully separated from political concerns that arise in the everyday world, since practicing scientists live in concrete societies and are vulnerable to carrying societal prejudices into their scientific practices. One of the purposes of this book is to demonstrate how easily, on Peircean terms, this can happen. Second, Peirce was quite open to the idea that humans can often *informally* practice the scientific method outside any laboratory. In "Fixation of Belief," he observes, "Everybody uses the scientific method about a great many things, and only ceases to use it when he [*sic*] does not know how to apply it" (W 3:254). He is referring to the commonplace of testing one's beliefs against external reality, to determine whether or not they measure up. This everyday practice of science happens in individual practice as well as in communities, whether these communities are filled with formally practicing scientists or not. In the chapters to follow, I will not take pains to make strict distinctions between "real" science and "everyday" science, because such distinctions can create barriers to understanding just how prevalent deep-seated prejudices can be in any community of inquiry. Finally, I acknowledge that my project may apply Peirce's ideas beyond what he specifically had in mind about the boundaries between science and the everyday world. Yet Peirce was, after all, a synechist who thus embraced *continuity* and criticized dichotomous thinking. So I would like to think that he would give me a fair hearing in my efforts to read his work continuously with social criticism, even though such a reading blurs a line he himself liked to draw between formal science and the everyday world.

The second objection comes from Dwayne Tunstall, a classical American philosophy scholar and a race theorist, who has told me that my work is too easy on white people.[42] I agree with his assessment, and I think that, by implication, my work is also too easy on anyone belonging to a hegemonic group, such as those who are economically secure, heterosexuals, men, and so on. I bend over backward to give these groups the benefit of the doubt, as I use Peirce's work to articulate the prevalence of the unintentional perpetuation of various types of discrimination. At the same time, my experience as a formerly oblivious white person, coupled with my experience of sexism, shows me that hegemonic conceptual framing can shape human thoughts, language, and behavior so thoroughly that blunt approaches to consciousness-raising can be ineffective for those in hegemonic groups. They can lead to such strong defensiveness that the discussion is blocked (cf. Alcoff 2006, 13). My gentle treatment of those in hegemonic groups is designed to keep the road of inquiry open. It is a fallibilist effort to use my own membership in privileged groups to undermine this very privilege, especially in regard to my being white.[43]

On this front, let me comment on the broader genealogy of this project, which began with my own white, middle-class experience. I was born in 1969. My elementary, high school, and college education did not include discussions of racism except as a phenomenon that *used to* be prevalent in U.S. society. As a result of the work of Martin Luther King Jr. and the civil rights movement, racism was a thing of the past, or so I learned. As a white person, I thought this made sense. After all, I saw no evidence of racism in my own experience, except the racist comments my grandfather made. But he was just old and set in his ways, just an individual who had not caught on to the newly nonracist society the United States had become. I was not taught to see as problematic that my high school graduating class of 480 was only 1 percent people of color. At the primarily white, middle-class college I attended, I went to an extracurricular talk that was a small exception to the school's predominantly white, middle-class discourse. A panel of African American scholars spoke about the fruitfulness of identifying themselves as *African* American as opposed to simply "American." I do not recall their specific arguments, but they included an appeal to the cultural and historical accuracy of "African American," which "American" simply did not capture. I remember responding sincerely, respectfully, but naively by asking a question that missed the entire point. It went something like, "Why can't we all call ourselves 'American,' to underscore the unity of our all being U.S. citizens?"

I did not understand that the term "American" is normatively loaded. It is latently raced, sexed, economically classed, and so on. It refers primarily to white, middle-classed, heterosexual men. As George Lakoff puts it, "If I speak of a typical American, what comes to mind for many is an adult white male Protestant, who is native-born, speaks English natively, and so on" (2002, 9). I eventually learned this normative loadedness through my post-college experiences, beginning with a year spent in the Jesuit Volunteer Corps (JVC), from mid-1991 to mid-1992, teaching and living in an African American inner-city neighborhood in Milwaukee, Wisconsin.[44] My students were primarily African American, and we talked a lot, inside and outside of class. They told me about the everyday prejudice they experienced from white people and how much this hurt their feelings. For example, one African American girl noted how sad it made her when, as she walked through a parking lot to enter a mall, white people who were in their cars would rush to lock their doors as she walked by. From 1991 to 1994, I also volunteered as a math tutor for inner-city children, who were also predominantly African American. I was shocked at how poor their math skills were for their respective grade levels. Having studied elementary education (in addition to philosophy) as an undergraduate, I saw clearly that these students were not receiving adequate public elementary education. They were not learning the skills they needed to build on. This was in stark contrast to my own suburban public education in the premier predominantly white, middle-class Millard school district in Omaha, Nebraska. My eyes had been opened. "American" did *not* tell the whole story after all.[45]

My own experience with consciousness-raising about racism informs one of my objectives for this book: to help those in hegemonic groups *see* what a hegemonically loaded culture makes so difficult for them to see, namely, the prevalence of economic classism, heterosexism, racism, sexism, and other social ills. It is thus a contribution to work in epistemologies of ignorance, since it examines the "*lack* of knowledge" of many in hegemonic groups and the mechanisms that promote this absence of knowing.[46]

To some scholars, my incorporation of personal biography may seem irrelevant at best. I respond that the philosophy we each do is grounded in our individual experience, whether we are aware of it or not and whether we acknowledge it or not. One's experiences, as I argue in the chapters to follow, can provide inroads for understanding. In the absence of certain experiences—like being the target of economic classism, heterosexism, racism, or sexism (or other discrimination)—understanding can be harder to achieve. The inclusion of details from my life is a personal outreach that supplements my scholarship in this book. It may make the Peircean concepts easier to grasp, whether through comparison or contrast. It is also intended in a fallibilist spirit, to acknowledge where my own blind spots lie. As a woman, I belong to a non-hegemonic group. As a white, middle-class, heterosexual person who was raised as a Christian/Catholic, I belong to hegemonic groups in respect to people of color, the poor, GLBTQs, and those who practice religions or spirituality outside the Christian tradition. Moreover, I was born and raised and currently reside in the United States, a colonizing country whose standard of living among its privileged members perpetuates suffering for many within and beyond its borders. The middle-class standard of living that I enjoy, in stark contrast to many other people in the world, can be seen in the personal examples that I use to help illustrate Peirce's ideas.

I expect and welcome criticisms regarding my blind spots. I have done my best to counter tendencies to speak from a falsely universalized perspective, that is, a perspective that takes my own experience as representative of everyone else's experience(s). Nonetheless, I am a fallibilist in both a Peircean and a social critical sense, meaning that my very best efforts are always amenable to critique, revision, and growth.

ONE

PEIRCEAN AFFECTIVITY

Peirce viewed the individual human organism as a body-minded, social animal who interacts semiotically with the world outside of her. He had little patience for the Cartesian portrayal of the individual as a disembodied, solipsistic knower with immediate epistemic access to truth. I use the term "naive individual" to convey a Cartesian knower who ignores her situatedness as an embodied, socially shaped organism in constant communication with the external environment. I reserve the term "individual" to convey a Peircean knower who is inescapably situated (and who may or may not be aware of this situatedness). For emphasis, I occasionally refer to the Peircean knower as a "synechistic individual." I call on "synechism"—a term referring to the philosophical importance Peirce grants to continuity[1]—to highlight the continuity of the human individual's body and mind, self and society, and inner and outer worlds. These continua reflect the affectivity of the human organism, whereby she is in ongoing body-minded interaction with the external world, including the latter's socio-political dimensions.

My first objective in this chapter is to introduce and situate Peircean affectivity within a post-Darwinian context. I use the work of Antonio Damasio as a tool for elucidating the post-Darwinian themes in Peircean affectivity. I also introduce aspects of Peirce's thought—self-control, phenomenology, and socialized instinctive beliefs—that facilitate a rich dialogue between Peircean affectivity and social criticism. My second objective is to highlight the specific social criticism thematic of my project: Well-meaning people in hegemonic groups (such as heterosexuals, men, whites, and so on) can nonconsciously perpetuate discrimination toward those in non-hegemonic groups (such as GLBTQs, women, people of color, and so on). My focus is the unintentional perpetuation of racism and (to a lesser extent) sexism. I present a preliminary sketch of this problematic, the details of which will be taken up in subsequent chapters, as I bring Peircean affectivity further into dialogue with social criticism.

Post-Darwinian Evolutionary Context and Self-Control

Peirce's philosophy occurs within a post-Darwinian evolutionary context, in which human beings are animal organisms who must successfully navigate the external world in order to survive and grow. While his preferred model of evolution is Lamarckian,[2] the post-Darwinian thematic of embodied, survival-mediated habit-taking must be held firmly in place, even when Peirce is not explicitly highlighting it for us. In fact, drawing out the post-Darwinian connections and implications of his ideas is the type of work that Peirce prefers his readers to do on their own, impatient as he is with having to spell out the obvious.[3]

Accordingly, my working definition of Peircean affectivity is the following: *the ongoing body-minded communication between the human organism and her or his individual, social, and external environments, for the promotion of survival and growth. This communication is shaped by biological, individual, semiotic, social, and other factors.*[4] This definition embraces the nonconscious, social, and semiotic dimensions of human reasoning. It is also influenced by the work of

Antonio Damasio, to which I turn below. I offer it in a fallibilist spirit that welcomes further inquiry and suggestions. I should note that Peirce does not use the term "affectivity." Nonetheless, the affective dimensions of his work—including feeling, emotion, sentiment, interest, instinct, agape, and sympathy, as well as belief, doubt, and habit—are harmoniously interrelated within my working definition. I employ "affectivity" as a synechistic term that encompasses the continuum of the human organism's ongoing communication with its environments, from the subtle nonconscious[5] physiological and semiotic processes to the more obvious forms of habit-taking and habit-modification.

Human habit-taking is an affective venture whereby individuals and groups communicate with their various environments in order to successfully cope and grow without undue interruptions from environmental factors outside their control.

For Peirce and the other classical American pragmatists, human habits are not merely mechanical, repetitive behavior like one's routine of brushing her teeth before bed or like "bad habits"—that is, behaviors one would like to eliminate from conduct, like slamming doors or smoking. Instead habits are body-minded patterns of behavior by which human organisms intelligently interact with their physical, social, and internal environments.[6] Habits span a continuum from uncontrolled activity, like the body's homeostasis mechanisms, to self-controlled conduct, whereby humans self-consciously take on new habits and critique existing habits. Habits, therefore, inform all human conduct, whether we (humans) realize it or not, and whether we like it or not. Peirce describes habits as patterns of nerve firings and attributes to each one a particular feltness, which can be confirmed experientially. For softball/baseball players, one's batting stance has a feel, for example. As a piano player, I can attest that my habits of playing scales have a feel to them. So do the habits of signing my name, typing on a keyboard, and driving my manual-transmission (stick-shift) car.

Two additional points about habit need to be introduced. First, habits are *tendencies*; they are not absolute laws that regulate behavior without exception. Thus my habits represent patterns and generalities that are not *always* executed in behavior. For example, my habit of walking to my favorite coffee shop every weekend reflects behavior in which I engage often, even *very* often. This habit does not rigidly dictate my behavior, however. Some weekends I have obligations with friends or family that preclude my routine; other weekends I am out of town. Still other weekends I try new coffee shops, for a change of pace. The same notion of habit-as-tendency applies at the level of communal or societal habits. In the United States, for example, there is a mainstream cultural habit of forbidding men to wear skirts. There are exceptions to this tendency, such that kilts are generally considered acceptable for men.

Moreover, because habits are tendencies and not absolute laws of human behavior, they can be changed. This change can be initiated by humans, because they have the self-control to set purposes/goals/ideals for their conduct.

A second point to consider is that, for Peirce, our beliefs are habits—that is, embodied patterns of nerve firings. The significance of this point will unfold in subsequent chapters. For now, I note that in the discussions to follow, I often use the term "belief-habit(s)," in order to keep the embodiment of belief in the foreground as I trace the affective themes in Peirce's work.

This second point, that beliefs are habits, relates to the first point, just noted, that habits are tendencies versus absolute laws. How is it that *belief*-habits are tendencies? One answer to this question is that someone's behavior may go against her belief-habits, which shows that belief-habits do not dictate behavior absolutely. For example, I believe that eating healthfully is best for my health, and my usual behavior is to eat foods that are good for me. Nonetheless, my behavior does not always reflect this belief-habit, especially when buttered movie-theater popcorn is involved. When my behavior diverges from my beliefs, I may or may not be aware of it. In the case of eating, I often *know* when I am eating foods that are unhealthy. With other beliefs, I may not know that my behavior contradicts them. My belief that racism is wrong, for example, may be contradicted by *unintentional* racism on my part. For example, years ago, the first time I taught an introductory philosophy course, my syllabus had no readings from people of color, which perpetuated the racist view that only white people have made significant contributions to philosophy. I was not *trying* to be racist in this case. Instead my focus was to have the typical historical survey of Western philosophy accounted for, which my department wanted me to cover, and I forgot to make room. Nonetheless, my syllabus was all white. How this unintentional contradiction between belief and practice is possible will be addressed in this and subsequent chapters.

Let us return more specifically to the affectivity of habit-formation in humans. Keeping the working definition of affectivity in mind, note that habit-formation is affective because it is a *process of inquiry* whereby one's habits are consistently attuned to environmental feedback that may interrupt one's conduct. My own habit of walking, for example, "communicates with" the ground on which I walk and the traffic patterns I encounter. Failure to attune to either set of "feedback" could result in, say, slipping on a patch of ice or getting hit by an oncoming car. So accustomed are humans to this ongoing communication between their habits and their environments that they often fail to notice that it occurs. This is one of the reasons why Peirce's phenomenology, to be presented below, is indispensable to a study of Peircean affectivity. Attention to the firstness, secondness, and thirdness of experience highlights how humans learn (thirdness) to avoid unwanted obstacles in their environment (secondness), which often results in habits that become so automatic as to function without their awareness (firstness).

Throughout the following chapters I will address the subtle and often unnoticed influences on human belief-habits that stem from two interrelated sources, the unique embodiment of each person and social-shaping. These influences often occur underneath the radar of human consciousness (cf. Damasio 2003, 228). I will be using the term "nonconscious" to describe such influences. My working definition of "nonconscious" is *occurring without one's conscious awareness.* My use of "nonconscious" is *inclusive* of both the "just beneath

the surface" meanings often ascribed to "subconscious" and psychoanalytic treatments of the "unconscious."[7] While I will not be explicitly examining psychoanalytic work in the present project, I want to
keep inquiry open on this front. Thus in a synechistic spirit, I take
"nonconscious" to embrace shadings and ambiguities that span from
the subconscious belief-habits that are just shy of conscious attention,
like my habit of pacing while I lecture, to "unconscious" habits that
are repressed and thus not readily accessible to conscious attention.[8]

My use of "nonconscious" encompasses the following interrelated
dimensions of human experience: (1) the homeostasis-promoting
physiological processes that ensure survival as an animal organism;
(2) the human organism's ongoing homeostasis-driven object assessment; (3) each person's idiosyncratic associations with ideas, events,
and objects in her world; and (4) instinctive beliefs, which can also
be described as common-sense or background beliefs. This list is
compatible with Peirce's description of "instinctive mind," which is
discussed below. Each of these four experiential facets often occurs
outside of consciousness, with varying degrees of conscious accessibility. The possibility for conscious accessibility, especially regarding
facets 2, 3, and 4, allows someone to change unwanted nonconscious
behaviors. In this context, testimony from others can be a key resource in bringing such behaviors to one's conscious awareness. Like
my working definition of affectivity, my conception of "nonconscious" is offered in a fallibilist spirit that welcomes further discussion and critique.

Exploring Peircean affectivity within a post-Darwinian context
gives rise to a significant concern that must be addressed before we
proceed. It might be objected that this post-Darwinian affective context undermines a view of the human person as capable of self-controlled conduct, whereby she shapes her own ends. Mapping survival
concerns onto human projects may seem to reduce, to an unacceptable degree, human activity to mere animalistic concerns for staying
alive and propagating the species.[9] In response, I would argue that the
opposite is indeed the case. Attention to a post-Darwinian thematic
enlarges self-controlled human activity, by drawing explicit attention

to ways self-control can be undermined by factors that might otherwise escape conscious attention. Achieving awareness of these factors is a step toward bringing them under the domain of self-control. Let me explain this point much more fully, by placing it within the multifaceted context of nonconscious belief-habits, self-control, Critical Common-sensism, communal inquiry, fallibilism, agapic sympathy, and reasonableness.

Whether humans acknowledge it or not, their ends are shaped by factors outside of their complete control, including culturally mediated interests in the survival of self and species.[10] A primary focus of my project is the dependency of children on their caretakers and community for survival, which leaves children vulnerable to internalizing unreasonable belief-habits about how reality works. By "internalization" (and its derivatives), I mean the incorporation, by means of reinforcement or trauma, of a belief into one's personal comportment and worldview, such that the belief is difficult to eradicate rationally.[11] On the whole, adopting the spoken and/or behavioral belief-habits conveyed by her caretakers and community promotes the young child's survival (cf. A. Rorty 1980, 122; Dewey [1922] 1988, 43–53, 65–68). Yet some of these belief-habits may promote racism, sexism, or other discriminatory thinking, which may be reinforced at the societal level. The young child does not have the resources to determine which caretaker and/or community belief-habits are survival-rich (such as "Hot stoves are dangerous") and which convey mere socio-political prejudice (such as "Women are inferior to men"). I discuss this tension in Chapter 2. By the time critical thinking develops in the human organism, problematic belief-habits—like those that promote racism, sexism, and so on—may be so internalized as to escape conscious awareness. Failure to embrace humanity's post-Darwinian legacy implicitly blocks the road of inquiry into human conduct by leaving such influences unexamined. To neglect inquiry into nonconscious, growth-inhibiting individual or communal habits is to promote blindness to the limitations such habits can place on us. This blindness undermines self-control.

For example, neuroscientist Joseph LeDoux, drawing on work in social psychology, explains how we can be affected *without conscious awareness* by stereotypes that affect how we treat people whose race or gender is different from our own:[12]

> [E]motions, attitudes, goals, and intentions can be activated *without awareness*, and . . . these can influence the way people think about and act in social situations. For example, physical features (like skin color or hair length) are enough to activate racial or gender stereotypes, regardless of whether the person possessing the feature expresses any of the behavioral characteristics of the stereotype. This kind of *automatic activation of attitudes* occurs in a variety of different situations and appears to constitute *our first reaction to a person*. And once activated, these attitudes can influence the way we then treat the person, and can even have influences over our behavior in other situations. (1996, 61–62, my emphasis; cf. Alcoff 2006, 242–43)

Since these reactions can occur without one's awareness, they can undermine self-control. That is to say, if my ideals for myself include acting in a nondiscriminatory fashion, yet I am having prejudiced reactions to people of color, for example, *without noticing these reactions,* then my self-control is undermined. My actual actions do not square with my consciously intended ideals for conduct.

Social psychologist John Bargh notes, with a measured optimism, that when people are educated about the nonconscious influence that race and sex stereotypes can have, they can correct for it if they want to, although such correction is by no means a simple task:

> When one is aware of the possibility of stereotypic bias and one possesses values against such bias, one can control the influence of the stereotype. . . . But the exercise of this control depends critically upon the awareness of the preconscious influence, and except in such cases as racial and (to a lesser extent) sex stereotypes, about which they have been educated, people are not aware of most varieties of preconscious influence. Even if they were to be, it would not be a straightforward matter to adjust for them. One suspects only that one has been influenced but has no idea how

much weight the preconscious input had on the final judgment. (1992, 250)

Bargh notes the importance of education for making people aware of how stereotypes can nonconsciously influence their thinking and behavior. This newfound awareness then can be used, by those who repudiate the stereotypes, to work against their nonconscious influence. While Bargh notes that it is not "a straightforward matter to adjust for" nonconscious stereotyping, I do not find this point overly discouraging (250). In fact, given the overconfidence I have seen in both white people and men in the United States, who assume that they simply are not racist and/or sexist, I find Bargh's comments refreshing (albeit sobering), as they underscore that addressing racism, sexism, and other social ills in the United States is far from a simple matter. Ongoing humility and hard work are necessary, even for those who have been educated about the nonconscious influence of racism, sexism, and other discriminatory belief-habits.

On Peirce's scheme, self-control occurs within a communal paradigm where fallibilism and ongoing growth are embraced, and correcting for conflicts between ideals and behavior is an ongoing process that is not supposed to come to an end. Peirce's thought is thus hopeful in the face of contradictions between ideals and conduct, because of the capacity for self-control itself. Self-control allows humans to reflect on their behavior in order to improve on it. Peirce notes, "Among the things which the reader, as a rational person, does not doubt, is that he not merely has habits, but also can exert a measure of self-control over his future actions" (EP 2:337). Self-control allows humans to set aims or goals or purposes (such as, say, trying to be more patient) that go beyond narrowly survival-oriented purposes, such as daily nutrition, which is a purpose shared by many nonhuman animals. Self-control enables humans to criticize their past actions (as, say, not reflecting the ideal of patient behavior) in order to improve on them (CP 5.533–35; EP 2:245–48, 337–38). Self-control also enables humans to inhibit behaviors (such as impatiently rolling one's eyes or looking at one's watch during conversations) that undermine one's purpose (of being more patient) (W 2:261 n. 6; EP 2:342, 385).[13]

Self-control's critical reflection extends into the background beliefs that inform an individual's or group's "common-sense" sensibilities. Peirce's Critical Common-sensism (CCS) is an epistemological doctrine that calls for the examination of beliefs that are usually taken for granted in human conduct and reasoning. Engaging in CCS is thus an operation of self-control, whereby individuals and communities scrutinize belief-habits that may seem too obvious to require critique (CP 5.497–525; EP 2:346–54). My project calls attention to how "the obvious" is often circumscribed within hegemonic-group interests, such that CCS efforts take on socio-political import. My focus is the common-sense beliefs that can take root in childhood.

Regarding beliefs that stem from childhood, Peirce explicitly says that we should critically examine them. In an 1893 addendum to his well-known essay "Fixation of Belief," Peirce notes:

> It will be wholesome enough for us to make a general review of the causes of our beliefs; and the result will be that most of them have been taken upon trust and have been held since we were too young to discriminate the credible from the incredible. Such reflections may awaken real doubts about some of our positions. (CP 5.376 n. 3)

Here Peirce explicitly acknowledges the vulnerability of children regarding beliefs they adopt during childhood. Small children do not have the critical capacity to question the beliefs of their caretakers and communities. It is therefore important to undertake critical reflection on our beliefs as adults, which "may awaken real doubts about some of our positions."

In his essay "What Pragmatism Is" (1905), Peirce takes care to situate self-control within a communal context. Following a discussion of self-control, he tells readers it is "all-important to assure oneself of and to remember" that "the man's circle of society (however widely or narrowly this phrase may be understood) is a sort of loosely compacted person, in some respects of higher rank than the person of an individual organism" (EP 2:338). Peirce is well aware of the power of society to manifest social belief-habits, which in turn shape the belief-habits of individual members of society. Knowledge itself is shaped by *communal* inquiry into knowledge and reality, which is why Peirce also says that "to make single individuals absolute judges of truth is most pernicious" (W 2:212). It is folly for an individual to conceive her self-controlled efforts as occurring outside of a social context. Attention to the communal context of self-control is also essential to the critique undertaken by Critical Common-sensism.

Examination of a socio-political example shows the importance of engaging Critical Common-sensism as a communal effort. As a child who was born in 1969, I learned the belief that racism is largely over in the United States, because of the accomplishments of the civil rights movement in the 1960s. Any lingering racism of, say, a family member here or there did not really "count" but only reflected an individual's failure to grasp that large-scale racism in the United States, such as legalized segregation, was over. It did not occur to me to question this idea as a child. As an adult, however, it did occur to me to question it. My experience as a teacher in an alternative high school, in a predominantly African American neighborhood in inner-city Milwaukee, Wisconsin, created real doubts for me that racism was, for the most part, absent in the United States. The consistent testimony from the students of color with whom I worked made it clear to me that my belief needed revising. As a result of my capacity for self-control, I criticized my former belief and changed it radically. In this example, my self-control *relied upon* a learning experience that exposed me to consistent testimony from people of color about ongoing racism in the United States. Without this experience and testimony, I cannot be sure that my adult self-controlled, critical reflection would have noticed that this particular childhood-derived belief (that racism is not a problem in the United States) was in need of revision.

This example highlights an important limitation of naively individualistic self-controlled efforts to scrutinize background beliefs from childhood—that is, efforts undertaken by an individual isolated from conversation with others in her community. Self-control cannot effectively criticize belief-habits that do not surface (to the individual) as needing to be examined. How, then, can a person become aware of belief-habits occurring outside of consciousness? One answer to this question is rooted in openness to feedback from other people, as my experience in Milwaukee indicates. Others can reveal belief-habits one enacts without realizing it. My students' testimony about the prevalence of racism made me conscious of my false belief-habit that racism is largely over in the United States. Becoming aware of this belief was the first step toward changing it. Thus, openness to feedback can enhance self-control. Through feedback one can learn of her blind spots and, ideally, adjust her belief-habits accordingly, ever open to further feedback as she continually works to instill new belief-habits. In Chapter 5, I discuss testimony further in this context, while also highlighting that, for Peirce, efforts at changing belief-habits must address their embodied roots; one cannot change a belief-habit via mere intellectual proclamation.

The importance of openness to the perspectives of others is implied in a description Peirce makes of self-control in his essay "Grounds of Validity of the Laws of Logic" (1869), where he places self-control in a communal context:

> Self-control seems to be the capacity for rising to an extended view of a practical subject instead of seeing only temporary urgency. This is the only freedom of which man has any reason to be proud; and it is because love of what is good for all on the whole, which is the widest possible consideration, is the essence of Christianity, that it is said that the service of Christ is perfect freedom. (W 2:261 n. 6)

Peirce is highlighting both the purposeful and inhibitory dimensions of self-control in this passage, placing both within the communal context of "love of what is good for all on the whole." In the sociopolitical context under consideration here, "the widest possible consideration" is a general purpose that helps inform more-specific purposes, such as the importance of repudiating racism (and other social ills) in the United States. Self-control enables people to have these loving and social-justice-oriented purposes, in addition to purposes shared with nonhuman animals, such as individual survival and propagation of the species. It should be noted that, for Peirce, Christianity is not grounded in doctrine or dogma but rather in love and communal concern. Thus his religious references can be applied secularly, beyond any doctrinal commitments of Christianity, as I will be applying them in this book by focusing on love and mutual concern among community members.[14]

When Peirce says that "[s]elf-control seems to be the capacity for rising to an extended view of a practical subject *instead of seeing only temporary urgency*," the inhibitory dimension of self-control is prominent alongside the purposeful dimension (W 2:261 n. 6, my emphasis). To achieve goals (such as getting up earlier in the morning), we often must say no to the "temporary urgency" of existing habits that resist growth (such as hitting the snooze button on the alarm clock). Within the socio-political context, those in hegemonic groups may need to inhibit the "temporary urgency" of dismissing negative feedback about discrimination from someone in a non-hegemonic group. The inhibition of this dismissal can be especially difficult regarding racism and sexism in the United States, since U.S. mainstream societal belief-habits proclaim that racism and sexism have largely ended in this country.[15] These are beliefs that are often considered unassailable knowledge. Moreover, these societal belief-habits often translate into individual belief-habits that involve being so sure that one *knows* racism or sexism to be over that further input is dismissed as unnecessary. When a white person says of a person of color that he or she is "playing the race card," it is often a dismissal that reflects a failure of inhibitory self-control.

When self-control *succeeds* in this socio-political scenario, those in hegemonic groups who sincerely eschew injustice achieve "an extended view of [the] practical subject" that embraces the broader purposes of love and the repudiation of injustice (W 2:261 n. 6). This extended view is also informed by genuine sympathy for the person giving the negative feedback (about one's own or society's behavior), even though this feedback might be hard to hear. Self-control in this case results in *resisting* the immediate urge to reject this testimony. The feedback is held in place as a source of learning and growth. This holding-in-place is fueled by a loving concern for the individual voicing the feedback. In his essay "Evolutionary Love" (1893), Peirce explains that agape is the ideal for humans in community. Agape, to be discussed more fully in Chapter 4, is love whose signal characteristic is an embrace of the different, even when this difference seems threatening (EP 1:353). Agapic love strengthens the inhibitory dimension of self-control, whereby the urge to reject what is foreign or uncomfortable is resisted.

It should come as no surprise that successful self-control in this context mirrors Peirce's first rule of reason, "that in order to learn you must desire to learn and in so desiring not be satisfied with what you already incline to think," and its oft-quoted corollary, "Do not block the way of inquiry" (EP 2:48). If those in hegemonic groups are satisfied in their belief-habits that racism and sexism are over in the United States, this satisfaction undermines the learning process. If they *know* that racism and sexism are over, then they may be convinced that there is nothing else to learn. This attitude fuels disinterest, or outright unwillingness, in pursuing inquiry into how racism and sexism (and other social ills) might be alive and well. This closed-mindedness blocks the learning process and blocks growth, both individually and at societal levels.

For self-control to optimally promote growth, there must be an ongoing epistemological humility at the individual and societal levels. Peirce is a fallibilist who believes that knowledge is always open for revision at some future point. This revision can be due to the organic nature of the cosmos itself, which has an element of spontaneity that can never be completely captured in scientific laws. It can also be due to testimony from community members who enhance or even overturn conventional knowledge about how reality works, which is my focus here. As I will discuss in Chapter 2, for Peirce reality is articulated by a *community* of inquiry, not by isolated Cartesian knowers. And he notes that this community is infinite in scope: "[T]he very origin of the conception of reality shows that this conception essentially involves the notion of a COMMUNITY, without definite limits, and capable of an indefinite increase of knowledge" (W 2:239). The communal epistemological efforts by which reality is described, then, involve a community "without definite limits," which implies that any given communal efforts are always subject to revision from future community members whose voices have yet to be heard. This ever-present possibility for communal growth, coupled with the organic growth of the cosmos itself, means that knowledge is also subject to "indefinite increase." Thus humility toward one's beliefs is critical.

This humility goes hand in hand with the most admirable ideal for humans, which is to promote the concrete growth of reasonableness in the universe. For Peirce, reason "always must be in a state of incipiency, of growth," as reason consists in the generality that governs individual events (EP 2:255). This generality is manifest in habits. And since the cosmos itself is *living*, the habits that form its very fabric grow as well, whether they be the large-scale habits of nature, such as the cycles of the seasons, or the smaller-scale habits that govern an individual's behavior. Peirce notes, "The creation of the universe, which did not take place during a certain busy week, in the year 4004 B.C., but is going on today and *never will be done*, is this very development of Reason" (EP 2:255, my emphasis). This being the case, "the ideal of conduct will be to execute our little function in the operation of the creation by giving a hand toward rendering the world more reasonable whenever . . . it is 'up to us' to do so" (EP 2:255). One way humans can help the universe become more reasonable is by fostering the growth of the reasonableness of their own belief-habits, as individuals and as communities.[16]

To grow is to increase in diversity, to become more heterogeneous (EP 2:254–55, 343–44; CP 1.174; EP 1:310). In the context of my project, I focus on growth in reasonableness in the context of human belief-habits that inform conduct and knowledge. Growth in reasonableness entails rendering the general patterns, or belief-habits, that govern one's behavior and/or knowledge more diverse. In the introduction,

I used the example of my belief-habit about racism growing in reasonableness, beginning with the unreasonable belief-habit that racism
is no longer a problem in the United States. This unreasonable belief-
habit grew in reasonableness to accommodate the prevalence of racism against African Americans, growth facilitated by the testimony
from my African American students in the 1990s. Nonetheless my understanding at this point in my life still was unreasonable to the extent that my belief-habit conceived racism against people of color as
merely a "black-white" paradigm, as if African Americans were the
only people to experience racism from Euro-American white people.
My belief-habit that racism is prevalent in the United States has
grown, further, into a multifaceted paradigm, including racism
against Asian Americans, Latino Americans, Native Americans, and
others. In addition, I now understand that within each of these
groups there is further diversity to be considered, such as the varying
countries and/or tribes that are represented under group designations
such as "Asian American," "Latino American," and "Native American." In addition, still other factors need to be considered, such as
English as a second (and sometimes imposed) language, immigration
issues, mixed-race issues, and more.[17] In fact, I now understand that
my belief-habits about racism will *never* achieve full reasonableness. I
will never be "done" understanding racism.[18] That said, my understanding of racism is now far more reasonable than it started out
being. There has been concrete growth. To view my understanding of
racism as "never done" is to be fallibilist toward my knowledge of the
world around me, ever open to further feedback that can help me
achieve further growth.

The epistemological humility required by self-control and reasonableness is ideally paired with agapic sympathy, which helps me hold
in place feedback that might be hard to hear. My care for others in
my community aids me in holding their testimony in place when it
challenges my own. Such challenges are often necessary for growth,
as they can reveal unreasonableness I may not realize I am acting out.
My behavior may *unintentionally* ignore, disparage, stereotype, or undermine diversity concerns regarding membership in the community

of inquiry (Lugones 2003, 83). I may thus unwittingly promote a homogenous or less diverse community of inquiry. As threatening as it may be to hear that my behavior has been, say, racist, sexist, or otherwise discriminatory, I ideally *care* about the community member(s) sharing this feedback. Epistemological humility and agapic sympathy thus ideally foster a self-controlled response to feedback—a response that holds in place the larger purpose of justice and diversity and inhibits knee-jerk exclusionary reactions (such as an accusation of "playing the race card") that block the road of inquiry.

On the Critical Common-sensism front, fallibilism, epistemological humility, and agapic sympathy all should inform the ongoing efforts by which humans continually expand self-control by scrutinizing their common-sense belief-habits. Since knowledge involves a community of inquiry, Critical Common-sensism must be undertaken not by Cartesian individuals isolated from communal dynamics but by socially attuned individuals and by societies. This way more common-sense beliefs have a chance of being critically assessed, because each individual can be helped by others to see background beliefs of which she is not conscious. My focus is on the background beliefs to which those in hegemonic groups are blind. Those in non-hegemonic groups are often in a position to identify those beliefs, such as those promoting heterosexism, racism, sexism, and other social ills. Ideally the genuine concern those in hegemonic groups have for those in non-hegemonic groups leads to an embrace of their testimony about ongoing discrimination.

When I use the term "embrace" in this context, I am signaling the epistemological attitude of deep open-mindedness that Peirce requires.[19] To embrace something—such as an idea, a person, a group, or someone's testimony—includes *but goes beyond* not rejecting it. To embrace something is also to allow oneself to learn from it. I contrast this with merely tolerating something, i.e., merely being open minded enough to *not reject* it. Take, for example, the following brief letter from a heterosexual woman who writes about her attitudes toward gay and lesbian people. Her comments are addressed to contemporary U.S. psychologist Harriet Lerner's advice column, *Life Preservers*:

I have nothing against homosexuals and I deplore prejudice of
any kind. But I fail to see the importance of "coming out" for
gays and lesbians. My husband and I do not discuss our sex life
or sexual orientation in public, so why should homosexuals?
What ever happened to privacy and discretion? (Lerner 1996, 311)

On the one hand, this writer tolerates "homosexuals." One could
speculate that she would, for example, support hiring a qualified person regardless of her or his sexual orientation. She also would probably repudiate violence aimed at those who are gay or lesbian. On the
other hand, the writer does not *embrace* their perspectives. This lack
of embrace is manifested in her closed-mindedness toward "coming
out," which undermines her *learning from* the experience of those
who are gay or lesbian. For example, while she and her husband "do
not discuss [their] sex life" publicly, they most likely *do* discuss their
sexual orientation in countless ways, at least implicitly, such as unproblematically using terms like "husband," "wife," "marriage," and
"honeymoon" (311). In 2010 legalized same-sex marriage is still deeply
resisted across the United States, such that same-sex couples are often
not in a position to marry. Moreover, public displays of affection in
the United States are held to a heterosexual norm that can make simply holding hands socially problematic for gay and lesbian couples
(312). If the letter writer *embraced* the idea of "coming out," she
might learn how prevalent heterosexual norms are in the United
States, such that being in the closet requires much "silence and se-
crecy" (311). As Lerner explains, "To be gay and in the closet is to
watch oneself constantly" (311). These efforts can be exhausting, an
insight the letter writer resists.

As a contrasting example, an *embrace* of same-sex relationships is
demonstrated by social criticism scholar Peggy McIntosh, who self-
identifies as heterosexual. She critically reflects on her own experience
to see how it reflects heterosexual privilege: "The fact that I live under
the same roof with a man triggers all kinds of societal assumptions
about my worth, politics, life, and values and triggers a host of un-
earned advantages and powers" (McIntosh 1988, 297–98). Such as
"Most people I meet will see my marital arrangements as an asset to

my life or as a favorable comment on my likability, my competence, or my mental health" (298). And "I can talk about the social events of a weekend without fearing most listeners' reactions" (298). These comments show that, beyond merely tolerating same-sex relationships, McIntosh allows the experiences of same-sex couples to teach her about the prevalence of heterosexual norms in U.S. culture.[20]

The embrace of feedback I discuss throughout this book focuses on those in hegemonic groups in relationship to the corresponding non-hegemonic groups, such as whites toward people of color, men toward women, heterosexuals toward GLBTQs, and so on. And within this context, the scenario I examine is the feedback that non-hegemonic groups can provide that discriminatory practices are still in play in the United States, despite mainstream assumptions that—at least regarding racism and sexism—injustices on these fronts are no longer prevalent. It is important to note that, when the relationship is reversed—such that the feedback comes from hegemonic groups and targets those in non-hegemonic groups—embracing feedback does not always foster reasonableness. In scenarios ranging from ignoring diverse perspectives to stereotyping them or dismissing them as unworthy of engagement, feedback from hegemonic groups can be explicitly unreasonable, because it promotes a community of inquiry that is less diverse and less open to inquiry about injustices that persist in the United States (Lugones 2003, 83). This issue will be taken up in Chapter 4.

Let us return to the objection that initiated this lengthy discussion of self-control, nonconscious belief-habits learned in childhood, fallibilism, epistemological humility, and agapic sympathy. The objection, once again, is that a focus on the post-Darwinian aspects of Peircean affectivity undermines a view of humans as self-controlled organisms, reducing them, to an unacceptable extent, to animal organisms that operate merely from a concern for individual survival and propagation of the species. I argue, in response, that *not* paying attention to the post-Darwinian aspects of human affectivity turns a blind eye on belief-habits learned in childhood that can function nonconsciously in adulthood, *undermining self-controlled behavior.*

Often exclusionary belief-habits that promote racism, sexism, and other social ills can operate in just this fashion.

To *embrace*, rather than merely tolerate, the post-Darwinian context for human thought and behavior is to allow ourselves to learn from it, to *promote* self-control on individual and social levels. This embrace opens inquiry into how humans might reason best, given that some of their ends are unavoidably shaped by culturally mediated concerns for survival and propagation of the species. This open inquiry reveals how survival concerns are linked, through the vulnerability of young children, to the socio-politically derived belief-habits of caretakers and society. My project explores how socio-politically derived, exclusionary habits can become internalized by those in privileged groups—such as Euro-Americans, heterosexuals, men, etc.—such that they function nonconsciously and threaten the reasonableness of inquiry. It embraces the Critical Common-sensist mandate that communal efforts be made to criticize common-sense (or background) beliefs in order to promote growth in human self-control. These efforts must include embracing the testimony of those—including people of color, GLBTQs, women, etc.—who can identify heterosexist, racist, sexist, or other discriminatory background belief-habits that Euro-Americans, heterosexuals, men, and others may not notice.

It should be noted that communal persons (that is, communities or societies) as well as individual persons are subject to the blind spots, and their concomitant dangers, that nonconscious belief-habits create. Communities or societies that allow growth-inhibiting habits to function without critique can easily perpetuate oppression, thereby undermining the flourishing of their members. The individual and her community are closely related. Oppression does not reside only in socio-political structures that are external to community members, such as laws and institutions. It also may reside in the internalized habits of members of historically privileged and oppressed groups. The latter may internalize self-exclusionary habits, which are rooted in lack of confidence in one's perspective as a community member

(hooks 2003a; Mills 1997, 118–19). The former may internalize exclusionary habits that disparage the perspectives of non-hegemonic individuals or groups. This second phenomenon is my focus in this
project, that is, growth-undermining habits of privilege, which include mistrusting and dismissing feedback from those in non-hegemonic groups (Alcoff 2006, 40).

Now that I have, hopefully, laid to rest a significant objection to
studying Peircean affectivity through a post-Darwinian lens, the path
is clear to continue that study and to explain more fully how its socio-
political trajectories take shape.

Peircean Affectivity and the Work of Antonio Damasio

As outlined above, the affective dimensions of Peirce's work—
including feeling, emotion, sentiment, interest, instinct, agape, and
sympathy, as well as belief, doubt, and habit—are harmoniously interrelated under my working definition of Peircean affectivity: *the ongoing body-minded communication between the human organism and
her or his individual, social, and external environments, for the promotion of survival and growth. This communication is shaped by biological,
individual, semiotic, social, and other factors.* I use "affectivity" to capture the continuum of the human organism's ongoing conversations,
from subtle to obvious, with its varied environments. This continuum
is underwritten by a post-Darwinian survival thematic that informs the
human organism's conduct. As I will continually demonstrate in this
project, the Peircean human organism is *always* "emotionally susceptible" or affective.[21] Antonio Damasio's work helps explain why.

Damasio's work involves the scientific investigation of emotion
and feeling in their relationship to the body and mind of the human
organism. He operates from an evolutionary perspective that is sensitive to the embodied, semiotic, and social dimensions of the human
experience, which are inseparable from concerns for promoting the
survival and flourishing of self and species. In what follows, I draw
from his three books: *Descartes' Error: Emotion, Reason, and the*

Human Brain (1994), *The Feeling of What Happens: Body and Emotion in the Making of Consciousness* (1999), and *Looking for Spinoza: Joy, Sorrow, and the Feeling Brain* (2003).[22] While Damasio does not specifically highlight and define the term "affectivity," he uses the phrase "process of affect" to refer to "the complex chain of events" that are involved in emotion and feeling (2003, 27; cf. 1999, 342 n. 10). He also applauds Spinoza's use of the Latin *affectus* as " 'the modifications of the body, whereby the active power of the said body is increased or diminished, aided or constrained, and also the ideas of such modifications' (Spinoza, *The Ethics*, Part III)" (Damasio 2003, 301 n. 3).[23] I thus use the term "theory of affectivity" as a working description of Damasio's work in this context, with the proviso that his work is ongoing and grows from book to book. Damasio himself notes, in fallibilist fashion, "I have a difficult time seeing scientific results, especially in neurobiology, as anything but provisional approximations, to be enjoyed for awhile and discarded as soon as better accounts become available" (1994, xviii). Damasio's research is, nonetheless, aimed at formulating and testing his hypotheses scientifically, as he documents in each of his books.

The compatibilities between Damasio's work and Peirce's thought are striking.[24] While we should not force a point-for-point match between the two, Damasio's theory of affectivity sheds considerable light on affective themes in Peirce's thought, especially the implicit ones. What follows is a selective treatment of Damasio's work, as it pertains to Peircean affectivity.

a. Homeodynamics and Survival

Damasio pairs human affectivity with homeostasis. For Damasio the human organism is a "homeostasis machine" in constant body-mind interaction with its environment. "Homeostasis" refers to the *ongoing* environmental assessment an organism undertakes to promote its own survival and well-being (Damasio 2003, 35). Damasio describes homeostasis in the following way:

All living organisms from the humble amoeba to the human are born with devices designed to solve *automatically*, no proper reasoning required, the basic problems of life. Those problems are: finding sources of energy; incorporating and transforming energy; maintaining a chemical balance of the interior compatible with the life process; maintaining the organism's structure by repairing its wear and tear; and fending off external agents of disease and physical injury. The single word homeostasis is convenient shorthand for the ensemble of regulations and the resulting state of regulated life. (2003, 30, Damasio's emphasis)

Damasio suggests that "homeodynamics" is a more apt term, as it better suggests the constant activity of the body.[25] I agree with this suggestion and will, from this point forward, be using the term "homeodynamics" to convey the processes outlined in the above passage.

An organism depends, then, on the homeodynamic regulation of its internal life processes. Damasio's theory of affectivity starts with this biological truism. Human affect involves the ongoing appraisal of internal and external environments, whereby changes in environment are detected. Any given change signals either a potential threat or a boon to the organism's survival/flourishing. The organism then addresses "the problem" of either protecting itself from the situation at hand or capitalizing on it (Damasio 2003, 35–36). The changes and responses involved range from the subtle to the obvious, and from microscopic to macroscopic, all part and parcel of the human organism's ongoing homeodynamic assessment of the environment (55–56).

Affective behaviors involve an evolutionary continuum that spans from the behavior of single-celled organisms[26] to the self-controlled behaviors of human organisms (Damasio 2003, 40 ff., 51 ff.). They also involve stimuli occurring both outside the organism and within the organism. Internal stimuli, such as cues arising from hunger or hormones, contribute to the highly individualized interest(s) that characterize a human organism's intentionality toward the world (39).[27] External stimuli—i.e., the wide range of physical things and events that we encounter outside of our physical bodies—are filtered through personalized interest(s) as well. These dimensions of individuality will be discussed more fully in Chapter 2, in conjunction with human embodiment and Peirce's discussions of cognition.

The lowest levels of homeodynamic/affective behaviors include the operation of the immune system, metabolism maintenance, and "basic reflexes" (Damasio 2003, 37). The next highest levels include "pleasure and pain behaviors," as well as drives (32–34). These lower levels shade into the next higher level, which Damasio calls the "emotions-proper" (38 ff.). Emotions-proper include what are conventionally considered emotions, like fear and sadness. Damasio notes that "emotions *in the broad sense*" is an appropriate classification of all homeodynamic activity up to and including emotions-proper (35, my emphasis). If continued to its furthest human potential, affective behavior is accompanied by *feelings*, whereby the human is aware of the affect being experienced.[28] This awareness, in turn, allows for the planning of future actions, so that opportunities and obstacles can be anticipated (Damasio 2003, 51 ff., 176 ff.; 1999, 284–85). The complexity of affective appraisal and response increases with the increasing complexity of the organism and environment (Damasio 1994, 89–94; 2003, 30–42). The human brain and mind[29] are, from an evolutionary perspective, adaptations for survival and flourishing (Damasio 1994, 89–90).

The more basic affective/homeodynamic behaviors are nested within the higher forms (Damasio 2003, 37–38). Damasio stresses that evolution does not throw away the old as it brings in the new (1994, xiii–xiv). The complexity of human feelings is not freestanding but has roots in the most basic bodily processes. Homeodynamics does not consist of a "tidy" set of relations, such that a "simple linear hierarchy" could be established (Damasio 2003, 38). Damasio uses the metaphor of "a tall, messy tree with progressively higher and more elaborate branches coming off the main trunks and thus maintaining a two-way communication with their roots. The history of evolution is written all over that tree" (2003, 38). Thus the most sophisticated levels of human affectivity are rooted in a back-and-forth information exchange with the most basic survival-oriented biological regulation.

b. Homeodynamic Character of "Emotions-Proper"

Damasio's work on human "emotions-proper" is sensitive to their inborn, social, and semiotic dimensions, as well as to their varied and often subtle forms. He divides emotions-proper into three types—background, primary, and secondary.

Background emotions are a composite product of usually "invisible" processes:

> I imagine background emotions as the largely unpredictable result of several concurrent regulatory processes engaged within the vast playground that our organisms resemble. These include metabolic adjustments associated with whatever internal need is arising or has just been satisfied; and with whatever external situation is now being appraised and handled by other emotions, appetites, or intellectual calculation. (Damasio 2003, 44)

Background emotions reflect the body's general "state of being" based on the ongoing dimensions of life regulations on which survival or homeodynamics depend (44).[30] Much of the time the work of background emotions happens nonconsciously, occurring outside a person's conscious awareness (Damasio 1994, 152; 1999, 228).

Damasio describes *primary emotions*[31] as "innate, preorganized" (1994, 133). These are the emotions theorists often group together as basic emotions: "The frequent listing includes fear, anger, disgust, surprise, sadness, and happiness" (Damasio 2003, 44). They are cross-culturally identifiable and depend for their functioning on the brain's limbic system (2003, 44; 1999, 285; 1994, 133). *Social emotions* (or secondary emotions) are those emotions that have some degree of preorganized programming but depend for their full manifestation on the social milieu of the organism (Damasio 2003, 45–47). Damasio includes in this category embarrassment, jealousy, guilt, and pride (1999, 51). These emotions involve a sensitivity to *social* context (Damasio 1994, 138). He notes that they go beyond a dependence on the brain's limbic system. They are evolutionarily more complex, requiring "the agency of prefrontal and of somatosensory cortices" (Damasio 1994, 134).

Damasio stresses that homeodynamic behaviors are present at or soon after birth but that learning plays a more and more active role in their implementation. This is especially true for the more complex mechanisms of the emotions-proper:

> The package of reactions that constitutes crying and sobbing is ready and active at birth; what we cry *for*, across a lifetime, changes with our experience. All of these reactions are automatic and largely stereotyped, and are engaged under specific circumstances. (Learning, however, can modulate the execution of the stereotyped pattern. Our . . . crying *plays* differently in different circumstances. . . .) (Damasio 2003, 34–35, emphasis in original)

The social-shaping of affectivity is significant for my project. As we will examine in subsequent chapters, social influence plays an important role in the semiotic-affective interaction the Peircean human organism has with his or her world.

Damasio's account of emotions-proper is Peircean in its inclusion of nonconscious, innate, and socially shaped dimensions of bodily activity. Of particular interest, for my purposes, is Damasio's account of background emotions, which helps elucidate the continuum of bodily activity that holds between Peirce's conceptions of feeling and emotion, as discussed in his Cognition Series, which I examine in Chapter 2. Generally speaking, background emotions also help us to understand the continual bodily motion of the human organism. Peirce's conviction that cognition and semiotics are *processes* resonates with the ongoing homeodynamic/affective behavior the human must maintain in order to survive. And his conviction that the individual cannot be separated from her synechistic social context is validated by Damasio's point that learning plays a role in shaping our inborn affective orientation toward our environments (2003, 34–35).

c. Feelings and Semiotics

Damasio argues that feelings depend on having a brain with the capacity to represent to itself what is going on in the body (2003, 109). Human feelings involve a sophistication of representation whereby the brain is able to represent to itself both the body and the self (Damasio 1999, 279 ff.).[32] In what follows, I use "feeling" to convey "human feeling." Feelings are signs, then, and they require a brain with semiotic capacity and self-awareness. They allow us to feel our emotions (in the broad sense)—like thirst or sadness—and to be aware of these feelings.[33] This account resonates strongly with Peircean ideas about feelings, firstness, and semiotics.

Damasio explains that, given any affect, feelings occur based on the mapping (or representation) of the resultant bodily response in the somatosensory regions of the brain.[34] He offers the following "hypothesis . . . in the form of a provisional definition": "[A] feeling is *the perception of a certain state of the body* along with the perception of a certain mode of thinking and of thoughts with certain themes" (Damasio 2003, 86, my emphasis).[35] The primary source of feelings is "the brain's body maps" (85). The nature of feelings as *perceptions* is similar to Peirce's equation of feeling and sensation in his early writings, which will be discussed below. Note that Damasio highlights the reliance of feelings on information about the body.

Feelings allow humans to register, for future reference, the survival value of objects in their environment. In fact, Damasio considers virtually all objects to be affectively salient for the human organism. This should come as no surprise, given that our homeodynamic balance requires our constant appraisal of objects in our environment for signs of benefit or danger. Thanks to human memory, the affective salience of encountered objects is remembered, becoming part of the information we "take in" from the world regarding the objects we perceive, whether we are conscious of it or not (Damasio 1999, 47, 57–58):

> As far as I can fathom, few if any perceptions of any object or event, actually present or recalled from memory, are ever neutral in emotional terms. Through either innate design or by learning, we react to most, perhaps all, objects with emotions, however weak, and subsequent feelings, however feeble. (Damasio 2003, 93; cf. 309 n. 3)

The compatibility of this feltness of objects with Peirce's work will be elaborated in Chapter 2, in conjunction with the felt dimension of cognition and association. The nonconscious dimension of association will be discussed in Chapter 4. For now, I will note that Damasio helps to articulate the interweaving dimensions involved in the feltness of a sign, highlighting as he does that innate, individual, and social influences play crucial roles in the affective coloring of objects (cf. Damasio 2003, 48–49). In what follows, for the sake of simplicity, I construe "object" broadly to refer to events, as well as "entities as diverse as a person, a place, a melody, a toothache, a state of bliss" (Damasio 1999, 9).

Peirce's Phenomenology: The Categories of Experience

Peirce's phenomenology highlights the dimensions of human affective engagement in the world. Just as Damasio articulates the human's ongoing environmental assessment and adaptation, so too do the categories of experience, the ever-present dimensions of what Marcia Moen calls the "phenomenological richness" of human experience (1991, 435). There are three categories: firstness, secondness, and thirdness. Peirce's phenomenological account of these categories gives us tools with which we can elucidate the complexities of the personalized/socialized, affective experience of the human organism. The categories are especially helpful for articulating the socio-political dimensions of human experience and habit-taking. The following account of the categories, with foci tailored to my project, will be drawn on and added to in subsequent chapters.[36]

a. Firstness, Secondness, and Thirdness

"Firstness" refers to the pre-discursive awareness that underlies one's actions and thoughts. Peirce describes this category as

> a consciousness in which there is no comparison, no relation, no recognized multiplicity . . . no imagination of any modification of

what is positively there, no reflexion. . . . [A]ny simple and positive quality of feeling would be something which our description
fits,—that it is such as it is quite regardless of anything else. (EP
2:150, 1903)

Firstness involves a felt attunement to the world within and outside of one's body. In its purity it cannot be described, because it is
too immediate to allow for comparison or contrast to other experiences or thoughts. It is pre-reflective. It includes the harmonious
rhythms of breathing, heartbeat, and other inborn habits that maintain the human organism's biological flourishing. It also encompasses
other habits to which one is so accustomed that they function without one's thinking about them. Ironically, firstness is often most easily "spotted" when something disturbs it. Firstness, for example, is
the felt equanimity of a beautiful walk during a steady snowfall, during which there is a harmony between you and your surroundings.
You are part of the whiteness coming down around you. As Peirce
would do, I invite you—the reader—to imagine yourself on a stroll
in the snow. Try to tap into the background feltness that characterizes
your attunement to the snow and your surroundings . . . Then, imagine yourself slipping unexpectedly on a patch of ice and falling down,
or having your wheelchair become stuck in a patch of unshoveled
snow. *These* are examples of secondness.

Secondness at its most extreme occurs when one meets brute environmental resistance to her projects, like falling down or getting
stuck. It involves a non-ego element of one's experience, a "not me"
that resists one's movement in the world. Peirce describes secondness
as "the element that the rough-and-tumble of this world renders
most prominent. We talk of *hard* facts. That hardness, that compul-
siveness of experience, is Secondness" (EP 2:268, 1903, emphasis in
original; cf. EP 2:150–51, 153–54, 1903). Secondness is also characterized by immediacy, *hic et nunc*[37] (here and now), as Peirce is fond of
saying. This dimension of experience, the brute clash that occurs
when you fall, get stuck, are startled, stub your toe, etc., *has no explanation* in the immediacy of the moment. (For explanations, we must

look beyond secondness and into the experiential dimension of third-ness.) Secondness can involve less tangible disturbances, like having one's absorption in a piece of music be disturbed by a ringing phone, doorbell, fire alarm, etc. The disturbances can also shade off into sub-tle environmental resistances, like the ground that breaks one's steps or supports one's wheelchair, and other patterns of physicality to which an individual is familiarized in her everyday experience. At this subtle extreme, secondness shades into firstness.

One can become so habitualized to certain environmental resist-ances that they become part of one's attunement to one's everyday world. When I first was learning how to drive a car with a manual transmission, for example, the experience was filled with paradigma-tic secondness. I was forever meeting brute resistance from the car as I struggled to get the clutch, gas, and gear shift to work in harmony with the incline of the road. How I dreaded stopping at a red light on a hill! I have been driving a stick shift for more than twenty years now, and it has long since become a part of the firstness through which I am attuned to my world as I drive. The rhythm of changing gears is a lot like the rhythm of walking for me. I do not think about it unless something goes wrong; then I am back to secondness-proper again.

Two points can be made regarding this shading of secondness into firstness and vice versa. First of all, firstness and secondness are part of every experience, although their proportions will vary. Falling down and getting stuck are experiences in which secondness is prom-inent, but nonetheless they still involve a pre-discursive, preconcep-tual attunement to one's environment (firstness). This is because each of these experiences has the felt awareness of one's personalized, em-bodied experience—that is to say, the experience insofar as it is, say, *mine* or *yours*.[38] On the other hand, the majestic stroll *before* falling or getting stuck involved a preponderance of firstness, but also sec-ondness to the extent that the physical environment offered resis-tance, such as the sidewalk resisting one's footfalls or wheelchair.

Thirdness, for our purposes, is the felt sense of synthesis involved in learning and reasoning, and the new (or newly adjusted) habits that result from learning and reasoning (EP 1:260, 291, 296).[39] It is the category in which self-control finds its home. It is thanks to thirdness that I learned how to drive the manual transmission, so that the secondness of awkward gear-shifting evolved into *smooth* gear-shifting that became part of my firstness. It is thanks to thirdness that I could form the goal of learning to drive the stick shift in the first place. More generally, thirdness allows humans to creatively adapt to their environmental vicissitudes, so that the second-nature habits that have become part of firstness can be changed when survival and/or growth require it.

Thirdness involves the habit-formation that *mediates* between one's felt, embodied pre-discursive awareness of the world (firstness) and resistance from one's environments (secondness). To form habits is to learn the patterns by which we can best harmonize with the various secondnesses of our environments. Thirdness was prominent for my young niece, for example, when she learned that water, after being left awhile in the freezer, turns to ice. (She called me long-distance to tell me her discovery.) Thirdness is only subtly present in the beautiful stroll in the snow, manifested in your implicit reasoning as to which habits to execute (habits of walking, navigation, etc.). It is present in the falling on the ice or getting stuck as you search for the reason why the unexpected scenario happened and then hypothesize how to avoid the problem in the future. Perhaps you thought that your boots had suitable traction to prevent falls or that this stretch of sidewalk was always kept clear of accumulated snow. Now you know better and will adjust your habits of conduct and expectation accordingly.

Thirdness helps humans adapt in order to survive. Francisco Jiménez, for example, writes of how his family immigrated to the United States when he was a child, in order to escape the poverty of their homeland in Tlaquepaque, Mexico (1998, 1–8). He knew no English at first. Learning English (thirdness), for Jiménez, soon became a matter of survival, so he could succeed in the U.S. school system, and so he could more effectively help support his family financially.[40] Had Jiménez and his brother not become fluent English speakers, they would not have been able to secure the custodial work that supported their family after their father seriously injured his back in the fields as a migrant worker (2001, 83–90). The brothers were in high school at the time (70). The man who hired them specified that their fluency in English was a necessary job requirement, such that their father, who did not speak English, would be ineligible to work for him (85–86). Clearly Jiménez's ability to learn English enabled him to adapt to living and working in the United States, so that he could—even as a teenager—become a primary breadwinner for his family.

Thirdness also enables humans, apart from the context of immediate survival concerns, to self-consciously take on new habits.[41] Thirdness, for example, enabled me to pursue learning Spanish as an adult, through taking classes, and continual practice in reading, speaking, writing, and listening to what, for me, is a new language. Studying this language has not been a matter of survival for me, as it was for Jiménez. In fact studying Spanish reflects my economic, racial, and "First World" privilege, since I have the resources and the noncoercive socio-political climate in which to learn a new language because I want to.

When habits are first being formed, thirdness is prominent, often alongside disruptive secondness. Firstness often becomes prominent when habits have been mastered. Early in the learning process there is often an awareness of the execution of new patterns of behavior, as one familiarizes oneself with these patterns and works to stabilize them (in order to avoid disruptive secondness). When I was first learning to drive a manual transition, once again, I was very conscious of where the clutch and gas pedals were, as well as of my right hand on the stick shift. I worked to internalize the correct balance of these components to avoid the secondness of stalling (or "kangarooing") the car. As I became accomplished at driving the stick shift, these now familiar patterns faded from explicit awareness into automatic functioning. In other words, the thirdness of the habit gradually shaded into firstness.[42] This is to say that familiar, functional habits that meet with little obstructive secondness or resistance tend to fade from one's immediate awareness as specific habits. Firstness and thirdness are closely related in this respect. The formation of a brand-new habit involves a higher proportion of thirdness/learning/synthesis, and, as the habit becomes routine for us, it shades into firstness. Those with good health and able bodies do not tend to notice their habits of breathing, walking, writing, and managing daily tasks. These habits become part of the gestalt feeling of embodiment that characterizes firstness.

This relationship between firstness and thirdness creates a tension that will be explored below and in subsequent chapters. On the one hand, thirdness enables humans to critique their existing habits. Peirce notes that self-control is used to reflect on one's ideals, to ensure they are consistent with conduct (EP 2:246). Since, however, one's habits can function without one's awareness (in the second-nature gestalt of firstness), it is possible for one's conduct to undermine one's ideals without self-controlled critical reflection catching the inconsistency. In "What Pragmatism Is," Peirce describes how deeply rooted established beliefs are for humans: "Belief is not a momentary mode of consciousness; it is a habit of mind essentially enduring for some time, and mostly (at least) unconscious; and like other habits, it is (until it meets with some surprise that begins its dissolution) perfectly self-satisfied" (EP 2:336–37). In this context, Peirce is describing the belief-habits that have become part of firstness, such that they function automatically—so automatically as to escape one's awareness. Peirce's insistence on placing self-control in a communal context suggests that feedback from others can help the individual in her efforts at self-control, by helping her identify nonconscious belief-habits that reside, undetected, in the firstness of her experience.

b. Introducing Socio-Political Secondness

A specific application of Peirce's phenomenology that I employ for my project is what I call *socio-political* secondness. I highlight the influence its presence or absence has on habit-taking and the corresponding shaping of firstness.

Peirce does not use the term "social secondness," but his ideas are compatible with the term, by which I mean socially dictated environmental resistance. Secondness—which involves any type of environmental resistance—occurs not only because of physical constraint and the laws of nature, like tripping on a rock and falling down. It can also occur because of social conventions that are largely outside one's control. For example, no one living in the contemporary mainstream of the United States who was sincerely hoping to land a conventional job would *dream* of showing up at a job interview, say, naked—even if the temperature and humidity were so high that wearing clothes was uncomfortable. This dress code is due not to physical but to social constraint.

Socio-political secondness refers to social secondness that is not encountered equally by all members of society, like the convention of wearing clothes in public is. Rather socio-political secondness, in the context of my project,[43] involves constraint that is directed at non-hegemonic groups. It includes prejudice and discrimination based on factors such as economic class, race, sex, sexuality, and so on. One's daily experience is often characterized by socio-political environmental resistance if one is a member of socio-politically targeted groups, such as GLBTQs, people of color, the poor, women, and so on. People in these groups are often limited in their movement in the world for socio-political reasons.

For example, legal scholar Patricia J. Williams had the following experience in 1986, after buzzer systems had been installed in many New York City stores as a crime prevention measure. The basic idea was to deny entry to suspicious-looking people during business hours without denying access to upstanding customers. Williams writes:

> I was shopping in Soho and saw in a store window a sweater that
> I wanted to buy for my mother. I pressed my round brown face
> to the window and my finger to the buzzer, seeking admittance.
> A narrow-eyed, white teenager wearing running shoes and feast-
> ing on bubble gum glared out, evaluating me for signs that would
> pit me against the limits of his social understanding. After about
> five seconds, he mouthed "We're closed," and blew pink rubber

at me. It was two Saturdays before Christmas, at one o'clock in the afternoon; there were several white people in the store who appeared to be shopping for things for *their* mothers. (1991, 44–45, Williams's emphasis)

Williams's movement in the world was limited by a "non-ego" force that barred her entry into a store, Benetton's, based on the color of her skin. The door was locked and was thus a physical instance of secondness, but it *need not have remained locked* to Williams once she pressed the buzzer. Socio-political constraint is ultimately the reason she was denied entry. Brute resistance blocked her path and shattered her equanimity: "In the flicker of his judgmental gray eyes, that saleschild had transformed my brightly sentimental, joy-to-the-world, pre-Christmas spree to a shambles. He snuffed my sense of humanitarian catholicity, and *there was nothing I could do to snuff his*, without making a spectacle of myself" (45, my emphasis).

Larger-scale examples of socio-political secondness targeting people of color in the United States abound. In *Asian American Dreams*, for example, journalist Helen Zia details the numerous socio-political obstacles, past and present, encountered by Asian Americans in the United States (2000). Despite the "model minority" myth that is used to pit them against African Americans, Asian Americans have experienced blatant racism dating back to the nineteenth century and extending into the present, including the internment of Japanese Americans during World War Two and, more currently, glass ceilings, hate crimes, and racial profiling (23–52, 293–302).[44]

People who are Euro-American, born and raised in the mainstream of the United States, are often not familiar with socio-political secondness based on race.[45] This is because mainstream U.S. society remains socio-politically structured to support and promote whiteness. Thus whites often experience an *absence* of socio-political secondness. This absence promotes habits of false universalization, whereby a Euro-American experience—where race is not an obstacle—is conceptualized as the norm, both in mainstream U.S. society and in the belief-habits of white people. False universalization occurs when a person or group assumes their experience is representative for all of humanity. When false universalization of a Euro-American experience occurs, it can be difficult for whites to take seriously the testimony of people of color who report on the socio-political secondness they experience based on their race. Yet to deny the latter's input regarding racism perpetuates a hegemonic norm that blocks inquiry and obstructs societal growth.

In terms of the phenomenological categories, white privilege shapes the felt equanimity (firstness) of Euro-Americans within the white-promoting habits of mainstream U.S. society. Euro-Americans often receive no socio-political resistance (secondness) based on their race. Thus, their white-privileged habits, which are often introduced in childhood, easily slide into the complacent attunement of firstness, often functioning so automatically as to escape notice. While firstness feels so deeply natural that it is pre-discursive and pre-reflective, this naturalness can be a repository for pernicious, socio-politically shaped habits regarding race. Shannon Sullivan notes:

> Human beings could never survive if, for example, they had to consciously guide every muscular movement that it takes to get out of bed in the morning. While the nonconscious aspect of habit enables organic flourishing, it also can limit it by allowing all sorts of destructive habits to operate undetected. White privilege is one[46] such habit. (2006, 4)

Building on Sullivan's point about the undetected habits of privilege, I would add that humans also could not survive into adulthood if they did not receive adequate care as infants and small children. Child development is a phase where young human organisms form many belief-habits about the world that become part of their firstness. Once again, survival interests and societal norms can coalesce for the infant and child, shaping his or her belief-habits so fully that they function undetected in adulthood. We can describe such belief-habits as "socialized instinctive beliefs," which I will explain more fully below. Heterosexual, male, white, and other privileged belief-habits often fall into this category.

Peircean Semiotics, Evolution, and Feelings

It is not my intention to fully engage Peirce's semiotics in my project.[47] Instead, I focus on one fundamental semiotic insight that informs Peirce's thought and helps make sense of Peircean affectivity: all our cognitions are signs. The starting point for this semiotic cognition is, for Peirce, feelings. This section explores how feelings are *at once* a sight of firstness, secondness, and thirdness. Beyond the qualitative immediacy discussed above, feelings involve sensation and synthesis. They are the portal through which objects *outside* the human organism are rendered as cognitions or ideas *within* the organism. Since we cannot access the world outside our bodies except through signs, our interaction with the world around us is semiotically mediated. While Peirce's semiotic theory itself can be a daunting and highly technical study, this basic insight about our relations to signs makes good sense. *Of course* we do not access the external world except through signs, as they are rendered for us by our sense organs and the corresponding nerve firings. When I see the dirty dishes in my sink, for example, this seeing is mediated by a synthesis involving the cone and rod cells in my eyes.

Peirce's semiotic insight also makes good sense from an evolutionary point of view. Semiotic capacity promotes survival. Damasio notes that "the ability to display images internally and to order those images in a process called thought" reflects a complexity by which certain animals can better "predict the future, plan accordingly, and choose the next action" (1994, 90). Since Damasio uses the term "images" broadly,[48] I take his usage to be equivalent—for our purposes—to "signs" as they occur in the human mind on Peirce's scheme. Because of the complexity of their environment, humans require intermediary neural circuitry more sophisticated than simple stimulus-response mechanisms.[49] In addition to perceiving the external world via images or signs, humans also possess an array of neural organs and systems that monitor their ongoing interactions with the external world (90–94). This complicated scheme allows for sophistication in manipulating images, conceptualizing, and categorizing, all of which help us reason and make decisions (94).

For Peirce, the basic point of contact between the human organism and the external world is "feeling" or "sensation," terms he uses synonymously in this context.[50] This synonymous usage signals the inseparability of qualitative immediacy (firstness) and environmental confrontation (secondness). Feelings/sensations are continuously triggered by objects external to the human body, which stimulate nerve firings in the sense organs. Feeling, or sensation, involves the grouping of nervous impulses (by means of hypothetic synthesis) such that a rudimentary sorting of things can occur—e.g., these red objects are different from those blue ones, or these are "painful circumstances" and those are "pleasurable" (W 1:472, 495–96; W 2:197 ff.). To have feelings requires *both* body and mind. In his 1866 Lowell Lectures, Peirce says: "Feelings, we all know, depend upon the bodily organism. The blind man from birth has no such feelings as red, blue, or any other colour; and without any body at all, it is probable we should have no feelings at all . . ." (W 1:495). Feelings are also fully *mind*-derived for Peirce. They are the felt dimension of cognition (W 2:227), and they also involve the ideation that makes cognition possible in the first place.[51]

Peirce's rather abstract descriptions of firstness, of which feeling is paradigmatic, can obscure the secondness and thirdness that always accompany an instance of feeling. Recall the earlier description of firstness as "a consciousness in which there is no comparison, no relation, no recognized multiplicity . . . no imagination of any modification of what is positively there, no reflexion. . . . [A]ny simple and positive quality of feeling would be something which our description fits,—that it is such as it is quite regardless of anything else" (EP 2:150, 1903). Note that Peirce says there is "no *recognized* multiplicity" in firstness (EP 2:150, my emphasis). In fact, one cannot experience a "positive quality of feeing" without the synthetic processing by which elements of the external world become signs (thoughts, cognitions, ideas)[52] to one's mind.

To see something, as noted above, is to experience a synthesis made possible by the cone and rod cells in our eyes.[53] Regarding hearing, Peirce notes:

> The pitch of a tone depends upon the rapidity of the succession
> of the vibrations which reach the ear. Each of those vibrations
> produces an impulse upon the ear. . . . [T]he pitch of a tone de-
> pends upon the rapidity with which certain impressions are suc-
> cessively conveyed to the mind. These impressions must exist
> previously to any tone; hence, the sensation of pitch is determined
> by previous cognitions. Nevertheless, this would never have been
> discovered by the mere contemplation of that feeling. (W 2:197)

To have what Peirce would call the "feeling of a tone" means that an
abstraction is occurring, by which an element of my external environment is rendered into a sign—that is, a cognition, idea, or thought in
my mind. For the sign-making to occur, by which I experience
"tone" in its firstness, secondness must be at play, whereby sound
waves converge on my ears. Thirdness must also be at play, whereby
the sound waves are synthesized into a unified tone. The synthesis
involved in sensation is often so seamless as to escape notice, such
that there is "no recognized multiplicity" (EP 2:150).

I employ the above dimensions of Peircean semiotics in order to
highlight and scrutinize the intricacy of the more conspicuous dimensions of our thought processes. It is not only the physiological
processing of feelings/sensations that is generally unrecognizable to
humans. As noted in my socio-political reading of the categories,
socio-political factors can influence one's felt encounters with the
world (firstness), and thereby one's cognition, without one's awareness of such influence.

Socialized Instinctive Beliefs

This brings us to an important clarification regarding Peirce's use of
the term "instinct." He believes "instinct" can be broadly construed
to reflect inborn habits, as well as socialized ones. In a 1902 discussion
of logic, he notes:

> If I may be allowed to use the word "habit," without any implica-
> tion as to the time or manner in which it took birth, so as to be
> equivalent to the corrected phrase "habit or disposition," that is,

as some general principle working in a man's nature to determine how he will act, then an instinct, in the proper sense of the word, is an inherited habit, or in more accurate language, an inherited disposition. *But since it is difficult to make sure whether a habit is inherited or is due to infantile training and tradition, I shall ask leave to employ the word "instinct" to cover both cases.* (CP 2.170, my emphasis)

Thus, for Peirce, "instinct" can refer to both natural habits that have been determined from birth, like breathing, *and* socialized belief-habits, such as religious beliefs. This broad construal of instinct is reflected in his synonymous uses of "instinct" and "sentiment" in contexts where he conveys the social-shaping of sentiment that occurs in society (EP 1:119, 377 n. 22; RLT 110–11).

For example, in discussing the a priori method of fixing belief, Peirce makes two comments in which "instinct" and (socialized) "sentiment" are used synonymously as forces that shape our beliefs and actions. First, "Indeed, as long as no better method can be applied, [the a priori method] ought to be followed, since it is then the expression of *instinct* which must be the ultimate cause of belief in all cases" (EP 1:377 n. 22, my emphasis).[54] Second, Peirce notes how the a priori method is problematic:

[W]hen I come to see that the chief obstacle to the spread of Christianity among a people of as high culture as the Hindoos has been a conviction of the immorality of our way of treating women, I cannot help seeing that, though governments do not interfere, *sentiments in their development will be very greatly determined by accidental causes.* (W 3:253, my emphasis; cf. Hookway 2000, 242)

By implication, Peirce is noting that "instinct" can be socialized through religious or governmental channels. This blurring between sentiment and instinct, which allows for "socialized instinct," is also found in Peirce's writings of the 1890s, where he explicitly overlaps sentiment and instinct, again using the terms synonymously. In "Philosophy and the Conduct of Life" (1898), he makes the bold assertion that "[i]t is the instincts, the sentiments, that make the substance of the soul. Cognition is only its surface, its locus of contact with what is external to it" (RLT 110). He also uses "sentiment" and "instinct" interchangeably when referring to "vital interest[s]," such as one's "religious life" and "code of morals" (RLT 111).[55]

Instinctive beliefs therefore include *socialized* beliefs, not merely "natural" ones like the belief that "fire burns" or that there is "order in nature" (CP 5.498, 508, 516; Hookway 2000, 216; Ayim 1982, 19). In Critical Common-sensist vocabulary, socialized instinctive beliefs are often specific (versus vague) and dubitable (versus acritical). Nonetheless, they are shaped and reinforced from childhood onward, such that they take on common-sense certainty or "practical infallib[ility]" (CP 1.661). Religious beliefs are often instinctive in this socialized sense. In this context, Peirce discusses the dubitability of the belief, which is found in Christian societies, that "suicide is murder" (EP 2:349–50).[56]

Extrapolating socio-politically, I include in the category of "socialized instinctive beliefs" ideas about race, sex, and other socio-political classifications. Socialized instinctive beliefs are included in one's common-sense (or background) beliefs. Addressing sexist common-sense beliefs, Christopher Hookway notes:

> If we reject a wholly biological understanding of instinctive belief and recognize that common sense is largely an historical cultural achievement, we may still expect a time-lag: inherited assumptions about the capacities of men and women derive highly fallible authority from their entrenchment in common sense. (2000, 212; cf. Anderson 1995a, 110–11)

My project focuses on these socio-politically shaped common-sense beliefs, whose instinctive qualities derive from socialization. Peirce's discussion of the authority method of fixing belief, while it does not explicitly invoke socialized instinctive beliefs, highlights his conviction that socialization can take explicitly political forms that are transmitted to the young and perpetually reinforced (W 3:250–51).

Instinctive beliefs not only take on common-sense certainty; they also often function nonconsciously—that is, without one's conscious awareness. For Peirce, consciousness is *not* "a separate tissue, overlying an unconscious region of the occult nature, mind, soul, or physiological basis" (EP 2:347). Rather, "the difference is only relative and the demarcation not precise" (EP 2:347). This means that instinctive beliefs promoting racism, sexism, and other social ills can function without the conscious awareness of those acting on them. At the same time, instinctive beliefs—at least in some cases—can be raised to conscious attention and scrutiny, which is an exercise of self-control undertaken by Critical Common-sensists. I will argue in Chapter 5 that socialized instinctive beliefs are especially amenable to Critical Common-sensist consciousness-raising, since they do not meet the criterion of vagueness and since they can be called into doubt by community members who experience socio-political secondness corresponding to the beliefs in question.

There is a tension here, however, which was noted above. Nonconsciously functioning racism or sexism (or a combination of the two), for example, can result in the rejection of testimony given by the person experiencing the racist and/or sexist socio-political secondness. Such a rejection often takes a form resembling "She's playing the race card" (Bonilla-Silva 2003, 29, 179; hooks 2003b, 30–31, 35). On the one hand, blind spots by definition refer to things a person cannot see, such as the nonconscious and unintentional functioning of racism or sexism. On the other hand, habits of white and/or male privilege often involve rejecting the testimony of those who can identify these very blind spots because of their experience of corresponding socio-political secondness.

The following chapters apply insights from Peircean affectivity to explain how habits of privilege can become so entrenched as to *promote* blind spots and encourage *blocking* the road of inquiry. The socialization of children within a society's hegemonic norms is a key factor in this explanation. The personal takes shape within the social and starts the minute a baby comes into the world. Babies are born with natural instincts, and they proceed to acquire *socialized* instinctive beliefs. Peirce gives the following description of "the instinctive mind":

> We may be dimly able to see that in part it depends on the accidents of the moment, *in part on what is personal* or racial,[57] in

part *[on what]* is common to all nicely adjusted organisms whose equilibrium has narrow ranges of stability, in part on whatever is composed of vast collections of independently variable elements. . . . (EP 2:241, my emphasis, editorial brackets[58])

To say that the instinctive mind involves "in part . . . what is personal" is to underscore, ultimately, the *socialized* character of the instinctive mind. Since the personal takes shape within a social matrix, socialization of the personal is, for Peirce, inescapable.

This does not eliminate personal uniqueness by any measure. The Peircean human organism is a distinct source of experience and creativity—that is to say, a distinct physiological cosmos embodying a corresponding perspective on the spatio-temporal world. Such uniqueness informs differences between "all nicely adjusted organisms" (EP 2:241), who vary in the specificity of each one's flesh, including degrees of able-bodiedness, food sensitivities, metabolism, pain thresholds, and a host of other factors. Individuals also vary in how they exercise their self-controlled belief-habit formation, such as how they adapt to secondness in their environments, how they set goals and/or ideals for conduct, and how they approach learning and/or creative endeavors.

Nonetheless the personal *is* social for Peirce: "We naturally make all our distinctions too absolute. We are accustomed to speak of an external universe and an inner world of thought. But they are merely vicinities with no real boundary line between them" (CP 7.438). And, "Experience being something forced upon us, belongs to the [outer world]. Yet in so far as it is I or you who experiences the constraint, the experience is *mine* or *yours*, and thus belongs to the inner world" (7.439, Peirce's emphasis). The force of experience includes the force of community, such that socio-political secondness is as much a part of reality as are habits of nature, like gravity. Thus socio-political habits about gender, race, sex, and sexuality (to name a few) become part of one's personal firstness as surely as do habits relating to one's able-bodiedness (such as using a wheelchair or walking). That is to say, children are implicitly and explicitly socialized about gender, race, sex, sexuality, etc., and the corresponding instinctive belief-habits often develop deep yet, from the individual's point of view, *imperceptible* roots.

Examining the intricacies of childhood belief-habit formation through the lenses of Peircean affectivity and social criticism promotes the consciousness-raising and (thus) self-control of those in hegemonic groups who wish to scrutinize and change these evasive socialized instinctive beliefs, in order to bring conduct and ideals into better harmony.

TWO

THE AFFECTIVITY OF COGNITION

Journal of Speculative Philosophy Cognition Series, 1868–69

Peirce's *Journal of Speculative Philosophy* Cognition Series, published in the late 1860s,[1] portrays synechistic individuals whose
ongoing processes of cognition and habit-formation are inescapably
shaped by personalized and socialized interests. Because of the inescapable bias of human cognition, humans do well to realize the value
of *communal* inquiry into knowledge and to accept the limitations of
their individual points of view. At the same time, humans are vulnerable in relation to the communities of which they are members. In
particular, humans are vulnerable to internalizing growth-inhibiting
habits because of their dependency—especially as children—on the
testimony of others in their communities, testimony that articulates
"reality" itself, especially for the young child. Growth-inhibiting habits include those that promote racism, sexism, and other forms of discrimination. Peirce's sensitivity to this vulnerability, I argue, indicates
the value he *implicitly* (in this context) places on the uniqueness of
each community member, which arises even amid inescapable communal influence. In other words, one's unique perspective can be a

resource to the community, not merely a source of pernicious bias. In fact, in these essays Peirce plants a very small seed regarding the potential heroism of the synechistic individual, a seed that grows steadily throughout his later writings.

I arrive at these conclusions by reading the Cognition Series through two lenses that mutually inform each other: a post-Darwinian affective lens and a social criticism lens. I present Peirce's work in these essays in conversation with Antonio Damasio and with various insights provided by social criticism (focusing primarily on race theory and feminism). I incorporate points of intersection on the latter front, in order to give voice to the socio-political potential that is latent in these essays. Three interrelated issues emerge from the interplay among Peirce's ideas, affectivity, and social criticism, which correspond to the three main sections of the chapter: (1) the uniqueness of an individual's embodiment, cognition, and habit-taking; (2) the social, and therefore political, dimensions of reality, epistemology, and human survival; and (3) the politics of child development and habit-taking, in the midst of which children can internalize habits that promote racism, sexism, and/or other forms of discrimination.

Let me offer a point of clarification before continuing. For Peirce, beliefs are a type of habit, and habits are associations. And so I will be using the terms "habit" and "association" synonymously. When I think it is contextually helpful to remind the reader that beliefs are habits and/or that habits are associations, I will do so by using terms such as "belief-habit" or "belief/habit/association."

Prelude: Seeds of Critical Common-sensism

Peirce's doctrine of Critical Common-sensism (CCS), articulated in the 1900s, is foreshadowed in these early essays. In "Questions Concerning Certain Faculties Claimed for Man" (1868), he explains that there is always already a fund of previous cognitions that informs our reasoning process (W 2:193–200). Critical Common-sensism involves taking a critical attitude toward these grounding beliefs, to determine whether any of them can be doubted. The Cognition Series gives clues as to how personalized and socialized dimensions of experience can result in instinctive, and nonconscious, belief-habits that reside in the fund of common-sense beliefs from which a person or community reasons.

In "Questions Concerning," Peirce denies that humans have a Cartesian-style intuition-detector faculty with which they can determine whether a given cognition is mediated by other cognitions or not (W 2:193 ff.). By "intuition" Peirce means "a cognition not determined by a previous cognition of the same object, and therefore so determined by something out of the consciousness" (W 2:193). In other words, an intuition is an unmediated cognition—that is, a cognition that "refers immediately to its object," without being influenced by other cognitions (W 2:193–94). For example, if I (as a human) can tell whether my cognition, say, of a sunset is determined only by the sunset itself that exists outside of my thinking about it (and is *not* determined by any of my other cognitions—such as those relating to my spiritual attunement to nature), *then* I have the human faculty for distinguishing intuitions from other, mediated cognitions. Peirce rejects this intuitive ability with the following reasoning:

> [T]here is no evidence that we have this faculty, except that we seem to *feel* that we have it. But the weight of that testimony depends entirely on our being supposed to have the power of distinguishing in this feeling whether the feeling be *the result of education, old associations, etc.*, or whether it is an intuitive cognition. . . . (W 2:194, my emphasis)

The ability to make such a distinction, of course, assumes we have the very intuitive faculty in question. That is to say, the only evidence of the intuition-detector faculty is a feeling that such a faculty exists, yet this feeling itself could be mediated by other cognitions that reflect personal and social bias. So it would not be reliable evidence unless it could be shown to be an intuition, which would thus be uninfluenced by other factors and, presumably, shared by all humans. Making such a determination about the feeling in question (namely, whether it is an intuition or a mediated cognition) would require the very intuition-detector faculty whose existence has yet to be proved. Thus, since this feeling evidence cannot be used without begging the question, Peirce rejects that humans possess this faculty. The remainder of his discussion of this issue focuses on examples of cognition that seem to be intuitive premises from which cognition proceeds but that, in fact, are themselves conclusions, or syntheses, which have brought about unity to a manifold in sensation or in thought (W 2:195 ff.).

Of particular interest for my project is Peirce's point that our feelings may be "the result of education, old associations, etc." (W 2:194). With this comment he makes room for both social influence (via education) and individual idiosyncrasy (via old associations) to influence our feelings. Moreover, since "old associations" are strongly influenced by social as well as individual factors, Peirce also sets the stage for personal uniqueness to arise within a social context.[2] In addition, he also notes that these modes of influence can be virtually undetectable, because the felt sense of indubitability corresponding to each is so strong. What seem to be unmediated intuitions are, in fact, the result of unnoticed processes:

> [J]ust as we are able to recognize our friends by certain appearances, although we cannot possibly say what those appearances are and are quite unconscious of any process of reasoning, so in any case when the reasoning is easy and natural to us, however complex may be the premises, they sink into insignificance and oblivion proportionately to the satisfactoriness of the theory based upon them. (W 2:199)

There are seeds of social critique here. The "indubitable" quality of some feelings can promote oppression by cultivating prejudice about oppressed groups in a society. The following is taken from the personal correspondence of Louis Agassiz, the famous nineteenth-century naturalist and proponent of polygenesis, the theory that human races are different species, each with its own origin (Gould 1981, 39):

> It was in Philadelphia that I first found myself in prolonged contact with negroes; all the domestics in my hotel were men of color. I can scarcely express to you the painful impression that I received, especially since *the feeling that they inspired in me* is contrary to all our ideas about the confraternity of the human type

[*genre*] and the unique origin of our species. *But truth before all.* Nevertheless, I experienced pity at the sight of this degraded and degenerate race, and their lot inspired compassion in me in thinking that they are really men. Nonetheless, *it is impossible for me to repress the feeling that they are not of the same blood as us.* (Quoted in Gould 1981, 44–45, my emphasis)

In this passage, Agassiz appeals to the "truth" of "the feeling [the 'negroes'] inspired in" him. The strength of his feeling is used to ground the "indubitability" of his prejudice. It also holds in place a personally idiosyncratic view of the world that is *at the same time* socio-politically informed. Agassiz's reaction to "negroes" reflects the personal idiosyncrasy of a man who had never before seen someone whose phenotype reflected African descent. A native of Switzerland, he had recently taken up residence in the United States. His reaction also illustrates the socio-political influence of the discussions of polygeny in the nineteenth century in the United States, where the doctrine took root as a primarily American scientific theory (Gould 1981, 42). Stephen Jay Gould notes that polygeny occurred within a Euro-American scientific mainstream that took for granted the superiority of Caucasians (1981, 30–42). In addition, Agassiz was more specifically influenced by the work of Samuel Morton, whose skull-measuring experiments (which are now considered unsound) supported Caucasian superiority and the inferiority of non-Caucasian races (Menand 2001, 103–5).[3] Thus Agassiz's exclusionary thinking is informed by *both* idiosyncratic and socio-political factors.

Let us now examine the personalized embodiment issues that shape the idiosyncrasy of human associations, or habits. As socialized as one's encounters with the external world are, he or she can only encounter this world from the perspective of his or her body, so it makes sense to start there.

Part 1: Individualized Embodiment, Cognition, and Habit-Taking

a. The Unique Human Body

Using our not so indubitable feelings as a starting point, we may recall that Peirce's references to feelings take for granted that they occur in a body. Antonio Damasio provides a contemporary scientific validation of the linkage between feelings and the body by highlighting the connection between mind and nerve cells, a connection that Peirce made himself:

> [T]he mind arises from or in a brain situated within a body-proper with which it interacts; . . . due to the mediation of the brain, the mind is grounded in the body-proper; . . . the mind has prevailed in evolution because it helps maintain the body-proper; and . . . *the mind arises from or in biological tissue—nerve cells— that share the same characteristics that define other living tissues in the body-proper.* (2003, 191, my emphasis)[4]

If we are to appreciate fully the individualized dimension of associations/habits, however, we cannot stop with the insight that mind implies body. We must emphasize that *my* mind implies *my* body. This point is implicit in Damasio's comment that an organism's body provides a boundary between it and the world outside:

> Life is carried out inside a boundary that defines a body. Life and the life urge exist inside a boundary, the selectively permeable wall that separates the internal environment from the external environment. The idea of organism revolves around the existence of that boundary. . . . If there is no boundary, there is no body, and if there is no body, there is no organism. Life needs a boundary. (1999, 137)

My body encloses and includes the personal boundaries through which I interact with the external world. To simply discuss the body-*in-general* can eclipse the deeply individualized nature and perspective of human embodiment.[5] For all the shared types of homeodynamic functioning among humans, the bodily functions that promote life also take on individualized permutations. With respect to nutrition alone, food allergies, metabolic rate, and bodily chemicals (such as adrenaline and hormones) are some of the factors that individualize a person's nutritional needs and schedule. These factors are, in turn, influenced by external environmental factors such as the availability of food, difficulties in avoiding genetically and chemically treated foods, pressures to conform to a feminine or masculine body type, and so on. In addition, men and women have different bodily experiences that are, in turn, individualized for each person: "Sexually differential biological processes—menstruation, pregnancy, childbirth, lactation, and sexual maturation in women and phallic maturation, paternity, emissions, and so on in men . . ." (Grosz 1993, 202).[6]

Another passage from Damasio puts a crowning touch on this personalized embodiment of mind. This is especially pertinent given Peirce's stress, in the present essay series, on cognition as an ongoing semiotic process (W 2:209 ff., 223 ff.). Damasio says:

> I believe that the foundational images in the stream of mind are images of some kind of body event, whether the event happens in the depth of the body or in some specialized sensory device near its periphery. The basis for those foundational images is a collection of brain maps, that is, a collection of patterns of neuron activity and inactivity . . . in a variety of sensory regions. Those brain maps represent, comprehensively, the structure and state of the body at any given time. Some maps relate to the world within, the organism's interior. Other maps relate to the world outside, the physical world of objects that interact with the organism at specific regions of its shell. (2003, 197)[7]

This passage illustrates the highly individualized nature of the ideas that flow through each human's mind. It also highlights the semiotic nature of the mind's relation to external objects. In order to survive, a human organism must be aware of the potential threat or benefit represented by objects in its vicinity. This awareness varies in its level of consciousness but is ever present. Recall Chapter 1's discussion of the affective salience of virtually all objects (Damasio 2003, 93; cf. 309 n. 3). The external objects surrounding the individual are signs, and they affect her associations by virtue of the information they carry regarding her individualized experience with them. Colapietro addresses this point from a Peircean perspective: "[W]e are in continuous dialogue with the natural world," so that we may effectively "*read* our potentially hazardous environment" (1989, 21, emphasis in original).

For Peirce this personalized information, the affective salience of objects, is relayed through feelings and associations, which are part of the cognition process itself. His discussions in "Some Consequences of Four Incapacities" (1868)—of feeling, emotion, interest, and association—are particularly revelatory regarding homeodynamic-semiotic themes.

Recall that, for Peirce, the means of *connection* between the human organism and the external world are "feelings" or "sensations," terms he uses synonymously in the Cognition Series. In "Questions Concerning," for example, Peirce notes, "The pitch of a tone depends upon the rapidity of the succession of the vibrations which reach the ear. . . . These impressions must exist previously to any tone; hence, the *sensation* of pitch is determined by previous cognitions. Nevertheless, this would never have been discovered by the mere contemplation of that *feeling*" (W 2:197, my emphasis). This synonymous usage of "feeling"/"sensation" signals the inseparability of qualitative immediacy and environmental confrontation, even as the passage focuses on the *synthesis* involved. Feelings/sensations are continuously triggered by objects external to the human body, which stimulate nerve firings in the sense organs.

b. Peircean Homeodynamics

I. COGNITION

Peirce describes cognition as an ongoing semiotic process. It reflects his categories, exhibiting three dimensions: "material" ("how it feels"), "denotative" (how it is connected to external objects and/or internal associations), and "representative" of an object (W 2:227). "Thought" is used in two senses: first, as a synonym for cognition, and, second, as a cognition whose representative dimension is most prominent. In what follows, I will (for clarity) refer to thought only in this second sense, not as a synonym for cognition in general. Thought in this second sense, of having a prominent representative dimension, designates a cognition that is connected to preceding cognitions by "a relation of reason," such that it has a "rational character" (W 2:230–31).

Before discussing the other two dimensions of cognition, I want to place this description of thought firmly within a Peircean context, so as to more easily trace its trajectories here and in later chapters. For Peirce, a rational/reasoned connection between cognitions draws on generalization(s) or aim(s) regarding human conduct and/or the other habits of the natural world. In the Cognition Series, Peirce's focus is on grasping generalizations of nature that offer *explanations*. He describes this by contrast: "By there being no relation of reason to the determining thoughts, I mean that there is nothing in the content of the thought which explains why it should arise only on occasion of these determining thoughts" (W 2:230). The rationality of humans is demonstrated in their grasp of the generalizations/habits of nature, which account for why things occur as they do (cf. W 2:226, 229, 263–64, 272). For example, if one has the cognition "That is thunder," it would be rational to have the subsequent cognition "Maybe it will rain." The linkage of thunder and rain reflects a generalization about the natural world—namely, the meteorological patterns that explain why thunder and rain are connected. It would probably *not* be rational to have the cognition "That is thunder" followed by the subsequent cognition "Rocks are hard," because this connection does not reflect a generalization about the natural world that explains why "Rocks are hard" is connected to a cognition about thunder.

Often connections that are rational are shared by others in one's community, but with a significant qualification. Others in one's community are likely to agree that thunder could lead to rain. In fact, when it comes to scientific inquiry into the workings of the natural and social world, communal verification of the regularities/generalizations/habits of nature is *required*, characterizing Peircean objectivity itself (W 2:270–71).[8] Reality, on Peirce's scheme, exists outside of humans but cannot be described without human communities giving it voice. The linkage between "rational" and "communal agreement," however, needs to be temporarily suspended in contexts of creative insight. This qualification reflects Peirce's fallibilism, the view that knowledge is always open to future revision. The community that describes reality and often underwrites the rationality of cognition is, ultimately, "without definite limits, and capable of an indefinite increase of knowledge" (W 2:239). It is an *ideal* community, which is "indefinitely" subject to future epistemological growth. An important source for this growth is the individual community member who has insight into generalities not (yet) grasped by the rest of the community. In this case, the individual is a source of creative hypotheses that can be tested scientifically and embraced to the extent they are verified. In these creative scenarios, the insightful individual herself is *rational* even though in disagreement with her community. Peirce himself models this maverick rationality in his *Monist* "Cosmology Series" of the 1890s, where he presents innovative scientific views that challenge the mechanistic cosmological models popular among his scientific peers.

In the present Cognition Series, Peirce's focus is on rationality that *does* reflect communal agreement, with only subtle hints toward the maverick rationality that pushes a community toward epistemological growth. Here his concern with the rational flow of thought implies a community that agrees on how reality works. Disturbances to the rational flow of cognition—that is, disturbances to *thought's* flow—are rooted in the feelings that underwrite each cognition. These feelings, fueled by one's associations, can be the home of nonconscious prejudice.

Let us return to the other two dimensions of cognition, denotative and material. What Peirce calls "the pure denotative application" or "attention" refers to "the power by which thought [or cognition] at one time is connected with and made to relate to thought [or cognition] at another time . . ." (W 2:227, 232). It is the dimension of cognition whereby old associations, which are habits, are brought to bear on the current flow of one's cognitions. For our cognitions relate not only to external objects but also to our past experience with external objects. This will be discussed more fully below. For Peirce, associations/habits occur in one's nervous tissue and thus are embodied (W 2:232). The actual *feel* of the nerve firings specific to each association/

habit is what gives cognition its felt, or material, aspect. The ideas in our respective minds literally have a feel to them. Often it is so subtle as to escape notice, but not always. For example, think about the police. This idea probably has a discernible feltness to you based on encounters you, or people you care about, have had with the police.[9] Let us examine more closely the role of feeling in cognition.

II. FEELING

In a passage leading up to a description of *emotions* as producing "large movements in the body," Peirce makes three important comments about *feeling* (W 2:230). Each of these comments supports a homeodynamic account of the human organism:

> There is some reason to think that, [1] corresponding to every feeling within us, some motion takes place in our bodies. [2] This property of the thought-sign, since it has no rational dependence upon the meaning of the sign, may be compared with what I have called the material quality of the sign; [3] but it differs from that latter inasmuch as it is not essentially necessary that it should be felt in order that there should be any thought-sign. (W 2:230)

First, Peirce proposes that feelings involve bodily motion—that is, "corresponding to every feeling within us, *some motion takes place in our bodies*" (W 2:230, my emphasis). Since feeling is one of the elements of cognition itself, and cognition is an ongoing process, this means that our bodies are always in motion and that this motion corresponds, to some degree, to our cognition (W 2:211, 223–24, 227). Second, Peirce notes that the feltness of a sign has "no rational dependence upon the meaning of the sign" (W 2:230). This is compatible with the individualized, embodied reaction to an object, which serves as a sign *to my own* body-minded organism of its unique value to me, but not necessarily to anyone else. Think, for example, of your favorite childhood food. There is a *feel* to this object that is unique to you. My favorite food, for example, was macaroni and cheese. Some may argue that the feel of "macaroni and cheese" would be the same for anyone who also had this food as her or his childhood favorite.

Feelings, for Peirce, are not that simple, however. The feel of macaroni and cheese *to me* involves my personal associations, such as the kitchen of my childhood house, the plastic bowl with my favorite cartoon character on it, and my stirring extra milk into my helping to achieve that "just right" texture. This combination of associations informing my feeling is mine alone, involving the uniqueness of my embodied experience of the world. As I will continue to demonstrate below, the felt dimension of cognition lends uniqueness to *all* cognitions, even those that seem to evoke no bodily response. This brings us to the next point regarding the above passage.

Third, Peirce says that "it is not essentially necessary that [the bodily motion] should be *felt* in order that there should be any thought-sign" (W 2:230, my emphasis). What Peirce seems to suggest here is that it is not necessary that the bodily-motion aspect of a thought-sign be *noticed* in order that there should be any thought-sign. For example, barring extenuating circumstances, "The sky is blue" is unlikely to trigger a noticeable bodily response for many adults. Peirce notes that this felt dimension is less "prominent" compared to the feltness of other types of cognitions, such as emotions and "sensations proper"[10] (W 2:230). This is because the "relation of reason" between the thought and other cognitions "detracts from the attention given to the mere feeling" (W 2:230). This supports my interpretation of the third point highlighted in the above passage. Our thoughts have a felt dimension, but it is inconspicuous and so can easily escape notice.

Damasio notes that the work done by the body to maintain its homeodynamic balance is often unnoticed by the human organism. He notes, "The background state of the body is monitored continuously" (Damasio 1994, 153). This is the quiet humming of homeodynamics, and it results in "background feelings," which correspond to the background emotions discussed in Chapter 1 (Damasio 1994, 152–53). Background feelings are so named because the organism's focus at any given time is usually turned outward:

> But the fact that our focus of attention is usually elsewhere, where
> it is most needed for adaptive behavior, does not mean the body

representation [i.e., feeling] is absent, as you can easily confirm when the sudden onset of pain or minor discomfort shifts the focus back to it. The background body sense is continuous, although one may hardly notice it, since it represents not a specific part of anything in the body but rather an overall state of most everything in it. (Damasio 1994, 152)

Returning to the Peirce passage we are examining: He describes feeling/sensation in a manner compatible with Damasio's background feeling, despite Peirce's antiquated physiological account:

In the case of a [feeling or] sensation, the manifold of impressions which precede and determine it are not of a kind, the bodily motion corresponding to which comes from any large ganglion or from the brain, and probably for this reason the [feeling or] sensation produces *no great commotion in the bodily organism*; and the [feeling or] sensation itself is not a thought [i.e., cognition in general sense] which has a very strong influence upon the current of thought [i.e., cognition whose representative dimension is prominent] except by virtue of the information it may serve to afford. (W 2:230, my emphasis)

Note that Peirce says that "the [feeling or] sensation itself is not a thought which has a very strong influence upon the current of thought *except by virtue of the information it may serve to afford*" (W 2:230, my emphasis). This is a significant qualification, as it bookmarks (albeit with little elaboration) the possible influence of feeling on thought. I will demonstrate below that this influence is broader than it seems at first blush, since Peirce does not maintain the sharp distinction between feeling and emotion outlined at this point in "Some Consequences." For now, however, let us examine how Peirce *does* distinguish between feeling and emotion.

Peirce says that the process of cognition has an embodied element of feeling or sensation. This element usually stays in the background, but it may affect the flow of cognition if the information it carries requires a disruption. If Peirce wanted to be more reader friendly at this point, he might have reminded us that, for all our powers of cognition, humans are still animal organisms whose survival is not guaranteed. Humans need food, shelter, etc., and live in a complex environment that must be successfully navigated in order to secure individual and species survival. However sophisticated self-control becomes, it is still rooted in the physical survival of the human organism. When the information conveyed by feelings is of a disruptive nature, the affective state of *emotion* is triggered.

III. EMOTION

Contrasting emotion to feeling/sensation, Peirce says:

> An emotion, on the other hand, comes much later in the development of thought—I mean, further from the first beginning of the cognition of its object—and the thoughts which determine it already have motions corresponding to them in the brain, or the chief ganglion; consequently, it produces large movements in the body, and independently of its representative value, strongly affects the current of thought. (W 2:230)

Peirce links emotion and instinct by specifically attributing animality and lack of self-control to the emotions. As he puts it:

> The animal motions to which I allude, are, in the first place and obviously, blushing, blenching, staring, smiling, scowling, pouting, laughing, weeping, sobbing, wriggling, flinching, trembling, being petrified, sighing, sniffing, shrugging, groaning, heartsinking, trepidation, swelling of the heart, etc., etc. To these may, perhaps, be added, in the second place, other more complicated actions, which nevertheless *spring from a direct impulse and not from deliberation.* (W 2:230, my emphasis)

Emotion is not an episode that "happens" to an otherwise static body. Rather, in its paradigmatic occurrences, such as someone flinching in fear, emotion arises in an organism whose homeodynamics require a more pronounced bodily response than usual, because of environmental conditions. Moreover, Peirce links emotion to *instinctive* survival mechanisms, which makes sense. Disruptions in homeodynamics significant enough to disturb the flow of thought (as emotions do) *should*, in some contexts, be accompanied by an uncontrolled instinctive response. In his later work, such as his essay "Philosophy and the Conduct of Life" (1898), Peirce readily admits that we should not trust "vitally important" matters to reason, because of reason's fallibility (RLT 105–22). The instinctive automatic response triggered by an emotion, then, need not be problematic. But it *can* be, which is Peirce's concern in the Cognition Series, a concern that is compatible with social critical insights.

As survival-rich as emotions can be, in some contexts they can—to cite a familiar example—contribute to social oppression. Fear and anger can result in discrimination ranging from dirty looks to hate crimes to the courtroom. Legal scholar Patricia Williams notes, "[A]s long as they are not unlearned, the exclusionary power of free-floating emotions make their way into the gestalt of prosecutorial and jury disposition and into what the law sees as a crime, sees as relevant, justified, provoked, or excusable" (1991, 67).

Peirce's description of the bodily commotion involved in emotion goes beyond the above list of specific "animal motions" to include "other more complicated actions, which nevertheless *spring from a direct impulse and not from deliberation*" (W 2:230, my emphasis). These other actions, I would argue, include socially derived instinctive prejudices that can manifest through an emotional response to a person, a response that could be either conscious or nonconscious. Recall the example, from Chapter 1, of the Euro-American white store clerk's conscious refusal of entrance to Patricia Williams, based on the color of her skin (Williams 1991, 44–45). On the nonconscious front, recall (also from Chapter 1) that research in social psychology shows that

> emotions, attitudes, goals, and intentions can be activated *without awareness*, and . . . these can influence the way people think about and act in social situations. For example, physical features (like skin color or hair length) are enough to activate racial or gender stereotypes, regardless of whether the person possessing the feature expresses any of the behavioral characteristics of the stereotype. This kind of *automatic activation of attitudes* occurs in a variety of different situations and appears to constitute *our first reaction to a person*. And once activated, these attitudes can influence the way we then treat the person, and can even have influences over our behavior in other situations. (LeDoux 1996, 61–62, my emphasis)[11]

These examples, both of conscious and nonconscious prejudice, indicate that emotional responses can be both complex and impulsive,
overtaking the inclusiveness and self-control of reasonable behavior.
Peirce's attunement to the subtlety with which this emotional takeover can occur is reflected in his ultimate blurring between emotion
and feeling, which he introduces later in "Some Consequences."

c. Contextualizing the "Uselessness" of Emotions

In "Questions Concerning," Peirce asserts the idiosyncratic dimension of emotions:

> [A]ny emotion is a predication concerning some object, and the
> chief difference between this and an objective intellectual judg-
> ment is that while the latter is relative to human nature or to mind
> in general, the former is relative to the particular circumstances
> and disposition of a particular man at a particular time. (W2:
> 206).

Recall the above description of thought, as a cognition that is connected to preceding cognitions rationally or reasonably. Peirce's reference to an "objective intellectual judgment" is based on the same
idea, such that "intellectual" is synonymous with "rational" and
"reasonable" in this context. An "intellectual" judgment draws on
generalizations/habits of the natural world or human conduct and
thus offers explanation regarding the object (cf. W2: 226–27, 229).
And others would agree with this judgment, such that it is "objective." An emotion is *not* focused on generalizations that others would
agree with but is uniquely individual, "relative to the particular circumstances and disposition of a particular man at a particular time"
(W2: 206).

The apparent worthlessness of an emotion's idiosyncratic connection to the cognitions that precede it is asserted in the next essay,
"Some Consequences":

> That which makes us look upon the emotions more as affections
> of self than other cognitions, is that we have found them more

dependent upon our accidental situation at the moment than other cognitions; but that is only to say that *they are cognitions too narrow to be useful*. The emotions, as a little observation will show, arise when our attention is strongly drawn to complex and inconceivable circumstances. (W2: 229, my emphasis)

Peirce, I would argue, is not trying to deny the usefulness of the emotions insofar as they promote the human organism's survival in the present. The two passages just quoted imply that emotions are compatible with the homeodynamics of the human organism. Peirce says that emotions are "relative to the particular circumstances and disposition of a particular man at a particular time" and are "more dependent upon our accidental situation at the moment than other cognitions" (W2: 206, 229). I think Peirce is aware that we need, at times, privately tailored emotions to protect our well-being as animal organisms. "[C]omplex and inconceivable circumstances" can be dangerous and thus may call for tailored emotional responses to ensure survival, even and especially if an intellectual judgment is not ready to hand (W2: 229).

His exaggerated wording in this context—that emotions "are cognitions too narrow to be useful" (W2: 229)—stresses a *logical* point, which is made in the third and final essay of the Cognition Series, "Grounds of Validity of the Laws of Logic." In "Grounds," Peirce argues for taking a socialized stance in our reasonings when we *do* have time to deliberate. Ever the logician of science, he aspires after a communal pursuit of knowledge. From the standpoint of science, he cannot abide the self-centered immaturity of emotions or any other type of cognition that excludes the perspectives of others. This brings us to another important affectivity issue.

Peirce explicitly acknowledges the affectivity characterizing *all* cognitions, including thought. This should not come as a surprise, since feeling is the material dimension of any thought. It is still a point worth highlighting, in order to more easily trace its implications here and in later chapters, in conjunction with the semiotic nature of human experience and Peirce's theory of association. The following passage from "Some Consequences" was cited above. I include it again with different emphases:

> That which makes us look upon the emotions more as affections of self *than other cognitions*, is that we have found them more dependent upon our accidental situation at the moment *than other cognitions*; but that is only to say that they are cognitions too narrow to be useful. (W 2:229, my emphasis)

This passage tells us that thoughts are "affections of the self" (although less so than emotions are) and that thoughts are "dependent upon our accidental situation at the moment" (although less so than emotions are). Peirce says, as noted above, that a thought differs from an emotion because its material quality, or feltness, falls into the background, because attention is focused on the rational relation between the present thought and the cognitions that determine it (W 2:230). Nonetheless, our thoughts *are* personalized, reflecting the idiosyncrasies of our embodiment at the moment, our surrounding environments, and our unique associations.

Peirce's eventual blurring of the distinction between feeling and emotion underscores the affective dimension of all cognition, such that emotions are not the only cognitions that are too idiosyncratic to be of use logically. This blurring occurs in the context of Peirce's examination of the denotative aspect of cognition, where the affective-semiotic character of human experience comes more clearly into focus.

d. Affective-Semiotic Experience: Attention, Association, Habit

Attention, or the denotative aspect of cognition, is affective, reflecting ongoing communication between the human organism and the external world. All thoughts are "affections of the self" because of the personalized associations that each person has with the objects in her world (W 2:229). Humans do not simply represent external objects to themselves; they also represent their *experience* with these objects. Thus, objects are signs for each human *privately* in addition to being signs in public senses—that is, regarding meanings shared with others in one's community. Red licorice, for example, is a sign for me of my brother (because it is his favorite candy), in addition to its other more public meanings (as, say, a type of candy of a particular color).

The formation of "nervous associations" ("associations" for short) is made possible by *attention*, which Peirce describes as "the power by which thought at one time is connected with and made to relate to thought at another time" (W 2:232). Attention allows humans to focus on particular objects in their world and to "produc[e] an effect upon memory," which is a habit or association (W 2:232). Attention not only creates new associations/habits to guide future behavior; it also draws on past associations/habits to guide present behavior. Peirce gives the following description of habit-formation:

> A habit arises, when, having had the sensation [or feeling] of performing a certain act, *m*, on several occasions *a, b, c,* we come to do it upon every occurrence of the general event, *l,* of which *a, b,* and *c* are special cases.
>
> That is to say, by the cognition that
> Every case of *a, b,* or *c,* is a case of *m,*
> is determined the cognition that
> Every case of *l* is a case of *m.* (W 2:232)

Peirce is talking about the felt regularity, the "groove," that humans fall into when they perform or avoid a particular action on numerous occasions. When I was a teenager, for example, I took up year-round distance running. I learned that, if I ran in cold weather, I would develop severe chills shortly after finishing. I also learned—the hard way—that I was very susceptible to illness if I did not take a hot shower immediately after these runs. Mapping this onto Peirce's formula, the "sensation [or feeling] of performing a certain act, *m*, on several occasions *a, b, c*" involved the feltness of how effective the hot showers were after a few particular runs on particular occasions. This feltness/sensation went significantly beyond the feel of hot water. It was a gestalt feeling/sensation that included the felt effectiveness of the shower for preventing illness.[12] This sensation led me to *generalize* that "running in the cold"—in other words, "the general event,

I"—is a case of (and also a *sign* of) "needing to take a hot shower afterward." As a result, running in the cold has an affective-semiotic charge for me in this respect.

Phenomenologically speaking, the habit I formed (thirdness) *mediates between* my bodily equanimity (firstness) *and* the environmental resistance of cold weather (secondness).[13] Attention allows us to track the regularities of our world, as I did regarding my bodily responses to weather conditions, so we can adjust our behavior accordingly. It shapes our memory, via habit-formation, regarding future behaviors (W 2:232). Attention accomplishes its tracking by means of the information provided by feelings, which detail the success, or lack thereof, of the organism's interaction with the external world.

Attention also guides present activity by *drawing on* one's preexisting habits, such as those that, to this day, help keep me healthy after I run in the cold. Thus attention allows us to continually form new habits while also drawing on old ones. My running example, because it focuses on my physical health, hints at the survival value of both paying attention and attention's relationship, via feelings, to habit/association and memory. This survival connection will be discussed more fully below, in the context of child development, and in Chapter 3, in the context of scientific investigations.

The running example, premised on *my own* body-temperature issues, also hints at the *personalized* associations/habits that attention produces, in addition to more conventional ones. Peirce focuses on these personalized associations/habits toward the end of "Some Consequences" and, in the process, introduces a fruitful terminological ambiguity between feeling and emotion.[14] Recall that in "Questions Concerning," Peirce says that "old associations" may be factors that shape our *feelings* (W 2:194). Here in "Some Consequences," Peirce briefly elaborates on this issue, highlighting the semiotic dimension of human affectivity. Note the change from the term "feeling" to the term "emotion":

> Everything in which we take the least interest creates in us *its own particular emotion*, however slight this may be. This emotion is a

sign and a predicate of the thing. Now, when a thing resembling this thing is presented to us, a similar *emotion* arises; hence, we immediately infer that the latter is like the former. (W 2:237, my emphasis)

And,

All association is by signs. Everything has its subjective or emotional qualities. . . . (W 2:238)

Recall the red licorice–brother example. Also, I take "slight interest" in kelly-green Volkswagen "bugs," because they remind me of my childhood, as this was the kind of car my mother drove. This kind of car is a *sign* to me, representing not only rational ideas like "these cars were popular in the United States in the 1970s." It is also a sign of mother-daughter love, thus having its own particular emotion *for me*. If my mother had driven this car only one day during my childhood, I probably would not have a memory of it. The repeated exposure to my mother driving me around in this car, however, led to an association or habit, by which I learned to connect this type of car with my mother and the related feeling/emotion.

Peirce's change in terminology from feeling to emotion, I would argue, reflects his insight into the unique affectivity that characterizes the associations each person makes. He uses "emotion" in the above passages to convey a subtle affective resonance he earlier ascribed to "feeling." This blurring underscores that objects have differing affective, or felt/emotional, resonances depending on one's personal and socially mediated experience. Since my embodiment and homeodynamics are highly individualized, so are the affective semiotics that inform my associations. For example, some people associate airplanes with the pleasant, subtle feeling of convenient travel. Others associate airplanes with the unpleasant, not so subtle emotion of fear—say, of crashing or of a claustrophobia attack. Still others may associate airplanes with prohibitive monetary expense or environmental expense (that is, a large carbon footprint). We are, once again, reminded of Damasio's account of affectivity, semiotics, and homeodynamics, discussed last chapter. All objects have a personalized affective salience for the human organism, who is constantly monitoring her environment to promote the survival of her unique body (Damasio 2003, 93). Our survival is promoted through attention to external objects, in order to pursue those that promote our survival and to avoid those that threaten it. This, in turn, buttresses planning for the future and creative decision-making.

Attention and association/habit are linked to the secondness of our environments, physical and social. I am interested in the socio-political implications of this connection. Note in this regard that the affective associations people have with objects can be negative, as the airplane example indicates. They can also involve cues by which the avoidance of environmental resistance or danger is habitualized. Social critic bell hooks describes the experience of being black in the United States. Notice her use of *attention* for self-protection, in the effort to avoid what I would call racist secondness:

> Living in a world of racial apartheid where custom and conventions invented to separate black and white lasted long past an end to legal racial discrimination, those who are powerless—black folks—must be overly aware of small details as we go about our lives to be sure we do not enter forbidden territory—to be sure we will not be hurt. You learn to notice things. You learn where not to walk, the stores you don't want to go in. . . . [Y]ou cannot live the way other people live. (hooks 1997, 97)

Hooks's observations as a black woman underscore the power differential involved in socio-political secondness—in this case, racist secondness. Because U.S. society remains white-dominant, despite work done in the civil rights movement, black people must "learn to notice things." In Peircean vocabulary, they learn to make associations/habits whereby they can avoid racist secondness. Moreover, since white people, insofar as they are white, are supported by these mainstream societal habits of race, they are often unaware that other people "cannot live the way" that they themselves do (97). Thus white people often do not have the associations/habits that can identify racist secondness, because they so seldom experience or witness such secondness themselves. This phenomenological blindness that people in hegemonic groups (such as the economic middle class, heterosexuals, men, whites, and others) often have regarding those in the corresponding non-hegemonic groups (the poor, GLBTQs, women, people of color, and others) will be discussed more fully in Chapter 3.

Another example of how the power differentials between hegemonic and non-hegemonic groups shape associations/habits is the stereotyping of those in non-hegemonic groups by those in hegemonic groups. Using racism once again to draw examples, in the United States negative stereotypes abound regarding people of color. For example, Helen Zia notes that

> Geishas, gooks, and geeks have been the staples of the main characters of [U.S.] mass culture's Asian universe: the subservient, passive female; the untrustworthy, evil male; the ineffectual, emasculated nerd. As each stereotype gained a foothold in the popular culture, it brought on new prejudices that real-life Asian Americans would have to contend with. (2000, 119)[15]

These stereotypical associations play out in one-on-one encounters. Linda Alcoff relates the following:

> When I was much younger, I remember finding out with a shock that a white lover, my first serious relationship, had pursued me because I was Latina, which no doubt stimulated his vision of exoticism. We had grown up in the same neighborhood, attended the same schools . . . and shared similar ambitions. . . . Yet our first encounters, our first dates, which I had naively believed were dominated by a powerful emotional and intellectual connection, were experienced by him as a fascinating crossing over to the forbidden, to the Other in that reified, racializing sense. (2006, 193)

She clarifies: "I learned this because he has written a novel based on his experience of our relationship" (298 n. 11).

Another example is provided by Cornel West, who recalls:

> Years ago, while driving from New York to teach at Williams College, I was stopped on fake charges of trafficking cocaine. When I told the police officer I was a professor of religion, he replied, "Yeh, and I'm the Flying Nun. Let's go, nigger!" I was stopped three times in my first ten days in Princeton for driving too slowly

> on a residential street with a speed limit of twenty-five miles per
> hour. (And my son, Clifton, already has similar memories at the
> tender age of fifteen.) (2001, xxv)[16]

These examples demonstrate how easily stereotypical associations can
lead to socio-political secondness for people of color.[17] Unfortunately
the testimony of people of color, and of others in non-hegemonic
groups, is often dismissed regarding the socio-political secondness
they experience—a dismissal rooted in the same power differentials
that create the socio-political secondness in the first place. This theme
will be discussed more fully in subsequent chapters.

I end this section by explaining how affective-semiotics can influence the flow of cognition. Recall Peirce's comment that the information carried by feelings can influence the (rationally connected) flow
of thought (W 2:230). His discussion of attention and personalized
association/habit are revelatory in this respect. As we have just seen,
feeling and emotion can shade into one another, converging into a
personalized affective salience that applies to the objects in our environment. Thus, the information conveyed by the (often backgrounded) felt dimension of cognition can trigger a personalized
affective response that disturbs thought's rational flow. For example,
I used to serve as a grief-support person for college students who had
had a family member die. Many of them reported that, in the months
following their loss, they had trouble focusing consistently during lectures. Everything would be going fine during, say, a history lecture:
note-taking, understanding, etc. Then the professor would refer to
something associated with the loved one who had died—she might
mention, say, France. As a result, the rational connectedness of the
student's thought would be interrupted. France would be associated
with the loved one, and the felt dimension of "loved one"—the "information" conveyed by the feeling—would be intense grief. Students
in scenarios like this would often experience a debilitating surge of
emotion that would derail their formerly rational thought flow.

This is not to imply that this affective response is *purely* personal;
it reflects numerous social factors, including the cultural norms shaping the relationship with the family member, as well as norms dictating the appropriate expression of grief for men and for women. In

cases like the police officer's prejudice against West, this point is especially clear. We cannot simply refer to "personalized" affectivity overriding rational thought flow. "Socialized" affectivity needs to be invoked as well. Racism and other types of discrimination in the United States are bigger affective issues than merely the exclusionary habits of an individual here or there. Thus we need to invoke "*personalized/socialized* affectivity" regarding the unique affective-semiotic salience of the objects in our respective experiences. This is ultimately a Peircean reminder that the personal is inescapably socially shaped.

Part 2: Reality, Survival, and Sociality

a. The Politics of Reality

Near the end of "Some Consequences," Peirce unveils his conception of reality,[18] the real, as *communally* articulated and affirmed.[19] The implications of this view of reality are significant when paired with Peirce's conviction that humans must be social in their reasoning if they are to reason well.

Let us begin with the passage detailing Peirce's description of reality. The real is the product of a communal human, scientific investigation of nature, and the community involved is infinitely large and extends indefinitely into the future. Peirce contrasts this communal human articulation of reality to the idiosyncrasy of the individual human organism's perspective:

> [W]hat do we mean by the real? It is a conception which we must first have had when we discovered that there was an unreal, an illusion; that is, when we first corrected ourselves. Now the distinction for which alone this fact logically called, was between an *ens* relative to private inward determinations, to the negations belonging to idiosyncrasy, and an *ens* such as would stand in the long run. The real, then, is that which, sooner or later, information and reasoning would finally result in, and which is therefore independent of the vagaries of me and you. Thus, the very origin of the conception of reality shows that this conception essentially involves the notion of a COMMUNITY, without definite limits, and capable of an indefinite increase of knowledge. (W 2:239)

The real, then, does not revolve around one's private, idiosyncratic ideas, a lesson that humans learn as children—that is, "when we first corrected ourselves." Instead, the real is what is discovered by a *community* of humans inquiring about the world outside them. Reality consists, for Peirce, in the regularities—or habits—that give form to the cosmos itself, including nature and human conduct.

In this context, Peirce does not emphasize the secondness characterizing human interaction with the external world, although he does acknowledge that "things which are relative to the mind doubtless *are*, apart from that relation" (W 2:239, my emphasis). That is to say, humans do not simply "make up" reality whimsically, without grounding in the external world. It is the secondness of the external world, in fact, that—through the mediation of thirdness—teaches humans about reality. Peirce hints at this secondness (mediated by thirdness) in the above passage in his reference, again, to "when we first corrected ourselves" in relationship to external physical and social environments (W 2:239). This points to his discussion of child development in the essay "Questions Concerning," where the child experiences the natural and social secondness involved in learning about the world and coming to self-consciousness (W 2:202–3). I examine child development in Part 3 below.

The real is based on communal human inquiry into nature and requires input from an infinite number of perspectives (in conjunction with the scientific testing of hypotheses). It is like the metaphor of the blind people standing, in place, around an elephant. While they cannot *see* the elephant, they ideally pool their observations from their various perspectives (from the respective vantage points of trunk, ears, tail, legs, etc.), thereby gaining as accurate a description as possible, given their limitations. Humans are prevented from gaining a complete grasp of the external world because of the bodily semiotic filters through which they communicate with it. Humans can only perceive the external world according to the limitations of their sense organs. If our sense organs were different, our reality would be different.[20] Moreover, an individual human is also limited in time and space. One of the truisms of phenomenology is that I only encounter the world through the limited spatio-temporal perspective of my body. Finally, in his later writings, Peirce also elaborates on the fact that nature grows.[21] Thus we have a third dimension of the impossibility of a complete human grasp of the external world. Thus to achieve the best, even if fallible, articulation of reality requires a communal effort.

There is a fruitful tension in Peirce's account of reality, one that is more explicitly taken up in the Logic of Science essays of the late 1870s. The tension is this: This communal real is, in fact, *ideal*, since it is based on an infinitely large community extending its inquiry indefinitely into the future. This means that, in the here and now, reality can only be articulated by a finite community. Thus any particular articulation of reality is fallible and subject to future modifications. As Ann Margaret Sharp notes, regarding Peirce's thought, "the world captured in human inquiry and designated as factual is always something one can question" (1994, 202). Moreover, this socialized account of reality allows a political dimension of reality to be addressed. Since reality at any particular point in time is articulated by a *finite* group of people, it can reflect exclusionary biases that are shared by these people and/or power imbalances that result in excluding certain individuals or groups from the communal articulation of reality. Ideally such discrimination would not happen, but any particular articulation of reality occurs within a historical human community and is thus vulnerable to discriminatory biases.

It may be objected that my points about politics and power render Peirce's account of reality untenable, because to be really real, so to speak, is to be free from any bias. Such an objection begs the question of reality existing separately from human articulation in the first place. Peirce's fallibilist articulation is, in fact, innovative *just because* it presents reality as capable of growth and change, as well as subject to oppressive takeover by powerful groups. Peirce is ahead of his time in presenting a conception of reality that is humanly articulated as well as scientifically grounded and thus amenable to social critique, reform, and revolution. In the history of Western culture, for example, articulations of reality have reflected the exclusionary biases shared by Euro-American white, propertied men, who often excluded others from the community of inquiry. Unduly limited accounts of reality were a result. Marilyn Frye and Adrienne Rich discuss how women in general and lesbians in particular have historically suffered erasure[22] at the hands of patriarchal power structures (Frye 1983, 152–74; Rich 1986, 23–75). Charles Mills makes an analogous observation from the perspective of African Americans living within the structures of white privilege in the United States:

> The peculiar features of the African-American experience—racial slavery, which linked biological phenotype to social subordination, and which is chronologically located in the modern epoch, ironically coincident with the emergence of liberalism's proclamation of universal human equality—are not part of the experience represented in the abstractions of European or Euro-American philosophers. And those who have grown up in such a[n] [African-American] universe, asked to pretend that they are living in the other [Euro-American universe], will be cynically knowing, exchanging glances that signify "There the white folks go again." (1998, 4)

In terms of our discussion here, we can say that Mills is discussing a particular segment of reality—namely, human experience. He is highlighting that "human experience" *as described from* a Euro-American white perspective that excludes African American experience is *inaccurate* as an abstraction that is applicable to any human's experience. When Mills notes that African Americans are "asked to pretend they are living in the other [Euro-American universe]," this highlights the power differential between Euro-Americans and African Americans, such that Euro-Americans have historically been in a position to impose their articulation of reality as *the* reality.

Whether or not it includes imposed exclusionary biases like racism, sexism, or other forms of exclusion, reality affects habit-taking by means of physical and social secondness. The habit of stopping my car at red lights, for example, is shaped by the threat of both physical and social environmental resistance: I do not want to be hit by another car, and I do not want to receive a ticket. My focus in this project is on habits that are ultimately shaped[23] by the presence or absence of *socio-political* secondness that is rooted in racist, sexist, and/or other discriminatory articulations of reality. I have lived my entire life in the United States and have *never* been pulled over by the police for driving too slowly or on trumped-up drug charges. This *absence* of socio-political secondness has everything to do with my race (Euro-American white) and, arguably, my sex (female).

b. Survival, Synthetic Reasoning, and the Social Principle

In "Grounds of Validity of the Laws of Logic" (1869), Peirce argues that "the social principle"[24] is the logical underpinning for synthetic reasoning (W 2:271).[25] Since synthetic reasoning is the only kind of reasoning that can increase human knowledge, social reasoning is all the more important. Peirce is not just talking about abstract learning here. He is addressing knowledge of the external world, knowledge that human organisms need for survival—that is, knowledge about what to expect in the future (inductions) and why (hypotheses).[26]

Peirce says that the human organism is *illogical* to the extent that she reasons synthetically based only on her own perspective. To do so is to put most of one's eggs in the same basket. Peirce compares the individual human to an insurance company. The wise insurance company does not put the bulk of its risk into only one client, because, if that client incurs devastating loss, the insurance company cannot survive the blow to its own security. Instead the insurance company needs to spread its risk among many clients, so that, if any particular client is wiped out, this loss is counterbalanced by the security spread among the many other clients. The human is like an insurance company in the risks she takes in reasoning about the external world. If she places the bulk of her risk in her own perspective by considering her own interests as the primary source of truth, she is like the unwise insurance company. If she is wrong about how the world works, she has little to fall back on (W 2:270–71).[27] From the standpoint of animal survival, she could die. Recall Peirce's oft-quoted line, "to make single individuals absolute judges of truth is most pernicious" (W 2:212)

Jon Krakauer's book *Into the Wild* provides a contemporary example of Peirce's point (1996). Krakauer details the true story of Chris McCandless, a Euro-American, middle-class man in his twenties, who in 1992 traveled alone to Alaska with virtually no knowledge of how to live off the land, except for ongoing reference to an Alaskan field guide on edible plants (160). McCandless was otherwise a very bright, well-educated, conscientious person with a deep reverence toward nature. His story is an inspiring narrative of commitment to one's inner spirit and to leading an authentic life without false dependencies on material things or other people. Except for one thing. McCandless died alone in the wilderness, after about four months, because of gaps in his knowledge that his field guide could not fill. McCandless did not spread his risk evenly. He depended almost exclusively on his own intelligence, and then on his field guide. He did not solicit the input of others, especially those who knew the Alaskan wild. He also lacked a topographical map of the area, which would have shown him that the impassable, bulging spring river that prevented his leaving the wild when he had planned to would have been straightforwardly crossed had he merely walked a half mile downstream (173–74). Had he left according to schedule, it is likely he would have avoided the food-poisoning accident that cost him his life (174, 189–95).

Peirce puts it this way:

> If a man has a transcendent personal interest infinitely outweighing all others, then, . . . he is devoid of all security, and can make no valid inference whatever. What follows? That logic rigidly requires, before all else that no determinate fact, nothing which can happen to a man's self, should be of more consequence to him than everything else. He who would not sacrifice his own soul to save the whole world, is illogical in all his inferences, collectively. So the social principle is rooted intrinsically in logic. (W 2:270–71)

As McCandless's story illustrates, the individual human organism's own survival is promoted by embracing the interests of others. To be self-centered in one's reasoning is not only to be illogical; it is to put oneself at risk unnecessarily (W 2:270–71). This is because the inter-ests of others are rooted in their perspectives on the external world, which can better inform the limited perspective of the solitary human being. One of the men who picked up the hitchhiking McCandless and delivered him to his point of departure into the Alaskan wild tried to convince him to take proper gear with him, even offering to buy him the gear. He was worried about him. This man's interest in McCandless's safety was attached to a perspective on the Alaskan wild that McCandless did not have and from which he would have bene-fited. McCandless refused most of the man's help, accepting only a pair of rubber boots and a sack lunch (Krakauer 1996, 3–7).[28]

Why does Peirce state the case for the social principle so strongly as to speak of "sacrificing [one's] own soul to save the whole world" (W 2:270)? There are at least two reasons. First of all, as detailed above, the human organism's individual perspective involves affect-ive-semiotic communication with the external world, which is fueled by her interest in survival. To the extent that one's interests are linked to heightened affective response, it may be difficult to accommodate the interests of others. Clinical psychologist Harriet Lerner notes that—thanks to the fight/flight response in humans—when anxiety is present, even in small doses, dichotomous thinking can dominate, whereby interests different from one's own appear threatening, even when they might in fact be complementary (2004, 58, 60; 1995). When this occurs, it may well feel like *sacrifice* or surrender to allow other interests to hold sway along with one's own. Second, while Peirce pays his dues to evolution and animal survival, his primary concern is for the ongoing growth of scientific knowledge beyond survival in-terests. This kind of growth is not served by egoistic interests that block the road of inquiry. He wants team players, not Cartesian intu-itionists who assume they have the corner on the market of truth. Team players sacrifice individual ego for the good of communal inquiry.

Both of these reasons highlight Peirce's emphasis on self-control, which in the present essay series is explicitly referenced only in a foot-note, in "Grounds of Validity of the Laws of Logic." As noted in

Chapter 1, he says that a hallmark of self-control is the ability to take a perspective that is broader than one's personal immediate interest: "Self-control seems to be the capacity for rising to an extended view of a practical subject instead of seeing only temporary urgency. . . . [A]nd . . . love of what is good for all on the whole . . . is the widest possible consideration . . ." (W 2:261 n. 6). This generous love, which is manifest in agape, "is the essence of Christianity" (W 2:261 n. 6). Self-control involves an inhibition of exclusionary affective reactions that could be triggered because of an inappropriate sense of "temporary urgency," when one is confronted with a perspective different from her own. As this passage also indicates, self-control is at its best when enhanced by a loving embrace of "what is good for all on the whole." Agapic love, as an ideal, reflects one's sincere concern for other community members, such that she *wants* to hold their feedback in place so that she can both learn from it and promote their well-being and thus the growth of the community as a whole (EP 1:352–71). Agape will be discussed in further detail in Chapter 4.

c. The Politics of the Social Principle

We cannot leave the story of the social principle here, however. To do so would neglect the politics of reality discussed above. On the one hand, Peirce tells us that "the social principle is rooted intrinsically in logic"—namely, the logic of spreading one's risk by pooling one's perspective with those of others, regarding knowledge of the external world (W 2:271). On the other hand, what if the others in one's social milieu are part of an oppressive power structure, whereas he or she is a member of an oppressed group? That is to say, what if powerful and oppressive others are the primary "articulaters" of reality, so to speak? What if the interests and perspective of these hegemonic others involve the subservience of one's social group, since that is what "nature" supposedly dictates? What if, since the day a person was born, she has been inundated with messages of her subservience to another social group, such that her self-interest becomes linked with playing a subservient role within her

culture? Marilyn Frye would call this a double-bind, a signal characteristic of being oppressed (1983, 2).

In a double-bind, all of one's options involve "penalty, censure or
deprivation," thus imposing disempowering limits on one's movement and growth (Frye 1983, 2 ff.). On the one hand, a person needs
to embrace the interests and perspectives of others in order to promote her own survival, to protect against fatal lacunae in her knowledge of the external world, both physical and social. On the other
hand, if she is a member of an oppressed group, embracing the interests of others can involve embracing perspectives on herself and the
world that undermine her growth and sense of self-worth. Frye explores the ubiquity of patriarchal messages females receive, from
childhood on, regarding their "proper" comportment and behavior.
They are censured if they fail to adopt "appropriate" behavior. Yet
meeting standards of femininity subjects them to condescending and/
or disrespectful treatment (2 ff., 15). Moreover, since pressures to act
feminine begin so early in a girl's life, she is likely to *internalize* feminine behavior and standards. This internalization fuels arguments, by
some, that feminine conduct—for example, shaving body parts that
men do not shave—results from inborn tendencies, when it is really
a product of deeply ingrained habits that have been socially enforced.[29] Such arguments confuse with inborn habits the firstness
habits that result from socialization.

Those belonging to privileged groups can also internalize growth-
inhibiting habits, albeit different ones (cf. McIntosh 1988). To this extent we must move beyond Frye's conception of double-bind, since
this applies only to the oppressed, in order to describe the coercion
faced by *all* children in hegemonic communities, regardless of their
race, sex, etc. I call this broader conception a "coercive survival dilemma," because small children are too vulnerable to challenge the
perspective of their caretakers and larger community or society. Such
a challenge would threaten their survival. This being the case, children are coerced regarding many belief-habits passed on to them by
their caretakers and/or society. More on this shortly.

Peirce gives mixed messages regarding his sensitivity to the politics of reality and the social principle. In his defense of the latter, he argues against those who attribute an inescapable selfishness to human actions. He gives, however, a puzzling example of human "selflessness":

> [T]he constant use of the word *"we"*—as when we speak of our possessions on the Pacific—our destiny as a republic—in cases in which no personal interests at all are involved, show conclusively that men do not make their personal interests their only ones, and therefore may, at least, subordinate them to the interest of the community. (W 2:271, Peirce's emphasis)

Peirce argues here that humans *do*, in many cases, take other interests besides their own into account. They are not merely solipsistically focused on their idiosyncratic interests. His example is troubling, however, since "speak[ing] of our possessions on the Pacific" can involve the idiosyncratic interest of financial investments made by individuals who have a vested interest in calling another land and its people "our possessions." The colonization of what became the United States of America involved just such individualized interests, as did the African slave trade.[30] While his later writings are more amenable to addressing this concern, in the present context Peirce does not seem aware of the oppressive interests that can be hidden within a professed socially inclusive stance.

Nonetheless, in the above passage, Peirce does say that people "do not make their personal interests their only ones, and therefore *may, at least, subordinate them to the interest of the community*" (W 2:271, my emphasis). My focus here is this subordination of individual interests to the community. The influence of others on one's reasoning is not a factor over which one has complete control, especially if one is in a position of dependence on and/or subordination to others. Sociality is not merely an epistemological goal of mature adults, although it is that. The social principle is also developed by each person, from *childhood* on, as she matures within a community on which she is dependent. In fact, social influence can so override a person's idiosyncratic interests and perspective that her community could convince her that she is "mad" (W 2:202). Thus social influence can enhance *and* undermine growth, the latter which becomes clearer when the "coercive survival dilemma" is examined in the context of child development within hegemonic communities.

Part 3: The Politics of Child Development

Belief-habit formation begins in childhood.[31] An examination of child development shines light on the socialization that shapes the growth of the human organism from infancy into adulthood. The idiosyncratic filter of individualized embodiment is inescapably shaped by social factors. Peirce argues, in fact, that self-consciousness arises amid the environmental clashes through which the child comes to the awareness that she must trust the testimony of others. We see, coupled with his arguments for cultivating the social principle, that the human child *depends for her survival* on the testimony of others. Given that reality reflects a communal articulation of the how the world works, the internalized socialization that characterizes child development is formidable. The adoption of socially derived instinctive beliefs by the child is perfectly understandable in this context. Moreover, in a hegemonic culture that continually reinforces racist, sexist, and other exclusionary beliefs, such beliefs can easily remain intact into adulthood, operating nonconsciously and resisting rational attempts to challenge them. Peirce does not explicitly address this danger in the present Cognition Series, but he does give an important hint in this regard, noting that testimony from others is so powerful it can convince someone that she is "mad" (W 2:202).

Peirce addresses child development in order to answer the question of whether humans have "an intuitive self-consciousness" (W 2:200). By "intuitive," as noted earlier, Peirce means unmediated by other cognitions (W 2:193–94). By "self-consciousness," he means a *personal* "knowledge of ourselves," "the recognition of my *private* self" (W 2:200–201, Peirce's emphasis). Is self-consciousness intuitive—that is, is my knowledge of my unique existence independent of previous cognitions (such as those representing external experience)?

Peirce answers this question negatively, asserting that self-consciousness is *social* in its origin, arising through the conflicts children experience with others and the physical environment. Self-consciousness involves a "feeling . . . of our personal selves" (firstness) and an *inference* made by the child (thirdness) based on the evidence she gains from conflicts (secondness) experienced within her social and physical world (W 2:201). While Peirce's account of child development was written long before his mature phenomenology, I find it helpful to read this account through a phenomenological lens to help foreground the belief-habit formation involved.

In what follows, I thus frame Peirce's argumentation phenomenologically, showing how the thirdness of self-consciousness is reached after stages characterized by the primacy of firstness and secondness, respectively. The idiosyncratic bodily interests that were discussed in Part 1 of this chapter are subsumed under a developmental stage of firstness, in which the human infant is absorbed in the world of her body and what it reveals to her. The emergence of self-consciousness results from the next stage, which is characterized by secondness. And the child's conscious adoption of habits is a stage characterized by thirdness. After discussing these stages, I address the many socio-political implications of Peirce's brief hint about the power of testimony to convince someone of being "mad" (W 2:202). My goal here is to highlight the socio-political dimension of the secondness experienced by the child and how this affects the habits she adopts and internalizes. I end by noting that, despite the power of testimony and internalization, children (and adults) are never fully determined by their communities/societies, and thus there is always hope for growth beyond instinctive belief-habits.

a. Firstness

Firstness is a stage that reflects the natural immaturity of the human infant, the immaturity that comes from being a human animal at a certain age and stage of body-mind development (cf. CP 7.375). The infant demonstrates solipsistic absorption with her or his body and oblivion to anything outside of this purview:

> A very young child may always be observed to watch its own body
> with great attention. There is every reason why this should be so,
> for from the child's point of view this body is the most important
> thing in the universe. Only what it touches has any actual and
> present feeling; only what it faces has any actual color; only what
> is on its tongue has any actual taste. (W 2:201)

For the child, the sensory qualities that she experiences are all there
is. This stage in development is prior to self-consciousness. While the
adult may observe the child "watch[ing] its own body with great attention," the child has no awareness of herself *as watching*. There is
no separation between the subject perceiving and the quality perceived. As Peirce notes, "No one questions that, when a sound is
heard by a child, he thinks, not of himself as hearing, but of the bell
or other object as sounding" (W 2:201). From a phenomenological
perspective, this nonreflective bodily absorption in sense qualities is
firstness.[32]

   This is not to say that the firstness reflected in child development
is pure and exclusive of the other categories. Phenomenological richness is present. The same children who for the most part are fully
absorbed in their world still meet with conflict from their environment (secondness). These encounters are all the more likely *because*
of the absorption of firstness characterizing this early phase of development. The younger the child, the more naive she is in the face of
the potential harms or benefits in her environment. As for thirdness,
Peirce notes that *thinking* in some form seems to always be present in
children:

> Indeed, it is almost impossible to assign a period at which chil-
> dren do not already exhibit decided intellectual activity in direc-
> tions in which thought is indispensable to their well-being. The
> complicated trigonometry of vision, and the delicate adjustments
> of coördinated movement, are plainly mastered very early.
> (W 2:201)

Prior to self-conscious thinking, and later alongside such thinking,
the developing human organism's body-mind thinks at instinctive
levels, ensuring optimal communication with the external world.[33]

Language development also falls under this early thirdness. Peirce notes the seemingly instinctive efforts of children to learn language in order to communicate with "bodies somewhat similar" to their own (W 2:202). Such efforts are so automatic for children that they are unaware of having undertaken them: "In many cases, [a child] will tell you that he never learned his mother-tongue; he always knew it, or he knew it as soon as he came to have sense" (W 2:196). In this context Peirce does not pause to specify the social influence present at different points all along the spectrum. Obviously, however, language development is dependent upon social factors. Coordination of movement also involves social influence, such as caretaker responses to a child's learning how to explore the environment, learning how to walk, and so on.

b. Secondness

Language development provides a transition between the self-absorption of firstness and the secondness-prominent phase of a child's development, where she comes into more explicit communication with others and the external world. Conflict is prevalent, as the child comes to the awareness that she is not coextensive with the world outside her but rather clashes repeatedly with it.

Once children are capable of communicating, they are capable of learning from the testimony of others, finding that the latter provides a more certain account of reality than "reality" itself (cf. Colapietro 1989, 71 ff.). In other words, through the testimony of others, children learn that what seem to be "facts" are actually "appearances" (W 2:202). Peirce explains what happens as the child "learns to understand the language" and "begins to converse" (W 2:202):

> It must be about this time that he begins to find that what these people about him say is the very best evidence of fact. So much so, that testimony is even a stronger mark of fact than *the facts themselves*, or rather than what must now be thought of as the *appearances* themselves. (I may remark, by the way, that this remains so through life; testimony will convince a man that he himself is mad). A child hears it said that the stove is hot. But it is

not, he says; and, indeed, that central body is not touching it, and only what that touches is hot or cold. But he touches it, and finds the testimony confirmed in a striking way. (W 2:202, Peirce's emphasis)

A child who has never been burned by something hot is likely enough to ignore or take lightly warnings by adults—that is, their testimony about not touching a hot stove: "But it is not [hot], he says; and, indeed, that central body is not touching [the stove], and only what that touches is hot or cold. But he touches it, and finds the testimony confirmed in a striking way." This shocking and, from the child's perspective, traumatic encounter with his environment is an instance of secondness. It promotes the internalization not only of avoiding hot stoves but of trusting the testimony of others. The child is made unequivocally aware that his world does not revolve around his limited conceptions of it. In other words, "testimony [from other people] is even a stronger mark of fact than *the facts themselves*, or rather than what must now be thought of as the *appearances* themselves." Self-consciousness begins to emerge alongside the harsh experiences of secondness through which children learn of their *ignorance* of the workings of their environment, ignorance that is highlighted by the accuracy of the testimony of others.

What Colapietro calls the "second moment in the early emergence of self-consciousness" is the child's awareness of her world as *private* (1989, 72).[34] The awareness of privacy, in this context, differs from awareness of ignorance, the latter involving the absence of knowledge about, say, hot stoves. The awareness of the *privacy* of one's world involves how the uniqueness of one's judgments can signal the incorrectness of these judgments. This new awareness comes about as the child realizes that "there is a certain remarkable class of appearances which are continually contradicted by testimony" (W 2:202–3). These appearances are those that are based on idiosyncratically "emotional" judgments (W 2:203). The child's judgment, for example, that it is appropriate to smear her dinner on the kitchen wall does not meet with automatic validation by others. In fact, such a judgment is likely to be denied, not just in the case of the child but in the case of anyone who proclaims judgments based solely on private interests. In this second dawning, then, the child adds to the insight about the importance of testimony the "conception of [appearance] as something *private* and valid only for one body" (W 2:203). The child is now aware of herself as capable of *error*, an awareness that "can be explained only by supposing a *self* which is fallible" (W 2:203, Peirce's emphasis).

Peirce concludes his presentation of child development into self-consciousness by saying, "Ignorance and error are all that distinguish our private selves from the absolute *ego* of pure apperception" (W 2:203). "Ignorance" refers to gaps in the child's knowledge. The child's isolated perspective cannot provide her with all she needs to know, such that trusting testimony is crucial to keeping herself safe from dangerous environmental objects (such as hot stoves). "Error" in this context refers not to gaps in knowledge but rather to personal judgments so unique they are not corroborated by others, such as the judgment that it is acceptable to smear one's dinner on the kitchen wall. Both ignorance and error are evidence the child uses to draw the inference that a private self must exist (W 2:203).

Thus Peirce has answered negatively the original question of whether humans have an unmediated or intuitive self-consciousness. First, self-consciousness is *not* initially present in young children, as evidenced by their absorption and lack of self-awareness (firstness stage) (W 2:201–2). Second, the development of self-consciousness is clearly mediated through encounters of secondness that reveal to the child her separateness and uniqueness in respect to the world outside her. This revelation is grounded in her language development, which enables her to experience the power of testimony to reveal the insufficiency of her solitary perspective on the world (W 2:202–3).

The phenomenological richness of the secondness stage of child development is reflected in the transition from the child's oblivion about her separateness from the outside world, to her conclusion that she must, indeed, be separate from this world. The clashes with the outside world (secondness) experienced by the child imply the presence of firstness in at least two ways. First, secondness is experienced as *clash*, because of the felt equanimity (firstness) that it disturbs. The shock of burning one's hand on the hot stove, for example, ruptures the calm functioning of her everyday movement in the world. Second, the secondness is experienced by the child as happening *to her* as an embodied organism. This implies the presence of firstness as the felt embodiment that each one of us brings to our experiences.[35]

The thirdness within the secondness stage reflects a growth beyond (but still inclusive of) learning and thinking instinctively, as the child forms new habits based on the secondness she encounters. I call this "reactionary" thirdness, as it is triggered externally via secondness. The child who burns her hand on the stove (secondness) exhibits thirdness as she concludes that she should not touch a stove if told that it is hot, which probably leads to an internalized habit whereby she avoids touching hot stoves. Thirdness is also reflected in the inference, of a *"self* which is fallible," drawn by the child at the close of the "ignorance" and "error" movements of the secondness stage (W 2:203, Peirce's emphasis). In this case the conclusion that a unique self exists (thirdness) mediates between the secondness resulting from ignorance and error, on the one hand, and the equanimity of firstness that this secondness disturbs. Self-consciousness is the transition between the secondness and thirdness stages of child development, as self-consciousness makes possible the active pursuit of self-controlled habit-taking.

c. Thirdness

Self-consciousness brings children into a stage of thirdness, which builds on and is inclusive of the types of thirdness found in the firstness and secondness stages of child development.[36] In addition to instinctive thirdness and reactionary thirdness, self-consciousness makes possible proactive reasoning and proactively self-controlled habit-formation. I use the term "proactive" to capture the child's ability to intentionally make use of thirdness in order to learn, to form habits, and to set goals for herself. In other words, the self-aware child in the thirdness stage is what Colapietro calls "a center of purpose and power" (1989, 74). In this stage children ask questions, initiating the learning process. They also initiate the formation of habits. I have seen this many times in small children who want to do for themselves a task that the caretaker has been doing for them, such as putting on clothes or fixing food. Goal-setting is also present. A child who wants to accomplish a task by herself has a goal of independent behavior regarding that task. My four-year-old niece's experiment, mentioned in Chapter 1, to see what would happen to water if it were left overnight in the freezer reflected her goal of learning about water and freezing temperatures.

The thirdness stage never ends. Proactive thirdness remains a prominent feature of human experience as children grow into adults who proactively learn about the world, form habits, and set goals. This is not to imply that reaching the thirdness stage means that all subsequent experiences will have proactive thirdness as the most prominent element, with secondness and firstness always playing lesser roles. Rather, reaching the thirdness stage means that proactive thirdness is now an *option*, not fully available in the earlier two stages, for conscious and controlled interaction with the world, interaction that is directed by the child or adult for herself.

In circumstances where they have a choice, humans can opt *not* to learn, to form new habits, or to set goals for themselves. The habits of privilege that I am examining in this book often involve just such a refusal of growth. Peggy McIntosh, describing how her white privilege manifests in her experience in the United States, notes: "I can remain oblivious of the language and customs of persons of color who constitute the world's majority without feeling in my culture any penalty for such oblivion. . . . I can choose to ignore developments in minority writing and minority activist programs . . ." (1988, 294). With these observations, McIntosh highlights not only certain types of refusal to learn but also the fact that refusing to learn can be a function of privilege. People in non-hegemonic groups often cannot afford *not* to know the hegemonic culture's belief-habits, including language, communication style, dress code, politeness code, and so on.[37] If they are to survive within the dominant culture, they often do not have the luxury to consider learning such norms as *optional*; it is often a requirement.

The thirdness stage of child development must be understood in its deeply communal and post-Darwinian contexts. Infants and young children are vulnerable and dependent animal organisms. Their self-controlled habit-taking could not develop if they died in either the firstness or secondness stage, which would most likely happen without the nurturing of caretakers (Dewey [1922] 1988, 43–53, 65–68). The infant's survival and language development both depend on the presence of caretakers; so do her other learning experiences. The community in general also helps teach the child about how reality works. Thus the child's habits are socially shaped.

As the child enters into the thirdness stage, to the extent that her outer environments remain relatively stable, she relies on linguistic, cultural, and other habits taught to her in the firstness and secondness stages. And testimony still plays a key role. As Lorraine Code notes:

> Developmentally, children learn to negotiate the world through processes of establishing reasonably fixed, constant expectations about the behaviors and "natures" of the people and things around them. Could they not do so, their survival would be in constant jeopardy; could they do so only erratically, their sanity would be similarly in jeopardy. *Most of what people come to know*, from the language into which they are born and educated, to the manners, customs, and cultural expectations they ingest, *are items and ways of being that they learn from other people*; sometimes by example, sometimes from being told—*from testimony*. (1995, 71, my emphasis)

Code is highlighting the ubiquity of social influence on the learning process of children. In Peircean terms, their "learn[ing] to negotiate the world" involves thirdness, through which belief-habits about the world are established and revised as necessary (71). Yet even as thirdness becomes more and more self-controlled, the communal matrix is still present, requiring a dependence on testimony even as children grow into mature adults. Code notes how often adults trust the testimony of others—in life-and-death issues such as "[e]ating what others have prepared, trusting the labels on packages, stepping into a car or an airplane" (72). This dependency of *adults* on testimony underscores the increased dependency of children on testimony, given the latter's heightened reliance on others for survival and for rudimentary learning. Children belonging to hegemonic communities thus face the coercive survival dilemma. Needing to trust communal testimony coerces children into adopting growth-inhibiting habits alongside empowering ones.

In the Cognition Series Peirce gives only a slight hint of the coercive survival dilemma faced by children in hegemonic communities, focusing instead on the epistemological security communities provide. He presents the community of inquiry as a team whose members corroborate their perspectives in order both to eliminate the emotional or idiosyncratic and to elucidate the common—that is, the rational or intellectual—patterns grasped by all. His account of child development supports this corroborative picture by portraying the privacy of the child's perspective as a source of error (W 2:203). As noted earlier, in this series Peirce does *not* explicitly give an account of the maverick rationality by which an individual may have a unique insight that is correct even though different from the community's perspective. He does, however, note—in the passage quoted above in the secondness stage—that "testimony will convince a man that he himself is mad" (W 2:202, Peirce's emphasis). This comment, I would argue, is a very subtle hint that opens the door to the coercive survival dilemma and the possibility that disagreeing with one's community can reflect epistemological insight (versus error). In what follows, I use this hint as a springboard for examining Peirce's account of child development in light of the politics of reality, the social principle, and the coercive survival dilemma, drawing out implications regarding the internalization of socialized belief-habits. My examples focus on the individual in relationship to a hegemonic community whose habits are racist and sexist.

d. Testimony's Darker Side: The Coercive Survival Dilemma

Peirce troubles the waters of testimony considerably when he makes a parenthetical comment about the child's discovery of its importance.[38]As noted in the secondness stage discussed above, he states:

> It must be about this time [of comprehending language and start-ing to converse] that [the child] begins to find that what these people about him say is the very best evidence of fact. So much so, that testimony is even a stronger mark of fact than *the facts themselves*, or rather than what must now be thought of as the *appearances* themselves. (I may remark, by the way, that this re-mains so through life; testimony will convince a man that he him-self is mad.) (W 2:202, Peirce's emphasis)

Peirce does not elaborate on his comment that testimony can con-vince someone of being "mad." Presumably he has in mind the nega-tive potential of the social principle. Each person needs to depend on testimony from others to supplement her limited perspective on the world. Ignoring the testimony of others can be life-threatening, as the tragic story of Chris McCandless illustrates. Yet testimony can be used maliciously, to exclude a community member from the community, rendering her epistemological input "mad." Because testimony is so powerful to human organisms, the excluded individual could become convinced of her or his "madness." This point is all the more impor-tant since "madness" is a far-reaching term.[39] For the purposes of my project, I limit my treatment to how "madness" relates to the socio-political issues that are my project's focus. Two interrelated types of "madness" I want to highlight are, first, "madness" linked to speak-ing out against communal norms and, second, "madness" linked to simply being different from communal norms in the first place. This second type of madness is associated with presumed cognitive inferiority.

First of all, as Naomi Scheman notes, "It is frequently by 'disagree-ing' about things the rest of us take for granted that one is counted as mad, ignorant, or otherwise not possessed of reason" (1993, 146). Scheman's comment highlights the hegemony that communal "com-mon-sense" can take on, such that diverging from what is supposedly obvious to everyone can result in being classified as crazy. This connection relates to a comment Peirce makes when, in his essay "Fixation of Belief" (1877), he describes the authority method by which a state attempts to force its people to adopt only officially sanctioned belief-habits. As belief-habit formation is an affective venture, the authoritative state not only perpetually teaches and reinforces acceptable beliefs; it also appeals to the "passions" of the people, "so that they may regard private and unusual opinions with hatred and horror" (W 3:250). Peirce is saying that the state can manipulate the belief-habits of the people so that they will embrace the state's belief-habits and shun belief-habits that differ from these. It is only a small step from viewing dissenting voices "with hatred and horror" to viewing such voices as mad, abnormal, or inferior because they challenge the status quo.

Second, the term "mad" can have the sense, according to an older definition of the term, of being "uncontrolled by reason or judgement; foolish, unwise" (*OED Online* 2009).[40] In this sense, "mad" can be linked to the hegemonically enforced classification of groups of people as cognitively inferior because not fully human. "Mad" in this sense reflects being "abnormal" or "inferior" because of one's hegemonically presumed difference from the human norm. This linkage between madness, abnormality, and inferiority has occurred historically for people of color and women, who were presumed to differ from the "proper" Euro-American, white, male "human" type. Both groups were considered defective rationally and morally.

For example, Charles Mills uses the term "subpersonhood" to capture the multiplex ways people of color have been historically viewed from the perspective of white hegemony (1997, 53–62). Subpersons have been seen through a racist lens that imposes on them an inferior ontology, viewing them as "incapable of autonomy and self-rule": "Historically the paradigm indicator of subpersonhood has been deficient rationality, the inability to exercise in full the characteristic classically thought of as distinguishing us from animals" (57, 59–60; cf. Tunstall 2007, 160–65). Focusing on women, Nancy Tuana notes that, from the standpoint of the most influential philosophers of the

Western canon, the paradigmatic human was, in fact, *a man*. Thus "woman is seen as lacking in just those areas judged as distinctively human: the rational and moral faculties" (1992, 13).[41] In these cases of people of color and women, a type of intrinsic "madness" has been attributed to them because of their rational and moral "abnormality" and "inferiority" in relationship to what has been considered "properly human."

Clearly these two types of "madness/abnormality/inferiority"— based in challenging communal norms and differing from communal norms—are closely related, as it is often people of color and/or women, and others in non-hegemonic groups, who resist hegemonic messages about their inferiority. This resistance, however, can be harder to achieve because of the power of testimony to convince someone of her "madness/abnormality/inferiority," such that it is difficult to feel sufficient worthiness to fight the hegemony (Mills 1997, 118–19). Charles Mills explains, for example, that people of color who wish to fight the subpersonhood imposed on them by "global white supremacy"[42] must "fight an internal battle before even advancing onto the ground of external combat. One has to overcome the internalization of subpersonhood . . ." (1997, 3, 118). This overcoming takes considerable work, Mills argues, in order to "learn . . . basic self-respect" and to claim cognitive authority and aesthetic value (118–20). To articulate Mills's points in Peircean terms: The "internalization of subpersonhood" signals that belief in one's inferiority has become part of one's firstness.[43] To change such a belief-habit (via thirdness) takes concerted effort. This change is possible, however, which signals the hopeful note with which I conclude the chapter. For now, I turn to how the internalization of disempowering hegemonic messages can begin in childhood.

The power of testimony creates the coercive survival dilemma for *all* children in hegemonic communities. In this context, when post-Darwinian concerns are taken seriously, it makes sense that such children could internalize testimony-driven, growth-inhibiting habits, such as a belief in their inherent madness/abnormality/inferiority or *superiority* based on their membership in a particular group (such as females, males, people of color, and/or whites). First of all, implicit in Peirce's comment about the strength of testimony is the *vulnerability* of the individual human organism in respect to testimony. The child needs to embrace the interests of others for survival. She is very unlikely to survive if left only to her own epistemological perspective. This is even more the case for the very young child, since she is physically weak and very naive about how the world works. In this respect, the stove example discussed above illustrates not only how ignorant a child is compared to her adult caretakers. It also implies how *dependent* the child is on the testimony of her caretakers. If, for example, a young child's caretakers tell her not to go into the street by herself and she disregards the warning, she could be killed by an oncoming car. Children are unlikely to survive without trusting what they are told.

A child ignores her caretakers at her own peril, and they are likely the bearers of many enabling habits. Nonetheless, these caretakers—and the community in general—can also be the bearers of growth-inhibiting belief-habits. These are the two sides of the coercive survival dilemma. A child learns that her world is private and thus a source of error in relation to the testimony of her caretakers and community. Yet the testimony in question may involve pressures to believe and behave "correctly" in order to preserve an oppressive societal status quo. Fear of abandonment by their caretakers or community may make children reluctant to question their testimony, since being abandoned would signal death almost as surely as would a child's refusing to look both ways before crossing a busy street. Psychologist Joan Borysenko notes that, when a small child is reprimanded by her caretakers, it shakes her world to the core:

> At the moment of reprimand, the world stops working according to the rules. The interpersonal bridge is severed. Feeling scared and isolated, the child wonders what she did to bring this disaster about. Does it mean she will be abandoned? Does it mean that Mommy will stay angry forever? Does it mean that she will never be loved again? *To a small child who knows so little about the world, a fragile being whose life is totally dependent on parental care, broken bridges are as frightening as death.* (1990, 53, my emphasis)

The small child is not in a position to take on the world by herself without the support of her caretakers and, I would add, community. In Peircean terms, the reprimand is an experience of secondness that ruptures her sense of security. In this respect, secondness is a theme connecting Borysenko's comments and Peirce's account of the child who defies caretaker testimony by touching the hot stove. In the latter case, the child "touches it, and finds the testimony confirmed in a striking way" (W 2:202). Both getting burned by the stove and being scolded are instances of secondness, to which the child responds with thirdness on some level.

In relation to caretaker-secondness, the smaller the child, the greater the likelihood that her thirdness will work to *adapt* to this type of secondness without trying to challenge it, because caretakers are the primary arbiters and teachers of reality for the child. From a post-Darwinian point of view, the child's caretakers not only explain reality to the child; they also continually mediate and protect the child from environmental secondness. Thus the child's adoption of her caretakers' belief-habits, in many respects, fosters her survival (cf. A. Rorty 1980, 122). The social principle is integral to the young child's development through the testimony of caretakers and, by implication, the larger community that has shaped the caretakers' habits. The child is continually exposed to this larger community indirectly (via caretaker habits) and/or directly, through day care, school, neighborhood, and the media. In terms of Peirce's phenomenology, the adaptation to secondness ranges from nonconscious to conscious. For children who have not achieved self-consciousness (thirdness stage), thirdness would be functioning instinctively or merely in reaction to the caretaker- or community-secondness, without (yet) reflecting intentional habit-taking. For children who *have* reached self-consciousness, the younger they are, the more likely they are to acquiesce to, without challenging, the demands of reality as articulated by their caretakers/community/society, even if these demands foster the internalization of disempowering or exclusionary habits.

To grasp how this internalization can occur, we can examine the process of habit-formation (thirdness) that occurs in response to experiences of secondness that disrupt the harmonious equilibrium (firstness) of the child. Recall that internalization, for my purposes, is the incorporation, by means of reinforcement or trauma, of a belief-habit into one's personal comportment and worldview such that the belief-habit is difficult to eradicate rationally (cf. A. Rorty 1980; Bartky 1990, 63–82). In terms of Peircean phenomenology, internalization results from secondness that is continually reinforced and/or traumatizing, to the extent that the belief-habit formed in response becomes so deeply rooted in firstness that it is difficult to subject it to self-control (self-control being thirdness, in a critical self-reflection mode).

The reality that children, and adults, confront does not consist merely of hot stoves to be avoided. It also consists of a vast array of socio-political habits and norms. When these social structures are violated, sanctions are incurred. This is the domain of socio-political secondness, which, to the developing child, is every bit as real as burning her hand on the stove. Socio-political secondness influences the habit-taking of the child, just as "natural" secondness does. Take, for example, a little boy who is scolded regularly when he cries, because crying is "unacceptable" for boys. When I was around twelve years old, I was shocked to see one of the boys in my neighborhood, who was between five and ten years old, being harshly reprimanded by his father. The boy was crying at the time and his father was "in his face," so to speak, angrily telling him how inappropriate and girl-like this behavior was. My guess is that my young neighbor eventually formed a habit (via thirdness) of *not* crying when upset about something, a habit he is likely to have internalized by now (into firstness). Bell hooks notes, "Patriarchal mores teach a form of emotional stoicism to men that says they are more manly if they do not feel, but if by chance they should feel and the feelings hurt, the manly response is to stuff them down, to forget about them, to hope they go away" (2004, 5–6). Societal rules in mainstream U.S. culture repeatedly tell boys (and men) that it is inappropriate to cry. Messages of this sort can come from family, friends, other community members, and the media. In response to this socio-political secondness, boys and men often develop a habit (via thirdness) of *avoiding* crying when upset about something. In my own childhood experience, in contrast, I was not scolded for crying. I *was* repeatedly taught that sitting with my legs open was "unladylike," which was another form of socio-political secondness. I developed a corresponding habit (via thirdness) of sitting with my legs close together or crossed, "like a lady."

With consistent reinforcement through socio-political secondness, the corresponding habits—such as avoiding crying or sitting with legs crossed—can become internalized. Recall that the habits one develops through thirdness, when practiced sufficiently, often become part of one's firstness. In other words, internalized habits function so automatically as to be like "second nature." They are part of the firstness of one's implicit sense of embodied functioning in the world, so much so that they are resistant to rational appeal. Marilyn Frye notes that, regarding socialization as feminine or masculine, culture becomes biology by means of habits that are shaped from childhood (1983, 34–38). Changing these habits is possible, but this change cannot be accomplished through "just will[ing] it to happen" (38). Instead one needs "constant practice and deliberate regimens designed to remap and rebuild nerve and tissue" (37). Speaking from personal experience, I can say that sitting with my legs crossed was a habit of femininity that, as an adult, took me about two or three years to break. While I *knew* that it is better for my back and the circulation in my legs if I did not cross them, it was *so* deep seated for me that it resisted rational appeal.

As part of a human organism's firstness, internalized habits present a challenge to subsequent thirdness-efforts to change them. I wanted, as just mentioned, to stop crossing my legs and, by means of thirdness, set the goal of eliminating this habit. Merely setting this goal, however, did not automatically result in habit change, because crossing my legs was internalized, deeply part of my firstness and resistant to my own efforts to change. I did eventually change the habit, but it took a lot of work through reinforcing new patterns of posture, which eventually became habitualized into my firstness.

Let us return to Peirce's comment that testimony can convince a person that she is "mad," which I have expanded to "mad/abnormal/

inferior." Internalized habits include beliefs, since for Peirce beliefs are habits. When one's "inferiority" is continually reinforced by care-takers or community, this belief-habit can become internalized (part of one's firstness) and be difficult to change through efforts of third-ness. This is to say that the internalization of inferiority is not a per-manent condition but rather one that takes significant effort to change.

It should be noted that, for the child in a hegemonic community, messages from caretakers and community can be in tension with each other. Hence caretakers may teach their child that all people are in-herently valuable and worthy of respect regardless of the color of their skin. Yet these efforts can be undermined by wider mainstream soci-etal messages that project a white norm as the human norm or that portray people of color as more likely to commit crimes.[44] Patricia Williams, speaking as an African American parent, writes about how her son had to cope with arguments among children at his nursery school "about whether black people could play 'good guys'" (1997, 3–4). In addition, bell hooks makes the point that people of color can themselves unwittingly pass along the message to their children that nonwhite is inferior:

> [B]lack mothers frequently come to me to ask what they can do when their children come home from school saying they want to be "made white." Often these women will share that they have done everything to instill love of blackness. However, in every case the woman seeks to change her appearance to look lighter or to make her hair straighter. (2003b, 37)

Hooks is pointing out that, in these cases, trying to aspire to a white beauty ideal, through lightening efforts and/or hair-straightening, sends the message that white beauty is superior, which undermines efforts "to instill love of blackness." Consistent testimony, whether intentional or unintentional, explicit or implied, that reinforces the "inferiority" people of color can result in the internalization of this belief-habit, even when this negative testimony is offset by empower-ing testimony.

For children belonging to hegemonic groups—in this case, whites—I consider it obvious that explicit and intentional caretaker-prejudice against people of color can result in internalized prejudice. I therefore prefer to focus on the more subtle point that, even when caretakers explicitly teach the worthiness and value of all people, white children can still internalize belief-habits that perpetuate racism.[45] This is all the more likely when the wider societal and community messages often perpetuate racism.

Sociologists Debra Van Ausdale and Joe Feagin include the following example in their book *The First R: How Children Learn Race and Racism* (2001). It was given to them by a young mother whose race, given the context, is presumably white:

> This woman, whom we will call Maria, had two children, a toddler aged two and a half and a seven-year-old. Since she and her family lived in the heart of New York City, one of the preferred methods for getting around town was to bundle the toddler into his stroller and maneuver the city sidewalks that way. . . . In the family's neighborhood there were usually several panhandlers on the street, almost all of them Black men who solicited change from passersby. Maria made it a habit to sidestep the area that these men frequented, giving them a wide berth. She was not fearful of the men, she said, for they were invariably polite and never demanded money. However, she usually was not able to offer them change and did not wish her children to think that she was not kind. Over time her practice of avoiding the men became routine. . . .
>
> One afternoon, her two-year-old bounced down beside her on the couch and announced, "Black men are bad." Maria was horrified: Where did this come from? She had never told him anything like this. His older sister, sitting alongside them, was equally stunned. . . . Maria's husband was queried along with friends and other family members who had access to the little boy; all were shocked. (204–5)[46]

In this example, the parents and family have not consciously taught the child to hold racist beliefs, yet the toddler has clearly formed one, namely the belief that "Black men are bad."

How can this racist belief be accounted for? The mother hypothesizes that her young son formed this belief by observing her own behavior of avoiding the panhandlers on the street, alongside the parental admonitions he regularly received to avoid "bad" things, like "stray dogs, electric outlets, stuff like that" (Van Ausdale and Feagin 2001, 205). She suggests that the racist belief is an unintentional by-product of the child's synthesis of her own behavior pattern with the stroller and the more general lesson about avoiding "bad" things. I would suggest an additional influencing factor in the formation of the racist belief. The toddler might have picked up on his mother's *discomfort* about not wanting to give money to the panhandlers (because she did not want to seem uncharitable) and/or any additional nonconscious discomfort she may have felt toward the panhandlers due to their race. Shannon Sullivan discusses how messages can be sent to children through strong feelings that convey racial messages, even when no words are spoken (2006, 63–93, esp. 64–65). I fully acknowledge I am speculating regarding the mother's discomfort, but I think it is realistic speculation, especially in light of Van Ausdale and Feagin's challenge to her hypothesis about the racist belief in question. They suggest that the toddler may have formed his racist belief from general observations of his social world, where African American men are treated unfairly by the U.S. criminal-justice system and are unduly represented as committing, along with Latinos, the most crimes (Van Ausdale and Feagin 2001, 203–6).

I would argue that the toddler's racist belief involved a complex interplay of many or all of the caretaker and societal habits just suggested. The parents' inclusive conscious beliefs about race were probably contradicted by societal messages. The parents' own internalization of these societal messages, which associate African and Latino Americans with committing crimes, could lead to mixed messages the parents are unaware of sending. Moreover, society itself—apart from parental messages—can be a very effective teacher. Van Ausdale and Feagin's research with preschool children (three to five years old) suggests that the toddler's racist belief reflects a common tendency for very young white children to engage in racist behaviors, against the express teachings of parents and teachers.[47] In the case of the children they observed, Van Ausdale and Feagin note, "It is likely here that no adult has actively taught most of these three-, four-, and five-year-olds about white power, racial self-identification, racial-ethnic exclusion, and racial-ethnic discrimination" (2001, 200). They go on to point to the societal ubiquity of racist messages: "[The children] are surrounded with racial imagery, thinking, discourse, and behavior. They observe it, experience it, and absorb it in different places and from the people they encounter" (200–201). The various "social settings" that influence children are interwoven,[48] and "[c]hildren are not ordinarily disconnected from the larger social worlds" (206). In terms of Peircean child development, we can say childhood thirdness, whereby children learn to adapt to the habits of their caretakers and community, involves learning habits implicitly and explicitly taught by parents, teachers, and other adults, *as well as* more general habits portrayed by society at large. These more general communal habits are portrayed through the media and through countless other social encounters.

In my own white, middle-class childhood, I received consistent societal messages that racism was primarily over in the United States. My parents routinely taught me that racism was wrong and that all people are equal and deserving of respect. I do not remember receiving messages that people of color were in any way inferior to me. (Since my family lived in virtually all-white suburbs, I do not recall seeing my parents' behavior toward people of color, because our social communities were so white-dominant.) Clearly, however, societal messages of white-dominance got through to me, as reflected in an unflattering example from my high school years. I attended a predominantly white, middle-class public high school in Omaha, Nebraska, where my graduating class of 480 was roughly 1 percent African American. I clearly remember hearing one day that an African American classmate of mine said he was experiencing racism at school. I completely disbelieved him. I did not express my disbelief to his face, as I hardly knew him, and I learned of his grievance only

second- or thirdhand. Nonetheless, I did not believe racism was possible at my school, and I felt completely confident in my disbelief. It
did not even occur to me to investigate this report of injustice, either
on my own or with the help of my parents. Clearly racist thinking was
at play here, as I so easily discounted an African American person's
testimony about a very serious issue. Why did I not feel immediate
and deep concern for him, especially given how incredibly outnumbered he was, given the roughly 100-to-1 ratio of whites to people of
color in my class? Why was I so confident about my knowledge of
something—namely, racism—that I had never experienced myself? I
would argue that I internalized racist beliefs in my childhood, despite
my parents' best efforts, due to what they did not know to tell me
about the persistence of institutional racism in the United States. I
also received consistent societal messages proclaiming that racism is
largely over in the United States, as well as messages that people of
color cannot be trusted. Where these latter messages about trustworthiness came from I cannot pinpoint. As I watched a fair amount of
television and had other regular exposure to U.S. mainstream culture,
it is not a stretch to hypothesize that I picked these messages up from
my society without consciously being aware of it, forming stereotypical associations/beliefs/habits about people of color.

As a high school student I was not aware that I was being racist in
my knee-jerk assumption that my classmate was wrong. Far from it.
The stereotypical associations that undermined my classmate's trustworthiness in my eyes were functioning nonconsciously alongside my
conscious beliefs that racism is wrong. My work in the following
chapters offers further explanation of how the credulity of children
to the testimony of caretakers and society can result, for those in hegemonic communities, in the internalization of discriminatory habits
by those in hegemonic groups—habits that thereby become instinctive beliefs that function nonconsciously in adulthood.

e. The Seed of Hope

I conclude this chapter by giving a hopeful reframing of Peirce's comment that "testimony will convince a man that he himself is mad" (W

2:202). Hidden in this observation is the *potential* for the individual community member to *be at odds* with what her community tells her about reality, despite the strength of the social principle and the coercive survival dilemma. Indeed an older child, or adult, may begin to question reality as articulated by her parents and community. She may also face strong opposition in doing so. This opposition can take the form of being told she is crazy for questioning the way things work, and hence Peirce's dismal reference to madness. Recall Scheman's observation that "[i]t is frequently by 'disagreeing' about things the rest of us take for granted that one is counted as mad, ignorant, or otherwise not possessed of reason" (1993, 146).

Yet Peirce's very acknowledgment of the potential conflict between an individual and her community is a hint that there is hope for growth, even in the context of intense hegemonic pressure to conform. For all the likelihood that children may internalize the growth-inhibiting beliefs of hegemonic communities, there is room for resistance. Bell hooks's life is a paradigmatic example of resistance in the face of familial and cultural hegemony. Her comments on the challenges of being African American in the United States were cited earlier. Hooks also describes the pressures, which she faced during her childhood, to conform to feminine standards. Growing up in the South, hooks found herself in repeated conflict with her parents' patriarchal values, which they tried to instill in their family. Speaking of herself in the third person, she describes how unfit for marriage her parents found her:

> [S]he was too smart, men did not like smart women, men did not like a woman whose head was always in a book. And even more importantly men did not like a woman who talked back. She had been hit, whipped, punished again and again for talking back. They had said they were determined to break her—to silence her, to turn her into one of them. (hooks 1996, 99)

Hooks's life speaks boldly of her resilience to both familial and cultural pressures. She is an influential, successful social critic, teacher, and writer. She exemplifies the possibility of the human organism's affective resilience in the face of the coercive survival dilemma faced by children in hegemonic communities.[49]

In addition, for children and adults belonging to hegemonic groups, affective resilience is also possible, by which they can resist the exclusionary belief-habits that promote their privilege at the expense of others. Peggy McIntosh, in her article "White Privilege and Male Privilege: A Personal Account of Coming to See Correspondences through Work in Women's Studies," addresses—with a view toward changing—exclusionary belief-habits that accompany racism, sexism, and heterosexism (1988). As McIntosh herself is white and heterosexual, her work demonstrates the ability of those in hegemonic groups to work against the societal belief-habits that advantage them unfairly. These habits can be hard to identify, often remaining "invisible" to those who benefit from them, and hence the importance of efforts to bring these habits to conscious awareness (291). Last chapter, we examined habits of heterosexual privilege that McIntosh identifies. Her list of white privilege, addressed briefly above, also includes such habits of expectation as "I can if I wish arrange to be in the company of people of my race most of the time," "I can go shopping alone most of the time, pretty well assured that I will not be followed or harassed," and "My culture gives me little fear about ignoring the perspectives and powers of people of other races" (293–94). As prevalent as these expectations are, they can be hard—but not impossible—to grasp. McIntosh notes:

> I have come to see white privilege as an invisible package of unearned assets which I can count on cashing in each day, but about which I was "meant" to remain oblivious. White privilege is like an invisible weightless knapsack of special provisions, assurances, tools, maps, guides, codebooks, passports, visas, cloths, compass, emergency gear, and blank checks. (291)

Bringing such elements of privilege to consciousness is a crucial first step to working for change, which includes using privilege against itself. McIntosh uses her own racial and heterosexual privileges to undermine those very privileges, by calling out the often elusive mechanisms that support them (292, 294, 298, 299). Thus McIntosh exemplifies the Peircean potential for self-controlled critique to promote habit change at individual and societal levels.[50]

By way of transition into the following chapters, let us expand from the Cognition Series to view Peirce's work as a whole, in order to articulate two themes. The first is hope in the midst of oppression. As vulnerable as a child is to the habit systems of caretakers and society, these habit systems cannot fully stifle the organic spontaneity of the human person.[51] For Peirce the community itself is a person on the macroscopic scale, and each of its members is a source of homeodynamic spontaneity and fruitful disruption that can foster communal growth by challenging stagnant communal habits. While in the present 1860s series this theme is far from explicit, he has planted a seed by allowing for the possibility that a mature community member may be at odds with her community's beliefs. This possibility is fortified by Peirce's portrayal of the uniquely embodied affective-salience that colors each person's experience of the world, even in the midst of inescapable socialization. Being at odds with communal beliefs can reflect maverick rationality that can foster communal growth.

The second theme is communal habit-formation. The present chapter points beyond itself by raising the question of how habit-formation should occur in communities, so that the coercive survival dilemma can be minimized. While the hopefulness of individual resiliency is always a possibility, surely individual and communal growth are better served by communal articulations of reality that are inclusive and fallible *in the first place.* We are at the doorstep of Peirce's Illustrations of the Logic of Science series of the 1870s, where he argues for the scientific method of communal habit-formation in contrast to the method of authority that characterizes hegemonic communities. His valuation of the synechistic individual is more explicit in this series. So too is the potential tension that can arise between this individual and a hegemonic community.

THREE

THE AFFECTIVITY OF INQUIRY

Popular Science Monthly Illustrations of the
Logic of Science Series, 1877–78

I n his Illustrations of the Logic of Science series, published in *Popular Science Monthly* in the late 1870s,[1] Peirce presents a robust synechistic individual, one who stands up to her hegemonic
community whose belief-habits need to be challenged. He also presents the scientific method as the preferred method of communal belief-habit formation. The scientific method—unlike the hegemonic
authority method—encourages input from individual community
members, since such input fosters growth in knowledge about the external world. Scientific inquiry synthesizes many individual perspectives on the world, in order to solicit insight, compensate for bias,
and elucidate common elements. This way, regularities characterizing
the external world can be learned with as much accuracy as possible
within the limits of human finitude and fallibility.

In what follows, building on work done in Chapters 1 and 2, I
read this series through affective and social critical lenses in order to
explain in more detail how it is possible for community members

to internalize hegemonic exclusionary belief-habits that can function nonconsciously. Deepening my post-Darwinian portrayal of Peircean human affectivity, I merge the concept of socio-political secondness with false universalization, the latter of which involves asserting as true for everyone beliefs reflecting a particular perspective. I also demonstrate that hegemonically exclusionary accounts of reality result in societal-level exclusionary habits, which can be internalized *conceptually* by individual community members, such that the very concepts by which individuals think about their world can reflect hegemonic, exclusionary bias. I will be using the term "concept" in a relatively nontechnical sense, to convey the abstract generalizations by which humans come to understand the world.[2] Concepts are beliefs, and beliefs are habits. Where appropriate I use these three terms together to highlight this linkage (beliefs/habits/concepts). Socio-politically biased conceptualization occurs, for example, when the experience of a hegemonic group or groups (such as whites, men, the economically secure, etc.) becomes internalized as the falsely universalized concept of "human experience." A by-product of this exclusionary conceptual internalization, which can function nonconsciously or instinctively, is the perception that non-hegemonic perspectives (voiced by people of color, women, the poor, etc.) are problematic conceptually—that is, crazy, overreactive, off base, or simply irrelevant. This can lead to the dismissal of non-hegemonic perspectives.

In conjunction with the danger of nonconscious exclusion or dismissal of non-hegemonic perspectives, my work in this chapter also highlights a methodological issue that Peirce leaves unaddressed, in this series, regarding the scientific method. The background beliefs that inform scientific inquiry may include hegemonic, exclusionary beliefs regarding the non-hegemonic groups in a community. In the Logic of Science essays, Peirce does not require the scientific community of inquiry to scrutinize these beliefs. Left unaddressed, therefore, are nonconsciously operating hegemonic belief-habits that actual scientific-community members (even well-meaning ones) may have internalized. The implementation of the scientific method, in turn, can be undermined by exclusionary bias, such as racism, sexism, or other forms of discrimination. Discrimination, even if unintentional, undermines Peirce's epistemological ideal of an infinitely *inclusive* community of inquiry (W 3:273, 284; cf. Sharp 1994, 201–7). This application problem shows how the Logic of Science series points beyond itself to Peirce's 1900s doctrine of Critical Common-sensism, which requires the scrutiny of background (or common-sense) beliefs by the community of inquiry.

Part 1: The Synechistic Individual of the 1870s

In the Logic of Science essays, the affective process of cognition described in the Cognition Series has evolved into the rhythm of ongoing habit-taking, whose pulses are belief and doubt.[3] This is the continuous *inquiry* by which individual humans and human communities converse with nature to determine how best to fix, or establish, their beliefs (or habits). The fixation of our beliefs is only a temporary measure at any point in time, as the continuous flow of experience results in regular challenges (secondness) to our habits. Peirce describes belief as a "demi-cadence which closes a musical phrase in the symphony of our intellectual life" (W 3:263). Environmental resistance, which results in doubt, forces us to continually monitor, adjust, or change our habits accordingly or suffer the consequences.

Recall that the process of human cognition has an affective dimension of feeling, which stays in the background much of the time. This state of feeling is incorporated into "Fixation of Belief" as the feeling/sensation associated with belief, "a calm and satisfactory state which we do not wish to avoid, or to change to a belief in anything else" (W 3:247). In the Cognition Series, Peirce describes the bodily commotion that corresponds to emotion (W 2:230). In the present essay series, this commotion is described as the emotion of *doubt*, i.e., "an uneasy dissatisfied state from which we struggle to free ourselves" (W 3:247, 285).

Peirce portrays belief in its phenomenological richness—that is, its firstness, secondness, and thirdness. The firstness of belief includes both awareness and feltness (W 3:263, 247). I will discuss awareness below. That our beliefs *feel* a certain way was described just above; they are "calm satisfactory state[s]" (W 3:247). Peirce also notes that "[t]he feeling of believing is a more or less sure indication of there being established in our nature some *habit* which will determine our actions" (W 3:247, my emphasis).[4] This portrays the close relationship between firstness and thirdness within the organism. Habits are thirds, mediating between organism and environment, and they have a *feel* to them, which reflects their firstness. Belief, then, involves the feltness (firstness) of learning, synthesis, and mastery (thirdness) that we experience as we successfully gear our bodies into the external world.[5] Recall that each of our habits has a particular feel, its own affective signature. Seasoned baseball or softball players know there is a feel to their batting stance. For those who know how to type, "home row" has a feel beyond the touch of the keys themselves. Cooking techniques, such as flipping pancakes or over-easy eggs, can be felt as well. I have many felt rhythms to my teaching style, ranging from situating my notes and writing the class outline on the board before class begins, to pacing while I lecture. The reader is encouraged to think of her/his own habits and their felt signatures.

In its stronger form, the secondness of belief involves recovery from habit-rupture and thus struggle against doubt. When our habits are in working order, they feel stabilizing, even though we are not likely to pay attention to this stability. If a habit encounters disruptive resistance, however, the affective response thereby triggered betrays the calmness and satisfaction that has been disturbed. For example, about a year ago, there were about three minutes left before the start of a class I was teaching. We had a lot of material to cover that day in order to stay on schedule. So there was not much time to spare. I turned to the chalkboard to erase what was there (a good amount of writing, coving the entire board), so I could write my own topic outline for class. This pattern of erasing the board and then writing my outline is a very comfortable, long-standing habit of mine. On this day, however, there was no eraser. I could not execute my outline-writing habit, as the board was covered with someone else's writing.

The affective signature of habit-rupture is doubt, the feltness of which involves the shock or surprise of habit interruption or failure. It was definitely surprising to me that there was no eraser. Doubt is "an uneasy and dissatisfied state from which we struggle to free ourselves and pass into the state of belief" (W 3:247). The "state of belief" in this context refers to a state in which our habits are newly adjusted, and/or newly formed, and back in working order. I could not find an extra eraser on short notice, and I did not have a long sleeve or other such spare fabric available to use as a makeshift eraser. In the moment, I indeed felt "uneasy and dissatisfied" until my students helped me improvise by using a piece of notebook paper to erase the board, which enabled me to write my outline and subsequent lecture notes. (In hindsight, I wonder why none of us thought to run down the hall to the bathroom for paper towels.) Doubt reminds us that the world outside our bodies does not revolve around our personal desires. My expecting and wanting to have an eraser handy when I teach does not automatically translate into eraser-availability. My external environment does not always provide, so I need to be able to adjust.

As exemplified by our growing collection of socio-political secondness examples, habits (such as catching cabs or entering stores) can be ruptured for socio-political reasons. And, especially important for my project, habits can *be free from* rupture as well, for socio-political reasons. My being Euro-American, for example, is a socio-political reason why my habits of safely driving my car have never been ruptured by police harassment.

In its subtler forms, the secondness of belief involves more of a co-existence with doubt. As discussed in Chapter 1, our belief-habits are continually met with environmental friction, such as the feel of the computer keyboard beneath one's fingers or the feel of the sidewalk beneath one's feet or wheelchair. Peirce readily admits that calling these lesser doses of resistance "doubt" is overdone, but his point is that secondness is always part of human experience (W 3:261–62; cf. Anderson 1995b, 95). Our beliefs receive ongoing feedback, of varying intensities, from the external world. Another type of subtle doubt involves the avoidance of habit-rupture. For example, I habitually avoid touching hot surfaces. My steering clear of burning my hands is informed, however mildly, by the doubt (habit-rupture) that would ensue were such painful contact to occur.

Here, too, a socio-political read is possible. Recall, from Chapter 2, bell hooks's continual attention to racist environmental cues:

> Living in a world of racial apartheid where custom and conventions invented to separate black and white lasted long past an end to legal racial discrimination, those who are powerless—*black folks*—*must be overly aware of small details as we go about our lives to be sure we do not enter forbidden territory*—*to be sure we will not be hurt. You learn to notice things. You learn where not to walk, the stores you don't want to go in.* . . . [Y]ou cannot live the way other people live. (1997, 97, my emphasis)

This passage describes a *socio-politically informed* layer of coexistence with doubt that many Euro-American people in the United States do not regularly experience based on race.

The *absence* for many Euro-Americans of racist secondness is also socio-politically informed. My *freedom* from having to pay attention to certain environmental cues—cues that hooks must heed to avoid habit-rupture—is because of my race. It reflects white privilege. Included in Peggy McIntosh's description of white privilege are items that can be classed as *absences* of socio-political doubt, which characterize her experience as a white person. Two of these items: "I can be pretty sure that my neighbors [in whatever housing I have chosen] will be neutral or pleasant to me" and "I can go shopping alone most of the time, pretty well assured that I will not be followed or harassed" (McIntosh 1988, 293). That both of these examples, for people of color, can involve the potential escalation from subtle doubt (such as rudeness or suspicious looks) to outright attack (such as accusations or violence)[6] highlights another aspect of doubt for those in oppressed groups. While socio-political secondness might not result in full-scale habit-rupture, it can. When socio-political doubt is subtle, this subtlety does not preclude danger. In Part 3, I discuss how the absence of socio-political doubt from the experience of privileged groups can fuel their false universalization of the doubt-free dimensions of their experience.[7]

I end this section by highlighting the awareness that Peirce attributes to belief. In "How to Make Our Ideas Clear," he describes belief in this way: "First, [belief] is something that we are aware of; second, it appeases the irritation of doubt; and, third, it involves the establishment in our nature of a rule of action, or, say for short, a *habit*" (W 3:263, Peirce's emphasis). The second and third points relate to the secondness and thirdness of belief discussed above. Peirce's focus on awareness in this passage relates to both survival and self-control. It also relates to both firstness and thirdness, once again highlighting the close relationship between the two. Awareness, consciousness, can be subtle, in the background of firstness. I am aware that my body belongs to me, for example, and is sitting in a chair while I type these words, yet this awareness is often not a foregrounded awareness, unless health concerns (such as an aching back) or an environmental shift (such as an earthquake) bring it to my attention.

Awareness lies on a continuum from this backgrounded consciousness to the more explicit awareness characterizing the thirdness that enables humans to track their environment and learn about it. The thirdness-rich awareness makes possible the human organism's homeodynamics-inspired environmental assessment of external objects. It also allows for a person's attention to the consequences of her actions, so that she can make adjustments when her habits fail to harmonize with the external world. Moreover, on the macrocosmic scale, thirdness-rich awareness makes possible communal human inquiry into the regularities of the external world, so that the survival of the human species can be optimized over the long run. Humans are not merely at the mercy of their external environments, forming only those belief-habits that are compelled through environmental clash. Due to their intellectual capacity, they have the ability to proactively form self-controlled belief-habits as they learn about the regularities of their world and as they formulate aims for conduct.

Part 2: Communal Fixation of Belief—Authority, A priori, and Science

The methods of fixing beliefs that Peirce discusses in "Fixation of Belief" occur against the backdrop of the ongoing affective flow of human experience, belief and doubt, within an external environment largely outside of human control. To the extent that one can control her or his belief-habit-taking, one can choose the method by which this occurs: tenacity, authority, a priori, or science. In terms of human survival over the long run, the scientific method is most effective. This is due to its attentiveness to both testimony and experience, an attentiveness that minimizes the risk involved in human interaction with the external world.

If one chooses the method of tenacity, one's own perspective alone is the ultimate touchstone for one's beliefs. Countervailing evidence from the testimony of others and even attention to the external world are shunned. This is the method of sticking one's head in the sand, come what may. Peirce attributes tenacity to "the instinctive dislike of an undecided state of mind, exaggerated into a vague dread of doubt, [that] makes men cling spasmodically to the views they already take" (W 3:249). This method is unlikely to hold water practically. Peirce notes, "The social impulse is against it"; to know others disagree with one's belief can undermine one's "confidence in his belief" (W 3:250). This point recalls the sociality[8] and child development discussions from the Cognition Series. The threshold of self-consciousness involves the realization that the testimony of others is just as valid, if not more so, than one's own. In the present essay, Peirce notes:

> This conception, that another man's thought or sentiment may be equivalent to one's own, is a distinctly new step, and a highly important one. It arises from an impulse too strong in man to be suppressed, without danger of destroying the human species. Unless we make ourselves hermits, we shall necessarily influence each other's opinions. . . . (W 3:250)

Children and adults ignore the testimony of others at their own peril. The inclination to trust this testimony is, general speaking, survival-promoting. Thus Peirce says that "the problem becomes how to fix belief, not in the individual merely, but in the community" (W 3:250). Adopting the beliefs of one's community, however, can result in the internalization of growth-inhibiting habits. Peirce's discussion of the method of authority illustrates this.

a. The Method of Authority and the Hegemonic
Articulation of Reality

The authority method of fixing belief involves the state's control of the beliefs of individuals. The authoritative state creates a hegemonic society, where social norms are dictated by those in power. Authority is a method that shuns inquiry, spontaneity, and freedom. It attempts to foreclose these elements of organic growth. When the authority method is followed,

> . . . an institution [is] created which [has] for its object to keep correct doctrines before the attention of the people, to reiterate them perpetually, and to teach them to the young; having at the same time power to prevent contrary doctrines from being taught, advocated, or expressed. . . . [A]ll possible causes of a change of mind [are] removed from men's apprehensions. . . . [They are] kept ignorant, lest they should learn of some reason to think otherwise than they do. (W 3:250)

The authoritative state aims to dictate the belief-habit formation of individuals so that their belief-habits conform to those sanctioned by the state. This is a manipulation of affectivity, which occurs through everyday saturation, as well as formal education, "to keep correct doctrines before the attention of the people, to reiterate them perpetually, and to teach them to the young." It is also reinforced through censorship, "to prevent contrary doctrines from being taught, advocated, or expressed."

To supplement these efforts, the authoritative state actively works to eliminate the possibility that, despite education and censorship, individuals might still hold beliefs differing from hegemonic norms. Note the affective efforts, which were cited last chapter:

> Let [people's] passions be enlisted, so that they may regard private
> and unusual opinions with hatred and horror. Then, let all men
> who reject the established belief be terrified into silence. Let peo-
> ple turn out and tar-and-feather such men, or let inquisitions be
> made into the manner of thinking of suspected persons, and,
> when they are found guilty of forbidden beliefs, let them be sub-
> jected to some signal punishment. (W 3:250)

The authoritative state wants unanimity. Peirce wryly notes that, if
the above strategies prove ineffective, "a general massacre of all who
have not thought in a certain way has proved a very effective means
of settling opinion in a country" (W 3:250). It is not always feasible to
kill off would-be dissenters, however, or even to make authoritative
strategies explicit. In such cases, social ostracism is brought into play:

> If liberty of speech is to be untrammeled from the grosser forms
> of constraint, then uniformity of opinion will be secured by a
> moral terrorism to which the respectability of society will give its
> thorough approval. . . . [L]et it be known that you seriously hold
> a tabooed belief, and you may be perfectly sure of being treated
> with a cruelty less brutal but more refined than hunting you like
> a wolf. (W 3:255–56)

The effects of social pressure on an individual's habit-taking are pronounced. In the Cognition Series, Peirce notes that testimony can
convince someone of being "mad" (W 2:202). I discussed this point
in relationship to the internalization of disempowering beliefs that
can occur when one is viewed as mad, abnormal, or inferior because
challenging or differing from communal norms.

In the present context, Peirce highlights an internalization-related
theme—namely, the *self-punishment* that can occur under communal
pressure to hold certain beliefs: "Singularly enough, the persecution
does not all come from without; but a man torments himself and is
oftentimes most distressed at finding himself believing propositions
which he has been brought up to regard with aversion" (W 3:256). I
define internalization as the incorporation, by means of reinforcement or trauma, of a belief into one's personal comportment and
worldview such that the belief is difficult to eradicate rationally (cf.

A. Rorty 1980; Bartky 1990, 63–82). The method of authority involves both reinforcement, by means of education and general environmental exposure (such as the media), and trauma, through socio-political sanctions. Thus it uses the coercive survival dilemma faced by children, as well as patterns of socio-political secondness, to ensure that "proper" beliefs are adopted, and internalized, by community members.

Those in power in the authoritative state include only hegemonic perspectives in the articulation of reality: "[T]hose who wield the various forms of organized force in the [authoritative] state will never be convinced that dangerous reasoning ought not to be suppressed in some way" (W 3:255). The "dangerous reasoning" involves diverging from hegemonic norms.[9] Peirce's portrayal of the authority method thus illustrates the possibility for a limited number of powerful people to *usurp* the articulation of reality and to enforce this hegemonic articulation upon others. He notes this method's historical precedence: "[F]rom the earliest times, [it has] been one of the chief means of upholding correct theological and *political* doctrines" (W 3:250–51, my emphasis). Reality can take on a politically unjust character when this usurping occurs.

The overall affective picture that Peirce paints of the authoritative society is bleak. Under the sway of exclusionary hegemony, the natural human sympathy that joins people together shows its darker side. Recall that sociality is "an impulse too strong in man to be suppressed, without danger of destroying the human species" (W 3:250). When fostered in an agapic fashion, the social impulse can manifest in a loving community that grows by feeling genuine concern for and embracing the diversity of each of its members. Everyone is on the same team, so to speak. I call this "agapic sympathy." In the authoritative setting, however, the manipulation of the social impulse results in "a most ruthless power" whereby committing "cruelties" in the name of exclusion becomes an internalized reaction to dissenting voices in one's community (W 3:251). I call this "exclusionary sympathy." This type of sympathy can produce the fear-driven polarity of the "us" against "them" outlook. Agapic and exclusionary sympathy will be discussed more in Chapter 4.

Despite its best efforts, however, the authoritative or hegemonic state cannot fully escape the growth-impetus provided by individuals who, for Peirce, have a more inclusive sensibility. Such synechistic individuals achieve perspective on the hegemonic beliefs of their cultures, seeing them to be *accidental*:

> [I]n the most priestridden states some individuals will be found who are raised above that condition. These men possess a wider sort of social feeling; they see that men in other countries and in other ages have held to very different doctrines from those which they themselves have been brought up to believe; and they cannot help seeing that it is the mere accident of their having been taught as they have, and of their having been surrounded with the manners and associations they have, that has caused them to believe as they do and not far differently. (W 3:251–52)

The existence of these individuals underscores a key point raised last chapter, namely that the dangers of disempowering internalization do not paint a fatalistic picture in Peirce's scheme. The seed of communal resistance planted in the Cognition Series has grown significantly, as Peirce places hope for communal growth in the hands of more socially attuned individuals.

b. The A priori Method

The a priori method reflects progress beyond the authority method, because it involves a more open and flexible communal inquiry. Peirce's depiction of this method highlights the value of trusting instinct in our beliefs and actions: "Let the action of natural preferences be unimpeded . . . and under their influence let men, conversing together and regarding matters in different lights, gradually develop beliefs in harmony with natural causes" (W 3:252). And, "Indeed, as long as no better method can be applied, it ought to be followed, since it is then the expression of instinct which must be the ultimate cause of belief in all cases" (EP 1:377 n. 22).[10] Peirce is well aware of the potential survival value of our instincts. Here he is noting that instincts can guide us to an intellectual understanding of the world as we "gradually develop beliefs in harmony with natural causes" (W 3:252).

The problem with the a priori method is that our instincts are not completely trustworthy; they do not necessarily reflect the regularities of nature. Instead, instincts in some cases overlap with sentiments, such that inquiry becomes "something similar to the development of taste," which is easily swayed and not conducive to communal agreement (W 3:253). Since sentiments can be influenced arbitrarily, instincts cannot be appealed to reliably. Thus, on the one hand the a priori method is superior to the method of authority because it involves a flexible, intellectual, communal inquiry. On the other hand, Peirce notes that the a priori method "does not differ in a very essential way from that of authority. . . . [T]hough governments do not interfere, sentiments in their development will be very greatly determined by accidental causes" (W 3:253; cf. Hookway 2000, 242).

The a priori method is not assured of being geared toward human survival over the long run, because our "natural preferences"/instincts/sentiments do not necessarily reflect the regularities of the external world (W 3:252–53). Since these natural beliefs cannot be relied on without some measure of critique, Peirce turns to the method of science.

c. The Scientific Method

Of all the methods of fixing belief-habits, the method of science best promotes human survival in the long run, because it esteems testimony and takes seriously the consequences that stem from belief-habits and other habits in nature. Scientific method is an ongoing and self-revising communal process. Its ideal practitioners embrace the fallibilism of beliefs and are thus open to revising beliefs in light of testing. That is to say, the ideal scientific community embraces organic *growth*. This embrace is essential in the complex environment with which humans must cope.

While the other methods allow for the denial of the external world, the scientific method considers this world to be a continuous touchstone for the truth of beliefs. It maintains that beliefs are caused not merely by human will but "by some external permanency—by something upon which our thinking has no effect" (W 3:253). While the external world can be articulated only via human thought,[11] it cannot be fully controlled by human thought (cf. Hausman 1993a, 144–45). The scientific method requires a community of inquiry that generates explanatory hypotheses, deduces the expected patterns of consequences that follow from said hypotheses, and then tests the hypotheses against experience.[12] This testing optimizes learning, enabling humans to minimize risk and plan for the future most effectively. The other methods do not require this testing and so do not manage risk well over the long run.

Recall the Cognition Series discussion of the relationship between risk and epistemology in terms of the social principle. Peirce's requirement that a *community*, not merely an individual, undertake scientific inquiry reflects this endorsement of communal epistemology. Indeed, Peirce reaffirms the risk of solitary, as opposed to communal, reasoning in the third Logic of Science essay, "The Doctrine of Chances." Over the long run, we most effectively reduce the risk of life-threatening surprises from the external world if our beliefs about it are informed by as many perspectives as possible (W 3:282–85).

The ideal scientific community of inquiry is infinitely large and extends over an indefinite period of time. This breadth of scope is required so that humans may have the best grasp possible of the regularities (or habits) of nature, which are infinitely complex, grow, and elude capture in absolute laws. Since scientific inquiry is not a finite endeavor, it is immature for an individual person or a finite community to decide they have a lock on truth. Such hubris would be in violation of Peirce's oft-repeated admonition: "Do not block the way of inquiry" (EP 2:48). Peirce says of the ideal community of inquiry, "This community . . . must not be limited, but must extend to all races of beings with whom we can come into immediate or mediate intellectual relation. It must reach, however vaguely, beyond this geological epoch, beyond all bounds" (W 3:284). This ideal of infinite inclusiveness and infinite projection into the future has significant implications regarding social justice and truth.

On the social justice front, while Peirce does not make the point explicitly, his ideal community of inquiry requires justice toward all human beings, as potential participants in scientific inquiry. Science and politics meet on this point, despite the colloquial belief that science can separate itself completely from political interests. Peirce's use of "intellectual" is inclusive of all human beings as animal organisms ("logical animals") who have the capacity to grasp the regularities of nature and to establish aims for conduct (W 3:244, 285; EP 2:348). Indeed, Peirce is not just limiting his discussion to *human* beings; he includes "all races of beings with whom we can come into immediate or mediate intellectual relation" (W 3:284).[13] Thus when Peirce specifies the "intellectual relation" that characterizes the infinitely inclusive community of inquiry, this is meant as a point of *inclusiveness*, not exclusivity (W 3:284). His account of cognition and his articulation of the ideal community of inquiry do *not* support the rendering of some human groups "unintellectual" and others "intellectual," as has commonly occurred in the history of Western thought. On this point it is important to recall that we are separating Peirce's personal racism and sexism from his philosophical ideas.

For Peirce, truth is "[t]he opinion which is fated to be ultimately agreed to by all who investigate" (W 3:273).[14] While the terms "fated" and "ultimately agreed to" can give the impression that it is merely a matter of time before truth is reached, truth can never be finished on Peirce's terms, due to the infinite nature of the community of inquiry. That is to say, "all who investigate" is not a finite group of people operating within a finite time frame. Once again, Peirce says, "This community . . . must not be limited, but must extend to all races of beings with whom we can come into immediate or mediate intellectual relation. It must reach, however vaguely, beyond this geological epoch, beyond all bounds" (W3:284). The community that underwrites truth extends "beyond this geological epoch, beyond all bounds." Thus truth must be an ongoing journey, due to the community's infinite inclusiveness and indefinite extension into the future (cf. Sharp 1994, 203). Carl Hausman describes the community required by the scientific method:

> [T]he method of science is other-directed and dependent upon a standard that transcends finite determination. . . . [T]his standard consists in a community that has no assignable, actual boundary. It is the drive toward the realization of this community that guarantees the growth of thought and the survival of mankind itself. At the same time, however, this community remains unknown to the finite mind. It cannot be envisaged as a defined goal, for it remains to be given form and it lies in an infinite future, a future not wholly free of surprises and irregularities within a growing system of laws. (1974, 18; cf. Anderson 1995a, 108–9)

Hausman is describing the unfinished and growing character of the community of inquiry that pursues truth within an organic universe that itself grows. Since this community cannot be finished, neither can truth itself. Instead, truth requires a community's consistent revision of its beliefs in light of both new experience and new perspectives. This reflects Peirce's fallibilism: "[I]t is conceivable that what you cannot help believing today, you might find you thoroughly disbelieve tomorrow" (EP 2:337, 1905).[15]

Peirce's conception of truth does retain a sense of unitary agreement, despite his fallibilism and his infinitely growing community of inquiry. As he succinctly puts the point in 1907, "I hold that truth's independence of individual opinions is due (so far as there is any 'truth') to its being the predestined result to which sufficient inquiry would ultimately lead" (EP 2:419–20). This comment holds in place both fallibilism and ultimate agreement. I am unconvinced, however, that truth, on Peirce's own terms, needs to involve ultimate agreement in the infinite future. I would argue that this unitary characterization of truth could be challenged by further inquiry conducted over a long enough time frame by communities that are far more diverse than the narrow Western cultural circles with which Peirce was most familiar. Hausman notes, in the passage cited above, that inquiring communities can encounter "surprises and irregularities" in the future (1974, 18). I would add that inquiring communities— that reflect deep and broad diversity, free from exclusionary bias— can themselves be sources of surprise regarding how truth itself is best conceived, especially considering the infinite time frame allowed by Peirce himself. This point requires far more attention than I can give it here, but I do think that Peirce's ideas about truth do potentially point beyond themselves—that is, beyond the necessity of unitary agreement—in ways that merit exploration.[16]

Let us return more specifically to Peirce's discussion of the scientific method in "Fixation of Belief," where he says that the "fundamental hypothesis" of the scientific method is the following:

> There are real things, whose characters are entirely independent of our opinions about them; those realities affect our senses according to regular laws, and, though our sensations are as different as our relations to the objects, yet, by taking advantage of the laws of perception, we can ascertain by reasoning how things really are, and any man, if he have sufficient experience and reason enough about it, will be led to the one true conclusion. The new conception here involved is that of reality. (W 3:254)

In this passage, Peirce says "any man" acting according to the scientific method is following the path to truth. This is an unfortunate choice of words, which reflects Peirce's appeal to individuals to exhibit self-control in choosing the best method of fixing their beliefs. Scientific method does *not* revolve around an individual's pursuit of truth about reality. It is a *communal* inquiry into reality that, ideally, includes all possible perspectives. Recall his description of reality in the Cognition Series:

> [W]hat do we mean by the real? It is a conception which we must first have had when we discovered that there was an unreal, an illusion; that is, when we first corrected ourselves. Now the distinction for which alone this fact logically called, was between an *ens* relative to private inward determinations, to the negations belonging to idiosyncrasy, and an *ens* such as would stand in the long run. The real, then, is that which, sooner or later, information and reasoning would finally result in, and which is therefore

independent of the vagaries of me and you. *Thus, the very origin of the conception of reality shows that this conception essentially involves the notion of a* COMMUNITY, *without definite limits, and capable of an indefinite increase of knowledge.* (W 2:239, my emphasis)

For Peirce, reality exceeds finite human thought. It is something outside any single person's control or articulation. It is also outside the grasp of any particular group of people. Even if we rounded up all the scientists living today, we would still have a *finite* group and thus an incomplete grasp of what lies external to human thought. Once again, the pursuit of truth cannot be finished.

The community provides varied perspectives that give information about reality, in the manner of the blind persons and the elephant. The varied perspectives also help identify and eradicate exclusionary bias, including false universalization. In the passage about reality in "Fixation of Belief," Peirce notes both the regularity with which external objects affect human organisms, *and* the fact that "our sensations are as different as our relations to the objects" (W3: 254). This is an acknowledgement of the inescapability of human bias. Scientific inquiry synthesizes many perspectives on the world, in order to solicit insight, compensate for bias, and elucidate common elements. This way, regularities characterizing the external world can be learned with as much accuracy as possible within the limits of human finitude and fallibility.

Note that there is a circle of influence between reality and science. One the one hand, science inquires into the nature of reality, based upon the effects of the external world on human organisms. Thus reality—in so far as it represents "external permanency"—is the starting point of scientific inquiry and its continual reference point, as scientists test their theories against it (W3: 253). On the other hand, science *influences* reality in so far as reality involves communal, human articulation. Thus, scientific inquiries *into the nature of* reality, since they are conducted by human communities, also *shape the articulations given* to reality, since these are *human* articulations. This reciprocity of influence represents the ongoing conversation between humans and the external world. If humans are to survive, they must pay attention to the regularities (or habits) of nature, that is, to reality in so far as it lies outside of human organisms. Science is rooted in this truism of human existence. At the same time, any particular articulation of reality is fallible, subject to revision based on factors such as the growth of nature itself, as well as new hypotheses generated by new or existing community members.

Of particular interest to my project are the socio-political implications of this fallible dimension of reality. Humans cannot survive if they wait for a perfect articulation of reality to occur, and reality always exceeds the complete grasp of present scientific inquiry. Thus humans must act from working knowledge. Yet reality can be hijacked by hegemonic groups who use the authority method to inculcate growth-undermining belief-habits. This hegemonic articulation of reality can be internalized as "the" reality. When this happens, the ideals of science can be undermined by hegemonic background beliefs that enter the scientific method through the back door.

d. Science Meets Authority and A priori: The Application Problem

Peirce's discussion of the scientific method, in these Logic of Science essays of the 1870s, points beyond itself to his 1900s work on Critical Common-sensism. First of all, before outlining the four methods, in "Fixation of Belief," Peirce asserts that we reason from "a variety of facts" that must be "taken for granted" in the reasoning process (W 3:246). This echoes a comment, made in the Cognition Series, regarding philosophical investigation—namely, that "[w]e must begin with all the prejudices which we actually have when we enter upon the study of philosophy. These prejudices are not to be dispelled by a [Cartesian] maxim, for they are things which it does not occur to us *can* be questioned" (W 2:212, Peirce's emphasis). We cannot reason without beliefs already taken for granted. To assume we can simply detach ourselves from such beliefs is mere self-deception (cf. W 3:248). In "Fixation of Belief," Peirce notes that "common-sense, or thought as it first emerges above the level of the narrowly practical," needs to be subjected to "a severe course of logic" (W 3: 246).

Second, Peirce does not incorporate this concern about background or common-sense beliefs into his articulation of the scientific method. That is to say, in the Logic of Science essays, he does not explicitly *require* the scientific community of inquiry to examine its background beliefs in order to eliminate those that undermine the inclusiveness of the scientific pursuit of truth. Third, in concrete scientific communities, scientists reason from common-sense beliefs that may be shaped by the state, via the authority method, or through other accidental causes, via the a priori method. In other words, the scientific method overlaps with both the authority and the a priori methods. These background/common-sense beliefs will, in his later work, become the fund of instinctive, common-sense beliefs scrutinized by the Critical Common-sensist.

It is difficult to tell how aware Peirce is of the socio-political dangers that could threaten an actual community of inquiry and thus undermine the implementation of the scientific method. His discussions, in "Fixation of Belief," of the different methods for securing our beliefs-habits imply that the adoption of the scientific method reflects a maturity that has left behind the less mature tenacity, authority, and a priori methods (W 3:253 ff., 331). Peirce does not, however, adequately address the fact that any flesh-and-blood community of inquiry is situated historically. If a community of inquiry is located in an oppressive society, its members are likely to internalize the corresponding hegemonic beliefs. When this occurs, these *authoritative/ hegemonic* beliefs become part of the instinctive background beliefs that inform *scientific* reasoning. An analogous danger applies to a priori beliefs, since these are not easily separable from authority-derived beliefs, especially in a hegemonic society. In other words, on the plane of practical implementation, the authority, a priori, and scientific methods are intertwined regarding the fixation of belief-habits. In what follows I use the term "background belief(s)" as a general term to refer to beliefs that may have been shaped by either the authority or the a priori method, or a combination of the two.

As an example of this implementation issue, take the nineteenth-century study of craniology undertaken by Western scientists. This study of craniology reflects science conducted under the influence of background beliefs presuming the inferiority of women and non-European races. Nancy Tuana outlines the attempt by craniologist Hermann Schaaffhausen to establish the inferiority of women, an attempt that begs the question of the inferiority of both women and people of color:

> Schaaffhausen claimed that there were five characteristics of female skulls that proved that woman's development is imperfect in comparison to man's: "the projection of the parietal protuberances, the lesser elevation of the frontal bone, the shorter and narrower cranial base . . . the more elliptical dental arch and the inclination to prognathism [having a small facial angle]." Schaaffhausen argued that these characteristics were reliable indicators of more primitive skulls *because* they were traits possessed by women and non-European races. In other words, Schaaffhausen presupposed the inferiority of women and non-European men in order to obtain a list of characteristics by which to classify skull types as primitive. A more obvious example of unconscious, circular reasoning is difficult to find. (1993, 44–45, Tuana's emphasis; Schaaffhausen 1868)

Tuana's example illustrates that practicing scientists can be biased in their work by background beliefs, such as the beliefs informing racism and sexism (cf. Gould 1981). In this particular case, the logical fallacy of begging the question goes unnoticed by the scientist. Peirce's advice that common-sense be subjected to "a severe course in logic" can be applied here (W 3:246). It should be noted that Schaaffhausen's work occurred in a *community* of scientists reasoning from racist and sexist background beliefs. He was not merely a lone eccentric. Tuana's and Stephen Jay Gould's work on sexism and racism in nineteenth-century science shows the prevalence of these socio-political biases (Tuana 1993, 34–50; Gould 1981, chapters 2–4).

Let me be more specific about this application problem. The scientific method has ideals of infinite inclusiveness and truth, which go hand in hand. To this end the ideal scientific community of inquiry embraces the self-revision of its beliefs. Since, however, the scientific method does not call for an examination of background beliefs, it is possible for an actual community of inquiry to *think* it is being adequately inclusive when it is actually discriminating against groups who have little socio-political power. The background beliefs that form an inescapable grounding for scientific reasoning can be repositories for instinctive socio-political prejudices that can, and historically *have*, limited membership within communal inquiry. Euro-American white, propertied men in many cases held exclusive membership and perpetuated this exclusivity.

It should be noted that Peirce does acknowledge, in the Logic of Science essays, that human stubbornness can impede, to some extent, the progress toward truth (W 3:273–74). I doubt, however, that he was complacent about such a blockage occurring within an actual community of inquiry practicing the scientific method to the best of its ability. Thus Peirce's work in the Logic of Science essays points beyond itself to his mature doctrine of Critical Common-sensism.

Part 3: Interest, Survival, and Power:
Politicized Habit-Taking and Internalization

In this section, to further elucidate the application problem just outlined, I show how deeply background beliefs can shape the communal inquiry of science. I begin by examining the interest in regularities that characterizes the human species as a whole. Peirce's linkage of science, in this respect, to the promotion of human survival is marked. Humans must learn about the regularities (or habits) of their world if they are to survive and grow over the long run. Yet these regularities concern not only reality as a natural realm outside of human conduct but also socio-political interests. Focusing on the latter, we find that the regularities of reality can embody exclusionary, falsely universal beliefs/habits/concepts that undermine Peirce's epistemological ideal. In the case of children, whose interest in reality's regularities is especially pronounced in terms of survival concerns, the internalization of exclusionary, falsely universal beliefs/habits/concepts is all the more likely.

In "Fixation of Belief," Peirce describes humans as "logical animals" (W3: 244). I take this as a reminder that human reasoning, for all its glories, is rooted in survival interests. In their ongoing inquiry with nature, if humans are wrong about how the external world works, it can be life threatening. Recall the story of Chris McCandless from Chapter 2. His inquiry with nature in the Alaskan wild ended tragically when he misjudged the edibility of the seed pods of the *H. alpinum* plant (Krakauer 1996, 189–95).[17] Notwithstanding the human accomplishments that grow from the capacities for self-control and abstraction, the promotion of survival is fundamental (Damasio 1999, 309 ff.). Recall Peirce's tracing of scientific development to the human instincts for nutrition and reproduction. Physics is rooted in "instincts connected with the need of nutrition" and "psychics" in those linked to reproduction (EP 2:51, 1898). He goes so far as to say, "Now not only our accomplished science, but even our scientific questions have been pretty exclusively limited to the development of those two branches of natural knowledge" (EP 2:51).

In "The Order of Nature" (1878), the fifth essay of the Logic of Science series, Peirce discusses human *interest* in the regularities of nature (W 3:312). Recall that, for Peirce, interest has an affective charge. In the Cognition Series he notes that "[e]verything in which we take the least interest creates in us its own particular emotion, however slight this may be. This emotion is a sign and a predicate of the thing" (W 2:237). This makes sense in a post-Darwinian evolutionary scheme. Humans do not merely observe the world from a detached perspective. They are organisms that must successfully navigate the world around them in order to survive and grow. To this end, humans have the capacity to *learn* about the life-threatening and life-promoting regularities of the world, versus merely reacting to them each time anew. In an 1895 manuscript, Peirce links the "interesting" more closely to his evolutionary thematic:

> There are certain combinations of feelings which are specially *interesting*,—that is, they are strongly suggestive of thought. *What* combinations are interesting? Answer: those which are very near a reaction between mind and body, whether in sense, in the action

of the glands, in contractions of involuntary muscles, in voluntary outward acts, or in inward acts by which one part of the nerves discharge in an extraordinary manner upon another. (EP 2:23, "Of Reasoning in General," Peirce's emphasis)

This linkage of interest to "a reaction between mind and body" brings to mind the homeodynamic environmental assessment whereby humans perpetually monitor their environment to promote survival (EP 2:23; Damasio 2003, 30, 35).

In "The Order of Nature," Peirce presents the reader with a description of a hypothetical world that humans would find *un*interesting:

> In the first place, there would be nothing to puzzle us in such [an uninteresting] world. The small number of qualities which would directly meet the senses would be the ones which would afford the key to everything which could possibly interest us. The whole universe would have such an air of system and perfect regularity that *there would be nothing to ask.* . . . [T]here would be nothing to stimulate or develop either the mind or the will, and we consequently should neither act nor think. The *interest* which the uniformities of Nature have for an animal measures his place in the scale of intelligence. (W 3:312, my emphasis)

This brings to mind a plant, satisfied with light, water, and the nutrients in its soil. If humans were not interested in the world—that is, affectively invested—scientific inquiry would not arise.[18]

Peirce's point is that humans *are* interested in the regularities of the world, as evidenced by their levels of curiosity and intelligence. Later in the essay, Peirce re-examines an issue that arose in the Cognition Series, regarding synthetic reasoning. He asks how humans can have an edge in reasoning about the causes of nature's regularities, such that human synthetic reasoning[19] meets with success far more often than probability alone would allow. Peirce's examination of this issue in the present context is distinctly survival oriented. He notes, "It seems incontestable . . . that the mind of man is strongly adapted to the comprehension of the world" (W 3:318). His search for an answer includes the following exploration:

> How are we to explain this adaptation? The great utility and indispensableness of the conceptions of time, space, and force, even to the lowest intelligence, are such as to suggest that they are the results of natural selection. Without something like geometrical, kinetical, and mechanical conceptions, no animal could seize his food or do anything which might be necessary for the preservation of the species. (W 3:318)

Peirce does not, in this essay or series, reach an answer that fully satisfies him.[20] But his discussion of the question makes clear that scientific investigation is rooted in concrete human survival interests.

a. The Politics of Interest and False Universalization

Clearly enough, then, human interest in the regularities of nature is ultimately grounded in survival-promotion. To learn about nature's habits is to be able to anticipate them and plan future behaviors accordingly, so that humans can avoid danger and pursue resources most efficiently. The tapestry of learning woven together via human interest, however, includes socio-political strands.

To elucidate these strands, I highlight four points. First, to identify the regularities that characterize the external world is to articulate *reality*. Such an articulation, as argued by Peirce in the Cognition Series and reviewed in the last section, is *socially mediated*. That is to say, any articulation of reality is a *communal, human* articulation. Second, determining regularities involves identifying patterns that are at play. Third, this pattern-identification involves attention to *relevant* similarities. Peirce notes that any "plurality" of things has "some character in common" (W 3:310). To come to terms with the "order of nature," then, "it is requisite to consider the characters of things *as relative to* the perceptions and active powers of living beings" (W 3:311–12, my emphasis). This is where human interest in the regularities of nature comes into play. Human interests determine which commonalities are relevant, that is, which regularities *matter*. Fourth, in addition to regularity identification driven by interest in human survival, there can be regularity identification driven by exclusionary socio-political interests and power structures.

Someone might object that it is inappropriate to address socio-political concerns in the present context, because Peirce is talking about the logic of *science* in these essays. Scientific exploration into the regularities of the world is not a socio-political endeavor. There are many answers to this objection, including the points raised in the last two chapters, regarding the synechistic shaping of the human being. A person cannot simply put on a "scientist hat" and thereby distance herself from her embodied, socio-political, and other situatedness. In "Fixation of Belief," Peirce also identifies political applications of the methods of fixing beliefs, especially regarding the authority method (W 3:248–57). In addition, as mentioned in the discussion of the scientific method, Peirce himself requires an infinitely inclusive community of inquiry. By implication, this requires all humans to be given membership, which is a political issue, especially given the exclusionary history of science in the West. When it comes to communal inquiry, then, political concerns actually precede epistemological, scientific ones, due to issues of communal membership (cf. Babbitt 1996, 34). A socio-political critique of the scientific identification of regularities is, therefore, appropriate in a Peircean context.

In her book *Impossible Dreams: Rationality, Integrity, and Moral Imagination*, Susan Babbitt sheds light on this point by examining how human interest in regularities can take on pernicious socio-political forms (1996). While she does not draw upon Peirce, her discussion is compatible with Peircean themes, and thus helps enhance their social critical dimensions. She notes, "We cannot make sense of our experience or of information without applying unifying general concepts" (15). Identifying unities involves not only determining relevant similarities, but also relevant *differences*. This takes on socio-political urgency regarding one of the most basic regularities to human experience, namely "humanity" itself. Who is included in this regularity? Who is excluded?[21] (14–16). Babbitt explains, "When a concept such as 'the people' is rooted in traditions of racism and sexism, entire groups of human beings are typically unable to be understood, or even identified, as people at all" (2). She also poses a question that further demonstrates the socio-political import of

Peirce's point (outlined above) that identifying "uniformities" in nature requires attention to relevant characteristics, that is to say, "the characters of things *as relative to* the perceptions and active powers of living beings" (W 3:311–12, my emphasis). Babbitt notes, "The question to be answered is about how we can properly identify real similarities and differences given that the conceptual and practical traditions upon which we base such judgments are often, among other things, racist [and sexist]" (1996, 21).

Babbitt stresses that the identification of "relevant" similarities and differences among human beings "depends on general background beliefs about human experience" (1996, 24). She thus helps show the political implications in Peirce's own points about both regularity identification and background beliefs. In society's characterized by racism and sexism, Babbitt continues, "racist, sexist assumptions are *implicit* in fundamental meanings and ways of thinking" (26, 27). It is thus the case that socio-political questions *precede* epistemological ones in some cases, as just noted (34). That is to say, the very concepts by means of which humans come to know the world can be informed by exclusionary socio-political bias. In Peirce's scheme, these concepts—including humanity and personhood—*should* be informed by an infinitely inclusive community of inquiry, since an inclusive communal articulation is implied in the ideal articulation of "reality" itself. The fact that hegemonic interests can interfere with how reality is articulated and conceptually understood is acknowledged by Peirce in his discussion of the authority method of fixing beliefs. His discussion of the scientific method, in the present series, however, neglects addressing the socio-political prejudices that could undermine the implementation of this method, due to unexamined exclusionary background beliefs.

The issue can be explained this way. The scientific community of inquiry embraces self-revision if one of its beliefs or concepts becomes doubtful. This revision of beliefs is integral to pursuing truth and the growth of knowledge. The problem of application, however, can arise if communal inquiry is undertaken by a hegemonic, exclusionary group. Due to power imbalances, the group's exclusionary

beliefs—such as a conception of "humanity" that excludes non-hegemonic groups—*may not meet with environmental resistance* sufficient
to trigger doubt and self-revision. In the history of the United States,
for example, Euro-American propertied men with power and privilege formed an exclusionary community that excluded people of
color and women from "humanity."[22] These non-hegemonic groups
did not have the political power to fully enforce their inclusion in
"humanity." That is to say, they did not have the political power to
generate anti-racist/anti-sexist secondness sufficient to effect immediate change. In turn, the racist and sexist beliefs of these affluent Euro-
American men *did not meet with* secondness sufficient to generate
doubt.

It cannot be assumed that, in the absence of significant anti-dis-
crimination secondness, members of the exclusionary group would,
of their own accord, question their exclusionary beliefs/concepts.
They may either think the exclusion, as in the case of humanity, is
justifiable, or they may not be consciously aware that the exclusion is
occurring. These issues will be discussed more fully below and in
Chapter 5. I am not overlooking the fact that people of color and
women in the United States eventually gained considerable power to
effect change and to gain de jure equal rights. The length of time this
took, not to mention persisting systemic racism and sexism, underscore the problem of implementation I am describing. So does the
fact that many other groups still face discriminatory secondness stemming from disability, economic class, sexuality, and so on. After all,
the United States has been *from its inception* a self-proclaimed democratic country where all are equal and deserving of rights.

When a hegemonic group articulates reality by means of "conceptual machinery" that reflects only the experience of a particular
group, false universalization occurs (Babbitt 1996, 17). False universalization—whereby a particular perspective is attributed to all of humanity—has been prevalent in Western thought historically, as
affluent Euro-American men have rendered articulations of reality
that excluded the non-hegemonic perspectives of people of color, the

poor, women, and others. In terms of the blind persons and the elephant metaphor (where differing perspectives result in more information about the parts of the elephant, its trunk, ears, tail, legs, and so on), the exclusion of perspectives results in an unduly limited portrayal of the elephant. Marilyn Frye, who uses a similar metaphor, gives a humorous depiction of Euro-American patriarchal thinking:

> Imagine that a single individual had written up an exhaustive description of a sedated elephant as observed from one spot for one hour and then, with delighted self-satisfaction, had heralded that achievement as a complete, accurate and profound account of The Elephant. The androcentrism of the accumulated philosophy and science of the "western" world is like that. (1992, 59)[23]

That the accounts of these men are biased towards a particular race, sex, and economic class (among other favored factors) is not the ultimate problem, I would argue, since any account of reality will be biased to some extent, for Peirce. Their accounts of reality are problematic, because they have been hegemonically enforced as *neutral* accounts of reality. I do not mean to imply such men have agreed on all details regarding the regularities of the external world. Nonetheless, this group of privileged men has shared many biases that have become incorporated conceptually into a "reality" that rests upon the exclusion of many perspectives. Mills argues:

> The *universalizing pretensions* of Western philosophy, which by its very abstractness and distance from vulgar reality seemed to be *all-inclusive of human experience*, are . . . illusory. White (male) philosophy's confrontation of Man and Universe, or even Person and Universe, is really predicated on taking personhood for granted and thus *excludes the differential experience of those who have ceaselessly had to fight to have their personhood recognized in the first place.* (1998, 9, my emphasis)

Affluent Euro-American men are not the only culprits here; similarly situated *women* have enacted analogous false universalizations in feminist movements in the West, neglecting issues including economic class, race, sexuality, and other factors (Lugones and Spelman

1990; hooks 1984; Rich 1986). Generally speaking, anyone who is privileged on some axis, such as economic class, race, sex, sexuality, etc., can fall prey to falsely universalizing their experience to this extent (cf. Lerner 1993, 209–16; McIntosh 1988). Peirce's promotion of an inclusive, communal inquiry into reality and truth can be applied to address these blind spots that can characterize the articulation of individual and group experience.

An important point for my project, which Peirce's ideas help articulate and address, is the following: when false universalization occurs in a hegemonic context, the exclusionary articulation of reality is enforced as both neutral and authoritative, such that *divergent articulations are rendered conceptually problematic.* Since the hegemonic account is supposedly neutral, no one is supposedly excluded. Since it is authoritative, those who would challenge its neutrality—such as those who are indeed left out—are likely to seem, or to be portrayed as, crazy, overreactive, merely emotional, or simply irrelevant, in comparison to the supposedly ahistorical, transcendent, objective "Truth" (Williams 1991, 8–9). Thus divergent viewpoints can be readily dismissed as falling short of the "real standards" by which "Truth" is assessed (8–9). Recall the example from Marilyn Frye in Chapter 2. Historically speaking, "reality" in the West has excluded the lesbian perspective. Lesbianism has been rendered both conceptually and naturally impossible: Since sex and sexuality revolve around what occurs "with respect to the penis," women having sex is "unnatural" (Frye 1983, 157 ff.). Thus, according to the dominant view, if a woman were a lesbian, something would be wrong with her (159–60).[24]

We can describe this de-legitimizing phenomenon in Peircean terms, as a non-agapic stance towards what is different from oneself. For Peirce, the concepts involved in a hegemonic, or any other, articulation of reality are communal *belief-habits,* and the community itself is a macroscopic person. As we will discuss next chapter, both individual and communal persons *grow* by means of agapically embracing new perspectives, even and especially when these perspective are at odds with existing habit systems. A typical *non*-agapic stance is the rejection of diverse perspectives. For example, take the founding credo of the United States: "All men are created equal." In its application, this belief/habit/concept was proclaimed from the falsely universalized perspective of an elite class of Euro-American white, propertied men. It thus only reflected their experience of respecting equality *within this hegemonic group*. And it resulted in contradictory patterns of behavior that upheld their equality with each other, while perpetuating the oppression of people of color and women. Although there were exceptions, as a hegemonic group, these men primarily resisted the growth opportunities provided by people of color and women who protested being oppressed. Thus people of color and women were not embraced as part of "men" who shared "equality". The hegemonic group members did not succeed in fully foreclosing social growth over the long run, but they tried to through the non-agapic rejection of voices differing from their own.

As I will argue below and in Chapters 4 and 5, the de-legitimizing tendency described here is not merely a historical phenomenon linked to conscious racism, sexism, and other forms of discrimination. It can be enacted present day by individuals in privileged groups who are consciously anti-racist, anti-sexist, and so on. This is due to the internalization and reinforcement of exclusionary beliefs/habits/conceptual schemes still in play in mainstream society in the United States. This type of internalization can begin in childhood due to the coercive survival dilemma and can be fueled both by an absence of socio-political secondness and by mainstream cultural reinforcement of privileged beliefs/habits/concepts. In other words, the socio-political shaping of affectivity, via belief/habit/concept formation, can occur without one's awareness.

b. Revisiting the Politics of Child Development

The survival value of human interest in the regularities of the world takes on a special form for children. This is because these regularities often are mediated by the habits of caretakers and community. John Dewey makes this point nicely in *Human Nature and Conduct*: "[A]n individual begins life as a baby, and babies are dependent beings. Their activities could continue at most for only a few hours were it not for the presence and aid of adults with *their formed habits*" ([1922] 1988, 66, my emphasis).[25] Human infants and young children are utterly dependent on their caretakers and community for survival. And as the stove example from last chapter illustrates, part of this survival entails trusting the testimony of their caretakers and community.[26] Even if this testimony involves explicit or implicit prejudice,[27] small children are likely to trust it, since they are probably too dependent and naive to question it. This is the coercive survival dilemma. By means of it, I would argue, the needle is threaded with respect to exclusionary habits and other habits of privilege for those in hegemonic groups.

Shannon Sullivan notes the young age (by three years old) at which children are aware of patterns of race in their world (n.d., 15–22; cf. 2006, 63–93).[28] When these social habits are reinforced through personal experience, education, and cultural messages, they can become virtually impossible to detect, since they involve a self-validating false universalization. In this section, I focus on habits of white privilege, to simplify the presentation, but other forms of falsely universalized privilege, with respect to economic class, sex, sexuality, etc., can be extrapolated. My objective is to show how internalized habits of false universalization fuel the nonconscious operation of prejudice in people who, on a conscious level, are anti-racist. The hypothetical white child I refer to below is one who is raised in a middle-class, predominantly white environment, where racism is taught as morally wrong but where white caretakers do not discuss race issues, such as white privilege, beyond this.[29]

Communal habits/beliefs/concepts form the backdrop against which one's individual habits are formed. Building on ideas discussed above, we can say that falsely universalized, hegemonic communal beliefs translate power differentials into the concrete experience of community members. In the United States, for example, hegemonic

communal habits underwrite the privilege of whites by largely eliminating socio-political secondness tied to race, such as the inconve-
nience of being harassed by police. The experience of white privilege
is also hegemonically reinforced as a *neutral* depiction of human experience. This falsely universal neutrality promotes the *oblivion* of
Euro-American whites to the discrimination suffered by people of
color, and the former may thereby *unintentionally* act to reinforce the
false universalization of white privilege.

Peirce's account of belief and doubt provides phenomenological
insight into the roots of this oblivion. Whites are often unaware of
the *absence* of race-based socio-political secondness from their experience, an absence that white privilege affords them. This unaware-
ness is linked to the corresponding lack of socio-political secondness
(or doubt) in their experience. The habit of expectation regarding the
absence of race-based socio-political friction can be internalized, because of the continued experience of a lack of environmental resistance to one's race. In addition, since this type of absence may never
arise *as an absence* in the first place, it is all the more difficult to detect. For example, if a small child burns her hand on the stove, that
experience involves habit-rupture and doubt.[30] In the future, the
child probably conducts herself so as to avoid getting burned. In contexts where hot stoves are nearby, she will probably, on a conscious
and/or nonconscious level, experience the absence of hand-burning
as an absence. She will know what is absent from her experience in
this respect—namely, the pain, doubt, and habit-rupture of burning
her hand. In contrast, someone who is white may experience *only* unimpeded habit-execution insofar as race is concerned, without the
corresponding doubt that could highlight the socio-political nature
of her experience.

White privilege involves, then, the following affective factor: a
race-based *absence* of socio-political secondness, which is rooted in
the societal habits into which the white child is born. These same societal habits result in the race-based *presence* of socio-political secondness for people of color. This is tricky phenomenologically for the
white child, since the exclusionary, privileged habits are articulated as

reality itself. That is to say, the "neutral" view of "human experience" is, in fact, the hegemonic concept of white privileged experience. For the white child who has not been educated otherwise, her failure to experience race-based socio-political secondness can *appear* to reflect the way things are for everyone else. That is, after all, what the hegemonic messages reinforce; for example, "Anyone willing to work hard enough can make something of themselves in the United States," "Race is no longer an issue in this country," "Anyone can pull herself up by her bootstraps," etc. In other words, the white child's experience of race *not being an obstacle* for *her* can take the generalized form of "race is not an obstacle for anyone else either." After all, the civil rights movement in the 1960s supposedly eradicated institutionalized racism, such as legalized segregation in the South (Bonilla-Silva 2003, 2–4; Sullivan 2006, 4–5; Williams 1997, 41). This promotes the white-privileged false universalization, "I don't see racism, thus it doesn't exist."

For example, in a feminism class I taught in 2004, where about 85 percent of the students were white, we were discussing issues of white privilege and false universalization, in conjunction with writings by theorists who are women of color. During class discussion of an article by bell hooks, two or three white students voiced their frustrations with hooks's "complaining" about racism. It sounded "dated" to them. From their white point of view, racism issues in 2004 were obsolete, the implication being that the civil rights movement of the 1960s took care of everything in this respect. Several African American students in the class volunteered their perspectives on the negative race issues (socio-political secondness) that indeed *did* characterize their experience as African Americans living in the United States in 2004. This disparity was a by-product of false universalization. My white students did not experience race as an obstacle *for them* or see it being an obstacle for anyone else. They then falsely universalized their position as normative, declaring obsolete the class reading from the 1980s that addressed post–civil rights movement racism. It did not occur to them that other present-day accounts of experience were available—namely, from people of color.

To their credit, I must add, these white students were open to the African American perspectives voiced by their classmates. It is difficult to tell, however, to what extent this was influenced by my authoritative presence and classroom rules about respecting the input of other students. I mention this point not to take away from the integrity of my white students but to highlight the application problem plaguing the scientific method. I would argue that without some kind of check, whites—when in the majority of a community—can easily fall into nonconscious habits of dismissal toward input from people of color.

Formal and informal education lie at the intersection of the sociopolitical and the affective, since education influences the concepts/habits/beliefs learned by children and adults. This influence can cut two ways. Formal education can be used to raise awareness regarding white privilege, and it can just as easily be used to reinforce the "invisibility" of white privilege. The media can collude in this as well, depicting a homogenous white human experience as normative (cf. hooks 2003b, 38–39). McIntosh describes her white education in the United States: "My schooling gave me no training in seeing myself . . . as an unfairly advantaged person. . . . [It] followed the pattern which Elizabeth Minnich has pointed out: whites are taught to think of their lives as morally neutral, normative, and average . . ." (McIntosh 1988, 292–93).[31] McIntosh also notes:

> My life was reflected back to me frequently enough so that I felt, with regard to my race, if not to my sex, like one of the real people.
>   Whether through the curriculum or in the newspaper, the television, the economic system, or the general look of people in the streets, we received daily signals and indications that my people counted, and that others *either didn't exist or must be trying, not very successfully, to be like people of my race.* (1988, 295, emphasis in original)

Here McIntosh addresses the media in addition to curriculum—an important point. For many children in the United States, the media is a significant source of informal education by the community.[32]

In contrast, note Helen Zia's experience of television in respect to race:

> It was so rare to see a real Asian American on television when I was a kid that we had a family ritual when one was spotted. It constituted what I now call an "Asian sighting." A hoot went out: "Hey, come see this, look now!" . . . Asian sightings are more common now, but they are still infrequent enough to create a thrill whenever real Asians appear on the screen, as martial artists, for example, or television reporters. (2000, 252–53)

Whereas McIntosh, as a result of race privilege, saw her race reflected on television "frequently enough so that [she] felt, with regard to [her] race . . . like one of the real people," Zia's television viewing was an experience where her race was rarely represented (1988, 295). These "insider" reports from McIntosh and Zia represent the differential experience of white children and children of color with respect to the common media portrayal of human experience.

As an example of a well-intentioned white person's nonconscious perpetuation of white privilege, I offer an anecdote shared by the clinical psychologist Harriet Lerner. Lerner self-identifies as a white, middle-class, Jewish woman and mother (1993, 215–16). She describes being confronted by an audience member who took issue with a talk she had just given:

> . . . I gave a lecture on the West Coast that I called "Mothers and Daughters: The Crucial Connection." When I took questions from the audience, an African-American woman raised her hand and pointed out that what I had said was not accurate to her experience, and certainly not for black women in general. I told her quite frankly that I had little experience with black mothers and daughters. She said, "Well, if you're talking about *white* mothers and daughters, why don't you say so?" (215, my emphasis)

The title of Lerner's talk—"Mothers and Daughters . . ."—involved falsely universalizing her experience as a white mother. She had spoken as if her experience as a mother were true of all mothers, regardless of their race. The experience of the African American audience member was not represented in Lerner's talk.[33]

Interestingly enough, Lerner also shares how she once asked a famous runner for an autograph for her son. She was dismayed when the runner wrote: "To Ben, Run for Jesus" (Lerner 1993, 215). Recall that Lerner is Jewish. While the runner was possibly trying to use the autograph to explicitly preach his beliefs,[34] it is also likely enough that he was falsely universalizing his experience as a Christian, for whom "Run for Jesus" is unproblematically inspirational. A former student of mine, who is Jewish, has told me how her "white" skin earns her privileges like those listed by Peggy McIntosh (McIntosh 1988). Yet she has had many experiences with anti-Semitic secondness in the United States when she has revealed that she is Jewish. This includes classmates ridiculing her at school and friends not being allowed to come and play at her house. A striking example of enforced false universalization in this context occurred when she suggested using snowflakes instead of Christmas trees for a holiday party being planned by the varsity dance team at the public school she attended. Her input was rejected.[35]

The complexity of these examples underscores the value of Peirce's fallibilist, communal outlook. Each of us can be on the receiving end of false universalization, where our experiences are rendered invisible by assumptions that everyone is, say, white or Christian or middle class, and so on. At the same time, each of us may perpetuate false universalization. An infinitely inclusive, communal ideal requires embracing input from all community members. This promotes the identification of blind spots rooted in false universalization a person may not realize she is promoting.

This lengthy discussion of child development and falsely universalized privilege has a direct bearing on Peirce's scientific method. This method cannot be fully separated, in the realm of concrete application, from either the hegemonic belief enforcement of the authority method or the accidental factors of belief-shaping classed under the a priori method. The internalization promoted by authority and other factors can result in nonconscious or instinctive belief-habits of race, sex, and other forms of privilege that undermine the inclusiveness of an actual community of inquiry. These habits can become part of the background beliefs that influence scientific inquiry, a connection that Peirce does not sufficiently address in this context. Moreover, since false universalization promotes the dismissal of supposedly "non-neutral" perspectives as crazy, overreacting, irrelevant, etc., nonconscious privilege in an actual community of inquiry can be self-perpetuating.

Part 4: Pragmatic Maxim, Imagination, and Power

My treatment of Peirce's pragmatic maxim further elucidates the application problem outlined above, foregrounding the contrasting characters of the scientific and authoritative methods of fixing belief, as well as the troubling overlap between them (which also includes the accidental belief-fixing factors of the a priori method). Peirce introduces the pragmatic maxim in "How to Make Our Ideas Clear," to help us "know what we think, to be masters of our own meaning" (W 3:260). By locating the meaning of our ideas in *practice over the long run*, the pragmatic maxim can be a provocative tool for revealing strands of meaning of which a person or community may not be aware. Applying this maxim to concrete examples in human communities reveals how exclusionary background beliefs can inform practice such that a professed meaning is undermined or even rendered contradictory.

Peirce's pragmatic maxim weds thought to habitual action by asserting that an object's meaning lies in its conceivable patterns of effects: "[W]hat a thing means is simply what habits it involves" (W 3:265). In "How to Make Our Ideas Clear," we find the oft-quoted version of the maxim: "Consider what effects, which might conceivably have practical bearings, we conceive the object of our conception to have. Then, our conception of these effects is the whole of our conception of the object" (W 3:266). In his later writings, Peirce returns again and again to this articulation, to clarify that he is *not* reducing thought to the immediacy of one set of consequences. Rather, his focus is on *habits*, both human and nonhuman, that order the world. Carl Hausman gives a helpful explanation of Peirce's example,

"To say that a body is heavy means simply that, in the absence of opposing force, it will fall" (W 3:267). Hausman notes that the heaviness of the body refers to consequences that "are to be expected at any time in the future. Thus, a central condition for intelligibility is the continuance of patterns of consequences into an indefinite, perhaps infinite, future" (Hausman 1999, 196). So the pragmatic maxim finds meaning in the regularities of the behaviors that stem from the belief, concept, or aim in question. Thus meaning extends into the future (EP 2:339–41).

On the plane of human conduct, the pragmatic maxim applies to self-controlled, *aim-driven* behavior that manifests in habits that are subject to further self-control.[36] In this context, the "object" of thought is an aim. To assess the meaning of a human aim, we conceive or imagine all the possible consequences to which it leads in the long run. Peirce says, "Now, the identity of a habit depends on how it might lead us to act, not merely under such circumstances as are likely to arise, but under such as might possibly occur, no matter how improbable they may be—no matter if contrary to all previous experience" (W 3:265; EP 1:131, 378 n. 7).[37] Christopher Hookway, giving a problematically exaggerated interpretation of the pragmatic maxim, says, "Peirce claims that, if we apply the pragmatic principle, we become *completely aware* of the relevant features of the meanings of our terms" (2000, 143, my emphasis). I disagree with this reading, because its confident wording implies we can "completely" know ahead of time how our aims will grow. We cannot. Moreover, the initial imaginative enterprise cannot be exhaustive; it can only reveal features that are relevant to us at the time we are imagining. We might not catch everything. Finally, since our habits grow as our aim is implemented, the meaning of our aims is never complete.

Peirce notes the open-endedness of meaning when he discusses committing oneself to the meaning of a word:

> [B]esides the consequences to which the person who accepts a word knowingly commits himself, there is a vast ocean of unforeseen consequences which the acceptance of the word is destined to bring about, not merely consequences of knowing but

perhaps revolutions of society. One cannot tell what power there
may be in a word or a phrase to change the face of the world. . . .
(EP 2:256)

Peirce is highlighting the fact that meaning grows, and it can grow
unpredictably. His point that words and phrases can have the power
to "change the face of the world" brings to mind a phrase such as
"liberty and justice for all,"[38] whose meaning continues to grow and
to change the social fabric of the United States (EP 2:256).

The method of science embraces the pragmatic maxim, and the
method of authority rejects it. The former takes inclusion as its ideal,
embracing the ongoing growth in meaning that this implies. The latter takes exclusion as an ideal, in an effort to forestall growth. Let us
examine social aims in the context of each of these methods and then
within the overlapping that occurs between them because of background beliefs.

In a community that practices the scientific method, efforts to
imagine the habits to which social aims lead involve, to the extent
possible, the perspectives of *all* the members in the community.
Community members understand that, to the extent that any perspectives are excluded, the meaning of the social aim is unduly constrained. Thus feedback is solicited from as many of its members as
possible. It is fallibilistic in its outlook, realizing that there are always
more perspectives to be included and that the implementation of an
aim can result in unforeseen, unwanted consequences. For example,
a good friend of mine who lived in Los Angeles during the first Gulf
War, around 1989–90, lived in a small community where many were
overseas fighting. The community implemented an aim to support
the troops by placing yellow ribbons on trees throughout the community. An unforeseen consequence of these efforts was a marked
increase of crimes, such as burglary and rape, targeted against women
whose family members were away fighting. Some criminals were taking the yellow ribbons in trees of residential homes as a sign that the
occupant(s) would be easier crime targets. When these harmful consequences came to light, the community took the feedback about its

aim seriously. It held the aim in place, on the one hand, by maintaining the ribbon theme in public spaces. It also, however, responded to the unintended consequences with public announcements warning those vulnerable to attack, as well as through the action of various women's groups and college students who helped spread the warnings door-to-door in the neighborhoods themselves.[39] This communal response reflects the fallibilist and self-corrective spirit of the scientific method, where communal feedback is part of the process by which an aim grows and is modified if necessary. It also shows that any societal aim is really an experiment whose results are never fully collected. Just as laboratory experiments can overturn a hypothesis, large-scale social "experimentation" can challenge aims by presenting unanticipated data, like the unexpected crime in the current example. Ultimately, then, there is a healthful dialectic between feedback and the self-controlled growth of a community. The road of inquiry is kept open.

In a hegemonic community, where those in authority dictate the fixation of belief, there is a finite community of inquiry consisting only of those in power. In this sphere the pragmatic maxim is rejected. Aims affecting the community are not inclusive, and their meaning is dictated and reinforced by a group dedicated to *blocking* the road of inquiry. The only consequences of merit are those that promote the status quo. Any problematic feedback is suppressed—by suppressing the individuals who would bring the feedback to light. Inclusiveness toward a diversity of perspectives is shunned, because this would undermine the hegemony of those in power. For example, in the true story portrayed in the movie *Erin Brockovich*, Pacific Gas and Electric (PG&E) is an authoritative community that has an aim to maximize profit (*Erin Brockovich* 2000). It manipulates the beliefs of those living near one of its factories who are suffering serious health problems due to the hexavalent chromium that PG&E has introduced into the community's well water in the process of running its plant. These residents are led to believe, by PG&E, that their problems have nothing to do with the hexavalent chromium. Beyond this,

PG&E dismisses the feedback of the community residents, so its aim will not be challenged. It is likely that the health problems of the community residents were *unintended* consequences of PG&E's aim of maximizing profit. Even when it was made aware of these consequences, however, PG&E refused to take responsibility and alter its course, until a major lawsuit forced it to.

I argued above that we cannot simply separate communities where science is practiced from those where authority rules. This is because the former are situated in socio-political contexts where hegemonic norms may hold sway, even among conscientious practitioners of inclusiveness. The background beliefs that inevitably inform scientific inquiry could include, and historically *have* included, exclusionary bias. This dynamic has been at play in the United States since its inception. This brings us back to the example, discussed earlier, of "All men are created equal." One the one hand, the United States has always prided itself, theoretically, on the inclusiveness of its democratic, communal inquiry into practical affairs, which is compatible with Peirce's scientific method. On the other hand, authority has reigned. Racism, sexism, and other exclusionary social practices underscored the fact that "All men are created equal" was really a narrowly targeted concept, or aim, at the beginning. It was an aim of the founding fathers, who had the power to direct its meaning to include contradictory habits that supported their own equality, while oppressing other groups. For all its worthiness as an ideal, the *practice* of "All men are created equal" as an aim and a belief-habit reflected its false universalization. Inquiry was open only to those within the elite class of white, propertied men. Regarding the pragmatic maxim's focus on the habits to which a concept leads, only habitual consequences *to these men* were considered legitimate. Individuals and groups representing non-hegemonic perspectives were excluded from imagining the meaning of "All men are created equal." And they have been, and continue to be, excluded when voicing negative feedback regarding this aim—including its bold contradictions.

Throughout the birth and growth of United States as a new country, non-hegemonic groups have been uniquely suited to point out contradictions between ideals and behavior, contradictions that undermine the scientific spirit of the pragmatic maxim. For example, those African Americans who were brutally enslaved against their will could voice the contradiction between "equality" and enslavement[40] and, after the emancipation, legalized segregation. Native Americans could voice the contradiction between "equality" and genocide, broken treaties, and land theft.[41] From the hegemonic point of view, however, since "all" were created equal, then "all" could own slaves and stolen land. Owning slaves and stolen land were outrageously contradictory habitual consequences stemming from "All men are created equal." Because the community of inquiry was composed only of affluent, white men, however, these contradictions did not officially emerge as red flags sufficient to stop these barbaric practices. Instead they became part of the contradictory foundation upon which the United States was built. And alongside the "equality" of all has been the "*subpersonhood*" of people of color and women, a hegemonically imposed "inferiority" that has been used to justify their exclusion from the community of inquiry.[42]

Contemporary U.S. culture lives in this legacy, including the persistence of its conceptual false universalization of privilege. On the one hand, mainstream U.S. society embraces many ideals of inclusivity, including repudiations of both racism and sexism. On the other hand, deep-seated discriminatory habits undermine the efficient implementation of these ideals, because of persistent exclusionary bias. In terms of the methods of fixing beliefs, the Peircean scientific inclusive ideal is undermined by background beliefs that consciously and/ or nonconsciously perpetuate exclusion. These background beliefs allow the authority and a priori methods to enter the scientific method through the back door. My primary focus is on the shared, nonconscious exclusionary bias that occurs within communities of inquiry, where well-meaning men, white people, and/or others in hegemonic groups can nonconsciously perpetuate prejudices that, on a conscious level, they repudiate. Because of this application problem, the efforts of well-meaning scientists, formal or informal, can be tainted by exclusionary background beliefs.

For example, Marilyn Frye tells the story of her efforts, along with those of other white feminists, to address the problem of racism within feminism. Their plan was to first meet together as a group, namely, as a "white women's consciousness-raising group to identify and explore the racism in our lives with a view to dismantling the barriers that blocked our understanding and action in this matter" (Frye 1983, 111). Despite their well-intentioned efforts, which were informed by the "encouragement of various women of color—both friends and women speaking in the feminist press," Frye and her group were met with criticism (111). Frye notes that "one Black woman criticized us very angrily for ever thinking we could achieve our goals by working only with white women" (111). Frye explained that this consciousness-raising group was only an initial stage and that she and her white colleagues intended to "organize a group open to all women shortly after our series of white women's meetings came to a close" (111–12). Her critic was not satisfied with this explanation, as it still reflected the exclusion of women of color from the key decisions being made. Frye confesses her bewilderment at this woman's anger, because it seemed crazy to her. Frye caught herself, however. She recognized that attributing craziness to a non-hegemonic perspective can be symptomatic of privileged, exclusionary bias (112). Frye was thus able to modify her understanding of the woman of color's perspective. It seems that the key for Frye was that she herself, as a women in relation to men, had been on the receiving end of "you're crazy" (112). This is significant, as it points to empathy and the power of imagination to help a person bridge from her limited perspective to the perspective of others.

In Peircean terms, Frye could imagine that, even though it seemed crazy to her, the woman of color's testimony was a legitimate source of doubt of the belief, "I was not behaving in a racist fashion." Frye's efforts here are characteristic of Critical Common-sensist inquiry, whereby imaginative reflection is used as a tool for creating doubt about our background beliefs. In 1893, Peirce appended a note to his

"Fixation of Belief" essay, stating that we can bring about a state of doubt through the use of our imaginations. This kind of doubt occurs in the context of self-controlled habit change (CP 5.373 n. 1). In this example, Frye was engaged in self-controlled habit change, as she was consciously trying to correct racism in her behavior. To this end imaginative reflection helped her embrace the testimony that, despite her well-intentioned efforts, her behavior was still racist.

The scientific method's application problem involves cases where, in contrast to Frye, people in privileged positions *do not* "catch themselves" and instead dismiss non-hegemonic perspectives as crazy, irrelevant, overreactive, and so on, because these perspectives simply do not reflect "everyday human experience." Yet the concepts by which the privileged conceive this experience are often falsely universalized. The background beliefs from which scientists reason can include exclusionary beliefs/concepts that make it hard to respect input from non-hegemonic perspectives. And since these background beliefs often function without conscious awareness, well-intentioned people can unknowingly perpetuate exclusion, discrimination, and ignorance.

The Logic of Science essays describe a stronger synechistic individual than that presented in the Cognition Series, the latter being at odds with her community but also in danger of being convinced of her "madness" (W 2:202). The synechistic individual of the present series is in conflict with her hegemonic community and also *stands up to* this community, in the name of human sociality. The question arises, then, as to how the individual and her community are to be ideally related for Peirce, since implicit in this series is the irreducibility of both. Also implicit is the application problem of the scientific method, since the scientific, authority, and a priori methods are intertwined via background beliefs. How can communal growth occur that holds in place both the perspectives of individual community members *and* the holistic vision of the community itself? Peirce's ultimate answer involves his mature doctrine of Critical Common-sensism. His answer also includes a model of agapic evolution, to which we now turn, whereby individual spontaneity provides a creative impetus for a community to grow beyond its present habit systems. In stark contrast to the authoritative model's rejection of an individual's diversity from communal norms, the agapic model *embraces* this diversity. The inclusiveness of the spirit of science is, thus, ideally fueled by agapic love.

FOUR

THE LAW OF MIND, ASSOCIATION, AND SYMPATHY

Monist "Cosmology Series" and Association Writings, 1890s

For Peirce, agapic love is the ideal that communities should embrace in relationship to their individual members, especially when these members are at odds with the community itself.[1] Peirce's views on agape occur in the rich context of his 1890s *Monist* "Cosmology Series" and writings on association,[2] where the synechistic individual emerges as a potential source of novelty, as a result of her unique experience and creativity. This novelty is an important source of communal growth. In what follows, I give an affectivity- and social criticism–focused interpretation and application of these key insights, drawing on work done in previous chapters. I first take up the synechistic individual and then the community.

I demonstrate that, on the one hand, agape provides an insightful affective communal ideal, especially for those in hegemonic groups who need to practice loving concern and openness toward community members in non-hegemonic groups. On the other hand, however, analogous to the application problem faced by the scientific method, applying the agapic ideal in actual communities can also be undermined by the nonconscious functioning of exclusionary background beliefs. Thus the work in this chapter, like the work done in Chapter 3, points beyond itself to Peirce's mature doctrine of Critical Common-sensism.

Part 1: The Law of Mind and the Synechistic Individual: Association

Once again we take up the ongoing flow of human cognition and belief. In this 1890s context, Peirce's preferred vocabulary is "feelings"/"ideas," and the flow of human thought is described by the law of mind. He says, "The law of mind is that feelings and ideas attach themselves in thought so as to form systems" (CP 7.467). The systems formed are habits, habit-formation being one with the process of cognition, which Peirce describes as an ongoing "rhythm" (CP 7.412): "[T]he whole action of the soul [or mind], so far as it is subject to law consist[s] of nothing but taking up and letting drop in ceaseless alternation" (CP 7.410); "the whole activity of the mind consists of a drawing in and dropping out" (CP 7.414).

When the mind allows feelings and ideas to "drop," they do not simply disappear. Rather they fade from conscious awareness to become part of new or existing habit systems, which exert a subtle but powerful influence on subsequent connections among ideas. This influence often goes unnoticed. It is the sway of sympathy among one's own habit systems, whose influence can shape our beliefs without our even knowing it (CP 7.434–35, CP 7.447–48).

Feelings/ideas originate in the firstness, secondness, and thirdness of the human organism's experience, in her ongoing interaction with external and internal environments. The organism's firstness, in this respect, includes both the feltness of her habits and the automatic, harmonious functioning of undisturbed habits. Secondness involves the ongoing confrontation between the human organism and the external world, including socio-political secondness. And thirdness includes the learning and mediation (between firstness and secondness) involved in one's habits, as well as a sense of self over time. Firstness and thirdness continue to be closely related here. Thirdness is re-flected in habits, old and new, insofar as they continually mediate one's navigation of the external world. To the extent that this media-tion is or becomes automatic, pre-reflective, these same habits reflect firstness.

The unique relationships among an individual's habit systems—which are both idiosyncratically and socially shaped—are sources of novel ideas/feelings. Cooking is an everyday example, where one's habits regarding how and what one normally cooks can be the source for novel combinations and new dishes. Cooking habits are idiosyn-cratically shaped by one's likes and dislikes, food allergies, nutritional needs, and so forth. They are likewise socially shaped by factors such as conventions regarding meat and dairy products, availability of types of food, and religious and cultural traditions.

a. Feeling and Idea in the 1890s

In his 1890s writings, Peirce promotes feeling to a higher cognitive status than it had in the Cognition Series of the 1860s. In the earlier essay series, feeling is the felt dimension of cognition, which accom-panies but is different from the representational dimension of cogni-tion (W 2:227). In his 1890s work, by contrast, Peirce often uses "feeling" and "idea" in the same breath, as he describes the law of mind:

> The one primary and fundamental law of mental action consists in a tendency to generalisation. *Feeling tends to spread*; connec-tions between *feelings* awaken *feelings*; neighboring *feelings* be-come assimilated; *ideas* are apt to reproduce themselves. These are so many formulations of the one law of the growth of mind. (EP 1:291, my emphasis)

And

> [T]here is but one law of mind, namely, that *ideas tend to spread* continuously and to affect certain others which stand to them in a peculiar relation of affectibility. In this spreading they lose intensity, and especially the power of affecting others, but gain

generality and become welded with other *ideas*. (EP 1:313, my emphasis)

Peirce does not explain this apparently puzzling conflation of terms, although he does distinguish between feeling/idea, on the one hand, and a *general* idea on the other: "A finite interval of time generally contains an innumerable series of feelings; and when these become welded together in association, the result is a general idea. For . . . by continuous spreading an idea becomes generalised" (EP 1:325). When ideas/feelings become generalized, and this generalization is useful to the organism, a habit is formed (CP 7.498). From the standpoint of survival, this makes sense. Ideas/feelings result from the human organism's ongoing inquiry with the external environment. General ideas—or proto-habits—are formed to adapt to the secondness of experience. Successful generalizations become full-fledged habits, which promote survival and growth.

In the context of Peirce's synonymous usage of "feeling" and "idea" in the 1890s, feeling is a part of and makes possible the representative nature of cognition. That is to say, feeling plays a role in ideation or the representative abstraction that occurs in cognition. The firstness and thirdness attributed to human cognition in the Cognition Series have been intertwined in the 1890s writings. "Feeling" and "idea" *both* convey, within the mind, the semiotic-nervous representations of the external world. Feeling is itself representative and thus is an idea. This makes sense from the perspective of everyday semiotics. Recall Chapter 1's explanation of how feelings are the portal through which human organisms interact with external objects. The greenness of my car, for example, is at once *both* a feeling/sensation based on my eyes processing information *and* a sign of the object to my mind.

b. The Subject-ness of Feelings and Personality

Peirce's categorial depiction of an "idea" in the *Monist* series essay "The Law of Mind" (1892) portrays what I call the "subject-ness" of ideas/feelings.

> Three elements go to make up an idea. The first is its intrinsic
> quality as a feeling. The second is the energy with which it affects
> other ideas, an energy which is infinite in the here-and-nowness
> of immediate sensation, finite and relative in the recency of the
> past. The third element is the tendency of an idea to bring along
> other ideas with it. (EP 1:325)

Note that Peirce is *personifying* ideas/feelings. They have a felt quality,
energy to affect other ideas/feelings, and a "tendency . . . to bring
other ideas [or feelings] along with [them]" (EP 1:325). This personi-
fication is no accident for Peirce, who specifically compares ideas to
persons, "[E]very general idea has the unified living feeling of a person" (EP 1:350, cf. 354).

To convey this anthropomorphic nature, Peirce uses the term
"subjective" and its derivatives, attributing to feelings/ideas subjective extension and intensity (EP 1:324; CP 7.396–98, 496–97). There
are at least two senses of "subjective" at play here. First, feelings/ideas
are subjective because they belong to a particular person in whose
mind the nerves are firing, and thus reflect her or his particular biases. Second, feelings/ideas have what I call "subject-ness." They have
subjective extension and intensity, because they *are subjects*. In being
constitutive of the person, feelings/ideas are also microcosms within
the human organism, that is, little subjects within the human subject
her- or himself. The microcosmic subject-ness of the feeling/idea un-
folds under the influence of existing habits in the organism.

Peirce notes the subject-ness of feelings/ideas in several places. In
"The Law of Mind," he notes that a feeling has "a subjective, or sub-
stantial, spatial extension" that is "a *subjective*, not an objective, extension" (EP 1:324, my emphasis). By this he means that feelings are
themselves subjects within the mind, "subject[s] of inhesion" (EP
1:324). They take up physical space in the nervous tissue of the brain.
Elsewhere in the essay, Peirce describes "subjective" as "considered
as a subject or substance having the attribute of duration" (EP 1:315).
This means that the spreading of feelings/ideas, described by the law
of mind, manifests in nervous tissue belonging to a unique body.
Peirce does not elaborate on this insight, although he does note that

feelings involve "externality," by which he seems to mean an outside trigger of some sort (EP 1:324–25). This relates to the secondness of experience and the intentionality of feelings/ideas. They are triggered by and related to objects.

The uniqueness of the human organism's body/mind is a significant factor here. The way a particular feeling/idea takes up space in *my* nervous tissue will differ from the way a similar feeling/idea takes space in *your* nervous tissue. Peirce uses the term "subjective intensity" to describe the internal vividness of a feeling, such as the liveliness that the sound of thunder has for me personally. In fact, I find the sound of thunder to be thrilling, whereas someone else may find it terrifying in liveliness or, perhaps, neutral. Subjective intensity is thus distinct from the *objective* intensity, which in this case would be the loudness of the thunderclap itself (CP 7.396–98, 496–97). The subjective intensity of a feeling/idea reflects its subject-ness. As a subject inhering in nervous tissue, a feeling/idea has a personalized vivacity. This vivacity is related to existing habit systems and how the present feeling/idea relates to them. This is another way of saying that the subject-ness of present feelings/ideas is related to past feelings/ideas that have become welded together in habit systems. Peirce specifically notes this influence of past experience on the human organism's ongoing flow of feelings/ideas, noting that "every state of feeling is affectible by every earlier state" (EP 1:323). Since the influence of past feelings will be different for each person, Peirce's comment underscores the fact that the influence of our past feelings/ideas is unique to each one of us. My own habit systems reflect past experience with many, many intense thunderstorms, none of which ever threatened my safety, and many of which were accompanied by fascinating (to me) wind and rain patterns. All this past experience informs the subjective intensity that the sound of thunder has for me. For someone whose life, or the lives of loved ones, was threatened by a thunderstorm, the sound of thunder may have a more intense subjective intensity than it does for me. And for someone whose experience of thunderstorms was uninteresting to them from the standpoint of aesthetics or safety, the subjective intensity of thunder may be considerably less subjectively intense, even neutral.

The influence of past feelings on present ones is sophisticated, reflecting what Peirce would call personality or personal character. Personality involves a holistic picture that incorporates one's past habit systems, one's ongoing activity in the world, and one's aspirations for the future. The welding together of personal habit-systems is unique to each organism. Peirce does not elaborate on this uniqueness when he discusses personality in "The Law of Mind." Nonetheless I would argue that one's habit-systems-gestalt includes one's unique embodiment and spatio-temporal orientation toward the world, as well as the ways these irreducibly individual factors blend with social and, more specifically, socio-political environmental interaction.

Peirce's description of personality encompasses the dynamic interplay among one's personal history, current environmental interactions, and expectations and aims for the future. He says that "[p]ersonality is some kind of coördination or connection of ideas" (EP 1:331). It is the general idea and "living feeling" that results from the ideas/feelings that make up the human organism (EP 1:331). It includes the feltness of being oneself[3], which involves a grand and ongoing gestalt of the feltness of one's habits. Moreover,

> This personality, like any general idea, is not a thing to be apprehended in an instant. It has to be lived in time; nor can any finite time embrace it in all its fulness [*sic*]. Yet in each infinitesimal interval it is present and living, though specifically colored by the immediate feelings of that moment. (EP 1:331)

Personality involves the ongoing growth of the human organism, which reflects a special kind of coordination of ideas/feelings. Peirce calls this coordination a *developmental teleology*, in order to capture both the goal-oriented directedness (teleology) and the dynamic growth of the goals themselves (developmental) (EP 1:331). Our goals grow as we do. An example of this phenomenon is the frequency with which college students change their majors as their interests change and grow. Personality, or character, is dynamic and lived.

Peirce's portrayal of personality supports the insight that, no matter how socially mediated one's habits may be, she will always be irreducibly unique in her individualized embodiment, her spatio-temporal perspective, and the interrelationships among all her habits.

The principles of association—contiguity and resemblance—demonstrate this point as well. An examination of these principles shows in detail how, on Peirce's scheme, individuals are sources of creativity (including creative resistance) in their communities.

c. Inner and Outer Worlds and the Principles of Association

The law of mind manifests in the synechistic individual through association by resemblance and association by contiguity, which Peirce pairs with a person's inner and outer worlds, respectively:

> The ensemble of all habits about ideas of feeling constitutes one great habit which is a World; and the ensemble of all habits about acts of reaction constitutes a second great habit, which is another World. The former is the Inner World, the world of Plato's forms. The other is the Outer World,[4] or universe of existence. The mind of man is adapted to the reality of being. Accordingly, there are two modes of association of ideas: inner association, based on the habits of the inner world, and outer association, based on the habits of the universe. (CP 4.157, ca. 1897)

The flow of feelings/ideas by which our habits are formed and refined is governed by the interplay between an inner world of individuality, or association by resemblance, and an outer world of "not me," or association by contiguity.

I. ASSOCIATION BY CONTIGUITY

Association by contiguity ("contiguity," for short) groups feelings/ideas based on experience. My experience of the connection between thunder and rain, for example, leads me to link the two. Contiguity involves the realm of secondness and habits acquired based on our experience with the external world. It involves connections, between feelings/ideas, that are dictated by factors outside one's mind, either conventionally or naturally: "[I]n association by contiguity an idea calls up the idea of the *set* in which experience has placed it, and thence one of the other ideas of that set" (CP 7.392, Peirce's emphasis). This connection between ideas reflects a large-scale habit that preexists a particular person's mental activity and control. Contiguity involves "the suggestion by an idea of another, which has been associated with it, not by the nature of thought, but by *experience*, or the course of life" (CP 7.391, Peirce's emphasis).[5] Peirce gives the example of the judicial branch of government making someone think of the executive and legislative branches of government and then, perhaps, of the performance of the legislature (CP 7.391).

The course of life also includes associations driven by socio-political secondness. For example, Jean Shinoda Bolen, a psychiatrist, Jungian analyst, and writer, describes the feelings/ideas she experienced on visiting the Anne Frank Haus in Amsterdam:

> I . . . felt a sense of kinship with Anne. During those same wartime years, I had been a child, too. As a Japanese American living in California, whose family had managed to escape being in a concentration camp, I had felt only a fraction of the apprehension of attracting hostile attention that Anne Frank and her family must have felt. We didn't have to go into hiding, but we did have to move often during the evacuation and the relocation of everyone of Japanese ancestry, initially staying just one step ahead of martial law. During the war years, I went to seven elementary schools in five states. (1994, 204–5)

Anne Frank and her family were in hiding from the Nazis, to avoid being sent to a concentration camp. During the same "wartime years," Bolen and her family were also making efforts to escape concentration camps. Thus visiting the Anne Frank Haus suggests to Bolen her own family's experience. This connection reflects an association by contiguity, whereby external factors, in the form of socio-political secondness, led Bolen to connect the threat of concentration camps to her own experience as a Japanese American living in the United States during World War Two.

Humans not only make associations by contiguity, but also by resemblance, which provides a contrast, for Peirce, between human and non-human animals. Non-human animals are clearly seen to demonstrate associations by contiguity, which involves a less sophisticated form of reasoning than does resemblance: "The dog, when he hears the voice of his master runs expecting to see him, and if he does not find him will manifest surprize, or at any rate perplexity. This is as good an example of inference from connection in experience as could easily be given" (CP 7.454). The connections involved in resemblance, on the other hand, involve a degree of abstraction that "brutes" seem not to achieve (CP 7.455).

II. ASSOCIATION BY RESEMBLANCE

Peirce calls "association by resemblance" ("resemblance," for short) the mind's natural drawing into clusters of feelings/ideas.[6] This type of association "probably implies a higher degree of self-consciousness than any of the brutes possess. It involves a somewhat steady attention to qualities as such; and this must rest on the capacity for language, if not on language itself" (CP 7.455). Resemblance involves abstraction beyond the capacity, shared by many nonhuman animals, to learn from past experiences. It thus allows self-controlled habit-taking to reach greater sophistication in humans than it does in nonhuman animals.[7]

To be more specific: Resemblance allows humans to create habits that differ from those present at birth and from those learned through association by contiguity. Peirce uses the term "general idea" to describe a cluster of feelings/ideas created through resemblance. General ideas become habits or concepts when, on repetition, they are found useful to the organism (CP 7.498, ca. 1898). Note that the habits in question are based on the organism's *own* connections, as opposed to connections provided by the external world. For example, in the movie *Cast Away* (2002) the fictional character Chuck Noland, played by Tom Hanks, is a Federal Express manager who has recently become stranded on a desert island. Before the crash that maroons him, Noland experienced a white, male, middle-class mainstream U.S. lifestyle. After the crash, we witness Noland's attempts to create new habits of survival, given his starkly new environment. Contiguity is in play, as Noland continually learns from his new experiences. Creativity, or association by resemblance, also plays a primary role, as he tries new combinations of habits he formerly developed through contiguity. This is especially evident when Noland uses materials from several FedEx packages that have washed ashore from the wrecked plane. He uses the insides of videotapes as makeshift rope. He uses the blade from an ice skate for chopping and cutting and as a small mirror to inspect an aching tooth. Contiguity would have already told him how rope, blades, and reflective surfaces work. In the new environment of the uninhabited island, ropes, blades, and reflective surfaces are not readily available. The miscellaneous FedEx packages *are* available, however, and resemblance enables Noland to make novel combinations: videotape as rope, ice-skate blades as knife, ax, and mirror. These new combinations promote Noland's survival in a new environment, by helping him adapt his old habits to this new environment.

Peirce links association by resemblance with instinct, saying, "[I]t may be a natural disposition, which was from birth destined to develop itself whatever the child's outward experiences might be, so long as he was not maimed nor virtually maimed, say by being imprisoned" (CP 7.498, ca. 1898). As long as a human organism's sense organs are fully operative and he or she is not socially isolated, his or her associations by resemblance will develop naturally, regardless of environmental particularities. Those who have spent time with small children and witnessed their vast stores of creativity and imagination—expressed in improvised games, costumes, stories, drawings— can attest to the young age at which resemblance is already present in humans. The survival value of this instinct toward resemblance is rooted in the adaptability made possible by unique habit-formation (cf. Damasio 1994, 89–94). Chuck Noland's creative ingenuity makes it possible for him to adapt to a huge change in environment, despite the ineffectiveness of many of his old habits of securing food, shelter, and water.

Association by resemblance signals the mind's ability to make self-controlled, creative connections between ideas, connections that go beyond those rendered by experience. It involves "the free play of imagination" (CP 7.437). Resemblance promotes not only survival in complex environments but also artistic and scientific creativity through which aesthetic and epistemological pursuits can grow and flourish. The creativity made possible by resemblance manifests differently in each individual human, depending on factors including the uniqueness of her personalized embodiment and her corresponding spatio-temporal perspective on the world, as well as the interaction among her unique habits and habit systems. In addition to and alongside these factors, creativity is shaped by experience.

The creative, imaginative energies of resemblance *draw on* contiguity.[8] If there were no associations/habits/beliefs learned via contiguity/experience, association by resemblance would have nothing from which to work. My creativity in the kitchen, for example, depends on the associations/habits/beliefs I have learned through experience—regarding spices, flavors, textures, cooking techniques, etc. For someone who had never before cooked or set foot in a kitchen, "creativity" would not apply to her or his attempts at cooking. This person would be dependent on trying things from scratch and then learning from the experience. The potential for creativity/resemblance would then grow alongside the accrual of experience. Even someone fairly new to cooking could be creative, as soon as she had a little experience to go on.

III. RECIPROCITY OF INFLUENCE

For Peirce, a person's inner and outer worlds are continuous, they shade into each other. The human organism's inner world colors her outer world, making this outer world a world *for her*. On the other hand, the outer world colors her inner world as well, limiting the personal control she might have over ideas in that domain. Peirce observes, "We naturally make all our distinctions too absolute. We are accustomed to speak of an external universe and an inner world of thought. But they are merely vicinities with no real boundary line between them" (CP 7.438). And, "Experience being something forced upon us, belongs to the [outer world]. Yet in so far as it is I or you who experiences the constraint, the experience is *mine* or *yours*, and thus belongs to the inner world" (CP 7.439, Peirce's emphasis).

Recall that the inner world is the world of resemblance and that the outer world is the world of contiguity. Peirce is saying that association by resemblance and association by contiguity *mutually* affect each other. One's personalized resemblances are shaped by one's experience, and vice versa. For example, my experience of running competitively during my high school years (contiguity) resulted in my applying running metaphors to my life, which reflects association by resemblance. At graduation I even gave a speech whose theme was "the race of life." In turn, this association by resemblance shaped my experience of running, which became a deeply symbolic act for me, representing strength, discipline, and commitment. Moreover, this reciprocal contiguity-resemblance influence grew along with me. When I became injured in college and could no longer compete (contiguity), I began to see running through a more relaxed metaphor, as reflecting self-attunement and self-care (resemblance). This evolved metaphor shaped my experience (contiguity). It led to my running *only* for pleasure—versus "making" myself run to complete an exercise regimen—and, eventually, it led to my embracing walking instead of running as my primary form of exercise.

The reciprocity between resemblance and contiguity can grow beyond the sphere of the synechistic individual. For an example that also addresses socio-political issues, take Alice Walker's novel *The Color Purple* (1982). A Pulitzer Prize–winning work of fiction, it represents Walker's creative ingenuity and thus involves association by resemblance. At the same time, the novel draws on Walker's experience and family history and thus involves association by contiguity. Her characters were inspired by her paternal grandfather and grandmother, as well as by the friendship that developed between her grandfather's second wife and his mistress, Shug Perry (A. Walker 1996, 45; 1983, 355–56; White 2004, 334–36). Regarding Celie, the character based on her grandmother, Walker made a point to give her a "much richer life" than her grandmother was able to experience (2003). Celie leaves her abusive husband and experiences a passionate love relationship with Shug Avery. She also supports herself through designing and sewing specialty pants and eventually inherits a house of her own (A. Walker 1982). These plot themes reflect creative associations by resemblance. In addition, as she wrote the novel, Walker's own experiences (contiguity) were shaped by her creativity (resemblance), as she attended to the demands of her characters. This included a move from New York to a small town in northern California, whereby Walker transformed her living habits in order to serve her creative process (A. Walker 1983, 355–60; 2003; White 2004, 308–12).

On a communal scale, Walker's novel as a work of art reaches out to its readers' experiences. As Walker herself puts it, "Art is the mirror, perhaps the only one, in which we can see our true collective face. We must honor its sacred function. We must let art help us" (1996, i). The story of Celie, Nettie, Shug, Mr.——, Sophie, and Harpo reflects the suffering and transformation of African American characters living in the legally segregated Southern United States—and, for some of the characters, in Africa—during the first half of the twentieth century (A. Walker 1982). Discussing *The Color Purple*, the book and the movie, Walker notes that her work addresses the human condition, not only the African American one (1996, i; 2003). In *The Same River Twice* (1996), Walker includes letters from her readers about *The Color Purple*, letters that reflect how their experiences were shaped by the novel. I have excerpted from three of these letters that, based on context, seem to come, respectively, from an African American woman, a Euro-American woman, and a man whose race I could not determine:

> Ann Clyde wrote, "Through your writing, you have spoken to me. . . . I just want to say thank you for doing your part, for making me proud to be black, to be a black woman and for your contribution." (A. Walker 1996, 243)

> Donna F. Johnson wrote, "I was, and continue to be, profoundly affected by your novel. . . . In my own circle, the novel was very well received by women of all ages—even Catholic nuns! . . . . You have awakened in me a desire to know and understand the experience of Black women." (232)

> Jeffrey P. Rowekamp wrote: "I am writing to you out of thanks. I
> just finished reading your book . . . , and I feel like my chest is
> about to burst. I almost cried. It made so much sense to me; made
> me think about my life and the real meaning of love." (238)

These reader comments reflect the impact of Walker's work on her
community of readers. The interplay of resemblance and contiguity
that informed Walker's *The Color Purple* influences far more than
merely her own belief-habit systems.

d. The Communal Value of the Individual and of Non-hegemonic Perspectives

The synechistic individual is an invaluable source of novelty for the
community, as a result of the uniqueness of her or his experiential
and creative perspectives. Since each person has her or his own body
and her or his own spatio-temporal position in the world, each person's experience is unique. The habits that make up each person's
past, present, and projected future are a constellation of contiguities
and resemblances that, ultimately, revolve around that person alone.
For example, Peirce himself plays the role of the creative synechistic
individual in his *Monist* "Cosmology Series" essays, which hypothesize a synechistic universe in which consciousness, chance, and mind
have a rightful place versus the mechanistic necessitarianism held by
many of his scientific contemporaries. Alice Walker is also a creative
synechistic individual; no one else could have written *The Color Purple* (1982).

The fact that synechistic individuals are inescapably socially shaped
points to synechistic *groups* of community members also being
sources of novelty for the larger community, because of shared experiences among synechistic group members, experiences that are not
encountered by other community members. In other words, these
groups have certain type(s) of experiential secondness in common,
my focus being socio-political secondness. Peirce does not explicitly
address group membership in the 1890s association writings, but it is
a relatively straightforward extrapolation, given his general convic-
tions about the influence of society on the individual's habit-taking.

Moreover, in his 1901 review of Karl Pearson's *Grammar of Science*, Peirce shows a sensitivity to group membership on the basis of economic class, sharply criticizing the tendency of British society to harness science to its sense of "social stability" (EP 2:58, 61). Peirce also hints at a similar economic-based class elitism in his criticism of the Gospel of Greed in the "Cosmology Series" essay "Evolutionary Love," to which I turn in Part 2. He thus seems well aware that group membership can result in shared experience.

The socialization informing our individualized habit-taking involves our membership in various groups, including groups identified by race, sex, and a host of other factors. These groups are likely to reflect similar habit-taking in respect to societal forces that base privileged and oppressive treatment of people on group membership. Thus the similar habit-taking is not due to inborn instinctive habits shared by group members. That is to say, the similarity does not involve innate "essences" corresponding to each race, sex, and so on. Rather the commonality occurs because of shared experiences (or lack thereof) of discriminatory secondness. People of color and women, for example, often encounter racist and/or sexist secondness that targets them because of their group membership. Euro-American men do not often experience either of these types of secondness, and Euro-American women do not often experience racist secondness.

The Color Purple, beyond reflecting the experience of a unique synechistic individual, Alice Walker, also reflects the experiences of African American men and women living in the rural U.S. south in the early twentieth century (1982). The brutality of both racism during this era in the South and domestic violence are prominent themes, as are spirituality and love in the midst of suffering. Walker's portrayal of African American experience cannot be said to speak for all African Americans' experiences of racism and racism/sexism. Nonetheless, her novel is an invaluable contribution to socio-political inquiry in a country like the United States, which continues to suffer from racism and sexism.

Many people of color and women in the United States share experiences of racist and/or sexist secondness that highlight racist and sexist societal habits that are not yet fully eradicated despite the efforts of the civil rights and women's movements. Racist and/or sexist societal habits are the source of socio-political secondness experienced by these groups. For Euro-Americans, however, racist secondness is *not* commonly experienced. The same can be said for men and sexist secondness. Moreover, in the United States, human experience is falsely universalized by mainstream culture, according to a white male privileged norm that is supposedly not raced.[9] This promotes falsely universalized associations/habits/beliefs that racism and sexism are no longer significant factors in human experience in the United States. For Euro-Americans and men, these associations/habits/beliefs foster blindness to the ways in which U.S. society continues to operate according to background racist and sexist beliefs. Because of these phenomenological "blind spots," the testimony of non-hegemonic groups is all the more important for identifying unjust societal habits that are still in play. Of course, phenomenological blindness can happen on other fronts besides race and sex. The reader is invited to extrapolate regarding able-bodied privilege, economic privilege, heterosexual privilege, and so on.

In addition, regarding discussions among the politically powerful that *do* acknowledge the persistence of injustice in the United States, non-hegemonic synechistic groups can help challenge the false universalizations and conceptual misunderstandings that can characterize even this explicitly justice-promoting communal inquiry. For example, legal scholar Frank Wu writes about the prevalence of racism against Asian Americans in the United States, stressing that race issues are not accurately portrayed by a black-white paradigm (2003). Wu gives the following "modest suggestion":

> Whatever any of us concludes about race, we should start by including all of us. Whether we strive for moral principles or practical compromises, our vision must encompass everyone. Our leaders should speak to all individuals, about every group, and for the country as a whole. A unified theory of race, race relations,

and racial tensions must have whites, African Americans, Latinos, Asian Americans, Native Americans, and all the rest, and even within groups must include Arab Americans, Jewish Americans, white ethnicities, and so forth. Our theory is an inadequate account otherwise. (36)

Another example is provided by Linda Alcoff, who describes the problematic complexities for Latinos in the United States:

> The question of Latino identity's relationship to the conventional categories of race that have been historically dominant in the United States is a particularly vexing one. To put it straightforwardly, we simply don't fit. Racialized identities in the North have long connoted homogeneity and easily visible identifying features, but this doesn't apply to Latinos in the United States, nor even to any one national subset, such as Cuban Americans or Puerto Ricans. We have no homogeneous culture, we come in every conceivable color, and identities such as "mestizo" signify the very absence of boundaries. (2006, 229)

The non-hegemonic perspectives represented by Wu and Alcoff are sources of reasonableness, by which anti-racist inquiry can embrace diversity and complexity. I continue to invite the reader to extrapolate beyond the deep complexities of anti-racist inquiry to include the analogous complexities involved in anti-sexist, anti-heterosexist, and other forms of inquiry seeking justice for marginalized groups. If the United States is to live up to its ideal of justice for all, its inquiry must embrace the rich diversity of those who have suffered injustice past and present. This embrace is all the more important since these non-hegemonic perspectives are still often poorly represented in societal inquiry in the United States.

I do not mean to imply that non-hegemonic perspectives are useful only to the extent that they articulate blind spots in hegemonic discourse. Since my focus in this book is on revealing how these blind spots are created and sustained, I overrepresent the role of non-hegemonic voices in naming these oversights. Nonetheless, insights and experiences originating outside the hegemonically articulated reality can provide alternative visions of how reality may be articulated in the first place. This calls into question just how the United States and the "West" in general might look if others had shaped the mainstream discourse. For example, in his essay "Kinship with the World," Vine Deloria explains:

> In the Indian tradition we find continuous generations of people living in specific lands, or migrating to new lands, and having an extremely intimate relationship with lands, animals, vegetables, and all of life. . . .
>
> Indians do not simply learn survival skills or different ways to shape human utensils out of other natural things. In shaping those things, people have the responsibility to help complete their life cycles as part of the universe in the same way they are helping people. Human beings are not above nature or above the rest of the world. Human beings are incomplete without the rest of the world. Every species needs to give to every other species in order to make up a universe. (1999, 226)

It is beyond the scope of my project to give this passage the analysis it deserves. Given the current planetary crisis of global warming, however, the insights that humans are connected with, dependent on, and responsible to the rest of the natural world portray a deeply relevant alternative paradigm. Historically, however, this Native American vision was jettisoned by Euro-Americans who sought to appropriate land for themselves.[10]

The value of an individual's or synechistic group's perspective does not guarantee that the perspective will be embraced within hegemonic discourse in general or within a specific community of inquiry that is dominated by individuals belonging to hegemonic groups, such as Euro-Americans, heterosexuals, men, and so on. For example, as a result of internalized falsely universalized associations/habits/beliefs regarding race in the United States, testimony that racism is still present often faces dismissal. Bell hooks notes:

> Simply talking about race, white supremacy, and racism can lead one to be typecast, excluded, placed lower on the food chain in the existing white-supremacist system. . . . While more individuals in contemporary culture talk about race and racism, the power of

that talk has been diminished by racist backlash that trivializes it, more often than not representing it as mere hysteria. (2003b, 27)

Hooks also notes that Euro-American resistance to feedback about racism can occur because of habits that operate outside of consciousness, such that "liberal whites who are concerned with ending racism may *simultaneously* hold on to beliefs and assumptions that have their roots in white supremacy" (2003b, 30, my emphasis). For Euro-Americans, many of whom have not experienced racist secondness, the falsely universalized associations/habits/beliefs of human experience as *not* including racism can function nonconsciously. When this happens, testimony about racism can seem irrelevant, hypersensitive, overreactive, or crazy, because it runs against the hegemonic conceptualization of human experience. In "human experience" race is not a factor. To "make" race a factor, by testifying about racism, is thus problematic. The Euro-American making a dismissal, such as "You're just playing the race card," *may not realize* that he or she is acting according to a falsely universalized, Euro-American concept/association/habit/belief. This can make it difficult for Euro-Americans to come to terms with their unintentional racism, since they do not "see" it. This failure to see extends beyond unintentional racism to include many other forms of unintentional discrimination. Once again the reader is invited to extrapolate.

e. Nonconscious Dimensions of Association

Peirce notes that we are not always aware of why one idea is connected with another.[11] This can be because an association by contiguity can suggest an idea without being noticed. He examines "a fact of consciousness [that] usually . . . [passes] unnoticed in suggestions by contiguity, namely that when A suggests B, the compound idea AB intervenes" (CP 7.406; cf. CP 7.399). *A* in this case is an association/habit/belief, which suggests *B*, another association/habit/belief. For example, I am driving in my car and notice the light up ahead has just turned red. The association/habit/belief "red means stop" (R) suggests the association/habit/belief "braking enables me to stop"

(B). R suggests B, the intermediate RB intervening, something like "red light—need to brake." I do not usually *notice* the RB linkage, but it is there. Clearly the nonconscious suggestions fueled by contiguity give an evolutionary advantage. We need many of our habits to function automatically, as they suggest the firing of other survival-promoting habits, which suggest others, and so on. The complications would be prohibitive if humans had to think about every habit execution. Our homeodynamic maintenance directs a vast number of association-based suggestions that occur outside our awareness (cf. Damasio 1999, 228).

The degree of nonconsciousness varies. Nonconscious connections may reside at the margins of consciousness, so that they readily come into view when a conscious gaze is turned on them. Peirce gives the personal example of looking out from his writing table and seeing the family milking-cow. He soon thereafter thinks of bringing his wife a glass of milk. In hindsight he notes that his train of thought was unobtrusively informed by the idea of helping his wife, who was ill at the time and who would have benefited from the milk (CP 7.428–29, 435). The idea is readily available to him in hindsight, so that he can describe it:

> In my train of thought about the cow, I have no doubt that idea of *doing something* to help my wife was what made me notice the creature at all, and caused my thought to be active in that direction. The set *wife-milk* was in the deeper shaded part of consciousness. The set *cow-milk* joined itself to this and gave *wife-milk-cow*, and thence *wife-cow*. This did not emerge into the glare of attention but was working all the time. (CP 7.435)

Peirce can, with a little effort, readily identify the idea, or association/habit/belief—namely, "helping my wife," that guided the suggestions leading him from "cow" to "bringing my wife a glass of milk."

Other types of nonconscious associative suggestions are not so easily grasped by the individual thinker. My concern is with nonconscious associative suggestions that are driven by hegemonic associations, such as those informing racism, sexism, and other social ills. The specific type of nonconscious association I will be addressing more fully below is the subtle operation of exclusionary sympathy, by means of instinctive beliefs that are racist, sexist, or otherwise discriminatory. Hegemonic associations/habits/beliefs are often invisible to those who benefit from them, whether they function through individual behavior or institutional structures. Yet these same associations/habits/beliefs are often in plain view for many who are in non-hegemonic groups and experience corresponding socio-political secondness. Dismissal of testimony from these non-hegemonic groups often occurs, however, by means of the very associations/habits/beliefs they are in a position to identify. Voices of people of color and women, regarding racism and sexism, for example, are often characterized as, at best, mere complaining. On the one hand, such a summary dismissal reflects the hegemonic association/belief/habit that only the testimony of Euro-Americans or men counts, regarding racism or sexism, respectively (cf. Mills 1997, 60–61). On the other hand, this hegemonic belief about testimony is not likely to be *consciously* endorsed by the Euro-American or man who makes the dismissal. On the contrary, those who dismiss in this fashion often repudiate racism and sexism. I argue that these often well-intentioned individuals are acting from nonconscious racist and/or sexist beliefs.

Part 2: The Law of Mind and Society: Agapic versus Exclusionary Sympathy

"Sympathy" is the term Peirce uses to describe the law of mind as it functions in human communities. In its ideal agapic form, sympathy embraces as sources of growth the creative bursts of spontaneity that arise within the existing habit systems of a community. I call this "agapic sympathy." Sympathy can also play out non-agapically, excluding opportunities for growth by rejecting new elements that arise from existing habits. I call this "exclusionary sympathy." Similar to the problematic overlap among the authority, a priori, and science methods of fixing belief is the problematic overlap that can exist between exclusionary and agapic sympathy as they manifest in actual communities. The agapic ideal can be undermined by the instinctive, nonconscious functioning of exclusionary background beliefs.

a. Sympathy among Human Organisms

Peirce argues that, according to his law of mind, "corporate"[12] or communal personalities must exist (EP 1:350–51).

> It is true that when the generalisation of feeling has been carried so far as to include all within a person, a stopping-place, in a certain sense, has been attained; and further generalisation will have a less lively character. But we must not think it will cease. *Esprit de corps*, national sentiment, sym-pathy, are no mere metaphors. (EP 1:350)

In fact, if the right kind of experiments were conducted, Peirce suggests, there would probably be "evidence of the influence of such greater persons upon individuals" (EP 1:350). In addition, he notes that his account of the law of mind makes sense out of "the very extraordinary insight which some persons are able to gain of others from indications so slight that it is difficult to ascertain what they are" (EP 1:332).

The community is a macrocosm of the individual for Peirce. Interpersonal feelings among humans—*sym-pathy*—parallels the *intra*personal sympathy occurring within the human person's (body-)mind. At the individual level, a present feeling/idea is inescapably influenced intra-sympathetically by the community of existing feeling-systems (or associations/habits/beliefs) within the organism. Creativity arises from an individual's drawing insightfully on past associations/habits/beliefs. At the communal level, an individual community member is inescapably influenced sympathetically by other community members and by communal habits. At this level, the individual herself, as well as groups, can be sources of creativity, which arise amidst communal sympathetic influence and from which the community as a whole can benefit. Here, ideally, the community draws on the insights that arise among its members, viewing these insights as sources of growth.

b. God as Sympathetic Ideal: Agape

There are ambiguities in Peirce's use of the term "sympathy," which are elucidated by distinguishing between human sympathy and the divine agapic ideal. Peirce uses "sympathy" to convey the law of mind as it functions on the communal human plane—inclusively or exclusively. As noted above, I use the appellations "agapic sympathy" and "exclusionary sympathy" to convey this difference. At the level of the divine, the Christian God is agape. As such, God serves as a divine sympathetic[13] source that makes possible the growth of a universe. Let me note that Peirce does not conceive Christianity as rooted in strict dogmas or doctrines, a point that will be discussed more below. His emphasis on Christianity focuses on a loving community, whose role-models are God and Jesus Christ.[14] The spontaneous bursts of novelty through which the universe is created point back to God as an ultimate creative and loving agency that embraces these bursts as sources of growth (RLT 258–63; EP 1:297; Hausman 1999, 204). At the human level, however, the agapic ideal involves choice. Human communities have the freedom to adopt a non-agapic, exclusionary stance toward perspectives that differ from their own.

I. HOW AGAPE WORKS

Peirce's discussion of agape occurs in the final "Cosmology Series" essay, "Evolutionary Love." He suggests that agape characterizes the evolution of the universe, which he calls agapastic evolution or agapasm, noting that "[i]n genuine agapasm . . . advance takes place by virtue of a positive sympathy among the created springing from continuity of mind" (EP 1:362). He gives a detailed description of this type of evolution at the level of the individual human organism, who is herself a cosmos undergoing evolution. In agapastic evolution, generally speaking, new and growth-inducing elements enter into an organism's experience by means of "energetic projaculation" and habit: "energetic projaculation" describes the spontaneous creation of "new elements of form," and habit plays the dual role of both stabilizing the new form, so that it is not rejected by the organism outright, and harmonizing or adapting the new form into the "general morphology" of the organism (EP 1:360).

For example, a few years ago I unexpectedly came across a small community fair while I was out on a walk. Of the various community agencies that had display tables, one was the local chapter of the International Hospitality Council (IHC). The IHC was looking for native English-speaking women to facilitate international women's book groups for women new to the United States who were not fluent in English. The groups would be a way to meet people and to learn more about English in an informal setting. I signed up on the spot. This was an "energetic projaculation," a burst of newness into my experience (EP 1:360). Habit then played the role of stabilizing this newness, allowing me to incorporate it into my existing lifestyle, by regularly clearing my calendar and doing the footwork to coordinate and foster the group. A note of clarification is in order here. To the extent that I am directing the show in my microcosmic universe, I am analogous to God, as is every individual, on Peirce's scheme. Unlike God, I am embodied, my scope of creativity is vastly smaller, and agape need not be a mode of operation I embrace. Humans can reject an agapic response, as I do when I fail to embrace bursts of newness, such as the chance to join other new groups or to attend a lecture or rally, or any number of other opportunities.

Peirce notes that the movement of energetic projaculation and habit found in agapastic evolution is the same as the circular movement of agapastic love, which "at one and the same impulse project[s] creations into independency and draw[s] them into harmony" (EP 1:353, 361). The movement of God's agapic love creates while allowing for the independence of the created (cf. Hausman, 1999, p. 204). It also embraces the uniqueness of the created, harmonizing it through habit. Regarding the reading group, I tried to be as hands-off as possible, to let our group unfold naturally, independent of my preconceived expectations. The other group members decided what they wanted to read and how they wanted to build group community through social engagements beyond our regular meetings. I did my best to harmonize our group through habit, by serving as a reliable communication hub and securing copies of the readings for each of our meetings.

It is important to note that spontaneous bursts or energetic projaculations are not *purely* spontaneous—that is, uninfluenced by the backdrops against which they occur. At the level of the cosmos itself, this means that the spontaneous "firsts" that hail the dawning of a universe themselves arise out of the agapically infused original continuity, which is, arguably, God (RLT 258–63; EP 1:352–53). At the level of the human organism, spontaneity is informed by the inner-sympathetic influence of existing habit systems. My spontaneous desire to volunteer to facilitate the book group, for example, was influenced by my existing habits of doing community service, reading, and interest in women's issues.

Another way of expressing this point is to say that agape is *contagious*. The very love whereby God allows a universe to grow spontaneously is so attractive that the created is likely to take on its character, as my spontaneity took on the character of my habits (Ventimiglia 2001, 28–31). In his description of this phenomenon, Peirce appeals to the parent-child relationship, noting that agapastic evolution occurs "first, by the bestowal of spontaneous energy by the parent upon the offspring, and, second, by the disposition of the latter to catch the general idea of those about it and thus to subserve the general purpose" (EP 1:362). God is a parent-like presence (in a vague sense), who confers creative freedom on "children," be they the originary feelings out of which the universe is ultimately made or human organisms. In either case, God's creative love is probably attractive enough that it is adopted by the beloved. Probably. Agape does not force its purposes onto the beloved but rather influences the beloved through the beloved's own desire to imitate it (Ventimiglia 2001, 28–31). This is final causality at work, the causality of mind. God is agape, and agape provides the ideal model for the functioning of the human mind and community, a model that allows for organic growth through the "gentle force" of final causality.[15]

Agapastic evolution, then, allows for the *flow* of life, in which bursts of creativity play a significant role. This is a flow in which habit mediates between spontaneity and the secondness of the external environment. Whether it is the evolution of a universe, of a community, or of an individual human organism, agape provides an organic model for growth, a model in which spontaneity is embraced as an indispensable source of vitality.

II. AGAPIC VERSUS EXCLUSIONARY SYMPATHY

God's agape is an ideal to which human communities should aspire as they grow in mature self-control. Peirce stresses this theme through contrast in "Evolutionary Love," where he criticizes his culture's focus on greed instead of agape. His critique itself reflects the fact that humans are not preordained to embrace the agapic love modeled by God. Humanity has a choice regarding the agapic ideal. Were God to *force* humans to take an agapic stance toward others and themselves, God's agape would thereby be performatively contradicted. Agape does not force. Rather, it embraces what is different from itself, even and especially when that difference is contrary to its very nature (EP 1:353; Ventimiglia 2001, 28–31). God as agape, therefore, allows humans to reject agape. In its paradigmatic form, agape involves embracing what is "most bitterly hostile and negative to itself" (EP 1:353).[16]

In applying the agapic ideal to human communities, which I wish to do here, I must address a possible misunderstanding or (depending on context) manipulation of agape that is not explicitly acknowledged by Peirce. In fact, I think Peirce leaves himself open to this misunderstanding by not more explicitly outlining the differences between divine, infinite agape and human, finite agape. I agree with Carl Hausman that "Peirce's notion of agape must be modified when applied to finite contexts within the cosmos" (1974, 22).[17] I present such a modification here by showing, on Peircean terms, how the agapic ideal should be understood within human communities.

The possible misunderstanding/manipulation is this: Agape is characterized by embracing what is different, even and especially when this difference is threatening to oneself. Thus people in nonhegemonic groups who aspire to this ideal might think, or might be pressured by those in hegemonic groups to think, that it is appropriate to embrace growth-inhibiting belief-habits about themselves, such as "People of color are inferior," "Women are inferior," and so on.[18] I would argue that such an understanding of agape is incorrect on Peircean terms, even though on the face of it, agape seems to require an embrace of the different *no matter what*. Such an embrace might work at the divine level, but not on the human plane.

It is unreasonable on Peircean terms for a person in a non-hegemonic group to embrace growth-inhibiting beliefs about herself, especially when these beliefs promote her removal from the community of inquiry. It is also unreasonable for those in hegemonic groups to embrace such beliefs about others. Since Peirce requires the community of inquiry to be infinitely inclusive, it is unacceptable—and undermines reasonableness—to countenance beliefs that suggest that some humans do not belong.[19] While Peirce does not speak to this point explicitly in "Evolutionary Love," he does address it implicitly. In the same context as his discussions of agapic love, Peirce criticizes his culture's "gospel of greed" for excluding the "weak" from communal inquiry (EP 1:357–58, 362). He counters this ruthless, Darwinian "survival of the fittest" gospel with "[t]he gospel of Christ [that] says that progress comes from every individual merging his individuality *in sympathy with his neighbors*" (EP 1:357, my emphasis). The dynamics within this loving community manifest sincere care and concern.

At this point, let me pause to stress that Peirce's Christian community is not united by means of dogmatic or doctrinal beliefs. In fact, Peirce had many harsh words for the evolution of Christianity as an institution, even within the same essay as he praises the Christian ideal of agape (EP 1:352–53, 365–66; cf. Orange 1984, 48–49). I think this gives Peirce's ideas about agape a secular appeal that they would not have otherwise. The ideal community is Christian, not because its members are united via shared doctrines. Rather they are united in "life and feeling" and in the "positive sympathy" modeled by Christ and by God (EP 1:354, 362). As Hausman notes regarding Peirce's invocation of Christianity in "Evolutionary Love,"

> What Peirce stressed was a kind of altruism and concern for communities in contrast to a view that advocated self-interest for the individual. . . . [O]ne can treat the ideas Peirce proposed through the religious setting in ways that are, at least explicitly, nonreligious, unless *religion* is taken in a broad sense that excludes commitment to some institutional group or dogma and refers to any metaphysical commitment. (1999, 203)

In other words, Peirce's grounding of agape in Christian ideals does not assume a religious, in the sense of dogmatic or doctrinal, commitment on the part of his readers.

With that qualification in place, let us examine the general dynamics within Peirce's ideal Christian community. In this context, growth occurs through the contributions of all community members, not merely those considered strong, whatever "strong" might mean. Contrasting his Lamarckian evolution, which is fueled by agapic love, with the ruthlessness of Darwinian evolution that "rejects" the weak, Peirce notes, "In genuine agapasm, on the other hand, advance takes place by virtue of a positive sympathy among the created springing from continuity of mind" (EP 1:362). Human communities, created by God, grow by means of mutual care and concern among their members. As Doug Anderson notes, "We imitate God by expanding our realm of neighbors, thus . . . generalizing our concern" (1995a, 107, cf. 105). By means of mutual care and concern, reasonableness is promoted, as the uniqueness of individual community members is embraced by her community mates, which increases the diversity within the community.

This ideal caring community, then, does not expect its members to be united through *sameness*. Rather it expects them to be united in the midst of their differences. To understand what Peirce has in mind here, take an explanation he gives about colors along a spectrum, "There is in the nature of things no sharp line of demarcation between the three fundamental colors, red, green, and violet. But for all that they are really different" (EP 1:363).[20] Ideally community members do not erect "sharp lines of demarcation" between themselves but rather embrace their differences, even when these differences are threatening (EP 1:363, 353). This brings us back to a proper reading of agape, a reading that places the agapic ideal within a human community whose members respect reasonableness and thus (ideally) do not embrace belief-habits suggesting that they themselves or others should be excluded from the community.

Moreover, Peirce's discussion shows that the reasonableness that informs the agapic ideal involves genuine care. Community members ideally have sincere concern for each other. Thus the exclusion of some groups from communal membership or from communal respect and trustworthiness is viewed as unacceptable from the perspective of *caring about* those who would be affected by such exclusion. The agapic ideal manifests in a compassionate embrace of communal perspectives differing from one's own, even and especially when feedback from these differing perspectives is negative and might reflect negatively on oneself. In the context of my project, I see the agapic ideal as applying especially to those in hegemonic groups (such as Euro-Americans, heterosexuals, men, and so on) who have trouble honoring testimony about discrimination from those in non-hegemonic groups. In particular, testimony concerning *nonconscious* discrimination can be especially hard to hear, because the behavior was unintended and can challenge the hegemonic-group person's view of herself as *not* discriminatory—that is, not heterosexist, racist, sexist, and so on. Agape calls for an embrace of this testimony, even and especially when it is threatening in this way.

To demonstrate in detail how human sympathy can either reflect or stray from the agapic ideal, an extended example is useful. Recall that the motion of agape is circular, involving two movements: First, a creative projection of newness, and second, an embracing and stabilizing of this spontaneous novelty. When human sympathy is agapic, it completes the circle by allowing for both movements. An agapic analysis can be made of psychologist Harriet Lerner's efforts to organize "the first women's feminist conference at Menninger's Clinic" (Lerner 1993, 210). The directors were herself and another "white, middle-class, heterosexual" female colleague (211). Their objective was "to create a safe space in which to critique theory and share personal experience. We knew that the freedom to speak honestly and openly required a conference setting that offered a radical departure from patriarchal structures" (210). Lerner and her colleague followed this initial conference, which they named "Women in Context," with others "focused on such themes as 'Women and Self-Esteem' and 'Mothers and Daughters'" (210). In the midst of their satisfaction with the success of these conference meetings, a spontaneous burst came in the form of significant criticism about false universalization: "Minority women began to challenge the white, middle-class, heterosexual 'culture' of the conference" (210). This criticism was a creative projection of newness—it was the *first* movement of agapic sympathy.

The *second* movement involved Lerner and her colleague's embracing and stabilizing this spontaneity, by working to make subsequent conferences far more inclusive of diverse perspectives (Lerner 1993, 212–13). This second movement was all the more agapic since Lerner found it quite difficult to embrace the criticisms about lack of diversity. She felt defensive and overwhelmed, engaging in exclusionary self-dialogue: "I . . . said things to myself like 'But we *are* a white institution,' and 'I don't really know women of color who could lecture on this subject,' and 'Won't the quality of the conference suffer if we try to invite speakers of every race, class, and creed?'" (210, Lerner's emphasis). Despite her discomfort with embracing both the criticism itself and the diversity of future conferences, Lerner completed the second movement of the agapic circle by "co-direct[ing] an inclusive conference, giving real [versus merely token] space to those women's voices long silenced and oppressed" (213).

In addition, Lerner sustained her agapic attitude by accepting criticisms of this new inclusive conference:

> We did not all sit in a circle, hold hands, and sing "We Are the World." Significant differences emerged, including criticisms of our leadership. Some questioned whether a conference held in a white institution under the leadership of two white women was fully inclusive. Others questioned the politics of white women "giving space" in *their* conference to black women and others. In

keeping with the research on tokenism, these important challenges did not emerge (and probably wouldn't have been heard)
until there were significant numbers of minority women among
us. (1993, 213, Lerner's emphasis)

Lerner embraced this criticism. She notes:

I learned more about myself in that conference, albeit through my
errors, than I had in any other. And I gained a deeper appreciation of the fact that truth-telling . . . is, first and foremost, a matter
of context. For context determines not only what truths we will
feel safe to voice, but also what truths we can discover and know
about ourselves. (213)

These comments reflect Lerner's growth based on feedback from
women in non-hegemonic groups. Moreover, Lerner has written
about these experiences to help explain to others in hegemonic
groups how easily unintentional socio-political exclusion can happen
(210).

Thus, Lerner's practice of agape promoted her individual growth,
as well as the growth the community of feminists with which she was
working. Testimony from women of color and other non-hegemonic
perspectives helped her enlarge her understanding of unintentional
socio-political exclusion and unintentional false universalization. Her
corresponding associations/beliefs/habits expanded and became more
complex. So did the community of feminists with which she worked.
This growth was not easy. It involved significant habit change in
order to address the problems of false universalization. The second
round of criticism also showed Lerner that even her best efforts still
reflected white hegemony. Her openness to continued criticism reflects her openness to continued growth and to the fallible nature of
her best efforts.

Lerner's agapic stance needs to be put into perspective, lest it seem
that I am unduly glorifying those in hegemonic groups who "conde-
scend" to acknowledge non-hegemonic perspectives. My intent is not
to glorify Lerner but to use as a model her candid admission both
of her unintentionally exclusionary practices and of her difficulty in

hearing criticisms from non-hegemonic perspectives. Lerner's experiences show how Peirce's agapic ideal is *liberatory* in its call for open-heartedness. On the human plane, the agapic embrace of what is "most bitterly hostile and negative to" oneself includes being open to criticism that challenges one to the core (EP 1:353). Shannon Sullivan notes that white people often have difficulty coming to consciousness about white privilege, because it "disrupt[s] their sense of themselves as morally good" (2006, 128).[21] Racism and other "-isms" are viewed so negatively in contemporary mainstream U.S. society that it can be difficult for someone to hear that her behavior reflects "-isms" to any extent. This fear of being discriminatory is often problematically coupled with the common-sense mainstream assumption that one cannot behave in a heterosexist, racist, sexist, etc., fashion unless one intends too (Alcoff 2006, 188). Fear of a challenge to one's self-concept as "*not* heterosexist, racist, sexist, etc.," receives illegitimate reassurance from the assumption that unintentional "-isms" are not possible. In contrast, agape calls for the embrace of feedback that one's behavior is, however unintentionally, discriminatory. It calls for listening and for openness to change.

Agape can be applied as an affective tool that those in privileged groups, such as Euro-Americans, heterosexuals, men, and so on, can use to hold in place negative feedback from those in non-hegemonic groups. It is a tool, to borrow from Patricia Williams, for "listening across that great divide," for "allow[ing] oneself to be held in a state of suspended knowing" (1997, 74). Agape is a strategy that those in privileged positions can use to push past an initial, and often strong, urge to dismiss negative feedback from non-hegemonic groups. The resistance of this urge makes the completion of the second movement of the agapic circle possible, whereby associations/habits/beliefs expand, *grow*, to embrace diversity.

In contrast to agapic sympathy, exclusionary sympathy includes the first movement but rejects the second movement of agape's sympathetic circle. It acknowledges the creative newness but refuses to embrace and stabilize it. In terms of habit-taking, exclusionary sympathy involves clinging to present habit systems *as they are*. It rejects growth. Lerner would have been exclusionary in her sympathy if she had rejected the feedback about diversity by portraying it as mere complaining, overreaction, "playing the race card," etc.

The *first* movement—the spontaneous, creative burst of newness—is a part of human sympathy regardless of type, agapic or exclusionary. In addition, this spontaneity is not freestanding but, as noted above, emerges amidst the backdrop of existing habit systems. It results from the intricate sympathetic coalescence that exists among the various components of existing habits. The spontaneity of the feedback at Lerner's conference, for example, arose from habits of feminist discourse and the goal of the conference itself: "to create a safe space in which to critique theory and share personal experience. We knew that the freedom to speak honestly and openly required a conference setting that offered a radical departure from patriarchal structures" (1993, 210). The critical feedback—that the conference was too white, middle class, and heterosexual—arose from these same habits, reflecting honesty and openness, as well as critique of theory and of patriarchal structures.

This is a significant point for my project, because hegemonic or oppressive communities often entrench themselves against changes requested or demanded by non-hegemonic groups within the community. Yet these very changes, from a Peircean point of view, are *by-products* of existing social aims or other associations/habits/beliefs. Recall Chapter 3's discussion of "All men are created equal." The challenges that arose from people of color and women, who were excluded from the implementation of this ideal belief-habit in practice, were grounded in the very belief-habit in question, namely, that "All men are created equal." Their challenges were creative bursts (first movement) that were rooted in the very ideal in question, yet were rejected by a majority of the founding fathers, who thereby rejected the second movement, that is, the agapic embrace of the new element. Mills notes, for example, "A lot of black thought has simply revolved around the insistent demand that whites *live up to their own (ostensibly universalist) principles*, so that African-Americans such as David Walker could challenge American Slavery and white supremacy in the name of the Declaration of Independence . . ." (1998, 5, Mills's emphasis).[22]

The deciding factor for what type of human sympathy is at play is whether or not the *second* movement of the sympathetic circle occurs. Agapic sympathy completes both movements, as Lerner did with the conference feedback. Exclusionary sympathy involves only the first movement. That is to say, the spontaneous bursts occur, but without subsequent embrace. Peirce's depiction of the authority state in "Fixation of Belief" is a paradigmatic example of a community that routinely rejects this second movement. In fact, it takes precautionary measures to ensure the first movement never occurs in the first place. Through education and social threat, the authoritative state attempts to forestall or silence the emergence of perspectives differing from its hegemonic decree (W 3:250–51, 255–56). It attempts to foster the internalization of disempowering habits in individual community members, so that they will refrain from voicing unique perspectives that challenge hegemonic norms. It attempts to manipulate communal sympathy to its own ends, rallying community members around an exclusionary cause—namely, the hegemonic associations/habits/ beliefs dictated by those in power.

c. Communal Potential: Agapic Sympathy

Agapic sympathy promotes the internalization by community members of empowering habits, which fuel a vision of diverse others as valued participants in communal inquiry. In "Evolutionary Love," describing the ideal Christian community, Peirce writes, "The gospel of Christ says that progress comes from every individual merging his individuality in sympathy with his neighbors" (EP 1:357). As noted above, the term "merge" need not require the surrender of the unique characteristics of the individuals merged. Colors on a spectrum are distinct while blending with the colors on either side of them (EP 1:363). The merging of individuals, then, can mean that they become continuous, with no clear markings between them and in mutual concern for one another. If Peirce were striving for a stronger sense of merging, whereby all individuality was sacrificed, he would jeopardize the spontaneity that is required for the growth of human persons and human communities. Christ did, after all, tell the Christian not to hide her light and not to bury her talents.[23] Peirce stresses that "the ideal of conduct will be to execute our little function in the operation of the creation [of the universe]" (EP 2:255). This small part may involve serving as a source of communal spontaneity, where one's voice challenges the existing social structures.

As noted earlier, Peirce saw himself this way within the community of science. The *Monist* "Cosmology Series" itself involved the presentation and defense of novel cosmological hypotheses that he offered as creative contributions to scientific inquiry. He saw his ideas as sympathetically influenced by scientists and other thinkers present and past, as well as involving innovative connections. Peirce's work in this series constituted a direct challenge to the necessitarian determinism that was in vogue among his scientific contemporaries. For Peirce, the ideal community of science embraces the agapic ideal, since this community must be infinite and indefinite in scope. This way any present community remains open to new perspectives that promote growth in knowledge.[24]

Let me close this account of agape with an additional, and tragic, connection with Peirce's life. In his later years, Peirce experienced a distinctly non-agapic rejection by his academic and scientific communities of inquiry. In fact, at the time he was writing about agape, Peirce was coping with the loss of an academic post at John Hopkins University, in 1884, as well as the loss of his position (a scientific post) at the United States Coast and Geodetic Survey, in 1891 (Brent 1998, 202).[25] In both cases, the brilliance of Peirce's work could not withstand the critical gaze of those who disapproved of his social character and unconventional religious views, as well as (in the case of the U.S. Coast and Geodetic Survey) his erratic and undependable work habits. This loss of social and professional standing affected Peirce profoundly, sending him, eventually, into poverty.[26] Writing to William James, in 1897, Peirce notes that "a new world of which I knew nothing, and of which I cannot find that anybody who has written has really known much, has been disclosed to me, the world of misery" (quoted in Brent 1998, 259–60; cf. 261–62). This sensitivity to the poor (if not to people of color and women) is reflected in his critique of the Gospel of Greed characterizing his society and in his efforts to defend those whom society deemed "weak" (EP 1:357, 362; Brent 1998, 259–62).

d. Communal Critique: The Gospel of Greed

Peirce's critique of his nineteenth-century culture's penchant for greed, in "Evolutionary Love," is a critique of exclusionary sympathy. He notes that the most prominent characteristic of nineteenth century culture is profit-seeking economics: "Intelligence in the service of greed ensures the justest prices, the fairest contracts, the most enlightened conduct of all the dealings between men, and leads to the *summum bonum*, food in plenty and perfect comfort. Food for whom? Why, for the greedy master of intelligence" (EP 1:354). Greed, then, characterizes the evolutionary engine of nineteenth-century culture's progress.

> [T]he great attention paid to economical questions during our century has induced an exaggeration of the beneficial effects of greed and of the unfortunate results of sentiment, until there has resulted a philosophy which comes unwittingly to this, that greed is the great agent in the elevation of the human race and in the evolution of the universe. (EP 1:354)

Greed is a philosophy that endorses the doctrine of "survival of the fittest," such that the strong become stronger, and the weak become weaker or die off.[27]

The Gospel of Greed focuses on the prosperity of the individual while neglecting his or her social situatedness: "[T]he conviction of the nineteenth century is that progress takes place by virtue of every individual's striving for himself with all his might and trampling his neighbor under foot whenever he gets a chance to do so" (EP 1:357). This conviction is at odds with Peirce's portrayal of synechism, in which the individual and her community are continuous and interdependent. The Peircean human community is a macroscopic person, such that every individual member has a contribution to make, not unlike the cells in the human body, to the overall growth of the organism.[28] Thus, not only is it nonsensical for a human person to conceive of herself or himself as completely independent of other community members, it also undermines the growth of the community as a whole. In contrast to this naive individualism, Peirce's vision of the Gospel of Christ involves teamwork and compassion, whereby "progress comes from every individual merging his individuality in sympathy with his neighbors" (EP 1:357).

The Gospel of Greed is not as individualistic as it portrays itself to be. Peirce highlights the situatedness of the greed-individuals in a passage quoted above: "Intelligence in the service of greed ensures the justest prices, the fairest contracts, the most enlightened conduct of all the dealings *between men*, and leads to the *summum bonum*, food in plenty and perfect comfort. *Food for whom?* Why, for *the greedy master of intelligence*" (EP 1:354, my emphasis). In this context, Peirce falls shy of specifying the socio-economic and political elitism that underlies the Gospel of Greed. He does, however, seem to realize that underwriting the individualist selfishness of his culture was a hegemonic group. Charting the course of the Gospel of Greed in nineteenth century United States and Europe, was a *class* of wealthy, privileged people, most of whom were propertied men of European descent. The *individuals* who were ruthlessly exploiting or destroying the "weak" were, for the most part, members of this *group*. Peirce's criticism of their blindness to their social situatedness could have been rendered more specific, by naming their social group as powerful, affluent Euro-American men. It should be noted that Peirce's 1901 criticisms of Karl Pearson's *The Grammar of Science* (1900, second ed.), noted above, provide a more explicit naming of social situatedness, as Peirce criticizes Pearson for making the stability and happiness of "British society" the goal of science (EP 2:58, 61). This goal included, for Pearson, an endorsement of eugenics as a way to limit procreation among the "weak" of society (1892, 10, 33).[29]

In the context of his present critique, Peirce's group-oriented criticism of greed is also implied in a group-oriented articulation of the survival of the fittest—an articulation that he makes in the context of describing Darwinian, or tychastic, evolution (evolution driven by chance):

> [I]n the tychastic evolution progress is solely owing to the distribution of the napkin-hidden talent of the rejected servant among those not rejected, just as ruined gamesters leave their money on the table to make those not yet ruined so much the richer. It makes the felicity of the lambs just the damnation of the goats, transposed to the other side of the equation. (EP 1:362)

This particular articulation of greed-based evolution highlights the social consequences that can arise from the denial of both social situatedness and agapic sympathy. Exclusionary sympathy rejects creative, different perspectives, refusing the agapic embrace. In this passage, these rejected perspectives are those of the "goats," or "ruined gamesters." This rejection, if we apply more context from U.S. history, is possible because the "lambs" (or the unruined card players) are in a position of *power* that enables them not only to exclude the "goats", but to *exploit* them. The "goats" are not only denied a voice in the evolution of humanity; their resources are "transposed to the other side of the equation." It is striking that Peirce could have written this in the post–Civil War United States in 1893, yet without an acknowledgment of the parallel between his lamb/goats metaphor and the slavery of African Americans or the genocide, land theft, and treaty violation perpetuated against Native Americans.

I. EPISTEMOLOGY, "WEAKNESS," AND SCIENCE

By identifying the greed-promoters as a group, we can better trace their activity as a finite community of inquiry that practices exclusionary sympathy, shutting out perspectives that differ from their own. The greed-promoters ignore or demolish the perspective of those they deem "weak," on the assumption that weakness renders one's interest irrelevant, or even detrimental, to social inquiry.[30] Yet this social exclusivity undermines the epistemological soundness of communal inquiry. While a hegemonic group may have the power to ignore non-hegemonic perspectives, this ignorance does not nullify the growth-promoting value of those perspectives. Examples supporting this point abound. To give but two: A Native American view of humanity's kinship with the land, noted above, is poignantly relevant today, in 2010, in the midst of the global warming crisis (Deloria 1999, 226). W. E. B. Du Bois's essay "The Conservation of Races" (1897) provides another example. Du Bois argues that each human race has a unique contribution to make to human development on the world stage. This being the case, those of African descent in America need to throw off an identity that strives for absorption within Euro-American culture. They need to embrace their heritage, voice, and potential for contribution to humanity's growth:

> [I]f in America it is to be proven for the first time in the modern world that not only Negroes are capable of evolving individual men like Toussaint, the Saviour, but are a nation stored with wonderful possibilities of culture, then their destiny is not a servile imitation of Anglo-Saxon culture, but a stalwart originality which shall unswervingly follow Negro ideals. (Du Bois 2001, 87)[31]

A hegemonic culture practicing exclusionary sympathy cannot invalidate non-hegemonic contributions to cultural growth. Hegemony may refuse to listen to alternative voices, but the value of these voices is unaffected by this refusal. This is especially true when hegemonic culture is the *source* of claims of inferiority regarding non-hegemonic groups.

Because a hegemonic cultural group is often in the position to "tell the story" of how reality works, often to the detriment of non-hegemonic groups, the notion of "weakness" must be problematized in order to promote the agapic ideal. The label "weak," in the context of the Gospel of Greed, seems to serve as a one-word argument for the legitimacy of exploitation and oppression. Yet "weak" is a very relative term. Martha Nussbaum makes this point regarding disability, showing it be a matter of perspective and power:

[A] handicap does not exist simply "by nature," if that means independently of human action. We might say that an impairment
in some area or areas of human functioning may exist without
human intervention, but it only becomes a handicap when society
treats it in certain ways. Human beings are in general disabled:
mortal, weak-eyed, weak-kneed, with terrible backs and neck,
short memories, and so forth. But when a majority (or the most
powerful group) has such disabilities, society will adjust itself to
cater for them. (2004, 306)[32]

Labeling a group "weak" can serve the hegemonic purpose of dismissal, by placing a non-hegemonic group (along with its individual
members) *outside* the realm of legitimate participation in communal
inquiry. When this dismissal occurs, however, left unchallenged are
important dimensions of the supposed weakness. In what capacity is
the group in question considered weak? Have they been *rendered*
weak? If so, by what or whom? Was coercion involved? Was injustice
involved? All but the first of these questions can be appropriately answered only by those deemed "weak" themselves. They have, however, been hegemonically dismissed from communal inquiry. Their
testimony does not "count," even though they provide an important
epistemic perspective on the weakness in question. What is left is a
hegemonic story in which only socio-politically sanctioned voices
have a say.

In terms of the pragmatic maxim and U.S. history, note that
"weak" individuals and groups have provided information on the habitual effects of the aims/concepts devised and implemented by the
powerful. The aim of wealth shared by the hegemonic elite *resulted
in*, among other things, the barbaric treatment of African Americans
and Native Americans. When the voices of these non-hegemonic,
"weak" groups were dismissed or ignored, so were the epistemic perspectives they provided. Yet these perspectives revealed stark contradictions. Powerful Euro-American, propertied males proclaimed,
"All men our equal," yet their own freedom was premised on genocide, land theft, treaty violation and slavery.[33] In terms of the gam-
bling metaphor cited above, African American slaves and Native

Americans are some of the metaphorical "rejected servants," the "ruined gamesters" whose resources have made the propertied Euro-American males "so much the richer" (EP 1:362). The "felicity" of these Euro-Americans, in this case, has been "just the damnation of the" African American slaves and the Native Americans (EP 1:362). Included among the "rejected" are other groups that have been, and continue to be, exploited—such as the poor, women, and people living in "Third World" countries—in order to bolster the economic stability of those who profit most from capitalism.[34]

II. THE APPLICATION PROBLEM REVISITED

The Gospel of Greed undermines Peirce's agapic ideal for communal growth. Its embrace of social Darwinism results in the rejection of those considered "weak." This rejection, as noted above, undermines the community's potential for growth because the valuable perspectives of the "weak" are excluded. The promoters of greed are *unreasonable* in a Peircean sense, because their attitude toward the "weak" reflects a refusal to include diverse perspectives, the embrace of which reason requires. Moreover, taking the United States as our focus, "weakness" itself was projected onto groups like African Americans and Native Americans by those in power, a self-serving rationalization for oppressing and exploiting these groups.

What resulted historically was that scientific efforts made to verify the "weakness"—or "inferiority"—of African Americans and Native Americans involved circular reasoning, whereby the very racial hierarchies supposedly under investigation were assumed true by the investigating scientists. Stephen Jay Gould notes, "In assessing the impact of science upon eighteenth- and nineteenth-century views of race, we must first recognize the cultural milieu of a society whose leaders and intellectuals did not doubt the propriety of racial ranking—with Indians below whites, and blacks below everybody else" (1981, 31). Interestingly enough, Gould conducted extensive research into Samuel Morton's (1799–1851) infamous skull-measuring projects, which were widely acclaimed in their day and also "proved" the superiority of Caucasians, as a result of their supposedly larger skulls, over

Native Americans and African Americans. Gould found astonishing amounts of data manipulation and unduly biased fudging that favored Caucasians and/or disfavored non-Caucasian races (1981, 50–69). Yet he also notes that there was no evidence of *conscious* fraud on Morton's part. Gould concludes that Morton's biases were so deep seated as to function "*unconscious*[ly]" (55, Gould's emphasis; cf. 54–56, 69). The fact that such exclusionary background beliefs can function outside of conscious awareness (for which I use the term "*non*consciously") was discussed last chapter in the context of how the authority and a priori methods can shape the background beliefs that inform scientific practice. This scenario creates an application problem for the scientific method as this method is articulated in the Logic of Science series, because even sincerely anti-discriminatory scientists can unwittingly act against Peirce's ideal.

The presence of nonconscious beliefs that unwittingly inform scientific inquiry raises an analogous problem regarding the agapic ideal. Following Gould's interpretation, Morton is an example of a scientist who *did not realize* the exclusionary bias informing his reasoning. This points to the possibility that consciously *agapic*-minded scientists or other inquirers may *think* they are being inclusive (anti-racist, anti-sexist, etc.) while in fact they are nonconsciously acting out instinctive exclusionary (racist, sexist, etc.) beliefs. In other words, nonconscious exclusionary sympathy can short-circuit an agapic response without a person's or community's even realizing it.

For example, Linda Alcoff describes how a Chicana friend of hers, who was an untenured female faculty member at the time, was demoted at her third-year review by an all-white "department majority," based on the testimony of one disgruntled graduate student—a white male who was her teaching assistant (2001, 66–67). Alcoff's friend considered his complaints to be "groundless . . . actually based in his discomfort in the position of teaching assistant to a Chicana" (66). His testimony was honored over hers, however, despite the fact that she received consistently high teaching evaluations that were *above* the college faculty mean. In addition, she "acted as the beloved advisor of the Latina student group, . . . cooked for her students every semester, . . . had many great student-teacher relationships, and . . . had already published one book and received a major grant to write her second" (67). In fact, *no one else was consulted* about this complaint other than the student himself. The contract of Alcoff's friend was "reduced in length and made contingent on the condition that she prove herself a better teacher" (66).

Alcoff spoke to her friend's white male department chair, "urging him to consult" with other students and others at the university who "would be in a better position to evaluate the conflicting claims" (2001, 67). Alcoff believed that the chair, to some extent, had her friend's best interests in mind, wanting to treat her fairly, but he nonetheless "reject[ed] out of hand the possibility that cultural difference played any role" in the white male graduate student's complaint (67).

In this case we have one woman of color in the midst of—except for her—an all-white cast: the complainant, the department chair, and the remaining department members.[35] And both the complainant and the department chair are also male. The department chair wanted to treat Alcoff's friend fairly yet refused to consider issues of racism and sexism. Alcoff speculates that this was because he assumed fairness "meant treating her as an individual without social identity and resisting the possibility that such facts [about her social identity] might be relevant unless *he himself* could see without a doubt that they were so" (2001, 67, Alcoff's emphasis).

Applying a Peircean interpretation, I would argue that the department chair is, on a *conscious* level, trying to treat Alcoff's friend just as he would any other faculty member and thus sees himself as doing right by her. Again, *consciously* he is not trying to degrade her testimony or undermine her career. Arguably he is trying to act agapically, versus exclusively, by striving for fairness, not allowing her difference in race and sex to be used against her. He is embracing, versus excluding, her right to due process for her contract renewal. At the same time, however, exclusionary sympathy is strongly present. A white male student's word is taken over hers, despite her glowing teaching and publishing record. The chair assumes that appealing to his own, white male experience is sufficient to determine that racism and sexism are not at play. He excludes as irrelevant the perspectives of Alcoff's friend, Alcoff herself, and the others she urged him to consult about this case. In other words, he is rejecting testimony that comes from others whose experience and expertise about racism and sexism are fundamentally different from his own. The department chair *is* rejecting the different, but is, arguably, not aware that he is doing so. We could say that he sees himself as satisfying agape by treating Alcoff's friend as a colleague, even though as a woman of color she is different from him. Thus he secures due process for her. Yet he fails to recognize this situation as requiring a much stronger form of agape than he is practicing, one that truly embraces her differences as opposed to asserting that they are not relevant.

Peirce's association writings can be used to illustrate how nonconscious exclusionary sympathy can occur by means of hegemonic background beliefs. While Peirce does not explicitly mention this nonconscious influence, he does describe what I would call nonconscious *agapic* sympathy. I extrapolate from this account, knowing that Peirce is open to examining cultural structures that can undermine social growth.

As discussed above, Peirce's evolutionary engine is agapic love, which exerts a noncoercive influence on the beloved through a gentle and subtle sympathetic influence that shapes spontaneous creativity, but without force. In his 1890s association writings, Peirce discusses an agapic sympathetic influence that occurs without one's explicit awareness, by means of one's social matrix.

> Our daily life is full of involuntary determinations of belief. It is the egotism of the ego, or field of attention, which imposes on [us] with its . . . conviction that whatever is known is known through it. It is not so. *I converse with a man and learn how he is thinking [without his having "'stated' the fact in accurate forms of speech"] . . . . [H]ow I have found out his thought is too subtle a process for this psychologist writing to find out.* (CP 7.447, ca. 1893, my emphasis)

Peirce gives two more examples: (1) learning a new slang word without ever hearing a formalized definition but rather through "ironical, twisted, humorous sentences whose meaning is turned inside out and tied in a hard knot," and (2) our sympathetic attunement to animals in our care (CP 7.447).[36] The nonconscious influence at play here, I would argue, is *agapic* sympathy, because it involves the embrace of persons, words, and animals that exist outside oneself. While Peirce claims not to know how this influence could occur, it is likely to be fueled, at least in part, by nonconscious agapic background beliefs, which allow for subtle communication and a host of other affective-semiotic associations.

In this context, Peirce does not address the fact that sympathy can be exclusionary. But clearly there could be nonconscious exclusionary background beliefs that foster a *failure* to connect with other persons, words, and animals. From the standpoint of U.S. mainstream culture past and present, we can easily adjust each of the examples Peirce has given in the above passage. I will focus only on the first.[37]

Peirce and his male interlocutor, who understand each other through subtle references that neither can fully explicate, are experiencing the nonconscious influence of *agapic* sympathy. They are each *embracing* the perspective of the other. Implicit in this male bonding, however, are the usual suspects, such as race and sex, and probably education and social pedigree. We could easily adjust this scenario to include a Euro-American affluent man who invariably *fails* to understand someone outside of his circle of fellows. Here *exclusionary* sympathy would be at play.

For another example, in *The Souls of Black Folk* (1903), Du Bois gives a poetic description of the general sympathetic divide between African Americans and Euro-Americans in the U.S. South at the turn of the twentieth century:

> Now if one notices carefully one will see that between these two worlds, despite much physical contact, and daily intermingling, there is almost no community of intellectual life or point of transference where the thoughts and feelings of one race can come into direct contact and sympathy with the thoughts and feelings of the other. (Du Bois 1989, 128)

While I am not saying that Du Bois wrote this passage with Peirce in mind, it does arguably portray a nonconscious functioning of an exclusionary sympathy, which can shut down the possibility of the subtle harmony that Peirce finds with his male, presumably Euro-American, interlocutor. Du Bois notes that this estrangement between the races is fueled by beliefs each group has about the other: "[O]ne side thinks all whites are narrow and prejudiced, and the other thinks educated Negroes dangerous and insolent" (129). To the extent that such beliefs function in the automatic everydayness that Du Bois describes, they are arguably functioning nonconsciously, at least for many white people. Whites are not subject to the same racist secondness that targets African Americans, and thus whites have the luxury of not paying attention to large-scale racist dynamics that they themselves can unwittingly perpetuate. Habits of white privilege often function nonconsciously (in the automaticity of firstness). In such cases, the first movements of sympathy are the various points of "physical contact" and "daily intermingling" that are spontaneous occasions for connection and growth (128). But the work done by nonconscious exclusionary beliefs often rejects the second movement.

I am concerned with the exclusionary effects of nonconscious hegemonic privilege in particular, since it reflects a structural power imbalance that can undermine communal inquiry. The failure of people of color to connect sympathetically (either consciously or nonconsciously) with Euro-Americans, in a hegemonically white society, is not likely to result in the dismissal of the Euro-American, hegemonic perspective. In contrast, when Euro-Americans fail to understand people of color, the dismissal of the non-hegemonic perspective(s) can easily follow. Factors exacerbating this imbalance are the ongoing overrepresentation of the Euro-American perspective in various communities of inquiry in the United States, as well as the continued false universalization of the Euro-American, middle-class experience as general to all humans. In this respect, Ralph Ellison's prologue to *Invisible Man* provides a telling metaphor:

I am an invisible man. No, I am not a spook like those who haunted Edgar Allan Poe. . . . I am a man of substance, of flesh and bone, fiber and liquids—and I might even be said to possess a mind. I am invisible, understand, simply because people refuse to see me. . . .

. . . That invisibility to which I refer occurs because of a peculiar disposition of the eyes of those with whom I come in contact. A matter of the construction of their *inner* eyes, those eyes with which they look through their physical eyes upon reality. (1980, 3, emphasis in original)

Ellison's African American narrator speaks, from a non-hegemonic position, of the racist eyes that "refuse to see" him as a person. I interpret this refusal, in the context of my project, as at least in part a manifestation of the erasure that occurs when Euro-American white reality is falsely universalized and enforced so that the perspectives of people of color are excluded from personhood itself (Mills 1998, 8–9; Nussbaum 1997, 87–88). Yet many white people who perpetuate this false universalization have no idea they are engaging in exclusionary sympathy, because the belief-habits involved are nonconscious.

Historically speaking, nonconscious exclusionary sympathy has been prevalent with respect to the non-hegemonic perspectives of people of color, women, and others, because of racist, sexist, and other discriminatory background beliefs that are *shared by* Euro-Americans, men, and/or other hegemonic groups. This pattern is of special concern for scientific or everyday communal inquiry, since Euro-American men (and others in hegemonic groups) often continue to be overrepresented and to hold more power than do people of color, women, and others in non-hegemonic groups. These concerns are reflected in Linda Alcoff's description of her friend, a Chicana, being demoted, because of the unquestioned testimony of a white male, by an all-white committee headed by a white male department chair. I would argue that the *shared* hegemonic bias within the all-white—except for Alcoff's friend—cast fueled oblivion about the racism and sexism at play, such that the department chair could refuse to even consider these factors (Alcoff 2001, 67). Let me note once more that hegemonic imbalances do not occur only in the case of Euro-American men. Anyone who is privileged in some respect can render invisible the corresponding non-hegemonic perspective.

Since exclusionary beliefs can *nonconsciously* close down a sympathetic harmony between those in hegemonic groups and those in non-hegemonic groups, the latter's perspectives can be excluded *even by* people who—on a conscious level—are anti-racist, anti-sexist, etc. Hence the application problem that undermines the scientific method (of the Logic of Science essays) also manifests in the context of the agapic ideal. In other words, people who are consciously committed to the infinitely inclusive community of inquiry *and to the agapic ideal* can nonetheless perpetuate the exclusion of non-hegemonic groups.

e. Moving toward Critical Common-sensism

By way of transition into Chapter 5's discussion of Critical Commonsensism, let me highlight points from two of Peirce's essays: "Philosophy and the Conduct of Life" (1898) and "Pragmatism as the Logic of Abduction" (1903). Peirce's use of the terms "instinct" and "instinctive mind," respectively, in these essays highlights that background beliefs can be the repository of prejudice and can also function nonconsciously.

In "Philosophy and the Conduct of Life," Peirce stresses how often humans act from instinct even when they think otherwise:

> Men many times fancy that they act from reason when, in point of fact, the reasons they attribute to themselves are nothing but excuses which unconscious instinct invents to satisfy the teasing "whys" of the *ego*. The extent of this self delusion is such as to render philosophical rationalism a farce. (RLT 111, Peirce's emphasis)

In fact, it is completely appropriate to trust instincts in the immediacy of vitally important life issues. Yet it is *just as* imperative *not* to simply trust instinct in the context of scientific inquiry.

Peirce is calling for a scientific philosophical spirit in which thinkers subject their instincts to doubt and empirical testing. Granting that scientists often act from the abductive instinct when forming hypotheses about natural laws, he affirms that instinct alone does not rule in such cases but must be subject to careful testing: "True, we are driven oftentimes in science to try the suggestions of instinct; but we only *try* them, we compare them with experience, we hold ourselves ready to throw them overboard at a moment's notice from experience" (RLT 112).

Peirce uses the terms "sentiment" and "instinct" synonymously in this essay, which points to the social-shaping of instinct. He boldly asserts, "It is the instincts, the sentiments, that make the substance of the soul. Cognition is only its surface, its locus of contact with what is external to it" (RLT 110). Recall Chapter 1's discussion of how sentiments can be socially shaped for Peirce, and thus instincts can be socially shaped too.[38] There I cited from a 1902 discussion of logic, where Peirce notes,

> If I may be allowed to use the word "habit," without any implication as to the time or manner in which it took birth, so as to be equivalent to the corrected phrase "habit or disposition," that is, as some general principle working in a man's nature to determine how he will act, then an instinct, in the proper sense of the word, is an inherited habit, or in more accurate language, an inherited disposition. *But since it is difficult to make sure whether a habit is inherited or is due to infantile training and tradition, I shall ask leave to employ the word "instinct" to cover both cases.* (CP 2.170, my emphasis)

In the present essay, this social-shaping of instinct is implied in Peirce's use of "sentiment" and "instinct" interchangeably when referring to "vital interest[s]," such as one's "religious life" and "code of morals" (RLT 111).

Central to my project is Peirce's insistence, in "Philosophy and the Conduct of Life," that our instincts, outside of vitally important topics, must be subject to criticism. Since instincts are paired, at least to an extent, with social-shaping, this criticism includes socially shaped instinctive beliefs that may interfere with the reasoning process. Failure to scrutinize our instincts, among other things, leaves us open to the felt certainty of social prejudice, for example, such as the prejudice that drove racist and sexist pseudoscience in the eighteenth and nineteenth centuries, as discussed above (Tuana 1993, 34–50; Gould 1981, chapters 2–4).

In "Pragmatism as the Logic of Abduction," Peirce problematizes our perceptual judgments by noting that they lie on a continuum with *abductions*. Perceptual judgments, for our purposes, are simply our perceptions. But these perceptions are, Peirce argues, *interpretative*—they have a "for me" character built into them. Adopting the Peirce's terminology of perception, we can say that we have no direct access to the *percept*. The percept is the brute secondness by which a sensation/feeling comes to us *hic et nunc* (here and now). There is no perspective from which to contemplate it or even talk about it: "Given a percept, this percept does not describe itself; for description involves analysis, while the percept is whole and undivided" (CP 7.626). The only way we can think about or describe a percept is through the perceptual *judgment*, by means of which I can say something like "That appears to be a yellow chair" (CP 7.626).[39] Peirce also notes, "There is no objection to saying that 'The chair appears yellow' means 'The chair appears *to me* yellow'" (CP 7.630 n. 11). Our perceptions have an interpretive character, which reflects the perspective of the person perceiving, even though this "for me" character is often so subtle as to escape notice.

Abduction is the mode of reasoning by which we render explanations for surprising or unexpected facts in our experience. We are confronted with a puzzling or surprising effect, and reason back to the cause. For example, years ago I went to California for the first time, having lived in the Midwestern United States for all my life. At the beginning of my stay, I was awakened in the middle of the night by a loud rumbling sound and a shaking bed. This was a surprising set of facts. I proceeded to conduct a sleepy, and sincere, abduction process: *Thunderstorm?* No. A look out the window discounted this hypothesis. *Huge semitruck driving by?* Unlikely. *Earthquake?!* Maybe.

I learned the next morning that there had indeed been an earthquake (4.5 on the Richter scale) the previous night. Abduction, then, involves making explanatory guesses. I have just given a paradigmatic example. At its least pronounced, abduction involves one's ongoing guesses that the future will conform to the past. These are much less likely to be wrong but still involve residual guessing. If I go out to my car and find that the driver-side door is locked, I "guess" that the same key that has always unlocked this door will unlock it again. And this will hold true the vast majority of the time, although we could imagine exceptions involving switched or broken keys.

When paradigmatic examples are involved, perceptual judgments and abductions are distinguished by the criterion of conceivability of doubt (EP 2:229–30). For example, a sincere perceptual judgment that "my shirt is blue" *cannot be doubted* in its immediacy. On the other hand, paradigmatic examples of abductions allow for the conceivability of doubt, as evidenced by my California example: Storm? Truck? Earthquake? It was possible for me to doubt each of my guesses.

That abduction and perceptual judgments shade into each other is evidenced by the kind of dual pictures offered in many basic psychology books, where the picture drawn looks like, say, a flight of stairs going up. But, on second glance, it looks like a flight of stairs going down (EP 2:228). The perspective shifts and one's perception changes. I recall a picture from a psychology class, where the line of an older woman's nose (her face depicted close up) could also be construed as the jawline of a younger woman standing at a distance. The drawing had been designed to depict both. These examples show that perception involves interpretation, even though this often shades off into the recesses of "some unconscious part of the mind," or one's "instinctive mind" (EP 1:228, 241). This dimension of the mind is not conscious, and thus not controllable, in the immediacy of the present (EP 2:227, 240).[40] Once again, Peirce describes instinctive mind this way:

> We may be dimly able to see that in part it depends on the accidents of the moment, *in part on what is personal* or racial,[41] in

part *[on what]* is common to all nicely adjusted organisms whose equilibrium has narrow ranges of stability, in part on whatever is composed of vast collections of independently variable elements. . . . (EP 2:241, my emphasis, editorial brackets)

To say that the instinctive mind depends "in part on what is personal" is to point at the same time to the inescapable social and socio-political factors that shape each person's associations/habits/beliefs. This is because, for Peirce, a person's inner world and outer world intertwine. Instinctive mind thus includes socio-political shaping that occurs because of hegemonic large-scale associations/habits/beliefs about economic class, race, sex, sexuality, and so on.

Moreover, Peirce emphasizes that "our logically controlled thoughts compose a small part of the mind, the mere blossom of a vast complexus which we may call the instinctive mind" (EP 2:241). This highlights the fact that our instinctive socio-political associations/habits/beliefs can dwell outside of our immediate control. In a 1905 discussion of Critical Common-sensism, Peirce notes that consciousness is *not* "a separate tissue, overlying an unconscious region of the occult nature, mind, soul, or physiological basis"; rather "the difference is only relative and the demarcation not precise" (EP 2:347). This continuum between consciousness and "an unconscious region" complements Peirce's account of instinctive mind, showing the likelihood that this "uncontrolled" dimension of mind often functions *without our awareness*, especially in the present moment (EP 2:347, 241). On the socio-political plane, this means that racist, sexist, and other discriminatory instinctive associations/habits/beliefs can function nonconsciously.

Recall the discussion in Chapters 1 and 2 of the social psychological research that shows how we can be affected *nonconsciously* by stereotypes that affect how we treat people whose race or gender is different from our own (LeDoux 1996, 61–62, my emphasis; Bargh 1992, 1990; cf. Alcoff 2006, 242–43). Social psychologist John Bargh notes that control can be gained over the nonconscious influence of stereotypes when one has been educated about the danger of specific stereotypes. But he also notes that gaining this control is not a "straightforward" task, because of the complexities of nonconscious influence (1992, 250). His comments mesh with the problematic in consideration here regarding nonconscious discrimination by those in hegemonic groups who repudiate the very discrimination that they unwittingly perpetuate, but who may not be educated about the possible influence of nonconscious stereotypes. His comments also resonate with the hope found in Peirce's conception of self-control as an ongoing, fallible process that esteems growth and communal input.

In the present essay, "Pragmatism as the Logic of Abduction," Peirce notes that what is outside our control today may become controllable at a later time and that what seems inconceivable today may become conceivable tomorrow (EP 2:240, 230). Implicit in these points is that humans can and do grow in self-control, expanding their control over beliefs that were functionally indubitable at an earlier time. There is a tension here, however. When issues of racism, sexism, and other exclusionary instinctive beliefs are at play, those who are in hegemonic positions (such as Euro-Americans, heterosexuals, men, etc.) may not be aware of it, while those in non-hegemonic positions *are* aware of it. Again, consider Alcoff's story of her friend, a woman of color in a department full of white people. She saw the racism and sexism at play and the majority of her colleagues did not.

The general problematic is this: How best to navigate the relationship between the community and the individual, when the latter is either a person or a group representing a non-hegemonic perspective in relation to hegemonic communal norms? Those occupying non-hegemonic perspectives are uniquely suited to identify the functioning of exclusionary instinctive/background beliefs that undermine self-controlled scientific inquiry. This uniqueness *should* be an occasion for an agapic embrace of the different—namely, a unique, non-hegemonic perspective on exclusionary beliefs, which identifies that they *are* (still) in play. The arising of this uniqueness within a community of inquiry presents the first movement of the agapic circle. Yet the very exclusionary beliefs in question, functioning nonconsciously in hegemonic-group members, can result in the dismissal of these valuable non-hegemonic epistemological perspectives. Thus there can be a rejection of the second movement of agape, by means of nonconscious exclusionary sympathy. Moreover, since *nonconscious* influence is involved, racist, sexist, and other discriminatory exclusion can be perpetuated even by people who on a conscious level are *anti*-racist, *anti*-sexist, and so on. We have reached the doorstep of Peirce's mature doctrine of Critical Common-sensism, which calls on self-control to turn its critical gaze toward the background beliefs that inform reasoning at individual and communal levels. Critical Common-sensism offers tools for eliminating even nonconsciously functioning exclusionary instinctive beliefs that undermine the ideals of agape and science.

FIVE

CRITICAL COMMON-SENSISM, 1900S

Critical Common-sensism (CCS) is an epistemological doctrine that calls for a critical examination of the common-sense beliefs that underwrite human cognition.[1] It is thus uniquely suited to address social critical concerns about discriminatory beliefs that can become ingrained within one's background beliefs without her or his awareness.[2] The self-controlled scrutiny of background/common-sense beliefs called for by Critical Common-sensism provides the missing piece in terms of the application problem faced by both the scientific method and the agapic ideal. I foreground Critical Common-sensism's social critical potential by examining CCS in conjunction with the work done in previous chapters, as well as in conjunction with additional social critical insights.

The chapter culminates by showing that, when Critical Common-sensism is ideally applied, it does not leave scientific and agapic ideals behind. Rather the strands of science, agape, and Critical Common-sensism weave into a tapestry of loving reasonableness, where the embrace of diverse perspectives promotes growth in knowledge and self-control. Critical Common-sensism provides those in hegemonic groups with consciousness-raising tools that can help them address their blind spots with respect to discrimination faced by those in non-hegemonic groups. Scientific method and agape provide the episte-mological and loving motivations to put this awareness into practice by resisting exclusionary instinctive beliefs despite the strength of their influence.

In what follows I will continue to use "belief" and "belief-habit" interchangeably, depending on context, to highlight the CCSist caution that beliefs are *habits* that can be difficult to change or eradicate. I also use "background" and "common-sense" synonymously to refer to the instinctive beliefs from which one reasons.

Part 1: Critical Common-sensism

> We begin doing philosophy against the background of our com-
> mon-sense view of things, a set of often inchoate and unformu-
> lated assumptions about the nature of mind and the physical
> world, about the scope of our knowledge and its sources, and
> about values and rationality, which forms the background to our
> everyday actions and inquiries. In modern jargon, we begin with
> a folk physics and a folk psychology, and a common-sense view
> of morality and rationality which are more often embodied in our
> habits of belief, action, inference, and evaluation than in a care-
> fully set out body of principles. (Hookway 2000, 198)

Peirce's Critical Common-sensism holds in place *both* human self-controlled reasoning *and* the fact that this reasoning has to start from already-existing, background belief-habits. [3] It is an epistemological doctrine that addresses the common-sense belief-habits underwriting human cognition. Critical Common-sensism acknowledges that, for all their powers of reasoning, humans always already reason from be-lief-habits that are so deep seated as to function outside their imme-diate awareness and control. At the same time, CCS maintains that humans must scrutinize these background beliefs.

Our common-sense beliefs are practically indubitable—that is, they are not doubted in the everyday course of life (cf. CP 1.661). One reasons from them without questioning them. CCS endeavors to examine these common-sense beliefs, to determine whether any are, in fact, doutbtful. Those that are found dubitable—once this dubitability is confirmed through scientific testing[4]—must be changed or abandoned. It should be noted that, in this CCS context, Peirce explicitly links "dubitability" with falseness when discussing problematic common-sense beliefs. In what follows I employ "dubitability" in this same sense.[5]

To clarify this critical sorting of beliefs, I refer to those that are "legitimately" considered indubitable and those that are "illegitimately" so considered. Under the "legitimate" category are two types of common-sense beliefs: those that are so deeply taken for granted they are not even identified as background beliefs in the first place and those that are so identified, but attempts to doubt them are unsuccessful. Peirce describes both types of these "original beliefs" as acritical (EP 2:347). Original beliefs withstand CCS scrutiny, either by not emerging as beliefs in the first place or by emerging as beliefs that are impervious to current efforts to doubt them. Hookway notes, "[A]n acritical belief is one of which we are certain, which does not issue from the kind of process of deliberation or reasoning which can be subjected to critical monitoring. We do not know why we believe these things; we cannot imagine being able to doubt them; and they have a foundational role for our practices of inquiry and justification" (Hookway 2000, 150). Given a particular common-sense belief, if efforts to doubt it fail, then it is *acritical* for the time being. It is legitimately indubitable. Peirce stresses, however, that acritical beliefs are always subject to doubt at a later time: "[W]hat has been [acritically] indubitable one day has often been proved on the morrow to be false" (CP 5.514). This reflects Peirce's fallibilism, whereby any belief is conceivably wrong, even if a particular person or community finds it to be acritical for the time being. Acritical beliefs are also characterized by their vagueness, to be explained shortly.

Illegitimately indubitable common-sense beliefs are those that can be identified and that are simply taken for granted. Efforts to doubt them are insufficient or not even undertaken. Peirce warns Critical Common-sensists against carelessly allowing an illegitimately indubitable belief into their set of common-sense beliefs: "[A] philosopher ought not to regard an important proposition as indubitable without a systematic and arduous endeavour to attain to a doubt of it" (CP 5.498). To illegitimately render a common-sense belief indubitable undermines self-controlled reasoning, by giving place to an unsound premise.

a. Vagueness versus Specificity

Legitimate and illegitimate indubitability apply to vagueness and specificity, respectively, in relation to common-sense beliefs. One of the signal characteristics of acritical common-sense (or original) beliefs is that they are *vague*, not so vague as to convey nothing, but vague enough that the principle of contradiction does not apply to them.[6] Two examples Peirce gives are "fire burns" and there is "order in nature" (CP 5.498, 508, 516) These beliefs convey something about both fire and nature, but remain vague enough that they are each true in some respects and false in others. For example, it is true that fire burns dry paper, but false that fire burns water (EP 2:350 ff.; CP 5.505 ff.; Hookway 2000, 150, 211 ff.). To render a vague belief specific is to make it doubt-able. Peirce notes, "[E]verybody's actions show that it is impossible to doubt that there is an element of order in the world; but the moment we attempt to define that orderliness we find room for doubt" (EP 2:541 n. 10; cf. CP 5.507–8).

The importance of vagueness for my project is its use as a *criterion*: If a belief is not vague, then it must not be considered a legitimately indubitable common-sense belief. Peirce asserts that CCS "*insist[s]* that the acritically indubitable is invariably vague" and "*all* the veritably indubitable beliefs are vague" (EP 2:350; CP 5.505, my emphasis). He also warns against considering *specific* beliefs to be indubitable:

> [I]f we are to admit that some propositions are beyond our pow-
> ers of doubt, we must not admit any *specified* proposition to be of
> this nature without severe criticism; nor must any man assume
> with no better reason than because he cannot doubt it, that an-
> other man cannot do so. (EP 2:433, my emphasis)

Peirce's fallibilism prevents him from absolutizing this admonition. Hence his qualification that specified beliefs are to be admitted (as acritical) only with "severe criticism." This fallibilist signature not-withstanding, Peirce's warning against illegitimate indubitability is clear, and so is his reasoning on the matter. He wants to ensure against specified beliefs, which *are* amenable to doubt, becoming un-critically accepted and then internalized as such. If this happens, then a scientifically unsound belief—that has not been subjected to the scientific method—can become absorbed into the habitual scientific assumptions that ground reasoning processes.

Racist common-sense beliefs, for example, can be used to exemplify the contrast between a legitimately indubitable, vague common-sense belief and an illegitimately indubitable, specified common-sense belief. The belief that there is order to nature is a vague, legitimately indubitable common-sense belief. In Western history, a specific version of this belief was illegitimately assumed to be indubitable by many European and Euro-American white people. The specified belief went something like this: "Nature is ordered in such a way that nonwhite races are inferior to Caucasians." Many affluent white people routinely reasoned from this belief as an uncritically accepted premise. They thereby ranked their own Caucasian race as superior and other races as inferior. This racist assumption resulted in circular reasoning about the inferiority of non-Caucasian races. Johann Friedrich Blumenbach (1752–1840), for example, wrote the influential work *On the Natural Variety of Mankind*. For evidence of the superiority of the Caucasian race, he includes an aesthetic appeal, noting that whites possess "that kind of appearance which, *according to our opinion* of symmetry, we consider most handsome and becoming" (Blumenbach 2000, 28, my emphasis).[7] Clearly Blumenbach's presumed audience was white, and he felt comfortable appealing to a common-sense racist aesthetic to support his racial hierarchy. Charles Mills provides an informative sampling of white philosophers' comments on the inferiority of nonwhite races. Immanuel Kant (1724–1804) made his own appeal to a common-sense aesthetic when he noted that "a clear proof that what [a Negro] said was stupid" was that "this fellow was quite black from head to foot."[8] David Hume (1711–76) asserted that "the negroes, and in general all the other species of men," are "naturally inferior to the whites."[9] Recall the nineteenth-century pseudo-science of race, which took for granted the very racial hierarchies that it set out to prove. Stephen Jay Gould comments that "the pervasive assent given by scientists to [these] conventional [racial] rankings arose from *shared social belief*, not from objective data gathered to test an open question" (1981, 35, my emphasis).

White supremacist common-sense beliefs are illegitimately indubitable. They are specific beliefs that are dubitable and false. Had people of color been included in the community of inquiry historically, the dubitability of these racist beliefs could have surfaced more effectively (cf. Harding 1991, 148–49). As it was, communities of powerful whites acted from a hegemonic common-sense that helped enforce their racist agenda.[10]

b. The Instinctive Nature of Common-sense Beliefs

Peirce says that original beliefs are "of the general nature of *instincts*" (EP 2:349, my emphasis). He does not define what he means by instinct in this context but notes that he uses the term "in a broad sense" (CP 5.498), which seems to refer to the dimensions of common-sense beliefs that make them feel so "original" that we "cannot 'go behind' them" (EP 2:347). They are "irresistible," reflect "innate cognitive habits," and are "uncontrolled" (CP 5.499, 504, 522). They can also function nonconsciously—that is, without our conscious awareness. Recall that Peirce links the uncontrolled with the "not fully conscious" and that, for him, consciousness is *not* "a separate tissue, overlying an unconscious region of the occult nature, mind, soul, or physiological basis" (EP 2:227, 347). Rather, "the difference is only relative and the demarcation not precise" (EP 2:347). Common-sense beliefs can function without one's awareness of them. This is why some do not even emerge when CCS looks for them. Hookway notes that, "We may not be very good at identifying common-sense certainties" (2000, 207). This is because they can function nonconsciously, such that we simply cannot "see" them. They are blind spots in our reasoning process. This often holds true for racist, sexist, and other discriminatory common-sense beliefs, which is why it can be hard for well-meaning anti-racists, anti-sexists, and others to detect their own discriminatory behavior.

Instinct also conveys the reliability of original beliefs, yet this "reliability" is limited. On the one hand, "[N]othing is so unerring as instinct within its proper field, while reason goes wrong about as often as right—perhaps oftener" (CP 5.522). This reliability is grounded in "the total everyday experience of many generations of multitudinous populations" (CP 5.522). On the other hand, instinct is not foolproof, as (1) it can be outstripped by the human species' development of self-control, and (2) instinct can be socialized to reflect narrow cultural or socio-political bias.

Regarding the first point, Peirce believes that original common-sense beliefs can become outmoded, stripped of their legitimate indubitability by the growth of humans in self-control. In other words, Critical Common-sensist doubt is sensitive to the evolutionary nature of the world and of human progress in particular. Peirce notes that original beliefs are limited in their range, applying only to humanity in its *primitive* settings:

> [I]ndubitable beliefs refer to a somewhat primitive mode of life, and . . . while they never become dubitable in so far as our mode of life remains that of somewhat primitive man, yet as we develop *degrees of self-control* unknown to that man, occasions of action arise in relation to which the original beliefs, if stretched to cover them, have no sufficient authority. In other words, we outgrow the applicability of instinct—not altogether, by any manner of means, but in our highest activities. (CP 5.511, Peirce's emphasis)[11]

Peirce believes that humanity has attained such growth, through scientific achievement: "Modern science, with its microscopes and telescopes, with its chemistry and electricity, and with its entirely new appliances of life, has put us into quite another world; almost as much so as if it had transported our race to another planet" (CP 5.513). This being the case, it is especially necessary to examine common-sense beliefs for doubtfulness, in order to keep up with growth in self-control. Again, "what has been indubitable one day has often been proved on the morrow to be false" (CP 5.514). The legitimate indubitability of original beliefs must be checked against growth in self-control, not simply decided on once and for all.

For the sake of good science, each of us must exercise ongoing self-control over our common-sense beliefs, even those that have been acritical to us in the past. For Peirce self-control involves the capacity to achieve critical distance from one's beliefs so that one can orchestrate growth through ongoing critique and modification of her beliefs and ideals (CP 5.533–35; EP 2:245–48, 337–38). Critical Common-sensism is itself an exercise in self-control, whereby individuals and communities work to raise to awareness beliefs that might otherwise function uncritically. While not all common-sense beliefs can be raised to consciousness, some can. And of these, some are subject to control through reflection and critique. Peirce does not pretend that one can achieve control over a given belief in the immediacy of the present but asserts that reflection on past behavior can be brought to bear on future behavior (EP 2:245, 337). Thus, even if one cannot help acting on a particular belief today, tomorrow she may be able to reflect on and critique that belief. Critical common-sensism and self-control are *processes* that work within an organic paradigm where change is ongoing.

The second point about the unreliability of instinctive beliefs—that they can reflect exclusionary socio-political bias—relates to illegitimately indubitable, specified beliefs. While original beliefs "rest on . . . the total everyday experience of many generations of multitudinous populations," this very experience can reflect social injustices that perpetuate oppression, even over "many generations" (CP 5.522).

Injustice can take root in common-sense through the hegemonic imposition of specified beliefs that are illegitimately indubitable, but can nonetheless become ingrained as part of one's background beliefs, especially for those belonging to hegemonic groups (such as heterosexuals, men, whites and others). Indeed, the goal of the authority method of fixing beliefs is the internalization of hegemonic beliefs by community members, so that these beliefs become an unquestionable dimension of experience. As noted in Chapter 1, in an 1893 addendum to "Fixation of Belief," Peirce comments, "It will be wholesome enough for us to make a general review of the causes of our beliefs; and the result will be that most of them have been taken upon trust and have been held since we were too young to discriminate the credible from the incredible" (CP 5.376 n. 3). As argued in earlier chapters, Peircean instinctive beliefs include *socialized* beliefs, not merely "natural" ones like the belief that "fire burns" or that there is order in nature (CP 5.498, 5.508, 2.170; Hookway 2000, 216; Ayim 1982, 19).

The cultivation of socialized instinctive beliefs, which become rooted in common-sense, often begins in childhood (CP 2.170, 5.376 n. 3). The coercive survival dilemma described in Chapter 2 highlights the seriousness with which a dependent and vulnerable child must take the testimony of her caretakers and community, since doing so can be a matter of life and death. It makes sense to describe *as instinctive* socialized beliefs that have been formed so early and under the pressure of needing to trust in order to survive (CP 2.170). Chapter 3 highlights the continued reinforcement of hegemonic beliefs via socio-political secondness and/or lack thereof, such that they form the very fabric of one's reality and the backdrop from which one reasons.

In his paper "What Pragmatism Is" (1905), Peirce notes that "[b]elief is not a momentary mode of consciousness; it is a habit of mind essentially enduring for some time, and mostly (at least) unconscious; and like other habits, it is (until it meets with some surprise that begins its dissolution) perfectly self-satisfied" (EP 2:336–37). Thus it is not only original beliefs that can function nonconsciously; any of our beliefs can. For people belonging to hegemonic groups, such as whites and men, racist and sexist beliefs learned (implicitly or explicitly) in childhood might not meet with surprise/secondness, as a result of hegemonic norms that endorse discrimination. Unchallenged, such beliefs can easily become woven into common-sense, without the realization of whites and men. The same danger of internalization applies to others in hegemonic groups, such as able-bodied people, those who are economically stable, heterosexuals, and so on.

Framing what Peirce calls "instinctive mind" in terms of common-sense beliefs, we could say that it includes a continuum of background beliefs ranging from those that are so deep they do not surface when CCS looks for them, to those acritical beliefs that can be identified but not doubted, to those that can be identified *and* doubted (such as racist, sexist, and other discriminatory beliefs). Instinctive mind is the repository for vague, legitimately indubitable beliefs, as well as the specified, illegitimately indubitable ones.

> We may be dimly able to see that in part ["instinctive mind"] depends on the accidents of the moment, *in part on what is personal* or racial, in part *[on what]* is common to all nicely adjusted organisms whose equilibrium has narrow ranges of stability, in part on whatever is composed of vast collections of independently variable elements. . . . (EP 2:241, my emphasis, editorial brackets)

Peirce's inclusion of a personal dimension in the instinctive mind, as noted last chapter, signals that specified, illegitimately indubitable beliefs can indeed make their way into one's common-sense. We cannot understand the personal—or the racial—outside of the social matrices that shape them, a theme also discussed last chapter in conjunction with association by resemblance (inner world) and by contiguity (outer world). One's personal understanding of herself or himself and of her or his world—including factors like economic stability, race, sex, sexuality, and so on—is socially shaped from birth.[12]

c. Doubt

The Critical Common-sensist "has a high esteem for doubt. . . . Only, his hunger is not to be appeased with paper doubts: he must have the heavy and noble metal, or else belief" (CP 5.514). It is tempting to read an overly Cartesian spirit into CCS's admiration for doubt. This would be an exaggeration. Despite the fact that both Descartes and Peirce use doubt as a tool against slavery to authority, Cartesian doubt is too strong, as well as too naive (CP 5.517; Hookway 2000, 204–5, 209 n. 11). In a dialogue between an imaginary interlocutor and an imaginary pragmaticist,[13] Peirce responds to the challenge that a Critical Common-sensist's admiration of doubt is best served by a Cartesian approach:

> *Doctor X:* I should think that so passionate a lover of doubt would make a clean sweep of his beliefs.
> *Pragmaticist:* You naturally would, holding the infant's mind to be a *tabula rasa* and the adult's a school state, on which doubts are written with a soapstone pencil to be cleaned off with the dab of a wet sponge; but if they are marked with talc on man's "glassy essence," they may disappear for a long time only to be revived by a breath. (CP 5.519)

Peirce's point here is that Cartesian doubt assumes that doubting a belief is a superficial issue, unattached to the deep-seated habits that shape our worldviews. The Cartesian assumes that, through the mere assertion of doubt, a belief is "doubted." Beliefs, however, are *habits* that cannot be cast off at will by the human organism. Either experience or imagination has to intervene if the belief-habit is to be modified (CP 5.524).

To fully appreciate Peirce's insights about paper-doubt, we must not construe it too narrowly, as if paper-doubt involves only beliefs that are not really in question (such as belief in the existence of the external world). There are at least two types of Cartesian paper-doubt, corresponding to sincere and insincere doubt of beliefs. Drawing on Descartes' First Meditation, there is the paper-doubt of a belief that one does indeed doubt, such as the trustworthiness of sense data (Descartes 1998, 60).[14] Second, there is the paper-doubt of a belief that one does not truly doubt, such as the existence of the external world.[15] Peirce criticizes Descartes for assuming that Cartesian methodic doubt can successfully clear the ground of reasoning from both types of beliefs, through merely writing down or asserting the doubtfulness of these beliefs. Our everyday behavior will betray both sincere and insincere paper-doubt, showing that the belief-*habits* corresponding to the senses and the external world are alive and well. As conscientiously as I may try to implement Cartesian doubt, if I see a rock sailing toward my head I will most likely believe—and therefore act on—both the sense data and the external otherness that tell me so.

Paper-doubt, whether it is sincere or insincere, ultimately undermines self-control, because it ignores the *affectivity* of belief and doubt—that is, their embodiment in habit. Peirce says that it is "disastrous to science for those who pursue it to think they doubt what they really believe" (CP 5.498). This is because the belief-habits continue to function, while they are thought to be "cast into doubt." One cannot, as Peirce notes, simply wipe beliefs away as if they had no physiological and neural roots. Paper-doubt assumes this can be done, however, and thus leaves the belief-habits in place, "only to be revived by a breath" (CP 5.519). Proper doubt involves habit-rupture or modification based on experience and/or efforts in the imagination: "For belief, while it lasts, is a strong habit, and as such, forces the man to believe until some surprise breaks up the habit. The breaking of a belief can only be due to some novel experience, whether external or internal" (CP 5.524). In other words, doubt, like a belief-habit, is an affair of the mind *and body,* not merely the mind. Habits mold one's body, so that to change or eliminate them involves special efforts. As I will argue below, Peirce's insights regarding paper-doubt help explain the difficulty of eradicating discriminatory beliefs, which, because of their habitual nature, can still function without one's awareness, despite one's conscious disavowal of them.

I. TOOLS FOR DETERMINING DOUBTFULNESS

The CCSist strategies for determining the doubtfulness of a common-sense belief involve "logical analysis," experience, "experimenting in the imagination," and testimony (CP 5.517, 509). Logical analysis is necessary to bring to awareness, to the extent possible, the common-sense beliefs informing our reasoning. Experience is an important source of information about whether a common-sense belief is doubtful or dubitable. At a time in human history when a particular society or culture believed the earth to be flat, for example, an expedition that succeeded in circumnavigating the globe would have offered experiential proof of the dubitability (falseness) of the belief "The earth is flat."[16] When we do not have experiential evidence at hand, we may turn to the imagination.

By conducting inner experimentations in imagination, a person can determine whether it is possible for her of him to doubt the belief in question (CP 5.507, 517). This involves abstracting the belief from its present circumstances, in order to determine if it becomes doubtable in comparison with other circumstances. Peirce puts it this way:

> [The Critical Common-sensist] hold[s] that everything in the substance of his beliefs can be represented in the schemata of his imagination; that is to say, in what may be compared to composite photographs of continuous series of modifications of images; these composites being accompanied by conditional resolutions as to conduct.
>
> These resolutions should cover all classes of circumstances, in the sense that they would produce . . . determinations of habit corresponding to every possible pragmaticistic application of the propositions believed. (CP 5.517)

Experimentation through imagination involves the realm of association by resemblance (as rooted in association by contiguity), in which the person's own repertoire of habits is brought to bear on the belief in question. The person uses the resources of her or his own experience (that is, contiguity associations as they are reflected in the inner world of resemblance) in order to conceive whether or not there is a scenario in which the belief in question can be doubted. This is similar to the application of the pragmatic maxim, whereby imagination is used to conceive of all possible habitual effects of a belief or aim. In the CCS context, however, the imagination is used to conceive of any way possible a belief could be called into doubt.

It is important to note here that, while one's experience helps facilitate this imaginative process, this experience also reflects an unavoidable limitation. The less experience one has, the less her or his imagination can experiment to test for conceivable doubtfulness. For example, returning to a personal experience I described in Chapter 1: When I was in high school, I lacked the imaginative capacity to doubt the belief "Racism does not occur at my school," which was a common-sense belief for me at the time. Recall that my graduating class was 480 students, roughly 1 percent of whom were students of color. The school was situated in a middle-class, predominantly white suburb. In my junior or senior year (approximately 1986), I heard that an African American classmate, who I did not know except by name, said he was experiencing racism from his teachers. I could not imagine what he was talking about. My school was not a racist school, I thought to myself. My imagination failed me. My personal experience (associations by contiguity) did not provide me with resources to conceive, via association by resemblance, the plausibility of his claim. I had never experienced racism and had never seen teachers be racist. It did not occur to me that my classes were almost always exclusively white. I did not believe my classmate. With more than twenty years of hindsight, including deeply alienating experiences of sexism and sexual harassment (as well as current work to unlearn my unintentional racism), I can imagine how easily racism might have occurred for my classmate.

Lorraine Code discusses how important it is to be mindful of the limitations of one's imaginative capacities and of the importance of *not* presuming *one* social imaginary that applies to everyone in a community or society. To talk about what "we" all know is true, or about what life is like for "us," can unwittingly silence non-hegemonic voices that are marginalized from the dominant way of life (Code 2001, 267–72). She highlights how one's imagination can reflect the hegemonic reinforcement of false universalization: "The complex of interlocking assumptions that presume universal human sameness and discount singular experiences at the limits of what the society defines as thinkable is held in place by *a hegemonic imaginary*" (272, my emphasis). In the context of my project, I take the "hegemonic imaginary" to refer to what is "officially" conceivable or imaginable, drawing on the interrelationships among hegemonic societal belief-habits.[17] In mainstream U.S. discourse, oppressive forces such as racism and sexism are viewed as primarily resolved, social ills of the past. The prevalence of ongoing racism and sexism is, for the most part, not "officially" conceivable. This hegemonic imaginary can reinforce the imagination-limitation of individuals in hegemonic groups. In my own high school example, my personal inability to imagine racism was buttressed by public mainstream discourse that claimed (and still claims) that racism is a thing of the past, so that anyone "complaining" about it is held suspect.

When experimenting through imagination *does* succeed in revealing the doubtfulness of a common-sense belief, the belief has been brought under self-control, at least to an extent. This opens the door to testing and confirming the dubitability of the belief. Imagination is thus a means by which humans achieve critical and creative distance from the world. If I stamp my foot about a particular common-sense belief, insisting that it is "inconceivable" that it could be doubtful, I show my *inability* to imaginatively separate the belief from its felt concrete urgency.[18] This belief has control over me, *not* vice versa. Confirming a common-sense belief's dubitability is just the beginning, however. If the belief is to be changed or eliminated, efforts of self-control must move beyond this discovery stage (which is comparable to sincere paper-doubt) to address the belief's habitual nature. Below I examine discriminatory hegemonic beliefs in this respect. It is not enough to simply assert their dubitability, since these beliefs are deep-seated habits that can function nonconsciously despite one's conscious disavowal of them.

In addition to experience and imagination, testimony is a tool for determining the doubtfulness of common-sense beliefs. Peirce's discussion of this aspect of CCS hints at the fact that scrutinizing common-sense beliefs is supposed to occur in the context of *communal* inquiry. It also highlights the familiar tension, in the context of my project, regarding an individual's holding a belief that conflicts with a belief, or beliefs, held by the rest of her community. Peirce notes, on the one hand, "Could I be assured that other men candidly and with sufficient deliberation doubt any proposition which I regard as indubitable, that fact would inevitably cause me to doubt it, too" (CP 5.509). This recalls the comment in the Cognition Series, discussed in Chapter 2, that communal testimony could convince a person of her or his "madness" (W2: 202). It also recalls the Logic of Science essay "Fixation of Belief," where Peirce describes the social impulse that leads a person out of tenacity and into a communal method for fixing beliefs (W 3:250). On the other hand, as we might expect, Peirce follows up the current passage with this qualification:

> I ought not, however, lightly to admit that they do so doubt a proposition after the most thorough criticism by myself and anxious consideration of any other criticisms which I have been able to find and understand has left it quite indubitable by me, since *there are other states of mind that can easily be mistaken for doubt.* (CP 5.509, my emphasis)

This passage highlights the importance of the individual as a source of communal growth. One who has done the rigorous footwork of determining a belief's indubitability should not "lightly . . . admit" or easily surrender to the community's doubt of said belief. This is because "other states of mind that can be mistaken for doubt" include, I would argue, prejudice and fear of what differs from the norm. Everyone else's doubting, or believing, something does not necessitate that they are right and the exceptional individual is wrong. We can recall, once again, Peirce's reference in "Fixation of Belief" to the defiant community member who has "a wider sort of social feeling" (W 3:251). This wider social attunement can involve challenging a belief's dubitability or indubitability, depending on context. To return to an example examined above, a hegemonic community can promote specified (versus vague) beliefs as indubitable, such as the inferiority of non-Caucasian races. In such cases, it is right for the individual to maintain her own view of, in this case, the dubitability of the racist belief in question.

Peirce does not explain how to navigate the tension between the individual and the community when they are at odds. On the one hand, individuals without a sense of their synechistic context should not rule the day. Peirce warns against the hubris of assuming a solitary claim to indubitability: "... nor must any man assume with no better reason than because he cannot doubt it, that another man cannot do so" (EP 2:433). On the other hand, an authoritative community, with no respect for the insight of the synechistic individual, should not take precedence either. A healthy dialectic is necessary between the synechistically minded individual and the synechistically minded community, in conjunction with scientific testing, in the determination of a common-sense belief's dubitability or indubitability. Neither should assume a naive authority at the expense of the other. The synechistic individual must sincerely acknowledge the input of other community members. If she is at odds with her community, she cannot merely assert the authority of her own determination of (in)dubitability without thoroughly checking against experience, experimentation through imagination, and self-criticism (CP 5.509). The community, for its part, must not dismiss the perspective of a synechistic individual, or synechistic group, without careful consideration and application of the scientific method. A simple appeal to the majority is clearly not acceptable to Peirce. If a common-sense belief is found doubtful, then the reason for the doubtfulness can be articulated in the form of a hypothesis that can be tested against experience (cf. Hookway 2000, 43, 150–51, 192). This way, regardless of how many, or few, find a belief problematic, there is a common standard of evaluation of the claim. Moreover, since truth is an ongoing and fallible process for Peirce, the evaluation of the claim can itself undergo further revision in light of future experience and perspective. This is an important point, given the history of racist and sexist pseudoscience in the United States, which shows that evaluating claims, or testing hypotheses, can fall far short of Peirce's infinitely inclusive ideal.[19] There is always room, on Peirce's scheme, to correct for exclusionary reasoning practices.

II. FAILURE TO ACHIEVE DOUBT

If experience, imagination, and testimony fail to find a common-sense belief doubtful, then it is a legitimately indubitable, acritical belief. While such a belief might be found doubtful and dubitable in the future, if a community's sincere efforts have failed to shake its present indubitability, this must be accepted. The reasons for this were stated earlier. Casting a belief into mere paper-doubt leaves the belief-habit in place but makes its presence harder to consciously detect. When a belief is merely declared doubtful or dubitable, which is what paper-doubt entails, it *ostensibly* no longer influences the reasonings of an individual or community. Yet since the belief is rooted in habit, and these roots have not been modified or changed, the belief still functions. I can, for example, *say* I doubt that there is order in nature, but the belief-habit will not thereby be affected. Whenever I expect the future to conform to the past, and whenever I act on this expectation, I betray my paper-doubt.

If a community is hegemonic, however, its declaration of indubitable common-sense beliefs can be fraudulent, not reflecting a fully communal Critical Common-sensist effort. Thus we arrive once again at the doorstep of inclusion/exclusion issues, which highlight that the scrutiny of common-sense beliefs *must include* all possible perspectives within a specific community. If a community aspires to be truly Critical Common-sensist, it must address socio-political concerns of epistemological exclusion.

Part 2: Socio-political Application of Critical Common-sensism

With Critical Common-sensism in place, operating in conjunction with the scientific method and agape, Peirce has the resources to address the application problem outlined in Chapters 3 and 4. The problem, once again, is this. The ideals of both science and agape can be undermined in actual human communities, because of latent prejudices and power differentials that hegemonic community members do not see. More specifically, common-sense beliefs can be infiltrated by internalized, exclusionary beliefs that have been enforced by an authoritative, hegemonic society. Since these common-sense beliefs can function nonconsciously *and* can be shared by members of hegemonic groups, exclusionary beliefs can function even within communities that repudiate racism, sexism, and other discriminatory practices. Since communities of inquiry in the United States still reflect the overrepresentation of hegemonic groups, shared nonconscious discriminatory beliefs about non-hegemonic groups can be unintentionally perpetuated. A common form of nonconscious discriminatory behavior is the dismissal of feedback from non-hegemonic groups, such as reports of racism, sexism, or other forms of discrimination. In what follows I continue to focus primarily on racism (and sexism to a lesser extent) in order to draw out the nuances of the nonconscious discrimination phenomenon in the United States. Narrowing my focus in this way allows me to go deeper into the complexities of the argumentation without having to pause to make qualifications. It also makes sense to focus on racism, since it is (along with sexism) widely proclaimed to be "over" as a systemic problem in the United States, which makes it a good example for highlighting the nuanced conceptual tools provided by Peirce's Critical Common-sensism. I invite the reader to extrapolate regarding other types of nonconscious discrimination that can be enacted by those in hegemonic groups who repudiate the very type of discrimination they are unwittingly perpetuating, such as discrimination against the poor, GLBTQs, and so on.

I frame the application problem in the following CCS terms. There can be communal disagreement about whether illegitimate common-sense beliefs, such as racist beliefs, have been fully eliminated. On the one hand, members of a community may all agree that racist beliefs are dubitable and should not inform thought and practice. On the other hand, members may disagree about whether these beliefs have been fully eradicated. Some, often whites, may endorse the sincere (but naive) paper-doubt view that simply asserting the wrongness of the beliefs is enough to effect "doubt" of them. Others, often people of color, profess the ineffectiveness of this shallow doubt, as they experience the continued functioning of racist beliefs that whites do not notice. In this regard I analyze the issue of well-intentioned "color-blindness" in mainstream U.S. discourse. Many white people sincerely repudiate racist beliefs but remain unaware of the prevalence of racism in contemporary U.S. society. Often these same white people dismiss feedback from people of color that racism still persists. Before showing how CCS addresses this problem, I will discuss, at length, how CCS can *diagnose* the problem by highlighting important nuances that are at play.

a. Historical Loophole

First, let me place the application problem in historical context, drawing on points made in earlier chapters. What I call the "historical loophole" refers to how explicit, conscious prejudice undermines implementation of the ideal community of inquiry. Recall that "[t]his community . . . must not be limited, but must extend to all races of beings with whom we can come into immediate or mediate intellectual relation. It must reach, however vaguely, beyond this geological epoch, beyond all bounds" (W 3:284). Members of the *ideal* community are mature in their epistemic outlook, demonstrating self-control that is informed by an agapic embrace of diverse perspectives. Peirce is inclusive in his description of the "intellectual relations" that characterize the ideal community. Nonetheless, historically speaking, both people of color and women have been excluded from actual communities of inquiry because of their supposed intellectual inferiority. Thus the hegemonic biases of Euro-American propertied men promoted a *limited* community of inquiry, a limited community that has been perpetuated historically.

I call this a *historical* loophole because it involves *conscious* prejudice and the explicitly endorsed exclusion of non-hegemonic groups from the community of inquiry. Historically people of color and women *were* denied entry into scientific, educational, and political circles in the Western world. These exclusions were premised on hegemonic common-sense belief-habits that are not easy to eliminate. This means that the historical loophole can persist in a contemporary form, even in the wake of the civil rights and women's movements in the United States. I call this persistence the "contemporary loophole." Racism and sexism exist in the United States even though mainstream discourse says they should and do not. I argue that the "contemporary loophole" remains, *even if we grant the premise* that racism and sexism are no longer consciously practiced in the United States. I grant this premise for rhetorical purposes, in order to show how persistent *nonconscious* prejudice can be among well-intentioned people who truly believe racism and sexism are wrong. I believe that conscious, systemic racism and sexism (as well as other forms of oppression) are alive and well in the United States and internationally. Nonetheless, I think it can be fruitful to separate unintentional discrimination from the mix, in order to make the case that well-meaning people still have work to do to unlearn their unintentional racism and sexism.

Returning to the historical loophole: If the membership of the community of inquiry is limited, as it has been in Western history, to Euro-American privileged men, then these men may fail to identify doubtful common-sense beliefs that need to be subjected to the scientific method. They may so take for granted premises such as "Non-white races are intellectually inferior to the white race" or "Women are intellectually inferior to men" that their logical analysis either *does not reveal* these specified common-sense beliefs in the first place or reveals them as acritical. Western history bears this out, as discussed above and in earlier chapters. Since people of color and women were thus explicitly excluded from communal inquiry, they were not present to identify and challenge the common-sense beliefs that degraded them.

Had such groups of people been given *proportionate* representation and status in communities of inquiry, things might have been different. Instead of a shared oblivion to the functioning of doubtful exclusionary common-sense beliefs, perhaps there may have been a majority of community members, including people of color and women, who could identify and/or challenge the common-sense beliefs in question (cf. Harding 1991, 148–49). These members could have pushed to have the beliefs subjected to fair scientific inquiry. Or perhaps the beliefs would not have taken root in the first place. When the community refuses membership to non-hegemonic groups, it limits its resources in experience, imagination, and testimony. It thereby also limits its ability to identify common-sense beliefs that undermine the community's self-controlled functioning.[20] Sandra Harding's critique of objectivity as reflecting "value-free, impartial, dispassionate [scientific] research" dovetails with my Critical Common-sensist analysis of shared hegemonic background beliefs:

> The conception of value-free, impartial, dispassionate research is supposed to direct the identification of all social values and their elimination from the results of research, yet it has been operationalized to identify and eliminate *only* those social values and interests that differ among the researchers and critics who are regarded by the scientific community as competent to make such judgments. If the community of "qualified" researchers and critics systematically excludes, for example, all African Americans and women of all races, and if the larger culture is stratified by race and gender and lacks powerful critiques of this stratification, it is not plausible to imagine that racist and sexist interests and values would be identified within a community of scientists composed entirely of people who benefit—intentionally or not—from institutional racism and sexism. (1991, 143, Harding's emphasis)

Harding is not drawing on Peirce's Critical Common-sensism here. Nonetheless, she sheds light on how CCS can be applied socio-politically, by highlighting how shared discriminatory "values and interests" create what I would call shared blind spots regarding background beliefs that inform scientific communal reasoning.

Historically, when affluent Euro-American white men were assuming that people of color and women were inferior, the nonwhite perspectives were *not* given a voice in the inquiry. The exclusive community of inquiry ignored that these people had both experience and imaginative capacities (because of their experience) that the community of white men *did not have*. The experience and imagination of these non-hegemonic perspectives would have enhanced the scrutiny of common-sense beliefs, since it would have made more likely the identification of additional doubtful beliefs. As discussed in earlier chapters, members of non-hegemonic groups, such as people of color and women, have often experienced socio-political secondness that Euro-American white men have not. To refuse them membership is to surrender to the blind spots that are inevitable when diverse perspectives are rejected in favor of finite group interest.

Group interest, which often accompanies naive individualism, helps explain the exclusionary thought and practice so commonly exhibited historically by Euro-American propertied men. Recall that Peirce's critique of greed involves a *group* critique, not merely a critique of greedy individuals. The profit-seeking Euro-American white men who benefited from the nineteenth century's economic Darwinism were not a mere collection of unrelated individuals. They were a group sharing common interests. The same point can be made here regarding communities of inquiry in the West. Such exclusive communities were severely limited in their scope, representing the experience and imaginative capacity of *only* those privileged in terms of economic class, race, and sex. Peirce's earlier warning can be reread in the spirit of group membership: "[N]or must any man [or group] assume with no better reason than because he [or they] cannot doubt [a particular proposition], that another man [or group] cannot do so" (EP 2:433). To make such an assumption is to block the road of inquiry into the common-sense beliefs that may be impeding a community's development in self-control.

b. Contemporary Loophole

Let us return to the "contemporary loophole." I use the designation "contemporary" to convey the fact that the perspectives of people of color and women are now included in many communities of inquiry in the West. Issues of historical racist and sexist exclusion are still in play, however, as a result of the deeply systemic nature of racism and sexism, the corresponding overrepresentation of Euro-American whites and men in actual communities of inquiry, and the fact that racism and sexism involve deep-seated habits that are hard to break.

Critical Common-sensist issues of membership and (dis)agreement about common-sense beliefs take on a contemporary form, because of the *nonconscious* influence of racist and sexist common-sense beliefs. The historical loophole manifested in diverse voices being left out of the communal discussion altogether. The identification of certain common-sense beliefs, which were shared and unnoticed by the community members, *could not occur*. In contemporary communities in the West, issues of exclusion can still occur within a community, even when it both consciously repudiates racist and sexist common-sense beliefs and includes members belonging to non-hegemonic groups. The specific scenario I will examine is this: Community members may disagree about whether or not racist and sexist common-sense beliefs are still in play, even though the beliefs have been stamped "dubitable" by the community as a whole. Members of non-hegemonic groups may think they are still in play, and members of hegemonic groups may think they are not.

Peirce does not specifically indicate how such a disagreement is to be navigated, although he strongly implies that the individual or group with unique experiential and imaginative resources must not be overridden by an uncritical majority. We cannot simply appeal to the scientific method regarding such a disagreement, unfortunately. We are dealing with concrete communities and their decisions regarding which hypotheses are to be tested *in the first place*.[21] If one community member, who is a member of a non-dominant group or groups, voices the hypothesis that discrimination or prejudice is at play, her input could be dismissed as unworthy of being tested (hooks 2003b, 27). Recall the experience of Linda Alcoff's friend, who was a woman of color in a primarily white philosophy department with a white, male department chair. Her hypothesis that racism and sexism were at play—in the white, male graduate student's complaint about her—was dismissed with no efforts to test it by talking with other students or with those at the institution who had expertise on issues of racism and sexism in the classroom (Alcoff 2001, 66–67).

In concrete historical communities, when disagreements arise regarding the presence of dubitable common-sense beliefs, such as racist and/or sexist ones, there is often a temptation among those in hegemonic groups to dismiss the testimony of those in non-hegemonic groups. This dismissal is all the more likely when the majority of community members belong to overrepresented hegemonic groups and do not have the experience or capacity of imagination to detect the presence of discriminatory common-sense beliefs in their reasoning process and behavior. Such discriminatory common-sense beliefs include skepticism toward the testimony of people of color and women, which results in a multifaceted skepticism toward a woman of color (Code 1995; Mills 1997, 60–61). Alcoff comments on how the white, male department chair should have handled the situation with the Chicana faculty member:

> The chair should have second-guessed his ability to judge the case, given the fact that he has never himself experienced teaching as a woman of color, nor seen a woman of color alone in a classroom full of White students. Based on this, the chair should have done more consultation, with other students certainly, but also with those at the institution that would be in a better position to evaluate the conflicting claims. (2001, 67)

In other words, the chair should have held in place the racism/sexism hypothesis and subjected it to the testing appropriate to the context, in this case consulting other students and institutional resources. Since he did not do this, the "contemporary loophole" was allowed to manifest in the form of an *uncritical* white majority voting to demote a woman of color—based on one white, male graduate student's complaint about her—despite her own testimony that racism and sexism were at play in his complaint (66–67).

I. UNDERNEATH THE RADAR OF PRIVILEGED PERSPECTIVES:
"COLORBLINDNESS"

Bell hooks describes an exercise she does with college students in the United States to help them raise to conscious awareness their beliefs about race and sex:

> In classroom settings I have often listened to groups of students tell me that racism really no longer shapes the contours of our lives, that there is just no such thing as racial difference, that "we

are all just people." Then a few minutes later I give them an exercise. I ask if they were about to die and could choose to come back
as a white male, a white female, a black female, or black male,
which identity would they choose. Each time I do this exercise,
most individuals, irrespective of gender or race invariably choose
whiteness, and most often white maleness. Black females are the
least chosen. When I ask students to explain their choice they proceed to do a sophisticated analysis of privilege based on race (with
perspectives that take gender and class into consideration). *This
disconnect between their conscious repudiation of race as a marker
of privilege and their unconscious understanding is a gap we have to
bridge.* (2003b, 25–26, my emphasis)

Looking at this awareness/unawareness issue in terms of sincere
paper-doubt and legitimate doubt helps to clarify where the "disconnect" can occur between conscious and nonconscious belief-habit
patterns. To apply the discussion from Part 1, recall that, for Peirce,
beliefs are deeply rooted habits that cannot be changed or eradicated
at will; rather their modification requires work in experience or in
imagination (CP 5.524). Without sufficient practice, a belief can come
back into play rather easily (CP 5.519). In terms of racist, sexist, and
other discriminatory common-sense beliefs, it is not enough to assert
that those beliefs are dubitable and therefore no longer part of a person's or a community's worldview. Such a stance enacts mere paper-
doubt that does not address the embodied depth of the exclusionary
background beliefs. This is why Cartesian doubt is insufficient. It
treats beliefs as if they can be easily erased and thus leaves their roots
intact, so that they may be "revived by a breath" (CP 5.519). Cartesian
doubt also assumes that doubt is merely a solitary venture.

In *Seeing a Color-Blind Future*, Patricia Williams addresses the
frustration for many people of color, herself included, regarding the
credo of "colorblindness" that informs contemporary mainstream
white discourse on race in the United States and the United Kingdom
(1997).[22] In the post–civil rights era of the twentieth and twenty-first
centuries, racist beliefs are officially considered to be false and, therefore, illegitimate bases for reasoning regarding public policy and

individual conduct. In this spirit, white people often claim to be "colorblind," to reflect their sincere repudiation of racism against people of color. In the past, seeing skin color resulted in discrimination against people of color by many whites in the United States. Therefore, in the present, *not* seeing a person's skin color—that is, being "colorblind"—can reflect a conscientious condemnation, by white people, of discrimination against people of color.[23] Yet while the assertion of "colorblindness" can be a well-intentioned way for Euro-American whites to express the unacceptability of racism, "colorblindness" can also, ironically, promote a *racist* status quo.[24] This occurs when well-intentioned "colorblindness" is used not only to express the wrongness of racism but also to insist that racism is no longer a serious problem. The insistence goes something like this: "Racism cannot still be prevalent in the United States, we are colorblind now" (cf. Bonilla-Silva 2003, 177 ff.).[25]

From a Critical Common-sensist perspective, the well-intentioned assertion of "colorblindness" identifies racist beliefs as dubitable. Yet unaddressed are the manifold ways that racism still persistently functions in the United States, despite the progress made during the civil rights era. People of color still deal with everyday and systemic discrimination that is more covert than the blatant racism of the "Jim Crow," legalized segregation that was once prevalent in the Southern United States (Williams 1997, 41; Bonilla-Silva 2003, 2–4; Sullivan 2006, 4–5). Shannon Sullivan notes, "Race supposedly is not at issue in a society that obsesses over urban ghettoes, crime, the resale value of one's house, welfare queens, the drug war, the death penalty, and a massively growing prison industry" (2006, 5).

People of color are regularly confronted with racist cultural habits that have not been fully addressed. Williams writes,

> While I do want to underscore that I embrace color-blindness as
> a legitimate hope for the future, I worry that we tend to enshrine
> the notion with a kind of utopianism whose naïveté will ensure
> its elusiveness. In the material world ranging from playgrounds
> to politics, our ideals perhaps need more thoughtful, albeit more
> complicated, guardianship. By this I mean something more than

the "I think therefore it is" school of idealism. "I don't think about color, therefore your problems don't exist." If only it were so easy. (1997, 4)

Williams is calling for deeper work to be done on racism. Merely asserting that "color doesn't matter" or "racism is wrong" is not enough. Moreover, it can give the false impression that racism is being addressed, when it has merely disappeared from the conscious view of white people.[26]

"Colorblindness" in this context reflects sincere paper-doubt, the primary insight being this: When a belief is only paper-doubted, the belief-habit *both* is "cast into doubt" *and* probably continues to function without one's awareness. Comparing and contrasting "colorblindness" to power-outage behavior helps highlight the issues at play. A person used to living with electricity has probably experienced the sincere paper-doubt that often occurs during power outages. On the one hand, the belief "The power is on" is sincerely in doubt— electronic devices have suddenly stopped working. On the other hand, even while *knowing* the power is out, one may inadvertently try to turn on the television (or other electronic device). The belief-habit about the electricity is *both* being sincerely doubted *and* still functioning. This is because our belief-habits, especially common-sense ones, function so automatically—so *instinctively*—as to overrule a simple conscious assertion of doubt. In this scenario the impotent television provides a straightforward cue that one has just acted on a belief-habit that is supposedly in doubt.

"Colorblindness" is a more complex instance of sincere paper-doubt. Here we have, on the one hand, racist belief-habits that have been placed in doubt in mainstream U.S. discourse. On the other hand, there is consistent testimony that racist belief-habits are still functioning in U.S. society. In contrast to an *individual* confronting her belief-habits, however, "colorblindness" involves a *community's* confrontation of its belief-habits. It is much easier for one person to determine whether she is acting according to belief-habits about something as clear cut as the power being out. There is only one person to convince, the person herself. And the ineffectual television set is an indisputable cue that the belief-habit has been acted on. In the case of "colorblindness," a community is involved.

Moreover, environmental feedback about the belief-habits in question is not linked to an inanimate object that fails to "turn on." Instead, the feedback involves people giving testimony, and the testimony is mixed. Some community members—often white people—insist that they themselves and/or U.S. society are "colorblind" and that therefore racist belief-habits have been eliminated. Others—often people of color—insist that racist belief-habits are still in play.[27] What results is communal disagreement about whether or not racist belief-habits have been eradicated. In terms of paper-doubt, we could say the first group believes that sincere paper-doubt of racist beliefs, through conscientiously pronouncing their wrongness, is sufficient for eradicating racist behavior on individual and societal levels.

The second group grasps the ineffectiveness of sincere paper-doubt and testifies to ongoing racism in U.S. society despite supposed "colorblindness." The testimony of people of color about racism, however, is often dismissed within the white-dominated discourse in the United States, such that the paper-doubt of the first group (often white people) holds sway. This dismissal often occurs without serious or sincere consideration of the testimony about racism. It is also often coupled with the accusation, literal or figurative, of "playing the race card" (Bonilla-Silva 2003, 29, 179; hooks 2003b, 30 ff., 25–40). To borrow a phrase from Lorraine Code, people of color often do not have "rhetorical space" in which to voice and to receive uptake regarding their experience of racism (Code 1995, ix–x; cf. Tuana 2006, 13). This paper-doubt-fueled dismissal is underwritten by the assumption that a person cannot behave in a racist fashion unless she consciously intends to (Alcoff 2006, 188).

This brings us to another point, which is implied in Patricia Williams's criticism, described just above, of "colorblindness." Those who have been targeted by exclusionary common-sense beliefs, including racist ones, are in a unique position to report on whether or not the beliefs are still functioning.[28] This is not to say that those in non-hegemonic groups have a "god's eye" view on things. It is to say, however, that someone who is oppressed because of race has a perspective on experience that someone who is a Euro-American white probably *does not* have. The same point applies to other axes of oppression. In 2010, it is part of the public discourse in the U.S. mainstream that both racism and sexism are wrong. To this extent they have been cast into paper-doubt. Whether or not the deep-rooted habits associated with each are still in play *cannot be determined* without consulting people of color and women. These are the groups who encounter the most socio-political secondness resulting from societal racist and sexist beliefs. For whites to assume that they alone can determine that racism is a thing of the past is to block the road of inquiry and to silence those often in the best position to speak to these matters. The same reasoning applies regarding men and sexism.

This shows that the eradication of racist and sexist common-sense beliefs is especially hard work. Self-controlled habit-change takes more effort than a simple declaration of success before the work has even begun. That is to say, eradication of racist and sexist belief-habits cannot be a matter of simply declaring doubt—that is, sincere paper-doubt. Speaking about racism, Shannon Sullivan comments on how to address habits of white privilege appropriately:

> A white person who wishes to try to change her raced and racist habits would do better to change the environments she inhabits than (to attempt) to use "will power" to change the way she thinks about and reacts to non-white people. . . . A person cannot merely intellectualize a change of habit by telling herself that she will no longer think or behave in particular ways. The key to transformation is to find a way of disrupting a habit through environmental change and then hope that the changed environment will help produced [*sic*] an improved habit in its place. (2006, 9)

In other words, "intellectualiz[ing] a change of habit"—or sincere paper-doubt—is not sufficient to eradicate racist belief-habits. More is needed, such as the new experience that a change in environment would provide, so that the embodied roots of the belief-habits can be confronted: "For belief, while it lasts, is a strong habit, and as such, forces the man to believe until some surprise breaks up the habit. The breaking of a belief can only be due to some novel experience, whether external or internal" (CP 5.524). To change or eradicate exclusionary common-sense beliefs, practice in the external world and/ or in the internal world of imagination needs to occur. This is what *legitimate* doubt involves, efforts to change habits.

Moreover, eliminating racist and sexist common-sense beliefs cannot be accomplished by the solitary efforts of privileged individuals or specific privileged groups, such as Euro-American whites and men. A diverse communal effort is needed that *pays close attention* to the voices of those who have been oppressed by the beliefs in question. The perspectives of people of color and women, for example, are needed to report on the progress that is and is not being made on changing racist and/or sexist habits. This progress is reflected in the extent to which socio-political secondness is still at play, because, once again, this secondness is evidence that racist/sexist cultural habits are still intact. It reflects Cartesian naïveté for a white person or a man, or for whites or men as groups, to assume that they can eliminate racist and/or sexist belief-habits without the input of those who are negatively targeted by these habits, namely, people of color and women. This assumption involves a refusal of inclusive communal inquiry.

If an actual community of inquiry is to grow past its dubitable common-sense beliefs, it must make efforts to prevent these beliefs from cropping up nonconsciously in the future. It must take seriously the agapic ideal of embracing a diversity of perspectives on the common-sense beliefs in question (cf. Sharp 1994, 203–10). Members of hegemonic groups, such as whites and men, may *consciously* repudiate discrimination in all its forms and yet still fall prey to old habits they do not realize are informing their decisions. This scenario is further complicated by how often these hegemonic groups are overrepresented, because of the continued systemic injustice toward people of color and women in the United States. This creates situations where a single community member or small group of members may identify racist or sexist beliefs to which the majority of members are blind. Ideally those in the majority will respect a non-hegemonic per-spective as representing *experience*, of socio-political secondness, that the majority of community members have never had. They will real-ize that their own imagination-experiments are insufficient to the ex-tent that they are not informed by this non-hegemonic experience. This way, even though the non-hegemonic perspective may be poorly represented numerically, it can still hold legitimate sway regarding the common-sense belief(s) in question.[29]

Let me offer a hypothetical example to highlight this point, an ex-ample drawn from twelve years of volunteer work with children with muscular dystrophy at special summer camps designed to be power-wheelchair and power-scooter friendly. Say a group of fully able-bod-ied people had, with great care, designed blueprints for a summer camp for children in wheelchairs or power-scooters. Would it be rea-sonable for this able-bodied planning committee to dismiss feedback from someone who uses a power-wheelchair and who noted that the blueprints, while making due consideration for ramps instead of stairs, had doorways throughout the camp that were too narrow to accommodate power chairs? Would it be reasonable for them to say, "You are just playing the wheelchair card"? When I use this example with my classes, my students tend to guffaw or laugh when I give the "wheelchair card" line, because it is straightforwardly clear that the feedback in question reflects experience and perspective that the able-bodied people probably lack and that they *need* in order to success-fully bring about their end of a "barrier-free" summer camp. This hypothetical example shows the value of feedback from a single per-son who represents a non-hegemonic perspective that others in the community do not share. At the University of Portland, where I cur-rently teach, my colleague Fay Beeler, who is the assistant director of the Physical Plant, tells me that input from wheelchair-using students has been essential in making the campus accessible. The able-bodied Physical Plant staff simply cannot anticipate all the modifications necessary on this front, even though they are deeply committed to fully serving the wheelchair-using student population.[30]

Unfortunately, it is all too easy for a majority of community members, who represent hegemonic perspectives, to dismiss non-hegemonic perspectives. Moreover, this hegemonic dismissal is facilitated by the very blind spots the diverse members can help to detect. Returning to my focus on racism and sexism, nonconscious prejudice against people of color and/or women can emerge in the form of *dismissing* these perspectives as illegitimate. In this way the historical loophole overlaps with the contemporary one, as prejudices that have supposedly been overcome continue to operate nonconsciously.

In what follows, I outline two related mechanisms of hegemonic dismissal—first, an appeal to the craziness or irrelevance of the non-hegemonic perspective, and, second, an appeal to the lack of conscious discriminatory intent of those belonging to hegemonic groups. Before continuing, let me remind the reader that, as discouraging as the phenomenon of hegemonic dismissal is, describing and understanding its mechanisms reflect the self-control that can, in turn, criticize these mechanisms and work to change them.

II. TWO MECHANISMS OF HEGEMONIC DISMISSAL

(a) *Craziness or Irrelevance* Given the danger, discussed in Chapter 2, that someone's community could convince her that she is mad/abnormal/inferior, it is not entirely surprising that a mechanism of hegemonic dismissal involves an accusation of craziness or irrelevance. Marilyn Frye argues that a common mechanism for the exclusion of non-hegemonic perspectives is their dismissal as "crazy" (1983, 84–85, 112). Frye discusses this dismissal in the context of the anger of women and, implicitly, others in non-hegemonic groups.[31] This anger, as Frye conceives it, is a social act that makes a claim for respect regarding a domain in which one is experiencing unwarranted obstruction (85 ff.). She gives the example of a woman who "had gone to some trouble to adjust the carburetor on her car and shortly thereafter an attendant at a gas station started monkeying with it. She was dismayed and sharply told him to stop. He became very agitated and yelled at her, calling her a crazy bitch" (89). In patriarchal societies, it is common for women's anger to be dismissed as crazy if it is

expressed regarding domains that are outside of "the place and functions of Mother/Caretaker/Conserver/Helpmate," which are realms
considered "appropriate" to women (90 ff.). Outside of these realms
(such as the domain of cars), it is common for a woman *not* to receive
"uptake" regarding the domain of her complaint; instead the subject
can shift to her sanity (84, 88–89). She is "crazy," and her claim for
respect and legitimate inclusion in the domain is dismissed.

Broadening Frye's observations about dismissals of non-hegemonic claims, I do not think that the dismissal—as "crazy" or irrelevant—of testimony from women or others in non-hegemonic groups
is dependent on their being perceived as angry. That is to say, someone in a non-hegemonic group can be perceived as calm and unfazed
even while her input is seen as off the mark. In such cases, I would
argue, following Frye, that a claim for respect is still being made regarding the subject matter under discussion. In the context of my
project, the subject matter has been the presence of racism, sexism,
and other social ills. The corresponding claim for respect involves,
for example, the expertise of a woman of color on issues of racism/
sexism—expertise based on a wealth of experience of patterns recognized as racist and sexist secondness. Bell hooks recounts giving a talk

> . . . where many white students expressed their disdain for the
> ideas I expressed, and for my presence, by booing. I challenged
> the group to consider that what I was saying was not as disturbing
> to the group as was my embodied young-looking presence, a
> black female with natural hair in braids. I had barely finished this
> comment before a *liberal white male* in the group attacked claim-
> ing "you are playing the race card here." His immediate defensive
> response is often the feedback that comes when black people/peo-
> ple of color make an observation about the everyday dynamics of
> race and racism, sex and sexism that does not conform to privi-
> leged white perceptions. (2003b, 30, my emphasis)

Bell hooks's hypothesis was that her presence as a black woman triggered the booing from her Euro-American white audience. She was
accused of playing the race card, an accusation that summarily dismissed her hypothesis (hooks 2003b, 30–31). While it is clear that this

scenario was probably not the most ideal setting for inquiry, we can also recall the story of Marilyn Frye's reaction, discussed in Chapter 3, to the woman of color who accused her of racism (1983, 111–12).

Frye's scenario *was* a communal-inquiry setting, in which Frye and other Euro-American white women "formed a white women's consciousness-raising group to identify and explore the racism in [their] lives with a view to dismantling the barriers that blocked [our] understanding and action in this matter" (Frye 1983, 111). The larger objective was to address problems of racism within feminist circles. As Frye recalls, "[O]ne Black woman criticized us very angrily for ever thinking we could achieve our goals by working only with white women" (111). Frye explained to the woman that she and the rest of the white group had not meant to be exclusive and had planned to "organize a group open to all women shortly after [our] series of white women's meetings came to a close" (111–12). The woman of color was not satisfied by Frye's explanation, as it still revolved around *white* people calling the shots about how to handle racism issues. Frye thought the woman of color sounded crazy, at least at first. Then it occurred to Frye that thinking someone seems crazy can be a by-product of hegemonic privilege—in this case, Frye's white privilege. She therefore "backed off" to regain her "balance" about the dynamics that were really at play (112).

Calling someone crazy need not be a conscious rhetorical ruse that intentionally exploits a power differential. It also need not take the form either of a literal accusation of craziness or of a bold assertion such as "You are playing the race card!" This is because, once again, common-sense beliefs can shape one's worldview *nonconsciously*, including the concepts used to organize one's experience (Frye 1983, 112).[32] This means that, for example, a certain hypothetical white, male scientist may *sincerely* believe that a woman of color's feedback about racism/sexism is crazy or irrelevant. He may be a committed Critical Common-sensist who is dedicated to ending discrimination on all fronts. Nonetheless, her voice may have no place in his conceptual scheme, wherein neither race nor sex presents obstacles to

human experience. He may not have experienced socio-political secondness in either of these forms. The woman's point of view may be
"non-sensical," because it names perspectives and obstacles that *do
not exist* for him. His hegemonic privilege enables him to falsely universalize his perspective—that is, to assume that his obstacle-free experience regarding race and sex applies to everyone else (Frye 1983,
117). The woman of color's non-hegemonic perspective, from his
point of view, may thus be akin to a logical impossibility (158; cf. 152–
74).[33] This is not to say that this scientist *cannot* embrace her perspective. Rather, the "craziness"/"irrelevance" of her perspective is rooted
in nonconsciously operative common-sense beliefs that enable him
to dismiss her perspective instead of respecting it as a legitimate challenge to his own. Moreover, because of the scientist's hegemonic privilege, he is *not forced* to respect her marginalized perspective. He has
the *power to choose* whether or not to grant her respect (111). If she
were big and strong in some way, she could use her power to make
him listen. But often she is not.[34]

The example of Alcoff's Chicana friend and her white, male department chair exemplifies these points. Her non-hegemonic perspective, deeply informed by experiences of racism/sexism in the
classroom, was considered irrelevant by him in negotiating the white,
male graduate student's complaint about her. Her hypothesis, that
the graduate student's grievance was based on "his discomfort in the
position of teaching assistant to a Chicana," was dismissed (Alcoff
2001 66). The chair falsely universalized his experience as a white,
male faculty member, where race and sex do not enter the classroom
as obstacles. Recall that Alcoff spoke to this man and believed that he
was trying to treat this woman fairly (67). Yet he tried to do so by an
appeal to his own white, male experience, instead of "second-
guess[ing] his ability to judge the case, given the fact that he has never
himself experienced teaching as a woman of color, nor seen a woman
of color alone in a classroom full of White students" (67). The chair
was nonconsciously racist and sexist, I would argue, because he dismissed as irrelevant the woman of color's hypothesis without subjecting it to fair testing (by talking with other students and with

institutional officials who had expertise on racism/sexism in the class-room) (67). He fell prey to the fallacy of "I don't see racism and sex-ism at play, thus they are not present."

As noted earlier, I do not mean to point the finger only at Euro-American white men. In her list of Euro-American white privileges that she enjoys, Peggy McIntosh lists the following:

> I can be casual about whether or not to listen to another wo-man's voice in a group in which she is the only member of her race. . . .
> If I declare there is a racial issue at hand, or there isn't a racial issue at hand, my race will lend me more credibility for either position than a person of color will have.
> I can choose to ignore developments in minority writing and mi-nority activist programs, or disparage them. (1988, 293–94)

These privileges are often hard for Euro-American whites to recog-nize within a culture that falsely universalizes Euro-American white experience as the norm. McIntosh also highlights her heterosexual privileges, as noted in Chapter 1 (1988, 297–98). And she notes how privileges relating to "class, religion, ethnic status, or geographical lo-cation" are "intricately intertwined" (293). There are many ways that hegemonic privilege can take shape nonconsciously.

Also noted above, since the tendency to falsely universalize one's own experience—thereby perpetuating racism, sexism, etc.—is often nonconscious, it can be hard, if not impossible, to detect among members of a community who all *share* the same nonconscious ex-clusionary beliefs. In the case of Alcoff's friend, "the department ma-jority" was white, and this group failed to challenge the chair's dismissal of the racism/sexism hypothesis (Alcoff 2001, 67). The hege-monic majority can be tempted to override the non-hegemonic voice, because it seems, to them, not to measure up conceptually; it seems, to them, crazy or irrelevant to the inquiry at hand. This mechanism of dismissal is strengthened when paired with another, the appeal to lack of racist, sexist, etc., intent on the part of those in hegemonic groups.

(b) *Lack of Conscious Intent*   We return to the folk-assumption that, if one is not consciously racist, sexist, etc., then one cannot act in a racist, sexist, etc., manner (Alcoff 2006, 188). Take, once again, the *liberal* white male who accused bell hooks of "playing the race card" when she suggested that her audience gave her a poor reception be-cause of her race and sex. Presumably this man was both anti-racist and anti-sexist, and yet he dismissed her claim with vigor (hooks 2003b, 30–31). The white, male department chair described by Alcoff is presumably consciously anti-racist and anti-sexist too (Alcoff 2001, 67). These examples reflect the "disconnect" described above— between, on the one hand, one's conscious motivation, and, on the other hand, nonconsciously habitual behavior. The folk assumption looks only for conscious motivation. Finding none, it thereby *dis-misses* the hypothesis that behavior can nonetheless be racist, sexist, and so on.

My Peircean critique of this folk assumption resonates with Jeffrey Gauthier's critique of Kant's ethical theory (2004). While I do not think that either the liberal white male of hooks's story or the depart-ment chair of Alcoff's story are necessarily card-carrying Kantian eth-icists, I do think the folk assumption about racism and sexism reflects a Kantian legacy. Gauthier argues that Kant's ethical theory relies so heavily on the motive of duty that it cannot address societal preju-dices that may inform (and historically *have* informed) the applica-tion of the Categorical Imperative.[35] Moreover, making the motive of duty the fulcrum of moral concern actually *undermines* the detection of such prejudices. This is because Kantian ethical agents, in assessing the moral dimensions of a situation, look no further than their con-scious motives. Gauthier writes,

> One of the features of systems of oppression such as racism and sexism that makes them so difficult to change is the fact that even thoughtful and perceptive moral agents can perpetuate these sys-tems without consciously willing any racist or sexist principles at all. By making the good will the sole criterion of the right, Kant-ianism directs the agent's moral attention to the conscious inten-tions of [an] act rather than to its objective function as part of a

broader system. Perhaps just as importantly, because the conscientious moral agent who has tested his principles to the best of his abilities with Kant's formal test will believe that he has done all that is morally required, he may be unlikely to perceive concerns that escaped the net of that procedure as having great moral significance at all. (2004, 11, my emphasis)

Gauthier is highlighting how focusing on only conscious intention fosters a false confidence that one has done a sufficient check against discriminatory behaviors, since, on a conscious level, one finds no discriminatory intent. This false confidence often fuels the dismissal of feedback that one's behavior is/was, in fact, discriminatory.

This dismissal by means of good intentions assumes that sincerely paper-doubting common-sense beliefs is sufficient to ensure their eradication: "I find racism and sexism to involve dubitable beliefs, therefore they no longer inform my thought and actions." Ironically, this stance is itself an enactment of exclusionary privilege. It assumes that non-hegemonic voices, such as those of people of color and women, are not relevant to the question of whether racist or sexist acts are being committed. Built in to the habits of both Euro-American white privilege and male privilege is the prerogative to ignore the perspectives outside the circle of privilege (McIntosh 1988, 293–94). Therefore, the very efforts of those in hegemonic groups to be anti-discriminatory can involve a nonconscious exercise of discriminatory exclusion. Bell hooks comments on racism in this respect:

> Once we can face all the myriad ways white-supremacist thinking shapes our daily perceptions, we can understand the reasons liberal whites who are concerned with ending racism may simultaneously hold on to beliefs and assumptions that have their roots in white supremacy. (2003b, 30)

We are led once again to Peirce's inclusive communal ideal, in which efforts to eliminate racist, sexist, and other discriminatory common-sense beliefs should embrace the perspectives of those most affected by these beliefs. Good intentions cannot be allowed to block the road of inquiry if a community is to successfully implement Critical Common-sensism.

Part 3: Loving Reasonableness: Critical Common-sensism,
Science, and Agape

We are now in a position to see how the proactive interpretation of Critical Common-sensism I have offered in this chapter addresses the application problem that can undermine the practice of science and agapic love. The success of Critical Common-sensism on this front depends on its active interplay with both scientific and agapic ideals. It is likely, in the United States, for nonconscious racist, sexist, and other discriminatory beliefs to be shared by the majority of a community of inquiry, who are often members of hegemonic groups such as whites, men, and so on. This can occur even among well-meaning hegemonic-group members who repudiate racism, sexism, and other forms of discrimination. Critical common-sensism gives us the tools to identify this problem as the continued functioning of dubitable common-sense beliefs, which have only been sincerely paper-doubted, leaving their habitual, embodied roots in tact. Moreover, synthesizing CCSist analysis with the ideals of science and agape provides a way out of the impasse presented by these shared nonconscious hegemonic beliefs.

Critical Common-sensism carries with it both the spirit of science and the spirit of agape, which the pragmaticist embraces as part and parcel of his or her commitment to knowledge and truth. In a discussion of Critical Common-sensism, Peirce puts it this way:

> [W]hat he adores, if he is a good pragmaticist, is *power*; not the sham power of brute force, which, even in its own specialty of spoiling things, secures such slight results; but the creative power of reasonableness, which subdues all other powers, and rules over them with its scepter, knowledge, and its globe, love. It is as one of the chief lieutenants of reasonableness that he highly esteems doubt, although it is not amiable. (CP 5.520, Peirce's emphasis)

This passage synthesizes the interrelationship of Critical Common-sensism, science, and agape, highlighting the importance of embracing doubt, "although it is not amiable." In the context of the application problem, doubt occurs as a challenge to the hegemonic assumption that racist, sexist, or other discriminatory common-sense beliefs have been eradicated and thus cannot be present in a given community of inquiry. Doubt involves a non-hegemonic hypothesis that discrimination of some form is present, even though discriminatory common-sense beliefs have supposedly been eliminated. It is common for those in hegemonic groups to dismiss hypotheses about discrimination when voiced by those in non-hegemonic groups, a dismissal that is often fueled by false confidence in the effectiveness of sincere paper-doubt.

Both science and agape supplement this Critical Common-sensist diagnosis, echoing the demand that the non-hegemonic hypothesis be given a fair hearing. Science, for its part, pursues knowledge about reality. Its efforts are undermined by exclusionary instinctive beliefs that prevent the identification of large-scale racist, sexist, and other discriminatory habits. These habits play out through racist, sexist or other discriminatory secondness not usually experienced by those in corresponding hegemonic groups. It is of scientific interest to honor hypotheses from community members representing non-hegemonic groups, as the unique experiences of these members (compared to those in hegemonic groups) make them epistemological assets to the community as a whole. These non-hegemonic community members are necessary to the growth of knowledge. The scientific embrace of a hypothesis about discrimination goes hand in hand with both the ideal of an infinitely inclusive community of inquiry and the agapic imperative to embrace difference, even and especially when this difference feels threatening (EP 1:353; cf. Anderson 1995a, 108–9).

The agapic ideal works from the perspective of a loving concern that bolsters self-control. On the one hand, it can be *very tempting* for those in hegemonic groups to respond to a non-hegemonic hypothesis with the "brute force" of rejecting the doubt such a hypothesis creates, by labeling the hypothesis crazy or irrelevant (CP 5.520). The felt certainty of nonconsciously functioning common-sense beliefs can be so strong as to preclude self-control. Recall Peirce's rather phenomenological description of self-control in "Grounds of the Validity of the Laws of Logic": "Self-control seems to be the capacity for rising to an extended view of a practical subject instead of seeing only temporary urgency" (W 2:261 n. 6). This "temporary urgency" can involve protecting one's view of herself as morally good and therefore incapable of behaving in a racist, sexist, or otherwise discriminatory fashion (W 2:261 n. 6; Sullivan 2006, 128).[36] It can feel so uncomfortable to grant the possibility that one has unwittingly perpetuated racism, sexism, etc., that an appeal to good intentions can be, ironically enough, used as a tool of exclusionary sympathy. "Temporary urgency" can also manifest in the "need" to restore a comfort level for the majority of community members (W 2:261 n. 6). If the hypothesis of the presence of racism, sexism, etc., "goes away," then most of "us" will feel much more comfortable.

On the other hand, in the same description of self-control, Peirce links self-control with the expanded perspective of the loving community:

> Self-control seems to be the capacity for rising to an extended view of a practical subject instead of seeing only temporary urgency. This is the only freedom of which man has any reason to be proud; and *it is because love of what is good for all on the whole, which is the widest possible consideration, is the essence of Christianity, that it is said that the service of Christ is perfect freedom.* (W 2:261 n. 6, my emphasis)

Agape, as the Christian ideal, informs self-control by giving the human organism affective footing *beyond* the immediate urgency of restoring one's own comfort level, or the comfort level of the majority. This affective footing is a love that embraces what is different, even and especially when that difference feels threatening to it. In this case, one's *concern* for the community member reporting discrimination, and thus creating doubt, overrides the dismissal-temptation. If, for example, someone is experiencing racism, which I may not grasp as a result of my being white, then I *want* to hold that feedback in place, even if it means that I (or others) have acted in a racist manner. While this may not be a comfortable admission for me to make, my concern for my community-mate will, ideally, lead me to hold her testimony in place, so that it can be acted on.

One who loves reasonableness, then, "highly esteems doubt, although it is not amiable" (CP 5.520). Indeed, doubt is not "amiable" when it manifests as a jarring interruption of one's projects and/or as a shock to one's sense of oneself as a flawless promoter of justice. Nonetheless, embracing doubt promotes growth in reasonableness, and rejecting it undermines self-control. More specifically, embracing doubt—via embracing the hypothesis that racist, sexist, etc., common-sense beliefs are still in play—allows those in hegemonic groups to diversify their understanding of racism, sexism, or other discrimination as functioning in more settings than they imagined possible. Their understanding of these types of discrimination is rendered more complex and nuanced. To reject doubt, through rejecting the hypothesis, is to surrender to the nonconscious operation of dubitable common-sense beliefs. This surrender undermines self-control, because it turns a blind eye on belief-habits that are undermining one's thought and behavior. It blocks the road of inquiry, breaking Peirce's First Rule of Reason: "[I]n order to learn you must desire to learn and in so desiring not be satisfied with what you already incline to think" (EP 2:48).

Someone may object that this embrace of non-hegemonic perspectives allows for an "anything goes" attitude in science or everyday life—such that any feedback whatsoever can take center stage—which would erode the possibility of productive rational discourse. Several points can be made in response to this concern. First of all, the non-hegemonic perspectives under discussion involve oppression. *Groups* are being targeted by racism, sexism, and so on, not merely an individual here or there. The patterns of feedback are compelling in their revelation of large-scale hegemonic habits. Second, even if an individual *were* giving a completely unique hypothesis, this alone would not count against it. Peirce's philosophy is committed to embracing creative novelty, as long as the corresponding hypotheses are subjected to the scientific method, which is my next point. Finally, the Peircean community of inquiry adheres to the scientific method. Hypotheses generated by this community will be subjected to the rigors of that method: They must have explanatory power, for example, and pass through the stages of deduction and induction. Granting special status to historically underrepresented, non-hegemonic perspectives does not change this.

Moreover, their special epistemological status does not confer on non-hegemonic groups a "god's eye" view on things. It is to say, however, that someone who is oppressed because of race, for example, has a perspective on experience that a white person probably *does not* have. The same point applies to other axes of oppression. In 2010, it is part of the public discourse in the U.S. mainstream that both racism and sexism are wrong. To this extent they have been cast into sincere paper-doubt. Whether or not the deep-rooted habits associated with each are still in play *cannot be determined* without consulting people of color and women. These are the groups who encounter the most racist and sexist secondness stemming from societal racist and sexist beliefs.

Community members in hegemonic groups are called to follow Marilyn Frye's example. They can acknowledge that seeing a non-hegemonic perspective as "crazy" is often a knee-jerk, exclusionary reaction that signals the false universalization—and corresponding close-mindedness—that can accompany hegemonic privilege (Frye 1983, 112). Instead, they can aspire after what Patricia Williams describes as "the insight that comes with the lack of prejudice, the abandon of prejudgment, the willingness to see another viewpoint and be converted if only for a moment, to allow oneself to be held in a state of suspended knowing" (1997, 74). This profound humility described by Williams echoes the rigors of Peirce's self-control ideally practiced—as self-critical, scientific, fallible, reasonable, and loving toward others. Thus the application problem finds a Peircean response in the interwoven demands of Critical Common-sensism, scientific method, and agapic love, which all fuel the "creative power of reasonableness" (CP 5.520).

CONCLUSION

To build community requires vigilant awareness of the work we must continually do to undermine all the socialization that leads us to behave in ways that perpetuate domination.

bell hooks, 2003b, 36

For we have, built into all of us, old blueprints of expectation and response, old structures of oppression, and these must be altered at the same time as we alter the living conditions which are a result of those structures.

Audre Lorde, 1984, 123

These words from bell hooks and Audre Lorde underscore a problematic lack of social critical sensitivity that informs Peirce's philosophy, as he largely failed to address the oppressive dynamics that can undermine, in actual communities, the ideal of infinite inclusion.[1] While *infinite* inclusion itself cannot be literally achieved in flesh-and-blood communities, I would argue that the fallibilism and openness represented by this ideal *can* be achieved. This achievement requires work on the part of community members in hegemonic groups to unearth nonconscious exclusionary beliefs that can tempt them to inappropriately reject feedback that represents non-hegemonic perspectives. Resisting this rejection, through agape, *enacts* infinite inclusion as an ongoing epistemological ideal.

I have argued that Peirce's philosophy, especially its affective dimensions, has resources to contribute to discussions in social criticism when his work is proactively read in conjunction with social critical thinking. Had Peirce not been blinded by his own race, sex,

{ 273 }

heterosexual, and social class privilege, he might have made more explicit that a community of inquiry is epistemologically deficient to the extent that it refuses membership and/or input from non-hegemonic groups. His later work's focus on agape and the repudiation of greed is likely an outgrowth of his own experience of poverty in his later years, coupled with his exclusion from social, scientific, and other intellectual communities of inquiry (Brent 1998, 136–322, esp. 259–62).[2] These biographical factors are arguably experiential inroads that helped Peirce's philosophy grow into its incorporation of agape, which is a key affective strategy for those in hegemonic groups to employ when they have difficulty being open to non-hegemonic perspectives. Nonetheless, in order for its social critical potential to come to fuller voice, Peirce's philosophy needs input from social critical thinkers. Thus my project's proactive reading of Peirce has been fueled by insights from race theory and feminism.

While contributions and challenges from social criticism help render his ideas more attuned to justice and thus more consistent with his own ideals, Peirce can make contributions to social criticism as well. Primary among these contributions are conceptual tools that can help those in hegemonic groups come to awareness about nonconscious exclusionary belief-habits and the mechanisms through which these nonconscious belief-habits can shape their thoughts and behavior. Achieving this awareness is a crucial initial step for changing such growth-inhibiting belief-habits, for those who are so inclined.

Peirce's ideas can help those in hegemonic groups grasp the oppressive dynamics that a hegemonic society hides from their view, while also affirming the possibility for self-controlled growth beyond these dynamics. His account of reality acknowledges both the perniciousness of indurate, exclusionary socio-political habits *and* the possibility for humans to change these habits. The affective and phenomenological dimensions of his thought point to the subtle ways exclusionary socio-political bias can inform the very concepts one uses to understand her or his world and other persons. At the same time, his Critical Common-sensist ideals are underwritten by the ideals of science and agape, both of which are committed to embracing diverse perspectives. Actual communities of inquiry are challenged by Peirce to cultivate agape, especially those in which privileged groups continue to be overrepresented, such as Euro-Americans, men, heterosexuals, the economically secure, and other hegemonic groups in the United States. This cultivation of agape is enhanced by a flexible imagination schooled in coloring outside of conceptual lines, so to speak. This way when individuals from non-hegemonic groups identify ongoing discrimination, their input can be embraced as a source of communal growth out of oppressive habits.

Peirce's account of child development illuminates where the seeds of socio-politically shaped common-sense beliefs are first planted, and why these beliefs can be difficult to change. The preceding chapters have shown that the seeds planted in childhood—and reinforced by society—can grow deep roots, becoming some of the illegitimately indubitable background beliefs with which Critical Common-sensism contends. Young children are vulnerable and dependent upon their caretakers and communities to teach them how "reality" works. In hegemonic societies, children can internalize growth-inhibiting habits whether they belong to oppressed or to privileged groups. My focus has been on the latter. The coercive survival dilemma makes it difficult for privileged children to resist forming exclusionary socio-political habits, such as the false universalizing tendencies of white, male, heterosexual, middle-class, and other forms of privilege.

The effectiveness of Peirce's ideas for consciousness-raising has been shown to me repeatedly in my upper-level Self and Identity philosophy course, where I teach Peirce's phenomenology and his ideas about ideal communal inquiry. I present Peirce's thought alongside Antonio Damasio's work and insights from social criticism, as I have done in this book. My white students, who form the vast majority in these classes, have repeatedly demonstrated how helpful they find Peirce's ideas for articulating race dynamics of which they had not previously been aware. They talk with fluency about firstness, secondness, and thirdness, as they realize how their whiteness can operate within their firstness, causing secondness to people of color, even though they themselves have not intended to be the source of racist secondness. My students of color often use Peirce's ideas, alongside social criticism readings, to describe their own varied experiences with racism dynamics in the United States.

In this course (and others), I make efforts to incorporate a plurality of perspectives into my course material, in order to challenge the false universalization of the typical white, male, Western canonical philosophy syllabus. In conjunction with these curricular efforts, I also facilitate class discussions about racism, sexism, and other forms of discrimination. This facilitation includes coaching my students about agapic listening with respect to being in a hegemonic group. I also explain how Peirce's admonition not to block the road of inquiry involves careful and considerate contributions to class discussion. This means that each student who participates must work to frame her or his contributions to discussion—in tone and in word choice—so that others may still feel safe and comfortable responding, even if they disagree. This conscientiousness in communication helps keep inquiry open.

Beyond work in the classroom with college-age students who are primarily eighteen to twenty-two years old, I think that Peircean/affective/social critical insights can be fruitfully applied in *children's* classrooms. In fact, attention to how children are educated transforms the dependency and malleability of childhood habit-taking into a source of hope and social change. I am not suggesting that elementary school students be asked to read Peirce! I *am* suggesting that formal and informal elementary education can introduce children to an agapic social outlook that both embraces diversity and is attuned to invisibilities that result from hegemonic exclusions.[3] The trust children must place in their caretakers, as well as the corresponding belief-habit formation that occurs, can be the targets of growth-*promoting* guidance and reinforcement.

Does this promotion of agape involve a political manipulation of children's habit-taking? Yes. The linkage between politics and education, however, is a natural one.[4] Education is how a society passes on its values to future generations (Dewey [1916] 1944, 2 ff.). And this need not involve ideological indoctrination. As John Dewey and Paulo Freire each argue, education *can* involve the mere transference of facts or propaganda, but it can also be liberating. Students can be taught how to actively think about the world and to view it critically (Dewey [1916] 1944; Freire 1970 [1997]). In a democratic society, like the United States, education is all the more important, since voting citizens are ideally literate ones who can converse intelligently about the concerns of the state (Nussbaum 1997, 1–14).

Moreover, unlike the limited democracy of ancient Greece, the United States is a democratic society that "talks the talk" of including all people, regardless of their race, sex, sexuality, economic class, etc. (a marked exception, in 2010, being the social and legal resistance to same-sex marriage). It thus follows that childhood education should be seen as a way to invest in this inclusion (Sharp 1994; Greene 1997).[5] It should also be noted that educational experiences that either promote or overlook the false universalization of hegemonic experience (as white, male, heterosexual, economically secure, and so on) involve a political manipulation of childhood habit-taking too. Only in this case, nonconscious racist, sexist, heterosexist, economic classist, etc., belief-habits are being reinforced, and these same nonconscious belief-habits often render invisible the types of discrimination actually experienced by people of color, women, GLBTQs, the poor, and others in non-hegemonic groups. I have demonstrated how these nonconscious belief-habits can lead to the dismissal of feedback given by these groups, because of the continued overrepresentation of whites, men, heterosexuals, the economically secure, and other hegemonic groups in actual communities of inquiry in the United States. Because of the limited experience that whites and men, for example, have with racism and sexism, respectively, they often have limited capacities for imagining the continued presence of these social ills.

I suggest that the elementary school classroom is a place where cultivating children's imaginations toward the embrace of diversity can help break the cycle of perpetual false universalization and its corresponding blind spots. In classes where students belong primarily to hegemonic groups, the cultivation of the imagination can be a way to compensate for the lack of diversity among the students. With imaginations exposed to diversity, children belonging to hegemonic groups may gain an enhanced ability to spot economic classism, heterosexism, racism, sexism, and other forms of discrimination for themselves. They may also be better prepared to listen to the corresponding testimony of the poor, GLBTQs, people of color, women, and others in non-hegemonic groups.[6]

As Peirce scholars know, Peirce values the imagination as a source of creativity and growth. He says that "next after the passion to learn there is no quality so indispensable to the successful prosecution of science as imagination" (CP 1.47, ca. 1896).[7] He promotes musement as a state where one's imagination can engage in "Pure Play," understood as *freedom to roam about* without the constraints of control and purpose (EP 2:436 ff.). In other words, he promotes the cultivation of an imagination open to embracing what is different from existing belief-habit systems. The agapic embrace of difference is facilitated by an imagination exercised in welcoming ideas that are radically different from what has been experienced or thought of before. Peirce encourages the muser to let her imagination experience freedom from all rules (EP 2:436 ff.). It is this freedom that helps a person learn to step outside the familiar.

In the spirit of opening inquiry into how to cultivate imagination in the elementary school classroom, I suggest literature as one fruitful avenue. This avenue can be especially helpful for the relatively homogenous classrooms that often characterize the experience of Euro-American, white, middle-class, heterosexual children in the United States, who may grow into well-meaning adults who are unaware of the extent of racism, sexism, discrimination against the poor, heterosexism, and other social ills in this country. Let me be quick to acknowledge that educational reform is desperately needed in the United States, in order that these homogenous classrooms stop reflecting extreme racism-based disparities in funding and resources.[8] Until this reform is achieved, I would argue that interim measures should occur now in these hegemonic-group-dominant classrooms, to promote awareness in children, so that more future adults can be sensitized to the deeper issues at play.

To offer a brief sketch: Literature can address two dimensions of imagination that especially need cultivation in order for those in privileged groups to counter the false universalization of human experience that can occur in the United States. These two dimensions are the agapic ability to embrace the different and the ability to notice the *absence* of diversity. The first dimension involves an expansion of the capacity for empathy—that is, the ability to put oneself in another's shoes.[9] The second involves an attunement to the invisible, such that someone notices that, say, there were *no* people of color in the movie she just watched.

Regarding the imagination's appreciation of different perspectives, Martha Nussbaum contends that literature helps make empathetic knowledge of others possible, especially in instances where "[d]ifferences of religion, gender, race, class, and national origin make the task of understanding harder"—for literature provides a rich cast of characters who are different from oneself (1997, 85, 86). She uses the term "narrative imagination" to refer to sympathetic imagination that is developed via literature. Literature helps to develop in readers/ students an awareness of and respect for the complex and deeply meaningful inner worlds of others, a respect that carries with it a natural boundary of "respecting [the] separateness and privacy" of others (90). This is because, along with recognizing the inner worlds of others, the reader/student comes to understand that an inner world is not something that is fully "open to view" (90).[10] Important educational by-products of literary exposure, Nussbaum argues, are empathy and compassion, sentiments that are part of students' moral development (90 ff.). These sentiments fall under Peirce's portrayal of agapic sympathy, which involves a person's care and concern for others in her community.

Literature that portrays characters belonging to non-hegemonic groups can help the hegemonic-group student resist exclusionary beliefs that would otherwise fuel dismissal of non-hegemonic perspectives. It gives this student an opportunity to relate to the characters as human beings who share with her or him the basic experience of trying to move through life the best one can. Imagining what it might be like to be this character is an important educational moment, especially when the character embodies circumstances—and thus experiences types of secondness—that the hegemonic-group student has no way of experiencing personally, such as being of a different race or sex (Nussbaum 1997, 92, 87 ff., 95 ff.). Teachers can help facilitate narrative imagination, in this case, through discussions or writing assignments that elicit personal responses to the story and that explore what it might be like to have experiences similar to those of a particular character.

The detection of false universalization involves a second dimension of imaginative flexibility that can be cultivated through childhood education: an imaginative attunement to the invisible. It involves seeing what is not there, so to speak. Nancy Tuana coined the phrase "reading as a woman" as a strategy both men and women can use to engage texts with a critical awareness of any implicit, as well as explicit, gender issues at play (1992, 5 ff.). I would call "reading with an attunement to the invisible" a development in imagination that builds on the first dimension of imaginative growth.[11] Hegemonic-group students who are equipped with an appreciation for the richness of human experience represented by the diverse characters in literature can, in turn, learn to recognize the *absence* of richness when they encounter it. These students can be encouraged to *problematize* portrayals of human experience—in literature, textbooks, the media, etc.—that represent primarily, for example, Euro-American white, middle-class people (Greene 1997).[12]

Nussbaum brings together these two dimensions of imagination development (the embrace of different perspectives and the attunement to lack of diversity) and underscores the importance of the linkage between childhood and the imagination. She advises that the development of narrative imagination begin in childhood, as children engage with their caretakers in storytelling (Nussbaum 1997, 89 ff., 93): "A child deprived of stories is deprived, as well, of certain ways of viewing other people" (89). The more children are exposed to stories and the rich casts of characters that can be found in literature, the more they will be attuned to the richness of perspectives that humanity represents. Literature, then, by providing windows into different perspectives on human experience, helps children develop their imaginative expectations regarding both specific texts and reality in general. The attuned intentionality through which children engage the world will be one that, ideally, *expects* to see a plurality of perspectives accounted for in their world. It will thus problematize and, again ideally, work to change a reality in which perspectives have been rendered invisible (Greene 1997).[13] Cultivated imaginations in children can thus lead to growth toward social justice.

As nice as this all sounds, I need to qualify my suggestion of focusing on childhood education as an important part of fostering change in the United States. While it is true that cultivating agapic imaginations in children fosters inclusive habits that can contribute to societal growth in the United States, it is imperative to hold in place the larger tensions in which this suggestion is situated. As much as I appreciate Nussbaum's vision regarding the power of literature, I do not want to be complacent with its optimism. Children receive many more messages about the world around them than what they are explicitly taught in school. They are inundated with extracurricular education from caretakers, other adults, and society in general, an education often permeated by exclusionary beliefs toward those in non-hegemonic groups. Such exclusionary messages are often portrayed to children without the conscious intention of adults, who may be unaware of their own behavior and/or who may be unaware of the heterosexist, racist, sexist, and other discriminatory messages that children are receiving from society at large, especially through the media. I agree with sociologists Debra Van Ausdale and Joe Feagin, who conclude their book *The First R: How Children Learn Race and Racism* by noting, "Obviously, the realities of race and racism do not start with children, and programs to eradicate racism cannot begin there either. . . . It is not a mystery where [young] children get their ideas: We adults are a primary source. . . . *They will not unlearn and undo racism until we do*" (2001, 214, my emphasis). Thus, the elementary education classroom efforts that I suggest for helping to foster agapic imaginations must be coupled with the ongoing efforts of adults to "unlearn and undo" racism, as well as heterosexism, sexism, and other forms of discrimination. And such efforts must be informed by openness to the fact that discrimination often happens by means of nonconscious belief-habits.

I will be the first to admit that, as helpful as Peirce's work can be for consciousness-raising, it does not offer concrete social-activist solutions regarding the individual and societal discriminatory belief-habits that his philosophy helps identify. My book points beyond itself in relationship to such solutions, solutions that will foster more concrete reform in U.S. schools, other institutions, and mainstream society as a whole.

Nonetheless, Peirce's ideas can help those in hegemonic groups who are committed to unlearning nonconscious discriminatory belief-habits. I use a Peircean lens to frame my own efforts to unlearn discrimination. I view these efforts as an imperfect, ongoing, and open-ended pursuit of agape. I know I will never finish unlearning unintentional racist, sexist, heterosexist, economic classist, etc., behaviors. If I were to consider myself finished, I would thereby become part of the problem, unwilling to listen to feedback about work I may still need to do in any of these areas.

I actively work to continually educate myself about different forms of oppression, pursuing readings, workshops, and conferences, as well as cultivating personal and professional relationships. For example, in October 2008, I attended the fifth annual California Roundtable on Philosophy and Race, where María Lugones gave the keynote address, "Coloniality of Gender and the Colonial Difference." Her talk, as well as the other paper presentations I attended, made it clear to me that my efforts in the present book lack a deep enough attunement to the impact of colonialism, past and present, within and beyond the borders of the United States. At this point in my professional development as a philosophy scholar, I need to educate myself much more fully about these issues. My work in this book thus points beyond itself in this respect as well, toward a better sensitivity to colonialism-critique that highlights how many people around the world, again past and present, have not been considered "human" from the standpoint of dominant Western countries, such as the United States. Lugones helped me to see this blind spot in my thinking and research.[14]

I thus see the conclusion to this book as an opening, not a closing. There is much more for me to learn as I work to use my privilege against itself[15] to promote social change. My corresponding developmental telos will continue to be Peirce's ideal of "giving a hand toward rendering the world more reasonable," as I continue to unlearn my own nonconscious discriminatory belief-habits and to help others in hegemonic groups do the same (EP 2:255).

Notes

1. I use "Euro-American white" to designate someone of European descent. Euro-American whites are perceived to be Caucasian in phenotype (i.e., physical characteristics). In this book I will at times use simply "Euro-American" or "white" as shorthand, depending on context. I agree with Marilyn Frye that the term "white" does not simply refer to phenotype but also calls into play socio-political privileges denied to those considered (by those secure in their own whiteness) *not* white. See, in this regard, Frye's "On Being White" (1983, 110–27; cf. 1992, 149–52).

2. My students have reported this transformation both in reflection papers, where their name is attached to their work, and in end-of-term anonymous course evaluations. Sometimes they are very explicit in their articulation of their realization. Other times they underscore, more generally, that their eyes have been opened, presumably about racism and other forms of discrimination we address in class.

3. I view *race*, along the lines of Marilyn Frye and Charles Mills, as stemming from phenotype (i.e., physical characteristics) but also involving the social construction of privilege and oppression (Mills 1998, 11 ff.; Frye 1983, 113–14; Frye 1992, 149–52). Charles Mills notes that "race" does not have scientific validity, but nonetheless has social reality (1998, 11 ff.). While I will not argue the point here, I believe that "race" is *real* in the Peircean sense, as it is both external to the individual human being, involving communal-scale habits, and race is also a source of belief and habit formation.

4. By "consciousness-raising" I mean an epistemological shift whereby an individual becomes aware of environmental factors (e.g., natural, social, economic, and/or political) that were previously unnoticed and/or not experienced by her. My thanks to Jeff Gauthier and Alex Santana for pushing me to clarify what I mean by this term.

5. My title is inspired by one of Marilyn Frye's titles, namely, *The Politics of Reality* (1983).

6. By "race theory" I mean philosophical critique that identifies and problematizes the use of race as an instrument of oppression and dehumanization. My choice of the term "race theory" to describe the race-oriented dimensions of my work in this book is indebted to personal conversations with Shannon Sullivan and Dwayne Tunstall, both of whom have given me an appreciation for how my work is not "critical race theory" in the latter's technical, historical sense. For a formal discussion of terminological issues on this front, see Tommy Curry, "Will the Real CRT Please Stand Up? The Dangers of Philosophical Contributions to CRT" (2009).

7. "Oppression" as I will be using the term refers to socio-political structures that target certain groups, subjecting them to limited options, which all involve some sort of "penalty, censure or deprivation" (Frye 1983, 2). Individuals belonging to historically and systematically oppressed groups (such as people of color, women, etc.) can be so outnumbered as to be the *only* woman and/or person of color in a particular community. Thus I use the terms "individual" and "group" somewhat synonymously in the discussions to follow. It is important to keep the following point in mind, however: Individuals cannot be oppressed insofar as they are *individuals*. Oppression targets *groups*. Individuals are oppressed only insofar as they belong to an oppressed group (7 ff., 15–16). Individuals can be oppressed on multiple fronts. Women of color who are poor, for example, have historically been oppressed because of economic class, race, sex, and, often, "Third World" status.

8. A striking example of racist reasoning can be found in Peirce's 1866 Lowell Lecture VI, where he argues against the implications of the following syllogism:

"All men are equal in their political rights

Negroes are men;

[Thus] Negroes are equal in political rights to whites."

Noting that "[t]he Declaration of Independence declares that it is 'self-evident that all men are created equal,'" Peirce argues: "Now men are created babies and therefore, in this case, *men* is used in a sense that includes babies and therefore nothing can follow from the argument relatively to the rights of Negroes which does not apply to babies, as well. The argument, therefore, can amount to very little" (W 1: 444, Peirce's emphasis). It is beyond the scope of my project to analyze the problems with Peirce's reasoning here. Fortunately, Peirce's ideas can be fruitfully applied to social criticism, even though Peirce himself had shortcomings on this front.

9. My thanks to Cathy Kemp and Mitchell Aboulafia for suggesting that I highlight this point more fully for my readers, in order to help humanize Peirce. Joseph Brent's *Charles Sanders Peirce: A Life* gives a detailed treatment of Peirce's decline into poverty in his later years; see chapters 4 and 5 (1998, 203–322). William James was instrumental in helping keep Peirce afloat during these years, eventually organizing the Peirce fund, which coordinated monetary contributions from Peirce's friends and supporters (304–7). Peirce's descent into poverty can be traced to such causal factors as his refusal of social conventions regarding marriage, his unconventional religious views, and other complicating factors, which contributed to a reputation so dubious that the doors to a career in academia were closed to him (136–202).

10. *The Essential Peirce*, 1:357, 362. A note on subsequent citations of Peirce's work is in order. Hereafter references to *The Essential Peirce*, volumes 1 and 2, are referred to as "EP," followed by volume number, then page number (Peirce 1992a, 1998). References to the *Collected Papers* are "CP," followed by the volume number, then paragraph number. For example, "CP 5.441" signifies volume 5 of the *Collected Papers*, paragraph 441 (Peirce, 1958–65). References to the *Writings of Charles S. Peirce* conform to the standard notation "W," followed by the volume and page numbers (Peirce 1982–86). "W 4:134," for example, signifies volume 4 of the *Writings*, page 134. Finally, references to *Reasoning and the Logic of Things* are abbreviated "RLT," followed by the page number (Peirce 1992b).

11. I thank David O'Hara for bringing this passage to my attention.

12. In his book *Strands of System*, Anderson explains why "the notion of strands of system is appropriate to Peirce's life work," drawing on the cable metaphor of reasoning, as well as on the fact that because of "his employment, travel, and marital and economic difficulties, Peirce had to work wherever and whenever he could. In a very direct way, then, readers of Peirce's work are forced to take up the variety of strands he produced to reconstruct the architectonic he offered" (1995b, 26). My own use of the term "strands" is smaller in scope than Anderson's. I apply it to describe the various strains of Peirce's thought that interweave with insights of social criticism, to form a cable of compatibility that depends not on a linear linkage but rather on an "intimate connection" among the ideas presented (W 2:213).

13. My work in this book is inspired by Lorraine Code's *Rhetorical Spaces* (1995). The compatibilities between her work and Peirce's are as striking as they are numerous. In graduate school, I read *Rhetorical Spaces* side by side with Peirce, my first exposure to both thinkers.

14. Lugones's book *Pilgrimages/Peregrinajes* (2003) has had a significant influence on my thinking about social criticism issues.

15. My definition of internalization is influenced by Amélie Rorty (1980) and Sandra Bartky (1990, 63–82).

16. "White privilege," to which I will be referring often, refers to the societal benefits that are granted to those who are considered phenotypically Caucasian. See Marilyn Frye's "On Being White" for a discussion of whiteness as an issue of social privilege, as distinct from phenotypical characteristics (1983, 110–27; cf. 1992, 149–52). See also Peggy McIntosh, "White Privilege and Male Privilege: A Personal Account of Coming to See Correspondences through Work in Women's Studies" (1988).

17. I use "GLBTQ" to refer to those who do not consider themselves heterosexual—namely, those who are gay, lesbian, bisexual, transgendered, queer, or questioning. My thanks to Devon Goss for fielding my questions about non-heterosexual groups.

18. For an introduction to pragmatist-feminism, see Seigfried's *Pragmatism and Feminism* (1996) and "Feminism and Pragmatism," the special issue of *Hypatia* that she edited (1993). Shannon Sullivan also does work in pragmatist-feminism; see *Living Across and Through Skins* (2001) and *Revealing Whiteness: The Unconscious Habits of Racial Privilege* (2006). For treatments specific to Peirce and feminism, see Marcia Moen's "Peirce's Pragmatism as Resource for Feminism," which focuses especially on the feminism-compatible roles played by feeling, the body, and semiotics in Peirce's epistemology (1991); Ann Margaret Sharp's "Peirce, Feminism, and Philosophy for Children," which draws extensive comparisons between feminist theory and Peirce's conception of the self, communal inquiry, and creative love (1994); Maryann Ayim's "The Implications of Sexually Stereotypic Language as Seen through Peirce's Theory of Signs" (1983); and Kory Spencer Sorrell's *Representative Practices: Peirce, Pragmatism, and Feminist Epistemology* (2004).

19. It should be noted that the gender categories of femininity and masculinity are Western constructions. To apply them outside of a traditional Western understanding can undermine an appreciation for the social dynamics and issues faced by non-Western cultures. My appreciation of this issue is shaped by Oyèrónké Oyewùmí's "Visualizing the Body: Western Theories and African Subjects" (1997), as well as by María Lugones's presentation "Coloniality of Gender and the Colonial Difference" at the California Roundtable on Philosophy and Race in 2008.

20. I borrow the term "liberatory epistemology" from Nancy Tuana, who provides a helpful introduction to feminist/liberatory epistemology in *En-*

gendering Rationalities (Tuana and Morgen 2001, 1–20). For additional reading, see *Feminist Epistemologies*, edited by Linda Alcoff and Elizabeth Potter
(1993).

21. For readers interested in how Peirce distinguished his own pragmatism from that of his contemporaries, see his essay "What Pragmatism Is"
(1905), where he introduced the term "pragmaticism" to distinguish his own
particular formulation of pragmatism (EP 2:331–45).

22. For further introduction to classical American pragmatism, please see
the following treatments, which were of great help to me in crafting my own
brief introduction to pragmatism here: John Stuhr's introduction to the second edition of *Pragmatism and Classical American Philosophy*, which is an
excellent collection of primary-source readings (2000, 1–9); "The Theory of
Practice," in Seigfried 1996, 3–16; and "Transactional Bodies after Dewey,"
in Sullivan 2001, 1–11. Vincent Colapietro (2000) provides an excellent specific introduction to Peirce's thought in the Stuhr collection.

23. For Peircean and other pragmatist scholars who are unfamiliar with
feminist philosophy, I recommend Susan Bordo's *Flight to Objectivity*, where
she offers a cultural, psychological, and historical alternative read of Descartes' *Meditations* that resonates with the pragmatist critique of Cartesian-
ism (1987). In the final chapter of her book, Bordo links her project with
explicitly feminist themes, thus providing a bridge of sorts for those who
might need one (97–118).

24. As a by-product both of narrowing my focus to racism and sexism
and of my attempt to continually gesture to other forms of hegemonic group
discrimination, my treatment of racism against people of color is limited
almost exclusively to whites who are also economically middle class (or
richer). I regret this limitation, for it certainly does not tell the whole story.
The denials about the prevalence of racism in the United States can differ
between middle-class and working-class whites. It has been noted by bell
hooks, for example, that working-class white adults are comfortable discussing the everyday manifestations of racism in the United States, while economically privileged white adults often deny them (2003b, 30). Shannon
Sullivan and Patricia Williams each discuss the well-intentioned "colorblindness" promoted by white *middle-class* parents/caretakers, which asserts
that race/color should not and *does* not matter anymore in societies like the
United States that have supposedly overcome racism against people of color.
Both explain how such "color-blindness" acts to hide the manifestations of
white supremacy that are still at play (Sullivan n.d., 22–28; 2006, 5, 61, 78–79,
123, 127, 189–92, 196; Williams 1997, esp. 3–16). It is this latter, middle-class
white dynamic that is prominent in this book.

25. Peirce's preferred spelling is "semeiotic." I will keep the traditional spelling of this term in this book, however, for two reasons. First, I will not be fully engaging Peirce's semeiotic system, and, second, I will be discussing sign generation in the context of Antonio Damasio's work. Keeping the traditional spelling will be less confusing as I draw parallels between the two thinkers (in Chapter 1). For readers interested in learning about Peirce's semeiotics, David Savan provides a nice introduction, "An Introduction to C. S. Peirce's Full System of Semeiotic" (1987–88). Also see James Liszka's *A General Introduction to the Semiotic of Charles Sanders Peirce* (1996). My thanks to André De Tienne for the recommendation of Liszka's book, which is often easier to track down than Savan's text.

26. My treatment of sentiment is limited here to the overlapping that Peirce highlights between instinct and sentiment, which I discuss in Chapters 1 and 4. I am well aware that more exploration of sentiment is needed than I provide in this book, exploration that builds more explicitly on sentiments as cultivated affects. See, in this regard, Hookway 2000, 223–45; Kemp-Pritchard 1981; and Savan 1981, 331–33.

27. See, for example, "Mimicking Foundationalism: On Sentiment and Self-Control" (Hookway 1993); *Truth, Rationality, and Pragmatism* (Hookway 2000); "Peirce on Philosophical Hope and Logical Sentiment" (Kemp-Pritchard 1981); "Peirce's Semiotic Theory of Emotion" (Savan 1981); "Cognition and Emotion in Peirce's Theory of Mental Activity" (Stephens 1981); and "Noumenal Qualia: C. S. Peirce on Our Epistemic Access to Feelings" (Stephens 1985). Notable exceptions regarding the embodiment theme include Vincent Colapietro's *Peirce's Approach to the Self* (1989, 69 ff.), and Marcia Moen's "Peirce's Pragmatism as Resource for Feminism" (1991, 438–43). I also found Colapietro's paper "Bodies in Commotion: Toward a Pragmatic Account of Human Emotions" helpful when I was first beginning to think about Peirce and affectivity (2002).

28. See, for example, "Eros and Agape in Creative Evolution: A Peircean Insight" (Hausman 1974); "Philosophy and Tragedy: The Flaw of Eros and the Triumph of Agape" (Hausman 1993); and "'Evolutionary Love' in Theory and Practice" (Ventimiglia 2001).

29. A small list includes his explicit linkage, in the 1866 Lowell Lectures, between feelings and the body (W 1:495). He makes consistent reference to embodied feelings throughout the rest of his corpus. The body is also strongly present in his phenomenology. In the Logic of Science essays from the 1870s, Peirce describes the human organism as a "logical animal" and suggests natural selection as an explanation for humans' hopeful disposi-

tions and their ability to reason synthetically (W 3:244, 318–19). And in 1898 he argues that science is derived from the instincts for nutrition and reproduction (EP 2:51; cf. CP 6.500). These examples demonstrate that, for Peirce, the human organism is embodied and engages her environment with the ongoing end of survival promotion.

30. The growing interest in the compatibilities between classical American pragmatism and racism in the United States is reflected in the recent publication of *Pragmatism and the Problem of Race* (Lawson and Koch 2004). None of the articles in this book features Peirce, however, and he is given little more than a handful of passing references. On the pragmatism-feminism front, Peirce suffers neglect as well. Little has been written detailing the compatibilities between feminist and Peircean thought. Charlene Seigfried's *Pragmatism and Feminism* provides a helpful introduction to the general compatibilities between classical American pragmatism and feminist thought, yet Seigfried primarily excludes Peirce from her project as a whole: "[Peirce] hardly figures in my own reconstruction of pragmatism" (1996, 281 n. 20). The following four important exceptions were also described in note 18 above: Marcia Moen's "Peirce's Pragmatism as Resource for Feminism," which focuses especially on the feminism-compatible roles played by feeling, the body, and semiotics in Peirce's epistemology (1991); Ann Margaret Sharp's "Peirce, Feminism, and Philosophy for Children," which draws extensive comparisons between feminist theory and Peirce's conception of the self, communal inquiry, and creative love (1994); Maryann Ayim's "The Implications of Sexually Stereotypic Language as Seen through Peirce's Theory of Signs" (1983); and Kory Spencer Sorrell's *Representative Practices: Peirce, Pragmatism, and Feminist Epistemology* (2004).

31. For feminist readers who are not familiar with Peirce, the term "secondness" predates Simone de Beauvoir's work and should not be confused with the use of "second" in her title *The Second Sex/Le Deuxième Sexe* (1949). I thank Lorraine Code for raising this possible confusion in my application of Peirce's work to socio-political issues like sexism (personal conversation, February 2007, FEMMSS2 Conference, Association for Feminist Epistemologies, Methodologies, Metaphysics and Science Studies).

32. For example, in his book *Moral Politics: How Liberals and Conservatives Think*, linguistics professor George Lakoff discusses "prototypes" that are dominant in the United States (2002, 8–11). He notes that prototypes are "cognitive constructions" that play a role in the reasoning process; they are *not* "objective features of the world" (9). This is to say that prototypes reflect *human-generated* categorizations, not extra-human classifications that exist

prior to human thought. In explaining the "typical case prototype," Lakoff gives a telling description of the typical United States of American: "For example, what we consider to be typical birds fly, sing, are not predators, and are about the size of a robin or sparrow. If I say 'There's a bird on the porch,' you will draw the conclusion that it is a typical case prototype, unless I indicate otherwise. *If I speak of a typical American, what comes to mind for many is an adult white male Protestant, who is native-born, speaks English natively, and so on*" (9, my emphasis). Lakoff has highlighted here a common dominant pattern of thinking in U.S. mainstream society. This type of classification of the typical United States of American tends, as I will demonstrate in the chapters to follow, to erase from view obstacles faced by United States of Americans who are *not* adult, white, male, Protestant, native-born, native English speakers. We can also add to this list able bodied, economically secure, and heterosexual.

33. This recalls a connection made by Marilyn Frye in *Politics of Reality*, namely that culture *becomes* biology through habit-taking: "Socialization molds our bodies; enculturation forms our skeletons, our musculature, our central nervous systems. By the time we are gendered adults, masculinity and femininity *are* 'biological'" (1983, 37, Frye's emphasis).

34. Lisa Heldke and Stephen Kellert offer a helpful treatment of objectivity, which includes critiques of traditional conceptions of objectivity and offers a pragmatist-feminist informed re-conceptualization of objectivity, in their article "Objectivity as Responsibility" (1995). While Peirce is not named in their discussion, their ideas are compatible with Peircean objectivity.

35. Helen Zia's *Asian American Dreams* (2000) is a helpful resource for gaining an appreciation of the diversity within the designation "Asian American." For discussions of mixed race, see Linda Alcoff's chapter "On Being Mixed" in *Visible Identities* (2006, 264–84), as well as Rebecca Walker's *Black, White, and Jewish* (2001). While the social criticism connections are my own, my application of Peircean reasonableness and growth to human habits is deeply informed by Michael Ventimiglia's work and by personal conversations with him (2001, 51–52, 60–62; 2005).

36. For readers interested in accessing evidence of the racism and sexism still present in the United States, the following resources are helpful. Racism-focused sources include *White Racism* (Feagin and Vera 1995); *Two Nations: Black and White, Separate, Hostile, Unequal* (Hacker 1995); "Some Kind of Indian: On Race, Eugenics, and Mixed-Bloods" (Jaimes 1995); *Black Wealth/ White Wealth* (Oliver and Shapiro 2006); and *Asian American Dreams* (Zia

2000). And also see the multifocused *Latinas and African American Women at Work* (Browne 1999) and *Sweatshop Warriors: Immigrant Women Workers Take on the Global Factory* (Ching Louie 2001). Sexism-focused sources include *The Macho Paradox: Why Some Men Hurt Women and How All Men Can Help* (Katz 2006) and *Speaking of Sex: The Denial of Gender Inequality* (Rhode 1997).

37. For readers versed in race theory, I need to make some clarifications. First of all, I believe that there are many white people who knowingly help keep racism alive in the United States. My work in this book is not aimed at trying to convince these people to become anti-racists. My book *is* aimed, however, at those well-meaning white people who are ready and willing to do more work to unlearn nonconscious habits that promote racism. I do think that such white people exist. It seems that Derrick Bell does too, given his depiction of "White Citizens for Black Survival" (WCBS) in chapter 5 of his *Faces at the Bottom of a Well* (1992, 89–108). I must grant, however, that Bell's WCBS pushes me to take my work to a more *activist* level than I propose in this book. My thanks to Bill Lawson for recommending this book and this connection to WCBS, as he pushed me to clarify my objectives for my book. Second, I do not deny the intransigence of racism in the United States, much as I wish the intransigence did not exist. I find convincing Charles Mills's theory of the Racial Contract, which argues that the social contract established by the founding fathers of the United States and dominant countries of the West is, in fact, a racial contract, made *by whites* to enforce on peoples considered "nonwhite": "[T]he peculiar contract to which I am referring, though based on the social contract tradition that has been central to Western political theory, is not a contract between everybody ('we the people'), but between just the people who count, the people who really are people ('we the white people'). So it is a racial contract" (1997, 2, 3). Mills is not endorsing the racial contract he describes, far from it (4–6). Rather he works to make explicit that a racial contract of "white supremacy" has "made the modern world what it is today" (1). The normative work done by such a "nonideal," racial contract is done inversely: "[I]t does normative work for us not through its own values, which are detestable, but by enabling us to understand the polity's actual history and how these values and concepts have functioned to rationalize oppression, so as to reform them" (Mills 1997, 6). I also find Derrick Bell's "interest convergence" principle to be an accurate, albeit sobering, description of how racism reform occurs and does not occur in the United States. This descriptive principle states that "[t]he interest of blacks in achieving racial equality will be accom-

modated only when it converges with the interests of whites" (Bell 1980, 523; cf. 1992, 7–11). I do not agree with Bell that "racism is an integral, *permanent*, and *indestructible* component of [U.S.] society," because I think that even the most intransigent of societal habits can be changed in the long run (1992, xiii, my emphasis). Nonetheless I do agree that racism in the United States is a deeply "integral" part of society that cannot be changed easily (1992, xiii). My thanks to Bill Lawson, Marc Lombardo, and Dwayne Tunstall for challenging me to think more deeply about how I am framing my project in relation to white people.

38. Two helpful treatments of the explicit dimensions of racism that are consciously perpetuated by Euro-American whites are Charles Mills's *The Racial Contract* (1997) and Robert Bernasconi's "The Invisibility of Racial Minorities in the Public Realm of Appearances" (2001).

39. I agree with Marilyn Frye that, at best, white people can only be "anti-racist." Frye explains that "as a white person one must never claim not to be racist, but only to be anti-racist. The reasoning is that racism is so systematic and white privilege so impossible to escape, that one is, simply, trapped" (1983, 126). White privilege can be resisted, though, and this resistance takes ongoing hard work (126–27).

40. White people often do not understand or experience themselves as having a race (Williams 1997, 6–16; hooks 2003b, 26 ff.; Sullivan n.d., 1–2, 13–16, 22–28; Mills 1997, 53 ff.; Mills 1998, 9–10).

41. My thanks to Roberto Frega for raising this objection.

42. Personal conversation in March 2007, Annual Meeting of the Society for the Advancement of American Philosophy.

43. Shannon Sullivan makes a similar point about her own white privilege, and white privilege in general, in *Revealing Whiteness* (2006, 10–13, 161–63, 196).

44. As part of the JVC program, volunteers received training in social justice awareness at several retreats throughout the year of volunteer service. This training helped me understand the deeply systemic racial discrimination that still informs U.S. society, even though many white, middle-class people do not see this and are not educated to see it.

45. Jonathan Kozol's work is helpful for white, middle-class people who are unaware of the disparities in U.S. public education between inner-city neighborhoods and suburban ones, disparities that strongly reflect race; see *Savage Inequalities* (1991).

46. Tuana 2006, 2, emphasis in original. An excellent resource for this type of epistemological critique is "Feminist Epistemologies of Ignorance," the special issue of *Hypatia* edited by Sullivan and Tuana (2006).

1. As Peirce puts it, "The tendency to regard continuity . . . as an idea of prime importance in philosophy may conveniently be termed *synechism*" (EP 1:313).

2. Peirce describes Lamarckian evolution as "evolution by creative love" or agapastic evolution (EP 1:362). The Lamarckian model is distinct from the Darwinian or tychastic model (where "fortuitous variation" is the agent of evolution) and the anancastic model (where evolution proceeds according to "mechanical necessity") (EP 1:358, 360). Agapastic evolution is fueled by habit-formation and habit change, which allows for human endeavor to be an agent of evolution. See his essay "Evolutionary Love" for a fuller discussion (EP 1:352–71, esp. 360–63).

3. In a late essay (ca. 1904), Peirce complains that the academic audiences of his time have been spoiled. They expect the essays they read to connect *all* the dots for them. Peirce thinks readers should be required to apply their own powers of reasoning to draw out implications of what they read. This allows the writer more freedom to present a rigorous and concise articulation of ideas ("New Elements," EP 2:301).

4. My use of the term "affectivity" resonates with the *Oxford English Dictionary*'s (*OED*'s) definition of "affectivity" as "emotional susceptibility," while my use also specifies an ongoing body-mind-environmental interaction that informs this "emotional susceptibility" (*OED Online* 2004, "affectivity, *psychol.*," p. 1). According to the *OED*, "affectivity" is derived from "affective," an adjective strongly associated with the emotions (2004, "affectivity, *psychol.*," p. 1). Definitions of "affective" include "[o]f or pertaining to the affections or emotions; emotional" and "[o]f, pertaining to, or characterized by feelings or affects" (*OED Online* 2004, "affectivity," p. 1, and "affective, *a.*" p. 2). The term "affect" is derived from the Latin *afficere*, which means "to act upon, dispose, constitute" (*OED Online* 2004, "affect, n.," p. 1).

5. I follow Antonio Damasio's use of the term "nonconscious" to encompass all processing that occurs outside of human awareness. Like Damasio, I want a term that captures more than psychoanalytic understandings of "the unconscious" (1999, 228). I will be using the term "nonconscious" in place of "subconscious" and "unconscious." This issue will be discussed more fully below.

6. The following description of habit, found in John Dewey's *Human Nature and Conduct*, is especially helpful, since it consolidates many of the

dimensions at play: "human activity which is influenced by prior activity and in that sense acquired; which contains within itself a certain ordering or systematization of minor elements of action; which is projective, dynamic in quality, ready for overt manifestation; and which is operative in some sub-dued subordinate form even when not obviously dominating activity" (Dewey [1922] 1988, 31).

7. Despite the compatibilities of our projects, my term usage differs sig-nificantly from that of Shannon Sullivan in her *Revealing Whiteness: The Un-conscious Habits of Racial Privilege* (2006). She explicitly avoids the term "nonconscious," in order to focus her project on a psychoanalytically in-formed treatment of *unconscious* habits of white privilege, a treatment that takes seriously just how hard it can be to raise to consciousness and eradicate racist habits on individual and societal levels (5–13). I agree with her that eradicating racist habits is extremely difficult. At the same time I think that, for my own project, use of the term "nonconscious" as *inclusive of* Sullivan's use of "unconscious" better captures the complexity of the inquiry opened by my post-Darwinian analysis of Peircean affectivity and its contributions to social criticism.

I think this inquiry offers, arguably, a more hopeful outlook than Sulli-van's regarding the elimination of deeply entrenched racist habits, because it focuses on the importance of embracing communal feedback as a tool to catch nonconscious behavior and thus to promote habit-change. I am not convinced that Sullivan adequately engages communal feedback as a re-source on this front. In the opening pages of her book, she showcases an example in which she highlights the ineffectiveness of communal feedback regarding the "slip[s] of the tongue" of audience members at her presenta-tion of a paper about racism and the Roma: "I was presenting a paper on racism and the Roma at an international conference in Slovakia, and upon completion of the paper, a Czech member of the audience proceeded to ask critical but sympathetic questions about my analysis. When doing so, he re-peatedly referred to the Roma ('Gypsies,' as most people at the conference called them) as 'Jews' without hearing his slip of the tongue" (2006, 6). When corrected by other audience members, "he, embarrassed, said that yes, of course, he meant the 'Gypsies'" (6). Yet the same man, followed by another audience member, *repeated the same slip*, using the term "Jews" in-stead of "Gypsies" or "Roma." In each case the speaker's support of Sulli-van's presentation implied that, on a conscious level, he was not anti-Semitic. Nonetheless, each was engaging a *habit* of using the term "Jews," instead of "Gypsies" or "Roma," which reflects European socio-politically derived habits of association. That is, "the slips [of the tongue] are evidence of a habit of thought in the European mind that involves the scapegoat role that Jews and Roma have been assigned in Europe for hundreds of years. The most extreme example of this role can be found in Nazi Germany's attempted extermination of the Roma and Jews during World War II" (6). Sullivan notes that, when the second man echoed the same term switch as the first, "[t]he audience and I did not correct him since, by that time, such correction felt *pointless*. After five occurrences, the substitution of 'Jew' for 'Gypsy' seemed to have roots too deep and stubborn for *conscious correction to eliminate*" (6, my emphasis). I would argue that Sullivan need not draw so pessimistic a conclusion. Audience feedback, in fact, could have helped these men realize they had again slipped back into old speech-habits. To fail to change an ingrained habit of speech in the immediate aftermath of being made aware of it need not signal hopelessness. Rather it could merely signal that more work needs to be done to change the habit in question. Communal feedback is invaluable in this respect because, in a context like the one Sullivan describes, it brings to consciousness behavior of which one is unaware. This brings to mind people who are trying to change their speech-habits to avoid male-dominated language. Receiving feedback that one, despite conscious intent, has said "mankind" or "man" instead of "humanity," for example, can help catch slips of tongue and thus signal that more conscious practice is needed before the new habits of inclusive language have been mastered. My project brings to the foreground the value of communal feedback as a resource for helping people, especially those in hegemonic groups, change habits that contribute to social injustice.

8. "Unconscious" has various meanings within psychoanalytic discourse, and I want to leave inquiry open as much as possible on this subject. I do, however, agree with Sullivan that an atomistic conception of the unconscious will not do. In *Revealing Whiteness*, Sullivan presents "a transactional conception of the unconscious" that combines insights from classical American pragmatism and LaPlanchian psychoanalysis (2006, 13, 45–62). For work specifically on Peirce and psychoanalysis, see Colapietro 1995; De Lauretis 1984, 1994; and Muller and Brent 2000.

9. As a synechist, Peirce is not concerned to draw a hard, fast distinction between human and nonhuman animals, nor am I. Peirce does note that humans differ from nonhuman animals according to the higher degrees of self-control humans are able to achieve: "The brutes are certainly capable of more than one grade of control; but it seems to me that our superiority to them is more due to our greater number of grades of self-control than it is

to our versatility" (CP 5.533). And, "All thinking is by signs; and the brutes use signs. But they perhaps rarely think of them as signs. To do so is manifestly a second step in the use of language. Brutes use language, and seem to exercise some little control over it. But they certainly do not carry this control to anything like the same grade that we do. They do not criticize their thought logically" (CP 5.534). It is beyond the scope of my project to explore Peirce's thoughts on this issue more fully.

10. Peirce goes so far as to say that scientific development in general can be traced to the human instincts for nutrition and reproduction. Physics can be traced back to "instincts connected with the need of nutrition," and "psychics" to those linked to reproduction (EP 2:51, 1898). "Now not only our accomplished science, but even our scientific questions have been pretty exclusively limited to the development of those two branches of natural knowledge" (EP 2:51).

11. My definition of internalization is influenced by Amélie Rorty (1980) and Sandra Bartky 1990 (63–82).

12. LeDoux cites John Bargh 1990 and 1992, where extensive research reviews can be found. On stereotyping, see esp. Bargh 1992, 240, 243–47, 250. LeDoux's reference to Bargh's work occurs in LeDoux's own overview of research that details how "emotional processing can take place outside of conscious awareness" (1996, 58).

13. It is beyond the scope of my project to give a developmental account of self-control in Peirce's corpus. Vincent Colapietro provides such an account in *Peirce's Approach to the Self* (1989, chapters 4 and 5). In his discussion, Colapietro synthesizes the disparate comments Peirce makes about self and self-control, to present a coherent account that does justice to Peirce's ideas.

14. Carl Hausman puts the point this way: "What Peirce stressed was a kind of altruism and concern for communities in contrast to a view that advocated self-interest for the individual. . . . [O]ne can treat the ideas Peirce proposed through the religious setting in ways that are, at least explicitly, nonreligious, unless *religion* is taken in a broad sense that excludes commitment to some institutional group or dogma and refers to any metaphysical commitment" (1999, 203). This point will be discussed more fully in Chapter 4, in conjunction with Peirce's essay "Evolutionary Love" (EP 1:352–71); cf. Orange 1984, 48–49.

15. For discussions of these denials in the United States, see *Racism without Racists* (Bonilla-Silva 2003) and *Speaking of Sex: The Denial of Gender Inequality* (Rhode 1997).

16. There is a tension in Peirce's references to reason's ongoing development. On the one hand, he says, "the essence of Reason is such that its being never can have been completely perfected. It always must be in a state of incipiency, of growth" (EP 2:255, 1903). On the other hand, "the pragmaticist does not make the *summum bonum* to consist in action, but makes it to consist in that process of evolution whereby the existent comes more and more to embody those generals which were just now said to be *destined*, which is what we strive to express in calling them *reasonable*" (EP 2:343, Peirce's emphasis, 1904). We can resolve this tension by viewing reasonableness as what Peirce would call a developmental telos—that is, an end or "destiny" that grows along with humans and the universe itself (EP 1:331; cf. Anderson 1987, 111–21).

17. The following brief list includes resources I have found helpful: *Asian American Dreams* (Zia 2000), *Yellow* (Wu 2002), *Visible Identities* (Alcoff 2006), *Borderlands/La Frontera* (Anzuldúa 1987), *Pilgrimages/Peregrinajes* (Lugones 2003), *Custer Died for Your Sins* (Deloria 1988), and "Some Kind of Indian" (Jaimes 1995).

18. As noted in the introduction, while the social criticism connections are my own, my application of Peircean reasonableness and growth to human habits is deeply informed by Michael Ventimiglia's work and by personal conversations with him (2001, 51–52, 60–62; 2005).

19. I thank Daniel Campos for his suggestion that I explain what I mean by "embrace."

20. McIntosh's work serves as a bridge to broader socio-political contexts. The passages just cited are from her article "White Privilege and Male Privilege: A Personal Account of Coming to See Correspondences through Work in Women's Studies" (1988), in which she addresses how those in hegemonic groups are often unaware of the societal privileges that they receive. Identifying as a white woman in academia, she speaks to male privilege and white privilege, also noting that privileges are often intertwined, based on the different groups to which one belongs (293, 298). I will return to her work in subsequent chapters.

21. *OED Online* 2004, "affectivity, *psychol.*" p. 1.

22. I do not draw directly on Damasio's many research publications. Readers interested in citations for these articles will find them in the endnotes to each of his books.

23. Damasio also uses the phrase "emotions in the broad sense" to describe an organism's homeostasis-maintaining behaviors, to be described shortly (2003, 35).

24. Damasio does not seem to be familiar with Peirce's work. The only reference to Peirce I found in the three above books is a footnote citing, without elaboration on Peirce's ideas, the latter's "Spinoza's Ethic," in which Peirce makes the point that "Spinoza's ideas are eminently ideas to affect human conduct . . ." (*Nation* 59 [1894]: 344–45; cited in Damasio 2003, 333–34 n. 5). Damasio is, however, familiar with William James's work in psychology. He is also well versed in philosophy and is deeply appreciative of the impact philosophy has on our worldviews. In *Descartes' Error* he offers an insightful and detailed critique of the Cartesian mind-body dualism, including its effect on the practice of medicine in the West (1994, 247–52, 254–58). Peirce would likely approve of the spirit of this critique.

25. "The word homeodynamics is even more appropriate than homeostasis because it suggests the process of seeking an adjustment rather than a fixed point of balance" (Damasio 2003, 302 n. 5). Damasio credits Steven Rose for coining this term.

26. "There is abundant evidence of 'emotional' reactions in simple organisms. Think of a lone paramecium, a simple unicellular organism, all body, no brain, no mind, swimming speedily away from a possible danger in a certain sector of its bath—maybe a poking needle, or too many vibrations. . . . Or the paramecium may be swimming speedily along a chemical gradient of nutrients toward the sector of the bath where it can have lunch. . . . *The events I am describing in a brainless creature already contain the essence of the process of emotion that we humans have—detection of the presence of an object or event that recommends avoidance and evasion or endorsement and approach*" (Damasio 2003, 40, my emphasis).

27. Damasio notes that the concept of external-versus-internal stimuli is a common way of distinguishing typical examples of emotion (e.g., happiness, sadness, anger, etc.) from, say, hunger or thirst (2003, 35, 302 n. 7).

28. This awareness characterizes *human* feelings but not the feelings of all nonhuman animals. Technically speaking, following Damasio's account, there are two basic levels of feelings. First, there is the feltness of the bodily commotion itself. These types of feelings occur in many nonhuman animals. A scared squirrel, say, has feelings that correspond to its emotion. Second, there is the *awareness* of this feltness, or the *feeling* of a feeling. This awareness is found in humans but is not likely to be found in all nonhuman animals. The scared squirrel is not likely to *know* it feels scared. To have this kind of feeling—i.e., the feltness of "I am feeling scared"—there needs to be a "second-order" representation that brings together the first-order feelings (of the emotion itself) and a sense of self (Damasio 1999, chapter 9, "Feeling

Feelings," 279–85). Damasio explains this issue fully in his book *The Feeling of What Happens* (1999), but in his more recent *Looking for Spinoza* (2003) he leaves the issue to the side. It should be noted here that Peirce seems to use feeling in a sense that captures *both* of the levels of feeling that Damasio distinguishes (feltness and awareness). There is also a subtle difference in the timing each attributes to feeling and emotion. For Damasio, feelings follow immediately after emotions; feelings are neural representations of the bodily motions that occur in emotions (2003, 28 ff., 49 ff., 64–65, 80, and chapter 3, esp. 85–88 and 96–106). For Peirce, emotions in their paradigmatic form—where they "produc[e] large movements in the body"—occur immediately after feelings (W 2:230). This is because they are based on information conveyed by feelings, a topic that will be discussed in Chapter 2. This difference between Damasio and Peirce does not diminish the parallels I draw between them in my project. For both Damasio and Peirce, a feeling and its corresponding emotion involve human homeodynamics.

29. Damasio's conception of "mind" is narrower than Peirce's. For Damasio, it is due to the sophistication of their brains that humans have "mind," mind being a *process* by which humans can "[form] neural representations which can become images, be manipulated in a process called thought, and eventually influence behavior by helping predict the future, plan accordingly, and choose the next action" (1994, 90; cf. 1999, 337 n. 7). (For more on Damasio's treatment of "images," see 1999, 9, 317–23.) Neural representations of objects and events in their environments allow humans to creatively adapt to environmental changes. Human behavior is thus shaped not only by the immediate presence of concrete objects and circumstances, such as experiencing a storm as it seriously damages one's shelter. Human behavior is also shaped by *representations*, which make thinking possible, whereby we can plan behavior, such as building more adequate shelter once the storm is over, without the concrete presence of the objects/ circumstances in question (cf. Damasio 1994, 89–91). For Peirce, on the other hand, "mind" is inclusive of Damasio's conception, but it is much broader, referring to the characteristics of an organic system as contrasted with a purely mechanical one: feelings, reactions, and habit-taking (EP 1:290–93). Mind is thus found everywhere in the organic Peircean cosmos (EP 1:293, 297). As for what makes humans unique in contrast to other animals, it is the higher degrees of self-control they can achieve (CP 5.533–34).

30. Damasio notes that (as of 2003) the state of research is such that it cannot be specified just what homeodynamic processes are and are not involved in background emotions (2003, 44).

31. Cf. Damasio 1994, 131–34; 1999, 50–51; 2003, 44–45.

32. Ultimately for Damasio, representing the self to the brain in this context also involves signals from the body (1999, 154, 168–94).

33. Two counterexamples: (1) Feeling without awareness: The squirrel probably does have awareness of its feeling, as noted above. (2) Awareness without feeling (inspired by Descartes' Sixth Meditation): If we related to our bodies merely as a captain does to her ship, we would have consciousness (i.e., awareness) of the workings of our ship, but we would not *feel* them. Human feelings as the final stage of Damasio's affective process include *both* awareness/consciousness *and* feltness of the homeodynamic processes occurring in our bodies.

34. For those knowledgeable in neurophysiology: The somatosensory regions that pertain to feelings are the insula, SII, SI, and the cingulate cortex (Damasio 2003, 105 ff.).

35. Damasio's feeling-hypothesis has considerable experimental support (2003, 86, 96–104, 106, 123). While evidence is strong that feelings are fundamentally based on body maps originating in the brain's somatosensory regions, it is still not clear (as of 2003) just *how* these maps are translated into feelings (Damasio 2003, 88, 198).

36. A note for Peirce scholars: While Peirce's mature phenomenology does not crystallize until his later work, I would argue that reading his earlier essays (as I do in the following chapters) through a phenomenological lens helps highlight the insights these essays offer to Peircean affectivity and social criticism. My thanks to André De Tienne, whose informal critical comments on my paper "C. S. Peirce's Embodied Phenomenology and Racism" inspired the present clarification, which is meant to ensure that I am not naively collapsing Peirce's earlier and later work (2009).

37. See CP 1.212, 2.146, 7.532.

38. The sense of self underlying one's experience, such that it feels like *one's own* experience, is the topic of Damasio's *The Feeling of What Happens* (1999). See also Patricia Muoio's "Peirce on the Person" (1984, 174–75).

39. Peirce describes thirdness as "that element of cognition which . . . is *the consciousness of a process . . . in the form of the sense of learning, of acquiring, of mental growth. . . .* This is a kind of consciousness which cannot be immediate, because it covers a time, and that not merely because it continues through every instant of that time, but because it cannot be contracted into an instant. It differs from immediate consciousness, as a melody does from one prolonged note. Neither can the consciousness of the two sides of an instant, of a sudden occurrence, in its individual reality, possibly embrace

the consciousness of a process. This is the consciousness that binds our life together. *It is the consciousness of synthesis*" (EP 1:260, 1887–88, my emphasis).

40. In his autobiographical book *The Circuit,* Jiménez describes needing to learn English to cope with English-only classrooms in the United States (1998, 14–26, 80–83). He also describes being a migrant worker in the fields with his parents, in order to help make ends meet for the family (61–127). Throughout the sequel to *The Circuit,* entitled *Breaking Through,* Jiménez describes how he worked both before and after school to support his family financially (2001). In addition to his autobiographical work, Jiménez, who currently is the Fay Boyle Professor in the Department of Modern Languages and Literatures at Santa Clara University, has published extensively on education, literature, and social justice themes (http://www.scu.edu/ethnicstudies/fjimenez/).

41. In "El buen juego y la mala suerte: Habilidad, reacción y espontaneidad en el fútbol," Daniel Campos gives an excellent Peircean analysis of how thirdness is the dimension of experience whereby humans cultivate new habits through training and practice (2006, 132–35). Campos also offers an insightful discussion of the collective thirdness and firstness displayed by *fútbol* (soccer) teams that have cultivated *communal* habits through working and practicing together. This discussion sheds light on how communal sympathy plays out on a Peircean scheme, even though Campos does not himself explicitly highlight the "sympathy" connection (136–37, 140–42). Peirce's understanding of communal sympathy will be discussed at length in Chapter 4.

42. Habits can be formed through the efforts of the imagination, in addition to physical iterations of patterns of behavior. As Larry Hickman puts it, "self-training may also be conducted in the imagination" (1994, 16). Vincent Colapietro integrates this point into a wider discussion of the Peircean self (1989, chapter 5, "Inwardness and Autonomy," 99–118).

43. My students in my Self and Identity courses at the University of Portland have helped me see that "socio-political secondness" can also be used to describe the secondness felt by people in hegemonic groups when they receive feedback that their behavior is heterosexist, racist, sexist, etc. (my thanks especially to Betsy Grasham and Alison Burke for this point). To prevent ambiguity in the present presentation, I will not use the term "socio-political secondness" to describe this type of resistance experienced by those in hegemonic groups. I want to focus on socio-political resistance that comes from exclusionary mainstream societal and individual habits. None-

theless, building on my students' insights, I believe that a "taxonomy of socio-political secondness" could be constructed, whereby different factors such as socio-political power differentials and differing types of socio-political resistances could be tracked in their complexities and nuances. It is beyond the scope of my project to offer this taxonomy, but I raise the possibility of constructing one as an invitation to my readers. My idea for a taxonomy of socio-political secondness is inspired by the taxonomy of epistemologies of ignorance that Nancy Tuana offers in her article "The Speculum of Ignorance: The Women's Health Movement and Epistemologies of Ignorance" (2006).

44. This racist treatment occurs, frustratingly enough, alongside assumptions in mainstream U.S. discourse that racism is a "black-white" issue and so does not significantly affect Asian Americans (Zia 2000, 156–57, 190, 290–91).

45. This is not to deny that white people can and do experience racism in the United States. While racism against people of color remains entrenched in the mainstream societal habits of the United States, white people who find themselves in the minority in a city or neighborhood, for example, may experience anti-white racism. I thank Samantha Kolinski and a former student for their feedback on this point. Nonetheless, whites who experience racism in the United States are still members of a hegemonic group who receive privileges based on their perceived skin color. Thus anti-white racism cannot be equated with racism against people of color. When I teach this distinction to my students, I use capital-R "Racism" as a designation for Racism against people of color, as the capitalization represents the societal, institutional backing of this type of racism in the United States. I use lowercase-r "racism" to designate racism directed by people of color against white people, or racism among people of color. This latter type of racism is related to "Racism" but is qualitatively different because those who perpetuate it do not themselves receive widespread validation and institutional support of their race in mainstream U.S. culture. In the present book, since I discuss only racism against people of color, I use the uncapitalized "racism" in this context.

46. Sullivan seems to be speaking figuratively here, describing white privilege as "one" habit (2006, 4). She readily speaks of "habits of white privilege" on the very next page and throughout *Revealing Whiteness* (2006).

47. To do so would entail the application of Peirce's various trichotomies of signs. The level of technicality this would introduce, in my opinion, would render my project inaccessible to a more general audience. Bringing

a larger audience to Peirce's work is imperative, if his ideas are to be applied more widely to socially salient issues, as I think they should be. David Savan gives a much more fully semiotic approach to affective issues in Peirce in his article "Peirce's Semiotic Theory of Emotion" (1981).

48. In addition to visual images, "there are also 'sound images,' 'olfactory images,' and so on" (Damasio 1994, 89).

49. "As organisms acquired greater complexity, 'brain-caused' actions required more intermediate processing. Other neurons were interpolated between the stimulus neuron and the response neuron . . . but it did not follow that the organism with that more complicated brain necessarily had a mind. Brains can have many intervening steps in the circuits mediating between stimulus and response, and still have no mind, if they do not meet an essential condition: the ability to display images internally and to order those images in a process called thought. (The images are not solely visual; there are also 'sound images,' 'olfactory images,' and so on)" (Damasio 1994, 89).

50. In later writings, Peirce uses "sensation" in conjunction with reaction/secondness (e.g., "A Guess at the Riddle," EP 1:260, 1887–88), and with perceptual judgment/thirdness (e.g., "Pragmatism as the Logic of Abduction," EP 2:226–41, 1903). It is beyond the scope of this project to speculate on these shifts, although I think they reflect the phenomenological richness of Peirce's scheme. Feeling/firstness is equated with sensation, which is, in turn, linked with the categories of secondness and thirdness, if we view Peirce's corpus as a continuous whole.

51. The ideational nature of feelings—by which a physical object can be made into a corresponding idea in my mind—is not fully present in Peirce's earlier writings. In Chapter 4, I discuss its emergence in the *Monist* "Cosmology Series" of the 1890s.

52. Peirce uses all three of these terms, in varying contexts, to convey the representations that the mind makes of external objects.

53. Peirce says in this respect that "colour is not an impression, but an inference" (W 1:516; cf. Apel 1995, 41). Cf. Damasio 1999, 134.

54. This comment is a later addition to the essay "Fixation of Belief" (EP 1:109, 377 n. 22, ca. 1910; cf. Hookway 2000, 38).

55. A second version of this 1898 lecture underscores the reliability, regarding matters of "vital importance," of "hereditary instincts and traditional sentiments" (CP 1.661). Here he pairs religiously socialized sentiment with "practical infallibility": "The conservative need not forget that he might have been born a Brahmin with a traditional sentiment in favor of suttee—a reflection that tempts him to become a radical. But still, on the

whole, he thinks his wisest plan is to reverence his deepest sentiments as his highest and ultimate authority, which is regarding them as for him practically infallible—that is, to say infallible in the only sense of the word in which infallible has any consistent meaning" (CP 1.661). Peirce's Critical Common-sensism calls us to scrutinize these "practically infallible" beliefs, to see whether what holds sway "vitally" can nonetheless become doubtful when subjected to the rigors of reason and self-control.

56. It should be noted that, in some contexts, Peirce uses the terms "instinct" and its derivatives to refer strictly to belief-habits that humans are biologically predisposed to voluntarily (versus mechanically) embrace or perform (EP 2:473, 1913). In other contexts he uses the terms "instinct" and "sentiment" synonymously, as just described, to convey deep-seated belief-habits that are socially derived, like our religious beliefs (RLT 110–11, 1898; cf. W 3:253 and EP 1:377 n. 22, ca. 1910). Peirce's discussion of suicide uses "instinctive" in the *former* sense, asserting that "the belief that suicide is to be classed as murder" is "not an instinctive belief," because it is dubitable, not acritical: "[W]hen it comes to the point of actual self-debate, this belief seems to be completely expunged and ex-sponged from the mind" (EP 2:350, 1905).

57. We should not read too much into Peirce's use of "racial" here, as he uses the term inconsistently in his corpus. Sometimes race is used coextensively with humanity (e.g., EP 2:433, 1907). Other times he refers to races *within* humanity (e.g., EP 2:257, 1903). Nonetheless "race" as a socio-political reality is socialized into what is "personal" because of Peirce's conviction of the inescapable interplay between the inner and outer worlds (CP 7.438–39).

58. The editors of *The Essential Peirce*, Vol. 2, note: "Words appearing in italic brackets indicate that they have been supplied or reconstructed by the editors" (EP 2:*xiv*).

CHAPTER TWO

THE AFFECTIVITY OF COGNITION

1. For readers unfamiliar with Peirce's Cognition Series: It consists of three essays—"Questions Concerning Certain Faculties Claimed for Man" (1868), "Some Consequences of Four Incapacities" (1868), and "Grounds of Validity of the Laws of Logic" (1869).

2. Vincent Colapietro notes that, in Peirce's scheme, "The self is distinguishable but not separable from others; *indeed, the identity of the self is constituted by its relations to others*" (1989, 73, my emphasis).

3. Gould discusses Samuel Morton's work in his book *The Mismeasure of Man* (1981, 50–69). Morton hypothesized that racial superiority and infe-

riority could be determined by the size of human skulls. Gould argues that an assumption of the superiority of the Caucasian race nonconsciously informed Morton's infamous skull-measuring experiments. Morton's work, the records of which Gould studied closely, was riddled with bad methodology that unduly favored Caucasian "superiority," yet this same work shows no intentional fraud. There was no evidence of cover up, despite the egregiously biased and ad hoc efforts to skew the results toward white superiority (Gould 1981, 54–69). Thus Morton himself provides an example of thinking that is shaped by exclusionary, and arguably nonconscious, socio-political associations.

4. With these remarks, Damasio explicitly pits himself against the modern conception of mind-body dualism (2003, 187 ff.). The emergence of mind, Damasio argues, is grounded in representations made possible by different regions of the brain. In *The Feeling of What Happens*, Damasio suggests that human consciousness is the result of a triad of representations: organism, object, and their relationship (1999). This presents a striking parallel to Peirce's conviction that the human is a (triadic) sign. It is beyond the scope of this project to pursue comparisons and contrasts between the two on this point.

5. Amélie Rorty reflects this sensitivity to individualized embodiment when she argues that the causes of a person's experience of an emotion should include personal genetic factors—that is, "a person's constitutional inheritance, the set of genetically fixed threshold sensitivities and patterns of response" (1980, 105).

6. Grosz's list occurs in the context of a broader point than mine, as she highlights the socio-cultural meanings attached to these bodily functions for women and men (1993, 202). Our projects are compatible, as the individualized bodily functions I detail here occur unavoidably within social meanings. See Grosz's "Bodies and Knowledges: Feminism and the Crisis of Reason" for an exploration of how the body matters epistemologically, as well as for a detailed critique of Western canonical portrayals of reason as transcending bodily particularities to achieve neutral objectivity.

7. Damasio references several of his own scientific publications on this front (2003, 325 n. 10; Damasio and Damasio, 1994; Damasio 1989a, 1989b). He is, however, careful to qualify that he is *not* claiming to know exactly how the images in question are made: "There is a major gap in our current understanding of how neural patterns become mental images. The presence in the brain of dynamic neural patterns (or maps) related to an object or event is a *necessary* but not sufficient basis to explain the mental images of

the said object or event. We can describe neural patterns—with the tools of neuroanatomy, neurophysiology, and neurochemistry—and we can describe images with the tools of introspection. How we get from the former to the latter is known only in part" (Damasio 2003, 198, Damasio's emphasis).

8. Cf. CP 7.259 (ca. 1900); CP 7.266 (ca. 1900).

9. Donna Beegle, who writes on how to effectively advocate for those born into generational poverty, describes feelings that those in poverty link to concepts like "*Police*—Police often hurt the people we love; therefore, they act/feel like the 'enemy': unfriendly, out to get us, and to be avoided"; "*Teachers*—Teachers don't understand us. They also feel/look like the 'enemy' . . ." (2007, 54). Beegle's research begins from her own experience as someone who, born into generational poverty, made her way from a GED to a doctorate degree in educational leadership (3–19).

10. Peirce does not clarify what he means by "sensations proper" in this passage (W 2:230). Presumably he is referring to sights, sounds, smells, tastes, and textures as cognitions in which the sense data itself is the prominent feature. These sensory cognitions are different from the feelings/sensations constituting the material dimension of thought, since the bodily information of the feelings/sensations in this latter case is of a more general nature (i.e., the body in general versus a specific sense organ) and is much more subtle (W 2:230).

11. As discussed in Chapter 1, in this passage neuroscientist Joseph Le-Doux draws on social psychologist John Bargh's work, where research reviews and discussion can be found (Bargh 1992, 1990).

12. It should not come as a surprise that the feeling/sensation in this case involves the synthesis of multiple factors, as one of the primary themes in "Questions Concerning" is the synthesis that informs our cognition even though we are often unaware of this synthesis (W 2:195 ff, 199). Regarding feeling/sensation, Peirce gives the following example, which was quoted earlier: "The pitch of a tone depends upon the rapidity of the succession of the vibrations which reach the ear. . . . These impressions must exist previously to any tone; hence, the sensation of pitch is determined by previous cognitions. Nevertheless, this would never have been discovered by the mere contemplation of that feeling" (W 2:197). The feeling itself, in other words, involves synthesis of a multiplicity—in this case, of "the succession of the vibrations."

13. Technically, the secondness in this case also includes my bodily threshold for withstanding cold, since this contributes to my becoming chilled as much as the external temperature does. This is a type of *internal* environmental resistance.

14. Peirce makes a brief reference to these individualized connections as "association by resemblance" but does not elaborate on his use of this term in this context (W 2:238). In his later writings, he describes associations by resemblance as those involving creative connections between ideas, in contrast to the connections provided merely by experience (CP 7.392, 437, ca. 1893; CP 4.157, ca. 1897; CP 7.498, ca. 1898). Chapter 4 will discuss these ideas more fully.

15. The relationships among these stereotypes of different groups can be manipulated to pit different "nonwhite" groups against each other, with a Euro-American norm as the ultimate yardstick. For example, as noted in Chapter 1, the "model minority" stereotype of Asian Americans is used to disparage African Americans (Zia 2000, 117–18, Brown et al. 2003, x; cf. Alcoff 2006, 262–63). Linda Alcoff notes that, in U.S. mainstream discourse, ". . . Asians and Jews have been similarly grouped together in the representations of their cultures as superior, threatening, and monolithic. In other words, unlike for African Americans and Latinos, Asians and Jews are not seen as having inferior intelligence or primitive cultures, but as groups with collective goals to take over the world and/or evil intent toward those outside their groups (the 'yellow peril' and 'Jewish world conspiracy')" (2006, 258). (Alcoff also addresses how Jewish people do and do not relate to the phenotypical and political dimensions of whiteness; see 256–58.)

16. My thanks to David O'Hara for bringing this passage to my attention.

17. In her book, *Black Feminist Thought*, Patricia Hill Collins writes about how stereotypes can reflect oppression on several fronts (2000). In her chapter "Mammies, Matriarchs, and Other Controlling Images" she discusses how stereotypes of African American women reflect "the ways in which oppressions of race, gender, sexuality, and class intersect" (72, 69–96).

18. "The politics of reality," the head I give this section, is a phrase I borrow from Marilyn Frye's book of this title (1983).

19. A point of interest for Peirce scholars: Peirce's description of reality in "Some Consequences" comes after a considerable amount of work, on human cognition, that is presented according to an order of *discovery*. This means that, while Peirce's account of reality occurs about two-thirds of the way through this three-essay series, its implications reverberate both forward *and* backward. Peirce does not trace these backward-glancing repercussions in the context of the Cognition Series. It is important to do so, however, in order to better appreciate the socialized, and thus politicized, dimensions of human cognition, affectivity, and child development. Tracing these backward-glancing repercussions characterizes my work in this section and in Part 3 below.

20. On this front, Damasio notes, "Frogs or birds looking at cats see them differently [than humans do], and so do cats themselves" (1994, 235; cf. 96–97).

21. See his *Monist* "Cosmology Series" of the 1890s (esp. EP 1.297, 310, 331). See also CP 1.141–175 (ca. 1897).

22. Erasure, in this context, refers to various types of exclusion that, historically, have rendered women nonexistent according to patriarchal standards in various cultures. This includes both literal and conceptual exclusion. An example of the latter is rendering "lesbian" conceptually nonexistent via a logically impossible definition, such as "women who have sexual intercourse" (my paraphrase) where sexual intercourse—by definition—requires a penis (Frye 1983, 156 ff, 152–73).

23. With "ultimately shaped," I leave room for the overlap between social and physical secondness. Socio-political secondness often involves physical barriers and therefore physical secondness to this extent. Yet the physical barriers—like Williams's being locked out of the store—exist only because of the socio-political secondness of exclusionary bias (Williams 1991, 44–45).

24. The terminology with which Peirce refers to the social principle varies throughout his writings. In later writings he uses "social impulse," "sentiment," and "sympathy." The sociality to which Peirce is referring is most clearly articulated in his 1890s writings on sympathy, association, and agapic love, where we learn that sympathy can take on both exclusionary and agapic forms. Chapter 4 addresses these issues in detail.

25. Synthetic reasoning differs from deductive reasoning in that it involves risk. Deductive reasoning does not, for it involves drawing conclusions based strictly on the information contained in the premises of an argument. Synthetic reasoning involves moving beyond what can be known in the premises into the unknown. For example, reasoning that the future will conform to the past, or that a particular hypothesis explains a surprising or puzzling phenomenon, involves going beyond what is known. The Kantian contrast between synthetic and analytic judgments is implicit, for Peirce, in this distinction.

26. Humanity's uncanny success in its synthetic reasoning defies the odds. Mathematically speaking, humans should be wrong in their inductions and hypotheses about the external world far more often than they are. Natural selection must have something to do with all this, although Peirce is not exactly sure what (W 2:263–64). In his later work, Peirce argues that instinct is the source of guidance for human abduction (hypothesis formation). See EP 2:217–18 (1903) and EP 2:443 (1908).

27. This is similar to Peirce's well-known cable metaphor, because it refers to *epistemological* security. Like the insurance metaphor, the cable metaphor underscores the fruitfulness of an epistemological model that relies on many strands, any one of which can break without the whole structure collapsing. The cable is meant to replace "a chain [of arguments] which is no stronger than its weakest link" (W 2:213, "Some Consequences").

28. My thanks to Samantha Kolinski for helping me think through Chris McCandless's story in relation to Peirce's ideas (personal conversation).

29. See especially the chapters "Oppression," "Sexism," and "In and Out of Harm's Way" (Frye 1983). See also Bartky 1990, 75, 77.

30. Peirce seems to reflect a blind spot common to white, propertied male philosophers in the West. The blind spot involves failing to see the "disconnect" between theory and practice. Following Charles Mills's lead on this topic, we can take John Locke as a prime example of a white, propertied male philosopher (in the Western tradition) who argued for the equality of all human beings and who argued against slavery. At the same time, Locke *invested* in the African slave trade in the Americas (Mills 1998, 4 ff.; Farr 1986, 267). For more detail on the paradoxical relationship between Locke's writings against slavery and his involvement in the African slave trade in the American colonies, see James Farr's article "'So Vile and Miserable an Estate': The Problem of Slavery in Locke's Political Thought" (1986).

31. My appreciation of the importance of Peirce's discussion of child development is indebted to Vincent Colapietro's insightful treatment of the same in *Peirce's Approach to the Self* (1989, 69–75).

32. As noted in Chapter 1, Peirce describes this category as "a consciousness in which there is no comparison, no relation, no recognized multiplicity . . . no imagination of any modification of what is positively there, no reflexion. . . . [A]ny simple and positive quality of feeling would be something which our description fits,—that it is such as it is quite regardless of anything else" (EP 2:150, 1903).

33. In these early essays, Peirce does not use "habit" to refer to these instinctive patterns of behavior and physiology, preferring to associate habit-taking with conscious awareness. His later writings, however, expand habit to include both conscious and nonconscious domains, better enabling us to see a spectrum of habit-taking that spans from nonconscious instinct to human self-control (see, for example, EP 2:336–37).

34. Colapietro adapts the term "second moment" from James Crombie's discussion of Peirce's treatment of child development, where Crombie notes that "testimony gives the first dawning of self-consciousness" (Crombie 1980, 80; cited in Colapietro 1989, 72, with emphasis added).

35. As noted in Chapter 1, the sense of self underlying one's experience, such that it feels like *one's own* experience, is the topic of Damasio's *The Feeling of What Happens* (1999). See also Patricia Muoio's "Peirce on the Person" (1984, 174–75).

36. It should be noted that Peirce's discussion of child development in the Cognition Series, structured as it is on the specific question of "[w]hether we have an intuitive self-consciousness" (W 2:200), does not extend beyond his answer to this question. He thus leaves it to the reader to extrapolate the stage ushered in by the child's inference that her unique self must exist. I provide this extrapolation as the thirdness stage of child development. As Colapietro notes, "in order for the self to function as an agency of self-control, he or she *must* be something more than a locus of error and ignorance; he or she must be a center of purpose and power" (1989, 74, emphasis in original). For Colapietro's extended and insightful discussion of Peirce's account of the self, see chapters 4 and 5 of *Peirce's Approach to the Self* (1989).

37. My thinking on this front is deeply informed by María Lugones's work in *Pilgramages / Peregrinajes: Theorizing Coalition against Multiple Oppressions*, especially her chapter "Playfulness, 'World'-Traveling, and Loving Perception" (2003, 77–100). See also "Have We Got a Theory for You! Feminist Theory, Cultural Imperialism, and the Demand for 'the Woman's Voice,'" cowritten with Elizabeth Spelman (Lugones and Spelman 1990).

38. A note of interest for Peirce scholars: My reexamination of Peirce's account of child development in light of the politics of reality, the social principle, and the coercive survival dilemma is supported by a comment Peirce makes at the end of his discussion of child development: "The only essential defect in this account of the matter is, that while we know that children exercise as much understanding as is here supposed, *we do not know that they exercise it in precisely this way*" (W 2:203, my emphasis). At this point in the Cognition Series, Peirce has not yet addressed the communal articulation of reality or the social principle, which are discussed in essays 2 and 3, respectively. In light of Peirce's disclaimer about the accuracy of his account of child development, it makes sense to reexamine his account in light of these insights from the second and third essays in the Cognition Series.

39. For readers interested in pursuing the topic of madness more deeply than I can treat it here, the following selective list of titles can serve as a springboard: *Women and Madness* (Chesler 1989), *Madness and Civilization* and *History of Madness* (Foucault 2001, 2006), *The Faber Book of Madness* (Porter 1991), *Madness and Modernism* (Sass 1992), *Social Order/Mental Dis-*

order (Scull 1989), *The Myth of Mental Illness* (Szasz 1974). My thanks to Jeff Gauthier and Norah Martin for their suggestions for this list.

40. I am referencing the *Oxford English Dictionary (OED) Online*—see the second entry for "mad" used as an adjective: "2. Of a person, action, disposition, etc.: uncontrolled by reason or judgement; foolish, unwise. Subsequently only in stronger use (corresponding to the modern restricted application of sense 4a, from which it is now often indistinguishable): extravagantly or wildly foolish; ruinously imprudent" (*OED Online* 2009). This "sense 4a" is also listed under "mad, adj.": "4. a. Of a person: insane, crazy; mentally unbalanced or deranged; subject to delusions or hallucinations; (in later use *esp.*) psychotic."

41. See Tuana's *Woman and the History of Philosophy*, where she discusses Plato, Descartes, Rousseau, Kant, Hume, Locke, and Hegel and also addresses, to a lesser extent, the latent classism and racism in many classic Western philosophical texts (1992). See also Tuana's *The Less Noble Sex: Scientific, Religious, and Philosophical Conceptions of Woman's Nature* (1993).

42. Mills describes "global white supremacy" as "*itself* a political system, a particular power structure of formal or informal rule, socioeconomic privilege, and norms for the differential distribution of material wealth and opportunities, benefits and burdens, rights and duties" (1997, 3, Mills's emphasis).

43. Sandra Bartky's piece, "On Psychological Oppression," is also helpful in explaining how those in oppressed groups can come to believe messages about their "inferiority" (1990, 22–32).

44. Patricia Williams discusses the impression among many whites in the United States that this is indeed the case, when in fact *whites* perform the majority of the crimes in the United States: "Actually U.S. Bureau of Justice Statistics for 1986 show that whites were arrested for 71.7 percent of all crimes; blacks and all others (including American Indian, Alaskan Native, Asian, and Pacific Islander) account for the remaining 28 percent" (1991, 73).

45. Shannon Sullivan discusses these issues in "Reproducing Whiteness: How to Raise a White Child" (n.d.) and *Revealing Whiteness* (2006, 63–93).

46. This example was brought to my attention in Sullivan's "Reproducing Whiteness" (n.d., 25–26).

47. Van Ausdale and Feagin's research was based on Van Ausdale playing the role of a "non-sanctioning" adult, for about a year, in a preschool/daycare center for three- to five-year-old children (2001, 38). The school used a "popular antibias curriculum" and was fairly diverse: "The school's official data on children in the classroom we observed was as follows: white (twenty-

four); Asian (nineteen); Black (four); biracial (for example, Black and white; three); Middle Eastern (three); Latino (two); and other (three)" (39). Van Ausdale established trust with the children, who felt free to engage in behaviors with each other that they would hide from the view of their teachers, who would punish children for engaging in racist speech or actions (40). Also, "In no case did [Van Ausdale] ask the children predetermined questions about race or ethnicity or overtly demonstrate that she was interested in researching these concepts. She kept her involvement with the children relaxed and nonadversarial, generally responding to [the] children's questions and requests in a conversational manner" (40). As they discuss throughout their book, Van Ausdale and Feagin's findings show that very young children are extraordinarily savvy regarding issues of race and racism, in contrast to prevailing research and common-sense assumptions that young children simply do not understand race: "We argue that children as young as three and four employ racial and ethnic concepts as important integrative and symbolically creative tools in the daily construction of their social lives" (26).

48. "Schools are linked to neighborhoods, which are in turn linked to employment and patterns of crime and crime perception. One cannot understand the problems of schools in the absence of understanding economic or community problems. The proper unit of analysis, for an understanding of racial or ethnic oppression, is the entire society. In many cases, one component institution enables or constrains yet another institution, and all institutions enable or constrain the individuals operating within them. All U.S. institutions are shaped by racial and ethnic histories and concerns. This is a fact of American life. Children are certainly important actors in this broad expanse of societal activities, and they often experience many of the contradictions and quandaries that adults experience. Children are not ordinarily disconnected from the larger social worlds" (Van Ausdale and Feagin 2001, 206).

49. In *Rock My Soul: Black People and Self-Esteem*, hooks discusses the low self-esteem issues faced by African Americans living in United States, with its history of slavery and its present forms of racist oppression. Here too hooks sends a message of hope in the midst of these issues, suggesting resources for African Americans to build empowered self-esteem (hooks 2003a).

50. Another helpful article is Alison Bailey's "Locating Traitorous Identities: Toward a View of Privilege-Cognizant White Character" (2000).

51. Resistance to being oppressed is a prominent theme in María Lugones's *Pilgrimages/Peregrinajes: Theorizing Coalition against Multiple Oppressions* (2003).

CHAPTER THREE

THE AFFECTIVITY OF INQUIRY

1. There are six essays in this series: "The Fixation of Belief" (1877), "How to Make Our Ideas Clear" (1878), "The Doctrine of Chances" (1878), "The Probability of Induction" (1878), "The Order of Nature" (1878), and "Deduction, Induction, and Hypothesis" (1878).

2. The term "concept" brings Peirce into better dialogue with feminist thinkers like Susan Babbitt and Marilyn Frye, and it helps convey the extent to which our beliefs inform the way we view the world around us, including other people. For a technical discussion by Peirce of the term "concept" and its derivatives, see CP 5.402 n. 3.

3. Peirce discusses belief and doubt in the first two essays of the Logic of Science series, "Fixation of Belief" and "How to Make Our Ideas Clear."

4. Other references in this context: "belief is of the nature of a *habit*" (in "Fixation of Belief") and "[t]he essence of belief is *the establishment* of a habit" (in "How to Make Our Ideas Clear") (W 3:248, 263, my emphases). Belief is both habit and habit-*taking*, because thought is an ongoing process. Any habit is a "rule for action," which is consistently challenged by its surrounding environments (W 3:263).

5. I borrow the idea of embodied "gearing into" the world from Merleau-Ponty's work in *Phenomenology of Perception* ([1962] 2000). Marcia Moen's discussion of what she calls the "bodily-felt shift" involved in Peirce's phenomenology is also helpful here (1991, 438–43).

6. Patricia Williams cites a 1988 case where "[t]wo white men . . . heaved a six-pound brick and a two-pound stone through the front window of a black couple's house. They did so, according to the U.S. attorney, 'because they felt blacks should not be living in their neighborhood and wanted to harass the couple because of their race'" (1991, 118–19).

7. There are fruitful connections to be drawn between socio-political doubt and what María Lugones describes as the lack of "playfulness" that she often experiences as a Latina woman in the United States (2003, 77–78, 93–96). In addition, her discussion of various ways of "being at ease in a 'world'" can be used to illuminate how the *absence* of socio-political secondness is experienced by those in privileged positions (90). For example, knowing the language and norms of the culture where one lives, agreeing with those norms, being in the midst of loved ones, and sharing a history with others are different ways of feeling at ease (90–91). For each of these types of ease, I would argue, there corresponds an absence of socio-political secondness.

8. In the present essay series, Peirce shifts from "the social principle" to the use of several terms conveying human sociality: "the social impulse," "sympathy," and "sentiment."

9. Peirce acknowledges that some forms of divergence from authority are tolerated as long as they are not considered too threatening (W 3:255).

10. This second comment is a later addition to the essay, ca. 1910, found in manuscript 334 (EP 1:109, 377 n. 22; cf. Hookway 2000, 38).

11. Recall that, for Peirce, humans cannot have immediate knowledge of the external world. Efforts to know this world are always semiotically mediated.

12. The scientific method utilizes the sophistication of human abstraction and self-control, whereby we are not dependent on being surprised by experience as an impetus for learning. We can also *anticipate* how experience will play out. We can be proactive in our conversation with nature, not merely reactive (cf. EP 2:369–70).

13. In "The Doctrine of Chances," he refers to "the human race, or any intellectual race" (W 3:285; cf. W 2:271 and EP 2:348).

14. By "fated," Peirce means "can nohow be avoided. . . . We are all fated to die" (W 3:273 n. 2).

15. In his essay "What Pragmatism Is" (1905), Peirce discusses truth in terms of human belief and doubt: "All you have any dealings with are your doubts and beliefs, with the course of life that forces new beliefs upon you and gives you power to doubt old beliefs. If your terms 'truth' and 'falsity' are taken in such senses as to be definable in terms of doubt and belief and the course of experience (as for example they would be, if you were to define the 'truth' as that to a belief in which belief would tend if it were to tend indefinitely toward absolute fixity), well and good: in that case, you are only talking about doubt and belief. But if by truth and falsity you mean something not definable in terms of doubt and belief in any way, then you are talking of entities of whose existence you can know nothing, and which Ockham's razor would clean shave off. Your problems would be greatly simplified, if, instead of saying that you want to know the 'Truth,' you were simply to say that you want to attain a state of belief unassailable by doubt" (EP 2:336).

16. Shannon Sullivan, for example, outlines a pragmatist-feminist account of truth, in her book *Living Across and Through Skins* (2001). Drawing on Dewey, she argues that "[t]ruth occurs when humans and their environments respond to and transact with one another in such a way that flourishing is achieved for both" (144, 133–56). My thinking about truth in Peirce's

thought has been shaped by challenges posed by Ken Stikkers (Summer Institute for American Philosophy, 2006) and Roberto Frega (personal correspondence, 2008). I have also benefited from talking with Judith Green about related issues (Summer Institute for American Philosophy, 2008). In addition, my interpretation of Peirce's conception of truth is influenced by Doug Anderson's discussion of the developmental teleology of the Peircean cosmos (1987, 111–21). I think that Peirce's conception of truth is a developmental telos that grows along with communities of inquiry pursuing it and along with the universe itself. For Peirce's description of developmental teleology, see his essay "Law of Mind" (EP 1:331, 1892).

17. Krakauer admits that it is not certain that this is why McCandless died, but Krakauer has done extensive research into McCandless's final days, including botanical and chemical research of the properties of plants that would have been available for McCandless to eat. See his extended discussion for the details (Krakauer 1996, 189–95).

18. An organism's complete lack of interest in its environment would mean it had no attunement to the regularities of that environment, so that it would have no sense of how the world works. Peirce notes that the world is "almost a chance-medley to the mind of a polyp" (W 3:312).

19. Recall that synthetic reasoning, in contrast to deductive reasoning, involves risk. Deductive reasoning is not risky, because it involves drawing conclusions based strictly upon the information contained in the premises of an argument. Synthetic reasoning involves moving beyond the premises into the unknown. For example, reasoning that the future will conform to the past, or that a particular hypothesis explains a surprising or puzzling phenomenon, involves going beyond what is known. The Kantian contrast between synthetic and analytic judgments is implicit, for Peirce, in this distinction.

20. He explores the possibility of instinct but does not ultimately appeal to it, in "The Order of Nature," as an answer regarding human accuracy in making guesses about nature (W 3:318–19). He leaves the question open: "[I]t is probable that there is some secret here which remains to be discovered" (W 3:319). As noted in Chapter 2, in his later work Peirce *does* endorse instinct as the source of guidance for human abduction. See EP 2:217–18 (1903) and EP 2:443 (1908). Peirce also speaks of the instinctive nature of reasoning in general (EP 2:427, 1907; EP 2:470 and 472, 1913).

21. As discussed in Chapter 2, the domain of Western philosophy provides abundant examples of an exclusionary vision of humanity. See Charles Mills's *The Racial Contract* and *Blackness Visible* (1997, 1998). Nancy Tuana's

Woman and the History of Philosophy, also noted in Chapter 2, demonstrates that, among the most influential philosophers of the Western canon, the paradigmatic human was, in fact, *a man*: "[W]oman is seen as lacking in just those areas judged as distinctively human: the rational and moral faculties" (1992, 13). One of the most striking examples is Aristotle. In his *Generation of Animals,* he describes women as "mutilated male[s]"; they are "monstrosities" since they depart from the "proper form" of humanity— i.e., male (quoted in Tuana 1992, 25). Tuana includes discussions of Plato, Descartes, Rousseau, Kant, Hume, Locke, and Hegel. She also addresses, to a lesser extent, the latent classism and racism in many classic Western philosophical texts (1992). See also Tuana's *The Less Noble Sex: Scientific, Religious, and Philosophical Conceptions of Woman's Nature* (1993).

22. This is not to say there were no white propertied men who opposed such exclusionary views but rather to stress that members of this elite class who *were* exclusionary held power sufficient to enforce an exclusionary view of humanity (Mills 1998, 8–9).

23. Recall in this vein the passage from Charles Mills, quoted last chapter, describing the Euro-American white articulation of reality that leaves to one side the experience of African Americans: "The peculiar features of the African-American experience—racial slavery, which linked biological phenotype to social subordination, and which is chronologically located in the modern epoch, ironically coincident with the emergence of liberalism's proclamation of universal human equality—are not part of the experience represented in the abstractions of European or Euro-American philosophers. And those who have grown up in such a[n] [African American] universe, asked to pretend that they are living in the other [Euro-American universe], will be cynically knowing, exchanging glances that signify 'There the white folks go again'" (1998, 4).

24. María Lugones and Elizabeth Spelman discuss how conceptual domination has occurred within traditional feminist scholarship, because of the fact that "some women's voices are more likely to be heard than others"— namely, "in the United States anyway, those of white, middle-class, heterosexual Christian (or anyway not self-identified non-Christian) women" (1990, 20). Charles Mills's discussion of the "peculiar moral and empirical epistemology" of the "Racial Contract" is also relevant to a discussion of conceptual domination (1998, 17–19).

25. Cf. Dewey [1922] 1988, 43–53, 65–68; Colapietro 2002, 4–5.

26. Cf. A. Rorty 1980, 122.

27. In "Reproducing Whiteness: How To Raise a White Child," Shannon Sullivan notes that "deliberate lectures are not the only, or perhaps even

primary way that children learn from their parents." Rather, "everyday, non-thematized activities and practices" teach racial lessons (n.d., 9–10). Her paper is a good resource for ideas about how to raise issues of race with white children in ways that challenge the unconscious perpetuation of white privilege in U.S. culture. See also chapter 3, "Seductive Habits of White Privilege," in *Revealing Whiteness* (Sullivan 2006, 63–93).

28. Cf. Van Ausdale and Feagin 2001.

29. As noted in the introduction to the book, Sullivan and Williams each discuss the well-intentioned "color-blindness" promoted by white middle-class parents/caretakers, which asserts that race/color should not and *does* not matter anymore in societies, like that of the United States, that have supposedly overcome racism against people of color. Both explain how such "color-blindness" acts to hide the manifestations of white supremacy that are still at play (Sullivan n.d., 22–28; 2006, 5, 61, 78–79, 123, 127, 189–92, 196; Williams 1997, esp. 3–16). Bell hooks notes that working-class white adults are comfortable discussing the everyday manifestations of racism in the United States, while economically privileged white adults often deny them (2003b, 30).

30. Depending on the context, the habits ruptured could include the habit of trusting her own judgment over that of her caretakers, the habit of unrestricted movement, and the habit of expectation that her actions will not result in pain.

31. McIntosh does not cite a specific work from Minnich on this point, but Minnich's book *Transforming Knowledge* is a good resource (1990). Toni Morrison's novel *The Bluest Eye* points a finger at homogenized white reading primers, as each of Morrison's chapters—in the tragic, powerful story about an African American girl who longs for blue eyes—begins with an excerpt from the chronicles of Dick and Jane (1993).

32. Michael Moore's *Bowling for Columbine* calls attention to the mainstream U.S. media's portrayal of people of color as committing most crimes in the United States. He also calls attention to white-collar criminals who are not perceived as "true" criminals, like people of color supposedly are (*Bowling for Columbine* 2004; cf. Van Ausdale and Feagin 2001, 203–6). Patricia Williams discusses the impression among many whites in the United States that this is indeed the case, when, in fact, *whites* commit the majority of the crimes in the United States: "Actually U.S. Bureau of Justice Statistics for 1986 show that whites were arrested for 71.7 percent of all crimes; blacks and all others (including American Indian, Alaskan Native, Asian, and Pacific Islander) account for the remaining 28 percent" (Williams 1991, 73). See

also Angela Davis's discussion in her essay "The Prison Industrial Complex" (2003).

33. I cite and discuss this example from Lerner in "Attunement to the Invisible" (Trout 2008, 71–72). Discussing women's oppression, motherhood, and race, Audre Lorde notes: "Some problems we share as women, some we do not. You [white women] fear your children will grow up to join the patriarchy and testify against you, we [Black women] fear our children will be dragged from a car and shot down in the street, and you will turn your backs upon the reasons they are dying" (1984, 119).

34. I thank students in my summer 2007 Self and Identity course at the University of Portland for noting that the runner might not have simply been falsely universalizing in the manner Lerner seems to assume.

35. I thank Devon Goss for providing these personal examples.

36. This theme is understated in the original version of "How to Make Our Ideas Clear" (1878). Peirce's 1893 and 1906 comments on the essay draw out these implications (cf. CP 5.402 nn. 2–3).

37. Peirce added the latter phrase "no matter if contrary to all previous experience" in 1894 (MS 422; see editors' notes: EP 1:124, 378 n. 7).

38. I borrow this shorthand of the United States of American ideal from Joe Feagin and Hernán Vera's discussion of racism against African Americans in the United States (1995, 2).

39. I thank Samantha Kolinski for providing this example (personal conversation).

40. For a historical portrayal of the economic realities of the New World colonies, such that African slavery became institutionalized as a Euro-American answer to the problem of labor, see Winthrop Jordan's *White over Black: American Attitudes toward the Negro, 1550–1812* (1968, 47–63). See also Mills 1997, 21, 31–40. In a literary study of whiteness and blackness in American literature, *Playing in the Dark: Whiteness and the Literary Imagination*, Toni Morrison observes, "The rights of man . . . , an organizing principle upon which the nation [of the United States] was founded, was inevitably yoked to Africanism. Its history, its origin is permanently allied with another seductive concept: the hierarchy of race. As the sociologist Orlando Patterson has noted, we should not be surprised that the Enlightenment could accommodate slavery; we should be surprised if it had not. The concept of freedom did not emerge in a vacuum. Nothing highlighted freedom—if it did not in fact create it—like slavery" (1992, 38).

41. For an extended discussion of the historical mistreatment of Native Americans by the U.S. government, see Vine Deloria Jr., *Custer Died for Your Sins* (1988). See also Sullivan 2006, 129–36, 142.

42. As noted in Chapter 2, I borrow the term "subperson" from Charles Mills, who uses it in the context of race: "[T]he peculiar status of a subperson is that it is an entity which, because of phenotype, seems (from, of course, the perspective of the categorizer) human in some respects but not in others. It is a human (or, if this word already seems normatively loaded, a humanoid) who, though adult, is not fully a person. And the tensions and internal contradictions in this concept capture the tensions and internal contradictions of the black experience in a white-supremacist society" (1998, 6–7). Mills does not limit his discussion to the "black" experience but also includes any race considered "nonwhite" (1997, 11, 16–17). Cf. Tuana 1992, 1993.

CHAPTER FOUR

THE LAW OF MIND, ASSOCIATION, AND SYMPATHY

1. The socio-political application that I make of Peircean spontaneity, sympathy, and agape is my own. Nonetheless, my appreciation for and reading of Peirce's cosmological writings and agapic evolution is influenced by the work of Doug Anderson, Carl Hausman, and Michael Ventimiglia. See in this regard Doug Anderson's *Creativity and the Philosophy of C. S. Peirce* (1987), "Realism and Idealism in Peirce's Cosmogony" (1992), "Peirce's Agape and the Generality of Concern" (1995a), and "Peirce's Horse: A Sympathetic and Semeiotic Bond" (2004); Carl Hausman's "Eros and Agape in Creative Evolution: A Peircean Insight" (1974), "Philosophy and Tragedy: The Flaw of Eros and the Triumph of Agape" (1993), and "Evolutionary Realism and Charles Peirce's Pragmatism" (1999); and Michael Ventimiglia's "'Evolutionary Love' in Theory and Practice" (2001). My appreciation of communal sympathy has also been enriched by Daniel Campos's essay (which I also cited in Chapter 1) "El buen juego y la mala suerte: Habilidad, reacción y espontaneidad en el fútbol" (2006), in which he offers an insightful Peircean analysis of the collective thirdness and firstness displayed by *fútbol* (soccer) teams that have cultivated communal habits through working and practicing together. Campos's discussion sheds light on how communal sympathy plays out on a Peircean scheme, even though Campos does not himself explicitly highlight the "sympathy" connection (136–37, 140–42).

2. The *Monist* "Cosmology Series" essays were published between 1891 and 1893. They include "The Architecture of Theories" (1891), "The Doctrine of Necessity Examined" (1892), "The Law of Mind" (1892), "Man's Glassy Essence" (1892), and "Evolutionary Love" (1893). My focus will be on "The Law of Mind" and "Evolutionary Love." The specific association writ-

ings that I am using include the following: Peirce's ca. 1893 writings on association (CP 7.388–467) (These writings are part of a project Peirce entitled
Grand Logic. Paragraphs CP 7.451–62 are from a book on logic aimed at a
younger audience. They are undated but bear such close resemblance to the
ca. 1893 association writings that I class them under this date. See editors'
note in the *Collected Papers* [7.451 n. 25]), a passage (ca. 1897) on association
that appears in his mathematical writings (CP 4.157), and passages on association that occur in a ca. 1898 manuscript on habit (CP 7.495–504).

3. On the feltness of self, see Patricia Muoio's "Peirce on the Person"
(1984, 174–75).

4. Peirce equivocates on what he means by "outer world" (or "external
world"). In some contexts, he seems to refer to a world outside the body of
the human organism (e.g., EP 2:419, 550 n. 49). In other contexts, he seems
to refer to the *ideas* deriving from this "outside" world (e.g., EP 2:412–13,
369–70). For my purposes, this equivocation is not problematic, since we
can have access to an "outside" world only by means of our ideas about it,
in Peirce's scheme (CP 7.408 n. 19). I will be using the term "outer world"
of the human organism in the second sense just noted—that is, as an intra-
mental dimension of ideas that derive from the world external to the
organism.

5. Peirce prefers not to use a verb form of "association" when referring
to one idea suggesting another, as in "I associate A with B." This preference
is due to his respect for the English associationalists, whom he credits for
being the first to use "association" as a scientific term and who were "careful
never to extend it to the operation or event whereby one idea calls up another to the mind" (CP 7.495).

6. Cf. CP 7.392 (ca. 1893), CP 4.157 (ca. 1897), CP 7.498 (ca. 1898)

7. In a ca. 1905 discussion of Critical Common-sensism, Peirce notes
that humans differ from nonhuman animals in the higher degrees of self-
control that humans are able to achieve (CP 5.533–34).

8. I thank Daniel Campos for helping me appreciate this point in its
richness (personal conversation). Resemblance is the source of the spontaneity involved in creative, scientific, or everyday abduction, whereby the answer to a problem and/or an aesthetic insight arises for an individual. When
the abduction occurs, it is not by means of deductive or inductive reasoning
but rather involves a qualitative leap beyond known arguments and habits
(CP 7.498). It is beyond the scope of this project to trace out these abduction
themes more fully.

9. Regarding the tendency among whites to perceive the white experience as "not raced," see Williams 1997, 6–16; hooks 2003b, 26 ff.; Sullivan
n.d., 1–2, 13–16, 22–28; Mills 1997, 53 ff.; Mills 1998, 9–10.

10. Shannon Sullivan provides an extended discussion of Euro-American versus Native American relationships to land, also drawing on Vine Deloria Jr.'s work (2006, 129–36).

11. Cf. CP 7.395, 406, 417, 424, 431, 434–35, 447.

12. Peirce does not have business in mind when he uses the descriptor "corporate" (EP 1:351). His primary focus in this context is the religious community found in Christian communities (EP 1:350–51).

13. Sympathy can be attributed to God only analogically, since sympathy occurs through feelings, and feelings involve both body and mind. Peirce is loath to attribute to God human attributes as specific as "mind" or "body." He is wary of "God" as an overly determined conception with colloquial connotations. In an 1898 account of his cosmogony, he addresses those who would attribute creative "firsts" to the "mind of God": "I really think there is no objection to this except that it is wrapped up in figures of speech, instead of having the explicitness that we desire in science. . . . To apply such a word to *God* is precisely like the old pictures which show him like an aged man leaning over to look out from above a cloud. Considering the *vague intention* of it, as conceived by the *non-theological artist*, it cannot be called false, but rather ludicrously figurative" (RLT 259–60, Peirce's emphasis).

14. See EP 1:352–54, 362, 365–66; RLT 259–60; Hausman 1999, 203.

15. Peirce borrows the phrasing "gentle force" from Hume, appreciating the latter's depiction of the gentleness with which the law of mind operates (CP 7.389).

16. Peirce borrows this description from Henry James Sr., a Swedenborgian (EP 1:353).

17. What is ideal for God cannot be considered ideal for humans in the same way, since humans and God are different in significant ways. While Peirce does not conceive of God in a strictly definable way, he does see God as infinite and therefore unlimited in ways that humans are limited (CP 8.262; RLT 259–60; EP 2:447). Agape as a divine ideal must be modified on the human plane. Unfortunately Peirce does not address this discrepancy (Hausman 1974, 22). It is beyond the scope of my project to fully take on this lacuna in Peirce's thought. See Peirce's "The Neglected Argument for the Reality of God" (EP 2:434–50). For a developmental study of Peirce's ideas about God, see Donna Orange's *Peirce's Conception of God* (1984).

18. A version of the manipulation I have in mind is discussed by both Marilyn Frye and María Lugones. They do not address agapic love specifically, but they do discuss how "love" can be manipulated as an ideal that keeps certain people in subservience to others. Frye focuses on how women

have historically been taught that, to be properly loving, they must surrender their own interests to the interests of men: "Under the name of Love, a willing and unconditional servitude has been promoted as something ecstatic, noble, fulfilling and even redemptive" (1983, 72, 66–83). This type of love, which is "proper" to women, however, is the product of a patriarchal "arrogant" perception that views others only through the lens of its own interests, wishing to acquire "the service of" women (67). Lugones, building on Frye's work and also highlighting the racism of white women toward women of color, notes that women too can hold an "arrogant gaze" toward others (2003, 77–100). Both Frye and Lugones want to reconceive "love" in order to avoid its being co-opted by arrogant perception that promotes hierarchies of sex, race, and economic class (Frye 1983, 72–76; Lugones 2003, 78–83). It is beyond the scope of this project to detail the extent to which their respective reconceptions compare and contrast with Peirce's account of agapic love. I will note that Lugones's revisioning of love seems more Peircean than Frye's in that Lugones insists on the interdependence of the lover and beloved, while Frye focuses on their independence (Lugones 2003, 78–83; Frye 1983, 74–75). Lugones discusses this contrast between her revisioning of love and Frye's (2003, 82–83).

19. It should be noted that a community of inquiry does well to *examine* exclusionary beliefs, not in order to embrace them, but rather with the aim of learning about them in order to better resist their effects in thought and practice. This point requires more attention than I can give it here, and it is inspired by Timothy Beneke's framing of his essay "Intrusive Images and Subjectified Bodies: Notes on Visual Heterosexual Porn," where he says, "In what follows I attempt to shed light on heterosexual men and their visual experience of women, their sexual distress, their difficulty identifying with women's experience, and their use of porn[ography]. Since I seek to understand certain forms of male suffering that I take to be real and *that men use to justify sexism and rape*, I want to be clear: *To understand or even to empathize with someone's distress is not to legitimate what it is used to justify or what may appear to issue from it. Any such attempts to understand male sexual distress must be undertaken with an eye to gaining insight as to how men might finally stop doing the many horrible things they do—to women, to each other, and to themselves*" (1991, 169, my emphasis). I do not agree with all of Beneke's points in his essay, but I appreciate his efforts to engage and understand ideas and practices he disagrees with, as a means of ultimately mitigating the harm that may stem from such ideas and practices. I also appreciate that he admits: "My biases are white, middle-class, and no doubt

unconsciously inform the picture of men I present" (169), a qualification that reflects the spirit of my project.

20. Peirce makes this comment about the color spectrum in relation to the three types of evolution he discusses in "Evolutionary Love," tychasm, anancasm, and agapasm (EP 1:363). He notes that tychasm and anancasm are really "degenerate forms of agapasm," as agapasm involves both chance (which is tychastic) and development toward an end (which is anancastic) (EP 1:362). This color metaphor is fruitfully applied to the ideal community as well, which makes sense, as it is a metaphor to explain synechism or continuity, which Peirce believes pervades the cosmos.

21. See also Lugones 2003, 14–15, 72–74.

22. The wording of this passage may seem universalist regarding whites. Mills's general depiction of the historical and philosophical picture, however, allows room for white social reformers. He refers to the moral contradictions and silences perpetuated by "a lot" of whites, and he names especially problematic thinkers rather than simply lumping all white people together (1998, 3–5). In *The Racial Contract*, Mills also notes, "[T]here have always been praiseworthy whites—anticolonialists, abolitionists, opponents of imperialism, civil rights activists, resisters of apartheid—who have recognized the existence and immorality of Whiteness as a political system, challenged its legitimacy . . ." (1997, 107).

23. Regarding the reference to light, see Matthew 5:14–16. Regarding the reference to talents, see Matthew 25:14–30 and Luke 19:12–27 (*The Holy Bible* 1985). My thanks to Leigh Johnson for helping me track down these biblical references.

24. The communal embrace of agapic sympathy can be also be fruitfully applied in the classroom. Agapic sympathy creates an environment in which each student's voice is valued, and creativity is embraced. In this atmosphere students are more likely to take risks in expressing themselves and growing in their sense of themselves as empowered agents. Michael Ventimiglia has discussed this issue. The following papers are helpful: "Three Educational Orientations: A Peircean Perspective on Education and the Growth of the Self" (Ventimiglia 2005); "Agape and Spiritual Transformation" (n.d. [a], 9–10); "Three Models of Personal Evolution Derived from the Cosmology of C. S. Peirce" (n.d. [b], 15–16). See also Sharp's discussion of the compatibility of Peirce's agape and a community of inquiry in the classroom. Her ideas are tailored to the Philosophy for Children program, where philosophical discourse is explicitly engaged in the classroom (Sharp 1994, 203–10). Maxine Greene writes about an agapic classroom atmosphere (although not

by this name and not in reference to Peirce) in "The Passions of Pluralism: Multiculturalism and the Expanding Community" (1997). She promotes classrooms in which the diversity of students is embraced.

25. I thank Roger Ward for pushing me to highlight that Peirce wrote about agape during years in which he was coping with intense isolation from communities of inquiry.

26. As noted in the book's introduction, I thank Cathy Kemp and Mitchell Aboulafia for suggesting that I highlight the poverty suffered by Peirce, as a way to help humanize Peirce for my readers. Joseph Brent's *Charles Sanders Peirce: A Life* gives a detailed treatment of Peirce's decline into poverty in his later years; see chapters 4 and 5 (1998, 203–322). William James was instrumental in helping keep Peirce afloat during these years, eventually organizing the Peirce fund, which coordinated monetary contributions from Peirce's friends and supporters (304–7). Brent also provides excellent documentation and discussion of the various factors that led to Peirce's descent into poverty (136–202).

27. "Among animals, the mere mechanical individualism is vastly reën-forced as a power making for good by the animal's ruthless greed. As Darwin puts it on his title-page, it is the struggle for existence; and he should have added for his motto: Every individual for himself, and the Devil take the hindmost!" (EP 1:357). Lest his readers misunderstand him, Peirce makes it clear that Darwin's ideas did not precede the culture of greed but rather that his work emerged within this culture and was readily embraced "because of the encouragement it gave to the greed-philosophy" (EP 1:359).

28. Cf. RLT 121. This parallels, to some extent, Damasio's discussion of the "social homeostasis" that characterizes human communal life (2003, 166 ff.).

29. My thanks to Doug Anderson for bringing to my attention the relevance, in this context, of Peirce's critique of Pearson's work.

30. Peirce's later critique of Pearson's eugenic spirit is foreshadowed here.

31. "The Conservation of Races" was not Du Bois's last word on race. For a study of the development of Du Bois's ideas on this matter, see Tommy Lott's "Du Bois's Anthropological Notion of Race" (2001).

32. Nussbaum continues, "Thus we do not find staircases built with step levels so high that only the giants of Brobdingnag can climb them, nor do we find our orchestras playing instruments at frequencies inaudible to the human ear and audible only to dog ears" (2004, 306).

33. As noted in Chapter 3, for an extended discussion of the historical mistreatment of Native Americans by the U.S. government, see Vine Deloria Jr.'s *Custer Died for Your Sins* (1988). See also Sullivan 2006, 129–36, 142. For

a historical portrayal of the economic realities of the New World colonies such that African slavery became institutionalized as an Euro-American answer to the problem of labor, see Winthrop Jordan's *White over Black: American Attitudes toward the Negro, 1550–1812* (1968, 47–63). See also Mills 1997, 21, 31–40. In a literary study of whiteness and blackness in American literature, *Playing in the Dark: Whiteness and the Literary Imagination*, Toni Morrison observes, "The rights of man . . . , an organizing principle upon which the nation [of the United States] was founded, was inevitably yoked to Africanism. Its history, its origin is permanently allied with another seductive concept: the hierarchy of race. As the sociologist Orlando Patterson has noted, we should not be surprised that the Enlightenment could accommodate slavery; we should be surprised if it had not. The concept of freedom did not emerge in a vacuum. Nothing highlighted freedom—if it did not in fact create it—like slavery" (1992, 38).

34. Two articles that are helpful in introducing these issues, especially as they affect women of color, are Chandra Talpade Mohanty's "Women Workers and Capitalist Scripts: Ideologies of Domination, Common Interests, and the Politics of Solidarity" (1997) and Ofelia Schutte's "Feminism and Globalization Processes in Latin America" (2002).

35. It is unclear from Alcoff's story whether the department as a whole was white, except for Alcoff's friend, or whether the "White-only" descriptor applied only to the department majority that voted for the demotion. The relevant passage: "Against her account, and without speaking to anyone but the disgruntled student, the department majority formed the opinion that my friend was not a good teacher. . . . [S]he enjoyed not the slightest presumption of credibility with much of her department when it came to problems of discrimination in the classroom. They assumed that they, a White-only amalgam of faculty, could assess the situation" (Alcoff 2001, 66–67). Either way, a white-only majority has dismissed the hypothesis of racism/sexism by a woman of color, without subjecting it to fair testing.

36. "In riding a horse; rider and ridden understand one another in [a] way of which the former can no more give an account than the latter" (CP 7.447).

37. Regarding the learning of slang, Maryann Ayim analyzes the use of terms such as "chick" and "girl" (among others) to refer to women, applying Peirce's semiotic scheme to highlight the demeaning, exclusionary nature of such usage. See her article "The Implications of Sexually Stereotypic Language as Seen through Peirce's Theory of Signs" (Ayim 1983). Regarding the human-horse example, setting aside the problematic issues linked to the

taming and domestication of nonhuman animals, I give Peirce the benefit of the doubt and portray his relationship with his horse as agapic. For a general discussion of human-(nonhuman) animal sympathy in Peirce's work, see Doug Anderson's "Peirce's Horse: A Sympathetic and Semeiotic Bond" (2004). For examples of exclusionary sympathy toward nonhuman animals, we can note the blatant and cruel exclusionary sympathy that underwrote vivisection historically and currently underwrites the barbaric treatment of many nonhuman animals. Recall that vivisection is the practice of live dissection of nonhuman animals *without anesthesia* (Pence 2004, 247–48).

38. Chapter 3 addresses this point too. Recall that in "Fixation of Belief" (1877) Peirce says that "sentiments in their development will be very greatly determined by accidental causes" (W 3:253). He says this in his discussion of the a priori method, in which he also uses "instinct" and "sentiment" synonymously, later adding to the essay this comment about the a priori method: "Indeed, as long as no better method can be applied, it ought to be followed, since it is then the expression of instinct which must be the ultimate cause of belief in all cases" (EP 1:377 n. 22, ca. 1910).

39. Peirce's neologism "percipuum" signifies the percept plus the perceptual judgment (CP 7.629). This awkward term is designed to capture the phenomenon that discursive access to the percept comes only through the perceptual judgment. Richard Bernstein's "Peirce's Theory of Perception" gives a helpful treatment of the development of Peirce's theory of perception (1964).

40. Peirce links control with consciousness in a comment about perceptual judgments: "[T]he perceptive [i.e., perceptual] judgment is the result of a process, although of a process not sufficiently conscious to be controlled, or to state it more truly, not controllable and therefore not fully conscious" (EP 2:227).

41. Recall, from Chapter 1, that we should not read too much into Peirce's use of "racial" here, as he uses the term inconsistently in his corpus. Sometimes "race" is used coextensively with "humanity" (e.g., EP 2:433, 1907). Other times he refers to races *within* humanity (e.g., EP 2:257, 1903). Nonetheless, "race" as a socio-political reality is socialized into what is "personal," because of Peirce's conviction of the inescapable interplay between the inner and outer worlds (CP 7.438–39).

CHAPTER FIVE
CRITICAL COMMON-SENSISM, 1900S

1. I am grateful to many people for their critical comments on the material in this chapter. Thank you to Doug Anderson, Cornelis de Waal, Peter

Hare, Lisa Heldke, Robert Lane, Shannon Sullivan, Dwayne Tunstall, and an anonymous reader. I also benefited from audience feedback at conference presentations of this material at Feminist Epistemologies, Methodologies, Metaphysics and Science Studies (FEMMS2, February 2007); the Society for the Advancement of American Philosophy (March 2007); and the Pacific Division of the Society for Women in Philosophy (October 2006). Finally, I received helpful audience feedback at a presentation I gave at Lewis and Clark College in Portland, Oregon, in November 2006.

The "critical" of Critical Common-sensism has additional meanings for Peirce too, including an indication of CCS's Kantian legacy (EP 2:353–54; CP 5.525).

2. A note to Peirce scholars: In a discussion of Critical Common-sensism (CCS), in the *Monist* article "Issues of Pragmaticism" (1905), Peirce comments that he can only address about "two percent of the pertinent thought which would be necessary in order to present the subject as I have worked it out. I can only make a small selection of what it seems most desirable to submit to [the reader's] judgment. Not only must all steps be omitted which he can be expected to supply for himself, but unfortunately much more that may cause him difficulty"(EP 2:348–49). My efforts in this chapter take seriously that Peirce's CCS writings were only the tip of the iceberg. I present a proactive reading of Critical Common-sensism through a social critical lens. I do not pretend to present exactly what Peirce may have had in mind. Nonetheless the interpretations and applications I offer are supported by the text and by Peirce's ideal of an infinitely inclusive, agapic community of inquiry that is open to self-correction and growth.

3. For additional information on Peirce's Critical Common-sensism, see Hookway 1990, 1993, and 2000, esp. chapters 7 and 8. In "Mimicking Foundationalism: on Sentiment and Self-control," Hookway explains how Peircean epistemology sharply opposes Cartesian foundationalist epistemology while also "Mimicking Foundationalism" (1993). Any satisfactory epistemological model, Hookway argues and I agree, must acknowledge that *some* kind of foundation is needed in order for humans to have the confidence to reason at all. Without this, we would "feel estranged or alienated from our ways of carrying out investigations and deliberations" (1993, 170; cf. 2000, 225, 233 ff.). Critical Common-sensism calls for an examination of the background beliefs that form the platform from which reasoning proceeds.

4. On the relationship between scientific testing and common-sense beliefs, see Hookway 2000, 150–51, 192.

5. Peirce explicitly links dubitability and falsehood at the conclusion of a Critical Common-sensist scrutiny of the belief "that suicide is to be classed

as murder": He explains that this belief is "substantially confined to the Christian world" and does not withstand "actual self-debate" (EP 2:350). He concludes: "This belief, then, should be set down as dubitable; and it will no sooner have been pronounced dubitable, than Reason will stamp it as false" (EP 2:350).

6. For a discussion of the role vagueness plays in Peirce's thought, see "Vagueness, Logic, and Interpretation" in Hookway 2000, 135–58.

7. This quote is from an 1865 translation of the 1795 edition of *On the Natural Variety of Mankind* (Blumenbach 2000, 27, editors' notes).

8. This line is found in *Observations on the Feeling of the Beautiful and Sublime* (cited in Mills 1998, 202 n. 8).

9. This line is found in a footnote in the essay "Of National Characters" (cited in Mills 1998, 202 n. 8). Mills's catalog also includes John Stuart Mill, Hegel, Marx and Engels, and Voltaire (202 n. 8).

10. I do not intend to overlook the Euro-American whites who argued for the equal humanity of nonwhite races. It is, however, beyond the scope of my project to detail their efforts.

11. Those interested in promoting colonialist racism could manipulate this comment, by insisting that they can determine the degrees of self-control of peoples different—and therefore "inferior"—from themselves, using this difference/inferiority to justify colonization, slavery, or genocide. Peirce himself might have sympathized with such manipulation, from a personal perspective. Nonetheless, we must set aside Peirce's own racism and focus on his philosophical ideas themselves. On these terms, it is clear that such a manipulation of "levels of self-control" would be unreasonable, because it would involve exclusionary, circular reasoning about "inferiority" of self-control (i.e., assuming inferiority to prove inferiority). This is the type of circularity just highlighted, which characterized nineteenth-century racist pseudoscience. On Peircean terms, it is not acceptable to project inferiority onto others in order to exclude them from inquiry, as discussed last chapter.

12. A hopeful point can be inserted here. Because specified beliefs are illegitimately indubitable common-sense beliefs, it makes sense that they can undergo change more quickly than our original common-sense beliefs can. Presumably regarding original beliefs, Peirce notes, in "Philosophy and the Conduct of Life" (1898), that "[i]nstinct is capable of development and growth,—though by a movement which is slow in the proportion in which it is vital; . . . The soul's deeper parts can only be reached through its surface. In this way the eternal forms, that mathematics and philosophy and the other sciences make us acquainted with will by slow percolation gradually

reach the very core of one's being, and will come to influence our lives . . ."
(RLT 121–22). On the other hand, he also cryptically notes, in a 1905 discussion of Critical Common-sensism, that "[instincts] can be somewhat modified in a very short time" (EP 2:349). It is unclear what particular context Peirce had in mind with this later comment. Nonetheless, given his broad conception of instinct, it is plausible that Peirce believed that *some* of our instincts, such as specified ones that are a product of socialization, are amenable to a relatively quicker change than our original beliefs are. For a model of this quicker change, we can look to his description of Lamarckian evolution in the "Cosmology Series" essay "Evolutionary Love" (1893). Peirce's account of this type of evolution describes human effort as an agent of personal evolution, by way of intentional habit-change (EP 1:360). My presentation of this issue—namely, the speed with which instincts might change—is indebted to the questions and insights of both the audience and commentator, Robert Lane, for my paper presentation, "Colorblindness and Paper Doubt: A Socio-political Application of Critical Common-sensism," at the Society for the Advancement of American Philosophy (SAAP), Annual Meeting, March 2007.

13. Recall that Peirce coined the term "pragmaticism" and its derivatives to name his own particular formulation of pragmatism (EP 2:331–45).

14. "Surely whatever I had admitted until now as most true I received either from the senses or through the senses. However, I have noticed that the senses are sometimes deceptive; and it is a mark of prudence never to place our complete trust in those who have deceived us even once" (Descartes 1998, 60; ATVII 18). Analyzing Descartes' *Meditations* within the historical-cultural milieu in which they were written, Susan Bordo highlights that trust in the senses was deeply undermined by the invention of the telescope, which revealed the sun as so much larger than unaided human senses previously reported (1987, 13, 34–38). Her *Flight to Objectivity* makes a strong case for taking Cartesian doubt—as a whole—much more seriously than traditional scholarship on Descartes usually does (14–16). Drawing on psychoanalytical, historical, and cultural insights from Descartes' era, Bordo argues that Cartesian doubt reflects the sincere epistemological anxiety that resulted from the painful shift in worldview that occurred in the transition from the medieval world to the modern one.

15. Passages that support paper-doubt as having sincere and insincere forms include the following. Peirce notes that "man possess[es] no infallible introspective power into the secrets of his own heart, to know just what he believes and what he doubts. The denial of such a power is one of the clauses

of critical common-sensism" (CP 5.498). This comment can refer to both sincere and insincere doubt, as two ways in which a person may lack insight into her ability to sufficiently doubt beliefs. Peirce also notes, "The Critical Common-Sensist . . . [attaches] great value . . . to doubt, provided only that it be the weighty and noble metal itself, and no counterfeit nor paper substitute. *He is not content to ask himself whether he does doubt,* but he invents a plan for attaining to doubt, elaborates it in detail, and then puts it into practice . . ." (EP 2:353, my emphasis). Once again, one can assure oneself of doubting in a sincere or an insincere fashion, just as Descartes does. Both insincere and sincere paper-doubt neglect the depth of work that is needed to achieve the type of doubt that CCS values. My thanks to Robert Lane, once again, whose commentary on my paper "Colorblindness and Paper Doubt" helped me formulate a more rigorous textual grounding for my broadened conception of paper-doubt (Trout 2007).

16. At the historical time this belief held sway, it would have been *inconceivable* to most people that the earth was otherwise than flat. Note, however, that the belief's "inconceivability" was contextual historically. For Peirce all beliefs are ultimately doubt-able—that is, conceivably other than what they presently are. This reflects his fallibilism.

17. Code notes that she derives "hegemonic imaginary" from Cornelius Castoriadis, who "characterizes the instituted social imaginary as follows: 'The socialization of individuals—itself an instituted process, and in each case a different one—opens up these individuals, giving them access to a *world* of social imaginary significations whose instauration as well as incredible *coherence* goes unimaginably beyond everything that "one or many individuals" could ever produce. These significations owe their actual (social-historical) existence to the fact that they are *instituted*'" (Code 2001, 280 n. 11, Castoriadis's emphasis; Castoriadis 1991, 62).

18. Recall Peirce's comment about self-control from the third Cognition Series essay, "Grounds of Validity of the Laws of Logic" (1869): "Self-control seems to be the capacity for rising to an extended view of a practical subject instead of seeing only temporary urgency" (W 2:261 n. 6).

19. As noted in Chapter 3, the reader can consult Stephen Jay Gould's and Nancy Tuana's work on racism and sexism in nineteenth-century science for discussions of the prevalence of these socio-political biases (Gould 1981, chapters 2–4; Tuana 1993, 34–50).

20. In addition, excluding groups from membership in communal inquiry makes it more likely that socio-political action of some kind will have to occur in order for the membership "rules" to change (cf. Babbitt 1996; Gauthier 2004, 9–11).

21. Hookway notes that cognitive habits (like the capacity to doubt) "guide us in recognizing when an inference is a good one, when evidence is sufficient for belief in some proposition, *when hypotheses are so implausible that we need not take steps to eliminate them before accepting a rival*, and so on" (2000, 254–55, my emphasis). I would argue that nonconscious racism (and other forms of discrimination) can shape the determination of implausibility that Hookway describes here. The result of such shaping is that testimony from people of color and other non-hegemonic groups can be deemed implausible by white people and others in hegemonic groups who do not recognize the discrimination they are perpetuating, because the discriminatory habits in question are functioning nonconsciously.

22. "Colorblindness" is a prominent theme in Shannon Sullivan's *Revealing Whiteness*, (2006, 5, 61, 78–79, 123, 127, 189–92, 196; cf. Sullivan n.d., 12–16). See also bell hooks's *Teaching Community* (2003, "Talking Race and Racism," 25–40).

23. This reasoning is often naively premised on a colorless or unraced standard of whiteness. White people often do not understand or experience themselves as having a race (Williams 1997, 6–16; hooks 2003b, 26 ff.; Sullivan n.d., 1–2, 13–16, 22–28; Mills 1997, 53 ff.; Mills 1998, 9–10).

24. "Colorblindness" is not always used with good, although naive, intentions. It can also be used with racist intentions, as a strategy for cloaking racist thinking. See Charles Mills's *The Racial Contract* (1997, 76–77); Sullivan 2006, 5, 127; Bonilla-Silva 2003.

25. For sociological research on this phenomenon regarding antiblack racism, see *Racism without Racists* (Bonilla-Silva 2003). Bonilla-Silva's research indicates that "colorblind" whites often allow that *some* racism occurs but at the same time deny its systemic impact on education, employment, and residential choices for African Americans (see especially chapter 2: "The Central Frames of Color-Blind Racism," 25–52). Bonilla-Silva acknowledges that many *well-intentioned* whites subscribe to "colorblindness" (13–14, 15, 54).

26. For some Peirceans, it might be tempting to limit the CCSist diagnosis of the "colorblindness" issue to the fact that the well-intentioned white people to whom I continually refer have *false beliefs* about their successful elimination of racist common-sense beliefs from thought and behavior. While I agree with this diagnosis as far as it goes, I would argue that it should not be seen as a stopping point in a CCSist analysis of "colorblindness." Critical Common-sensism has so much more to offer. It can help us understand *why* racist beliefs can find their way into a well-intentioned anti-racist

white person's conduct. In addition, the white people in question often deny that they have false beliefs about their successful elimination of racism from their thought and conduct. The expanded CCSist inquiry I offer, supplemented with insights from social criticism, helps make sense of this point as well.

27. Note that I am *not* saying that *all* whites do not understand the continued presence of racism and that *all* people of color do. In "Talking Race and Racism" in *Teaching Community* (2003, 25–40), bell hooks discusses the complexity of the issues of awareness of racism and internalized racism for whites and people of color. Nonetheless it is common enough for there to be only one person of color in a room full of whites and for feedback from that person about racism to be dismissed by the white majority (27).

28. They are also in a position to internalize disempowering beliefs about themselves based on race, sex, and so on. Commenting on her novel *The Bluest Eye,* Morrison notes that it is based on a true experience in her life. As a young child, Morrison was horrified to hear the confession of a female classmate who, like her, was African American. The classmate wished she had blue eyes. Morrison writes: "Implicit in her desire was racial self-loathing. And twenty years later I was still wondering about how one learns that. Who told her?. . . . Who had looked at her and found her so wanting, so small a weight on the beauty scale? [*The Bluest Eye*] pecks away at the gaze that condemned her" (1993, 210). See also hooks 2003a; 2003b, 37–38; Mills 1997, 118–20; Williams 1997, 119–20.

29. Cf. Mills 1997, 109 ff.; Alcoff 2006, 179–94. This point, and work in this chapter more generally, threads the needle for a Peircean contribution to pragmatist-feminist standpoint theory, whose ground has been laid by Charlene Seigfried and Shannon Sullivan. It is beyond the scope of my project to fully discuss this point. See *Pragmatism and Feminism* (Seigfried 1996) and "Transactional Knowing: Towards a Pragmatist-Feminist Standpoint Theory" in *Living Across and Through Skins* (Sullivan 2001, 133–56). For a general introduction to feminist standpoint theory in its various forms, see *The Feminist Standpoint Theory Reader* (Harding 2004). Standpoint theorists often use standpoint in a technical sense, which does *not* signify mere "viewpoint or perspective" but rather "an achieved (versus ascribed) collective identity or consciousness, one for which oppressed groups must struggle" (Harding 2004, 14 n. 11). My own discussion of feedback from non-hegemonic groups, however, does not *necessarily* require an achieved standpoint, because such feedback can result from experiences of socio-political secondness that are obvious within one's experience. I see the often dismissed, phe-

nomenologically derived feedback from non-hegemonic groups as an important epistemological resource. My thinking on this front is influenced by Linda Alcoff's article "The Phenomenology of Racial Embodiment" (2006, 179–94).

30. Personal conversation, April 2009. Cf. Terri Elliott's "Making Strange What Had Appeared Familiar" (1994). It should be noted that able-bodied people can neglect to take into consideration the perspective of those who use wheelchairs. For example, a wheelchair-using student with whom I worked in the 1990s told me stories of having to repeatedly assert her right to navigate *unimpeded* to class as a college student, as her university repeatedly overlooked obstacles, such as snow accumulation, that blocked her path. Her needs were not fully grasped by the able-bodied university staff with whom she was dealing and thus were repeatedly not anticipated by them, making her self-advocacy necessary.

31. See also Lugones and Spelman 1990, 21–24.

32. Cf. Sullivan 2006; Flax 1979.

33. Cf. Williams 1991, 8–9. Susan Babbitt also notes that those in power have themselves defined the conceptual schema by which perspectives are articulated in the first place. Historically these schema have made it impossible to even conceptualize the humanity and thus personhood of people of color and women. This can force the marginalized to *act* against the systems that create this impossibility. These defying actions seem outrageous within the conceptual scheme itself but are in fact the only means for asserting personhood for those whose humanity/personhood is refused by the very conceptual scheme in question (Babbitt 1996; cf. Gauthier 2004, 9–11).

34. Regarding the *requirement* that persons in non-hegemonic groups pay heed to hegemonic perspectives, see Lugones and Spelman 1990; Mills 1998, 8.

35. The Kantian moral agent applying the categorical imperative relies on "background moral knowledge" (Gauthier 2004, 4). More specifically, rules of moral salience (RMS) underwrite the application of the categorical imperative by determining, for example, which situations are moral in nature and which elements in particular are morally charged. They help us "grasp why tying a noose around my neck raises moral questions that tying my shoes does not" (Gauthier 2004, 4) These rules, however, can reflect deep-seated prejudices, in which certain groups of people are not viewed as ends-in-themselves in the first place. This is reminiscent of Susan Babbitt's points, raised in Chapter 3, regarding who, historically, has been included in "humanity" (1996, 2, 14–16). When RMS reflect exclusionary socio-political bias,

a conscientious Kantian moral agent can commit, as Barbara Herman puts it, "errors of moral judgment that will not be caught by the CI [categorical imperative] procedure" (quoted in Gauthier 2004, 6). Gauthier disagrees with Herman's position that Kant's moral theory can withstand this critique, which highlights its vulnerability to perpetuating racism, sexism, etc. Herman maintains that RMS are always subject to critique and are themselves subject to the demands of the categorical imperative. As social change occurs, RMS must—*on Kantian principles*—be revised to reflect sensitivity to newly identified social ills (Gauthier 2004, 5–11). Yet, as Gauthier notes, Kant does not allow for the *discovery* of discrimination in the RMS in the first place (8–11).

36. See also Lugones 2003, 14–15, 72–74.

CONCLUSION

1. My thanks to Dwayne Tunstall and Amanda Mosher for their critical comments on earlier drafts of this conclusion.

2. As noted in Chapter 4, I thank Roger Ward for pushing me to highlight the isolation from community that Peirce experienced at the time he was writing about agape.

3. This suggestion is borrowed from a project in which I bring Paulo Freire's *Pedagogy of the Oppressed* ([1970] 1997) into conversation with Dewey's conception of habit. Much of the following discussion, through my treatment of Martha Nussbaum's work, is adapted from my article "Attunement to the Invisible: Applying Paulo Freire's Problem-Posing Education to 'Invisibility'" (Trout 2008) from *The Pluralist*. Copyright 2008 by the Board of Trustees of the University of Illinois. Used with permission of the University of Illinois Press.

4. My thanks to Claire Katz for helping me deepen my appreciation of this point (personal conversation).

5. Ann Margaret Sharp notes the compatibility of Peirce's ideas with the creation of a community of inquiry in the classroom (1994, 201–10). She is not merely interested in the relevance of Peirce's work to the education of children in general. She draws extensive parallels between Peirce's thought and the Philosophy for Children paradigm in particular, where philosophical discourse is explicitly incorporated into primary education classrooms (195–210).

6. Lorraine Code notes: "The role of the imagination in cognitive and moral lives is often underestimated in philosophical discussion. But the very impossibility of knowing everyone intimately and well points to the cognitive and moral importance of an educated imagination as a way for moral

agents to move empathetically beyond instances they have taken the trouble to know well to other, apparently related, instances" (1995, 92–93).

7. In this context he also hints at the importance of an agapic spirit indirectly, by saying that conservatism is not the proper disposition for the scientist, because it is not open to change (CP 1.50–51, ca. 1896). Moreover, in a 1903 manuscript, Peirce makes a passing comment that to give "support to the imagination" is to serve science (EP 2:185).

8. For readers seeking more information on this front, I suggest Jonathon Kozol's *Savage Inequalities: Children in America's Schools* (1991). Another helpful resource is Derrick Bell's *Silent Covenants: Brown v. Board of Education and the Unfulfilled Hopes for Racial Reform* (2004).

9. Martha Nussbaum describes empathy as "the ability to imagine what it is like to be in [another] person's place" (1997, 91).

10. This is an important point, as studying the experience of others can be undermined by a naive (and arrogant) sense of mastery regarding another's life. Code discusses the extent to which we can know or identify with another (1995, 120–43, "I Know Just How You Feel").

11. Nussbaum argues that exposure to other perspectives by means of literature can help raise one's consciousness toward people who are "invisible" to society in general as a result of the stereotypes that block an authentic seeing, as Ralph Ellison describes in *Invisible Man* (1980), which Nussbaum references in this context (1997, 87 ff., 95 ff.). On the themes of learning via characters who are different from oneself and of becoming familiar with invisible perspectives, I recommend the entire chapter "The Narrative Imagination" (Nussbaum 1997, 85–112).

12. These and related issues are discussed by bell hooks in *Teaching to Transgress* (1994, esp. chapters 3, 10, and 12) and *Teaching Community* (2003, esp. chapters 3 and 4).

13. Nussbaum's *Poetic Justice* discusses how the development of narrative imagination bridges into the sphere of political criticism and action, as students become attuned to the oppressive circumstances of characters and may become motivated to change these circumstances as they occur in real life (1995, 87, 90 ff.).

14. I learned from María Lugones's talk, as well as from her comments on the papers of other participants at the 2008 Roundtable on Philosophy and Race, Berkeley, California. I also benefited from Sarah Hoagland's paper, "Colonial Practices/Colonial Identities: White Academic Feminist Deployment of Gender," and from a personal conversation with her at this same conference.

15. Cf. Bailey 2000; McIntosh 1988; Sullivan 2006, 10–11.

Works Cited

Alcoff, Linda Martín. 2001. "On Judging Epistemic Credibility: Is Social Identity Relevant?" In *Engendering Rationalities*, ed. Nancy Tuana and Sandra Morgen, 53–80. Albany: State University of New York Press.

———. 2006. *Visible Identities: Race, Gender, and the Self.* New York: Oxford University Press.

Alcoff, Linda, and Elizabeth Potter, eds. 1993. *Feminist Epistemologies.* New York: Routledge.

Anderson, Douglas R. 1987. *Creativity and the Philosophy of C. S. Peirce.* Boston: Kluwer Academic.

———. 1992. "Realism and Idealism in Peirce's Cosmogony." *International Philosophical Quarterly* 32 (2): 185–92.

———. 1995a. "Peirce's Agape and the Generality of Concern." *International Journal for Philosophy of Religion* 37 (2): 103–12.

———. 1995b. *Strands of System.* West Lafayette, Ind.: Purdue University Press.

———. 2004. "Peirce's Horse: A Sympathetic and Semeiotic Bond." In *Animal Pragmatism*, ed. E. McKenna and A. Light, 86–96. Bloomington: Indiana University Press.

Anzuldúa, Gloria. 1987. *Borderlands/La Frontera.* 2nd ed. San Francisco: Aunt Lute Books.

Apel, Karl-Otto. 1995. *Charles S. Peirce: From Pragmatism to Pragmaticism.* Trans. J. M. Krois. Atlantic Highlands, N.J.: Humanities Press.

Ayim, Maryann. 1982. *Peirce's View of the Roles of Reason and Instinct in Scientific Inquiry.* Meerut City, India: Anu Prakashan.

———. 1983. "The Implications of Sexually Stereotypic Language as Seen through Peirce's Theory of Signs." *Transactions of the C. S. Peirce Society* 19 (2): 183–97.

Babbitt, Susan. 1996. *Impossible Dreams: Rationality, Integrity, and Moral Imagination.* Boulder, Colo.: Westview Press.

Bailey, Alison. 2000. "Locating Traitorous Identities: Toward a View of Privilege-Cognizant White Character." In *Decentering the Center: Philosophy for a Multicultural, Postcolonial, and Feminist World,* ed. U. Narayan and S. Harding, 283–98. Bloomington: Indiana University Press.

Bargh, John. 1990. "Auto-motives: Preconscious Determinants of Social Interaction." In *Handbook of Motivation and Cognition,* ed. T. Higgins and R. M. Sorrentino, 93–130. New York: Guilford.

———. 1992. "Being Unaware of the Stimulus vs. Unaware of Its Interpretation: Why Subliminality Per Se Does Matter to Social Psychology." In *Perception without Awareness,* ed. R. Bornstein and T. Pittman, 236–55. New York: Guilford.

Bartky, Sandra Lee. 1990. *Femininity and Domination.* New York: Routledge.

Beegle, Donna. 2007. *See Poverty . . . Be the Difference!* Tigard, Ore.: Communication Across Barriers.

Bell, Derrick. 1980. "Brown v. Board of Education and the Interest-Convergence Dilemma." *Harvard Law Review* 93 (3): 518–33.

———. 1992. *Faces at the Bottom of the Well: The Permanence of Racism.* New York: HarperCollins.

———. 2004. *Silent Covenants: Brown v. Board of Education and the Unfulfilled Hopes for Racial Reform.* New York: Oxford University Press.

Beneke, Timothy. 1991. "Intrusive Images and Subjectified Bodies: Notes on Visual Heterosexual Porn." In *Men Confront Pornography,* ed. Michael Kimmel, 168–87. New York: Crown.

Bernasconi, Robert. 2001. "The Invisibility of Racial Minorities in the Public Realm of Appearances." In *Race,* ed. R. Bernasconi, 284–99. Malden, Mass.: Blackwell.

Bernstein, Richard. 1964. "Peirce's Theory of Perception." In *Studies in the Philosophy of Charles Sanders Peirce: Second Series,* ed. E. C. Moore and R. S. Robin. Amherst: University of Massachusetts Press.

Blumenbach, Johann Friedrich. 2000. "On the Natural Variety of Mankind." In *The Idea of Race,* ed. R. Bernasconi and T. Lott, 27–37. Indianapolis, Ind.: Hackett.

Bolen, Jean Shinoda. 1994. *Crossing to Avalon.* New York: HarperCollins.

Bonilla-Silva, Eduardo. 2003. *Racism without Racists: Color-Blind Racism and the Persistence of Racial Inequality in the United States.* Lanham, Md.: Rowman and Littlefield.

Bordo, Susan. 1987. *The Flight to Objectivity.* Albany: State University of New York Press.

Borysenko, Joan. 1990. *Guilt Is the Teacher, Love Is the Lesson.* New York: Warner Books.

Bowling for Columbine. 2004. Videorecording. Produced by Michael Moore et al. Written and directed by Michael Moore. Santa Monica, Calif.: MGM Home Entertainment.

Brent, Joseph. 1998. *Charles Sanders Peirce: A Life.* Bloomington: Indiana University Press.

Brown, Michael K., Marin Carnoy, et al. 2003. *White-Washing Race: The Myth of a Color-Blind Society.* Berkeley: University of California Press.

Browne, Irene, ed. 1999. *Latinas and African American Women at Work.* New York: Russell Sage Foundation.

Campos, Daniel G. 2006. "El buen juego y la mala suerte: Habilidad, reacción y espontaneidad en el fútbol." In *¿La pelota no dobla?: Ensayos filosóficos en torno al fútbol,* ed. C. Torres and D. Campos, 121–47. Buenos Aires, Argentina: Libros del Zorzal.

Cast Away 2002. Videorecording. Produced by Steve Starkey et al. Directed by Robert Zemeckis. Twentieth Century Fox and DreamWorks LLC.

Castoriadis, Cornelius. 1991. "Individual, Society, Rationality, History." In *Philosophy Politics, Autonomy: Essays in Political Philosophy,* ed. D. A. Curtis, 47–80. New York: Oxford University Press.

Chesler, Phyllis. 1989. *Women and Madness.* San Diego: Harcourt Brace Jovanovich.

Ching Louie, Miriam. 2001. *Sweatshop Warriors: Immigrant Women Workers Take on the Global Factory.* Cambridge, Mass.: South End Press.

Code, Lorraine. 1995. *Rhetorical Spaces.* New York: Routledge.

———. 2001. "Rational Imaginings, Responsible Knowings: How Far Can You See from Here?" In *Engendering Rationalities,* ed. N. Tuana and S. Morgen, 261–82. Albany: State University of New York Press.

Colapietro, Vincent. 1989. *Peirce's Approach to the Self: A Semiotic Perspective on Human Subjectivity.* Albany: State University of New York Press.

———. 1995. "Notes for a Sketch of a Peircean Theory of the Unconscious." *Transactions of the Charles S. Peirce Society* 31 (3): 482–506.

———. 2000. "Charles Sanders Peirce: Introduction." In *Pragmatism and Classical American Philosophy,* ed. John Stuhr, 43–54. 2nd ed. New York: Oxford University Press.

———. 2002. "Bodies in Commotion: Toward a Pragmatic Account of Human Emotions." Paper presented at the annual meeting of the Society for the Advancement of American Philosophy, Portland, Maine.

Collins, Patricia Hill. 2000. *Black Feminist Thought: Knowledge, Consciousness, and the Politics of Empowerment.* Rev. ed. New York: Routledge.

The Color Purple. 2003. Based on the novel by Alice Walker. Produced by Steven Spielberg et al. Directed by Steven Spielberg. Warner Home Video. Videorecording.

Crombie, James E. 1980. "Peirce and Our Knowledge of Mind." In *Two Centuries of American Philosophy*, ed. Peter Caws, 77–85. Totowa, N.J.: Rowman and Littlefield.

Curry, Tommy J. 2009. "Will the Real CRT Please Stand Up? The Dangers of Philosophical Contributions to CRT." *Crit* 2 (1): 1–47.

Damasio, Antonio. 1989a. "The Brain Binds Entities and Events by Multiregional Activation from Convergence Zones" *Neural Computation* 1 (1): 123–32.

———. 1989b. "Time-Locked Multiregional Retroactivation: A Systems-Level Proposal for the Neural Substrates of Recall and Recognition." *Cognition* 33 (1–2): 25–62.

———. 1994. *Descartes' Error: Emotion, Reason, and the Human Brain*. New York: Avon Books.

———. 1999. *The Feeling of What Happens: Body and Emotion in the Making of Consciousness*. San Diego, Calif.: Harcourt.

———. 2003. *Looking for Spinoza: Joy, Sorrow, and the Feeling Brain*. Orlando, Fla.: Harcourt.

Damasio, Antonio, and Hanna Damasio. 1994. "Cortical Systems for Retrieval of Concrete Knowledge: The Convergence Zone Framework." In *Large-Scale Neuronal Theories of the Brain*, ed. Christof Koch, 61–74. Cambridge, Mass.: MIT Press.

Davis, Angela. 2003. "The Prison Industrial Complex." In *Are Prisons Obsolete?* 84–104. New York: Seven Stories Press.

De Beauvoir, Simone. 1949. *Le Deuxième Sexe. I. Les Faits et Les Mythes, II. L'Expérience Vécue*. Paris: Librairie Gallimard.

De Lauretis, Teresa. 1984. "Semiotics and Experience." In *Alice Doesn't: Feminism, Semiotics, Cinema*, 158–86. Bloomington: Indiana University Press.

———. 1994. "Sexual Structuring and Habit Changes." In *The Practice of Love: Lesbian Sexuality and Perverse Desire*, 298–312. Bloomington: Indiana University Press.

Deloria, Vine, Jr. 1988. *Custer Died for Your Sins*. Norman: University of Oklahoma Press.

Descartes, René. 1998. *Discourse on Method and Meditations on First Philosophy*. Trans. Donald Cress. 4th ed. Indianapolis: Hackett.

Dewey, John. [1916] 1944. *Democracy and Education: An Introduction to the Philosophy of Education*. New York: Simon and Schuster.

———. [1922] 1988. *Human Nature and Conduct: The Middle Works of John Dewey: 1899–1924*, ed. Jo Ann Boydston. Vol. 14. Carbondale and Edwardsville: Southern Illinois University Press.

Du Bois, W. E. B. 1989. *The Souls of Black Folk*. New York: Bantam Books.

———. 2001. "The Conservation of Races." In *Race*, ed. R. Bernasconi, 84–91. Malden, Mass.: Blackwell.

Elliott, Terri. 1994. "Making Strange What Had Appeared Familiar." *Monist* 77 (4): 424–33.

Ellison, Ralph. 1980. *Invisible Man*. New York: Random House.

Erin Brockovich. 2000. Produced by Danny DeVito et al. Directed by Steven Soderbergh. Universal Studios. Videorecording.

Farr, James. 1986. "'So Vile and Miserable an Estate': The Problem of Slavery in Locke's Political Thought." *Political Theory* 14 (2): 263–89.

Feagin, Joe, and Hernán Vera. 1995. *White Racism*. New York: Routledge.

Flax, Jane. [1979] 1999. "Women Do Theory." In *Women and Values: Readings in Recent Feminist Philosophy*, ed. Marilyn Pearsall, 9–13. 3rd ed. Belmont, Calif.: Wadsworth.

Foucault, Michel. 2001. *Madness and Civilization*. London: Routledge.

———. 2006. *History of Madness*. London: Routledge.

Freire, Paulo. [1970] 1997. *Pedagogy of the Oppressed*. Trans. Myra Bergman Ramos. Rev. ed. New York: Continuum.

Frye, Marilyn. 1983. *The Politics of Reality: Essays in Feminist Theory*. Freedom, Calif.: Crossing Press.

———. 1992. *Willful Virgin*. Freedom, Calif.: Crossing Press.

Gauthier, Jeffrey. 2004. "Feminism and Philosophy: Getting It and Getting It Right." Paper presented at Society for Women in Philosophy, annual Eastern Division meeting of the American Philosophical Association, Boston, Mass.

Gould, Stephen Jay. 1981. *The Mismeasure of Man*. New York: Norton.

Greene, Maxine. 1997. "The Passions of Pluralism: Multiculturalism and the Expanding Community." In *Classic and Contemporary Readings in the Philosophy of Education*, ed. Steven Cahn, 510–21. New York: McGraw-Hill.

Grosz, Elizabeth. 1993. "Bodies and Knowledges: Feminism and the Crisis of Reason." In *Feminist Epistemologies*, ed. Linda Alcoff and Elizabeth Potter, 187–215. New York: Routledge.

Hacker, Andrew. 1995. *Two Nations: Black and White, Separate, Hostile, Unequal*. 2nd ed. New York: Ballantine.

Harding, Sandra. 1991. *Whose Science? Whose Knowledge?* Ithaca, N.Y.: Cornell University Press.

———, ed. 2004. *The Feminist Standpoint Theory Reader*. New York: Routledge.

Hartsock, Nancy. 1997. "The Feminist Standpoint." In *Feminist Social Thought*, 462–83. New York: Routledge.

Hausman, Carl. 1974. "Eros and Agape in Creative Evolution: A Peircean Insight." *Process Studies* 4:11–25.

———. 1993a. *Charles S. Peirce's Evolutionary Philosophy*. Cambridge: Cambridge University Press.

———. 1993b. "Philosophy and Tragedy: The Flaw of Eros and the Triumph of Agape." In *Tragedy and Philosophy*, ed. N. Georgopoulos, 139–53. New York: St. Martin's Press.

———. 1999. "Evolutionary Realism and Charles Peirce's Pragmatism." In *Classical American Pragmatism: Its Contemporary Vitality*, ed. S. Rosenthal, C. Hausman, and D. Anderson, 193–208. Chicago: University of Illinois Press.

Heldke, Lisa, and Stephen Kellert. 1995. "Objectivity as Responsibility." *Metaphilosophy* 26 (4): 360–78.

Hickman, Larry. 1994. "The Products of Pragmatism." In *Living Doubt*, ed. G. Debrock and M. Hulswit, 13–24. Dordrecht, Netherlands: Kluwer Academic.

Hoagland, Sarah. 2008. "Colonial Practices/Colonial Identities: White Academic Feminist Deployment of Gender." Paper presented at the fifth annual California Roundtable on Philosophy and Race, Berkeley, Calif.

The Holy Bible. 1985. New International Version. Red Letter Edition. Grand Rapids, Mich.: Zondervan.

hooks, bell. 1984. *Feminist Theory: From Margin to Center*. Cambridge, Mass.: South End Press.

———. 1994. *Teaching to Transgress*. New York: Routledge.

———. 1996. *Bone Black*. New York: Henry Holt.

———. 1997. *Wounds of Passion*. New York: Henry Holt.

———. 2003a. *Rock My Soul: Black People and Self-Esteem*. New York: Washington Square Press.

———. 2003b. *Teaching Community*. New York: Routledge.

———. 2004. *The Will to Change: Men, Masculinity, and Love*. New York: Washington Square Press.

Hookway, Christopher. 1990. "Critical Common-Sensism and Rational Self-Control." *Nous* 24 (3): 397–411.

———. 1993. "Mimicking Foundationalism: On Sentiment and Self-Control." *European Journal of Philosophy* 1 (2): 156–74.

———. 2000. *Truth, Rationality, and Pragmatism*. Oxford: Oxford University Press.

Jaimes, Annette. 1995. "Some Kind of Indian: On Race, Eugenics, and Mixed-Bloods." In *The Feminist Philosophy Reader,* ed. A. Bailey and C. Cuomo, 312–29. New York: McGraw-Hill, 2008.

Jiménez, Francisco. 1998. *The Circuit: Stories from the Life of a Migrant Child.* Albuquerque: University of New Mexico Press.

———. 2001. *Breaking Through.* Boston: Houghton Mifflin.

Jordan, Winthrop. 1968. *White over Black: American Attitudes toward the Negro, 1550–1812.* Kingsport, Tenn.: Kingsport Press.

Katz, Jackson. 2006. *The Macho Paradox: Why Some Men Hurt Women and How All Men Can Help.* Naperville, Ill.: Sourcebooks.

Kemp-Pritchard, Ilona. 1981. "Peirce on Philosophical Hope and Logical Sentiment." *Philosophy and Phenomenological Research* 42 (1): 75–90.

Kozol, Jonathan. 1991. *Savage Inequalities: Children in America's Schools.* New York: HarperCollins.

Krakauer, Jon. 1996. *Into the Wild.* New York: Random House.

Lakoff, George. 2002. *Moral Politics: How Liberals and Conservatives Think.* 2nd ed. Chicago: University of Chicago Press.

Lawson, Bill E., and Donald F. Koch. 2004. *Pragmatism and the Problem of Race.* Bloomington: Indiana University Press.

LeDoux, Joseph. 1996. *The Emotional Brain.* New York: Simon and Schuster.

Lerner, Harriet. 1993. *The Dance of Deception.* New York: HarperCollins.

———. 1995. *On Anger.* Boulder, Colo.: Sounds True. Sound cassette.

———. 1996. *Life Preservers.* New York: HarperCollins.

———. 2004. *Fear and Other Uninvited Guests.* New York: HarperCollins.

Liszka, James. 1996. *A General Introduction to the Semiotic of Charles Sanders Peirce.* Bloomington: Indiana University Press.

Lorde, Audre. 1984. *Sister Outsider.* Berkeley, Calif.: Crossing Press.

Lott, Tommy. 2001. "Du Bois's Anthropological Notion of Race." In *Race,* ed. R. Bernasconi, 59–83. Malden, Mass.: Blackwell.

Lugones, María. 2003. *Pilgrimages/Peregrinajes: Theorizing Coalition against Multiple Oppressions.* Lanham, Md.: Rowman and Littlefield.

———. 2008. "Coloniality of Gender and the Colonial Difference." Keynote Presentation at the fifth annual California Roundtable on Philosophy and Race. Berkeley, Calif.

Lugones, María, and Elizabeth Spelman. 1990. "Have We Got a Theory for You! Feminist Theory, Cultural Imperialism and the Demand for 'The Woman's Voice.'" In *Hypatia Reborn: Essays in Feminist Philosophy,* ed. Azizah Al-Hibri and Margaret A. Simons, 18–33. Bloomington: Indiana University Press.

McIntosh, Peggy. 1988. "White Privilege and Male Privilege: A Personal Account of Coming to See Correspondences through Work in Women's Studies." In *Critical White Studies: Looking Behind the Mirror*, ed. R. Delgado and J. Stefancic, 291–99. Philadelphia: Temple University Press, 1997.

Menand, Louis. 2001. *The Metaphysical Club*. New York: Farrar, Straus and Giroux.

Merleau-Ponty, Maurice [1962] 2000. *Phenomenology of Perception*. Trans. Colin Smith. New York: Routledge.

Mills, Charles W. 1997. *The Racial Contract*. Ithaca, N.Y.: Cornell University Press.

———. 1998. *Blackness Visible: Essays on Philosophy and Race*. Ithaca, N.Y.: Cornell University Press.

Minnich, Elizabeth Kamarck. 1990. *Transforming Knowledge*. Philadelphia: Temple University Press.

Moen, Marcia. 1991. "Peirce's Pragmatism as Resource for Feminism." *Transactions of the C. S. Peirce Society* 27 (4): 435–50.

Mohanty, Chandra Talpade. 1997. "Women Workers and Capitalist Scripts: Ideologies of Domination, Common Interests, and the Politics of Solidarity." In *The Feminist Philosophy Reader*, ed. A. Bailey and C. Cuomo, 379–401. New York: McGraw-Hill, 2008.

Morrison, Toni. 1992. *Playing in the Dark: Whiteness and the Literary Imagination*. New York: Random House.

———. 1993. *The Bluest Eye*. New York: Penguin.

Muller, John, and Joseph Brent, eds. 2000. *Peirce, Semiotics, and Psychoanalysis*. Baltimore: Johns Hopkins University Press.

Muoio, Patricia A. 1984. "Peirce on the Person" *Transactions of the C. S. Peirce Society* 20 (2): 169–81.

Nussbaum, Martha. 1995. *Poetic Justice*. Boston: Beacon Press.

———. 1997. *Cultivating Humanity: A Classical Defense of Reform in Liberal Education*. Cambridge, Mass.: Harvard University Press.

———. 2004. *Hiding from Humanity: Disgust, Shame, and the Law*. Princeton, N.J.: Princeton University Press.

Oliver, Melvin, and Thomas Shapiro. 2006. *Black Wealth/White Wealth*. New York: Routledge.

Orange, Donna. 1984. *Peirce's Conception of God: A Developmental Study*. Lubbock, Tex.: Institute for Studies in Pragmaticism.

OED (Oxford English Dictionary) Online. 2004. Oxford University Press.

OED (Oxford English Dictionary) Online. 2009. Oxford University Press.

Oyěwùmí, Oyèrónké. 1997. "Visualizing the Body: Western Theories and African Subjects." In *The Feminist Philosophy Reader,* ed. A. Bailey and C. Cuomo, 163–77. New York: McGraw-Hill, 2008.

Pearson, Karl. 1892. *The Grammar of Science.* London: Walter Scott.

———. 1900. *The Grammar of Science.* 2nd ed. London: Adam and Charles Black.

Peirce, Charles S. 1958–65. *Collected Papers of Charles Sanders Peirce,* ed. C. Hartshorne, P. Weiss, and A. Burks. Cambridge, Mass.: Belknap Press, Harvard University Press.

———. 1982–86. *Writings of Charles S. Peirce: A Chronological Edition,* ed. M. Fisch, C. J. W. Kloesel, E. Moore, et al. Vols. 1–3. Bloomington: Indiana University Press.

———. 1992a. *The Essential Peirce: Selected Philosophical Writings.* Vol. 1, *1867–1893,* ed. N. Houser and C. J. W. Kloesel. Bloomington: Indiana University Press.

———. 1992b. *Reasoning and the Logic of Things,* ed. Kenneth Laine Ketner. Cambridge, Mass.: Harvard University Press.

———. 1998. *The Essential Peirce: Selected Philosophical Writings.* Vol. 2, *1893–1913,* ed. Peirce Edition Project. Bloomington: Indiana University Press.

Pence, Gregory. 2004. *Classic Cases in Medical Ethics.* 4th ed. Boston: McGraw Hill.

Porter, Roy, ed. 1991. *The Faber Book of Madness.* London: Faber and Faber.

Rhode, Deborah. 1997. *Speaking of Sex: The Denial of Gender Inequality.* Cambridge, Mass.: Harvard University Press.

Rich, Adrienne. 1986. "Compulsory Heterosexuality and Lesbian Existence (1980)." In *Blood, Bread, and Poetry,* 23–75. New York: Norton.

Rorty, Amélie O. 1980. "Explaining Emotions." In *Explaining Emotions,* ed. Amélie O. Rorty, 103–26. Berkeley: University of California Press.

Sass, Louis. 1992. *Madness and Modernism.* New York: HarperCollins.

Savan, David. 1981. "Peirce's Semiotic Theory of Emotion." In *Proceedings of the C. S. Peirce Bicentennial International Congress (Graduate Studies No. 23),* ed. K. L. Ketner, 319–33. Lubbock: Texas Tech University Press, 1982.

———. 1987–88. "An Introduction to C. S. Peirce's Full System of Semeiotic." *Monograph Series of the TSC* [Toronto Semiotic Circle]. Toronto: Victoria College in the University of Toronto.

Schaaffhausen, Hermann. 1868. "On the Primitive Form of the Human Skull." *Anthropological Review* 6:412–31.

Scheman, Naomi. 1993. "Though This Be Method, Yet There Is Madness in It: Paranoia and Liberal Epistemology." In *A Mind of One's Own*, ed. L. M. Antony and C. Witt, 145–70. Boulder, Colo.: Westview Press.

Schutte, Ofelia. 2002. "Feminism and Globalization Processes in Latin America." In *The Feminist Philosophy Reader*, ed. A. Bailey and C. Cuomo, 401–12. New York: McGraw-Hill, 2008.

Scull, Andrew. 1989. *Social Order/Mental Disorder*. Berkeley: University of California Press.

Seigfried, Charlene Haddock, ed. 1993. "Feminism and Pragmatism." Special issue, *Hypatia* 8, no. 2.

———. 1996. *Pragmatism and Feminism: Reweaving the Social Fabric*. Chicago: University of Chicago Press.

Sharp, Ann Margaret. 1994. "Peirce, Feminism, and Philosophy for Children." In *Children, Thinking, and Philosophy: Proceedings of the 5th International Conference of Philosophy for Children, Graz, 1992*, ed. Daniela Camhy, 195–212. Sankt Augustin, Germany: Academia Verlag.

Sorrell, Kory Spencer. 2004. *Representative Practices: Peirce, Pragmatism, and Feminist Epistemology*. New York: Fordham University Press.

Stephens, G. Lynn. 1981. "Cognition and Emotion in Peirce's Theory of Mental Activity." *Transactions of the C. S. Peirce Society* 17 (2): 131–40.

———. 1985. "Noumenal Qualia: C. S. Peirce on Our Epistemic Access to Feelings." *Transactions of the C. S. Peirce Society* 21 (1): 95–108.

Stuhr, John, ed. 2000. *Pragmatism and Classical American Philosophy*. 2nd ed. New York: Oxford University Press.

Sullivan, Shannon. 2001. *Living Across and Through Skins*. Bloomington: Indiana University Press.

———. 2006. *Revealing Whiteness: The Unconscious Habits of Racial Privilege*. Bloomington: Indiana University Press.

———. n.d. "Reproducing Whiteness: How to Raise a White Child." Computer printout.

Sullivan, Shannon, and Nancy Tuana, eds. 2006. "Feminist Epistemologies of Ignorance." Special issue. *Hypatia* 21, no. 3.

Szasz, Thomas. 1974. *The Myth of Mental Illness*. Rev. ed. New York: Harper and Row.

Trout, Lara M. 2007. "Colorblindness and Paper Doubt: A Socio-political Application of Critical Common-sensism." Paper presented at the annual meeting of the Society for the Advancement of American Philosophy.

———. 2008. "Attunement to the Invisible: Applying Paulo Freire's Problem-Posing Education to 'Invisibility.'" *Pluralist* 3 (3): 63–78.

———. 2009. "C. S. Peirce's Embodied Phenomenology and Racism." Paper presented at the twelfth International Meeting on Pragmatism, São Paulo, Brazil.

Tuana, Nancy. 1992. *Woman and the History of Philosophy*. St. Paul, Minn.: Paragon House.

———. 1993. *The Less Noble Sex: Scientific, Religious, and Philosophical Conceptions of Woman's Nature*. Bloomington: Indiana University Press.

———. 2006. "The Speculum of Ignorance: The Women's Health Movement and Epistemologies of Ignorance." *Hypatia* 21 (3): 1–19.

Tuana, Nancy, and Sandra Morgen, eds. 2001. *Engendering Rationalities*. Albany: State University of New York Press.

Tunstall, Dwayne A. 2007. "Why Violence Can Be Viewed as a Legitimate Means of Combating White Supremacy for Some African Americans." In *Radical Philosophy Today*. Vol. 5, *Democracy, Racism, and Prisons*, ed. Harry van der Linden, 159–73. Charlottesville, Va.: Philosophy Documentation Center.

Van Ausdale, Debra, and Joe Feagin. 2001. *The First R: How Children Learn Race and Racism*. Lanham, Md.: Rowman and Littlefield.

Ventimiglia, Michael. 2001. "'Evolutionary Love' in Theory and Practice." Ph.D. diss., Pennsylvania State University, University Park.

———. 2005. "Three Educational Orientations: A Peircean Perspective on Education and the Growth of the Self." *Studies in Philosophy and Education* 24 (3–4): 291–308.

———. n.d. (a). "Agape and Spiritual Transformation." Computer printout.

———. n.d. (b). "Three Models of Personal Evolution Derived from the Cosmology of C. S. Peirce." Computer printout.

Walker, Alice. 1982. *The Color Purple: A Novel*. New York: Harcourt.

———. 1983. *In Search of Our Mothers' Gardens*. San Diego, Calif.: Harcourt Brace Jovanovich.

———. 1996. *The Same River Twice*. New York: Scribner.

———. 2003. Interview. "Conversations with the Ancestors: *The Color Purple* from Book to Screen." *The Color Purple*, special ed. Videorecording. Warner Home Video.

Walker, Rebecca. 2001. *Black, White, and Jewish: Autobiography of a Shifting Self*. New York: Riverhead Books.

West, Cornel. 1989. *The American Evasion of Philosophy*. Madison: University of Wisconsin Press.

———. 2001. *Race Matters*. New York: Random House.

———. 2004. "Afterward: A Conversation between Cornel West and Bill E. Lawson." In *Pragmatism and the Problem of Race,* ed. B. E. Lawson and D. F. Koch, 225–30. Bloomington: Indiana University Press.

White, Evelyn. 2004. *Alice Walker: A Life.* New York: Norton.

Williams, Patricia J. 1991. *The Alchemy of Race and Rights.* Cambridge, Mass.: Harvard University Press.

———. 1997. *Seeing a Color-Blind Future: The Paradox of Race.* New York: Farrar, Straus and Giroux.

Wu, Frank H. 2002. *Yellow: Race in America beyond Black and White.* New York: Basic Books.

Zia, Helen. 2000. *Asian American Dreams.* New York: Farrar, Straus and Giroux.

Index

Michael Epperson, *Quantum Mechanics and the Philosophy of Alfred North Whitehead*.

Kory Sorrell, *Representative Practices: Peirce, Pragmatism, and Feminist Epistemology*.

Naoko Saito, *The Gleam of Light: Moral Perfectionism and Education in Dewey and Emerson*.

Josiah Royce, *The Basic Writings of Josiah Royce*.

Douglas R. Anderson, *Philosophy Americana: Making Philosophy at Home in American Culture*.

James Campbell and Richard E. Hart, eds., *Experience as Philosophy: On the World of John J. McDermott*.

John J. McDermott, *The Drama of Possibility: Experience as Philosophy of Culture*. Edited by Douglas R. Anderson.

Larry A. Hickman, *Pragmatism as Post-Postmodernism: Lessons from John Dewey*.

Larry A. Hickman, Stefan Neubert, and Kersten Reich, eds., *John Dewey Between Pragmatism and Constructivism*.

Dwayne A. Tunstall, *Yes, But Not Quite: Encountering Josiah Royce's Ethico-Religious Insight*.

Josiah Royce, *Race Questions, Provincialism, and Other American Problems, Expanded Edition*. Edited by Scott L. Pratt and Shannon Sullivan.